Hometown Memories . . .

Morning Chores
and
Soda Fountains
Tales from the Good Old Days
in The Texas Hill Country

A TREASURY OF 20TH CENTURY MEMORIES

Cow Chips in the Cook Stove—Tales from the Lower Panhandle of Texas
Moonshine and Mountaintops—Tales from Northeast Tennessee
When We Got Electric…—Tales from Northwest West Virginia
Outside Privies and Dinner Pails—Tales from Southwest Iowa
Milking the Kickers—Tales from Southwest Oklahoma
Rolling Stores and Country Cures—Tales from Northeast Alabama
Penny Candy and Grandma's Porch Swing—Tales from North Central Pennsylvania
Rumble Seats and Lumber Camps—Tales from Northern Michigan
Lye Soap and Sad Irons—Tales from Northwest Missouri
Almost Heaven—Tales from Western West Virginia
Hobos and Swimming Holes—Tales from Northern Wisconsin
Saturday Night Baths and Sunday Dinners—Tales from Northwest Iowa
Sod Houses and The Dirty Thirties—Tales from Northwest and North Central Kansas
Coal Oil Lamps and Cattle in the Crops— Tales from Northern and Mountain West Idaho

Hometown Memories . . .

Morning Chores
and
Soda Fountains
Tales from the Good Old Days
in The Texas Hill Country

A TREASURY OF 20TH CENTURY MEMORIES
Compiled and edited by Todd Blair and Karen Garvey

HOMETOWN MEMORIES, LLC
Hickory, North Carolina

Morning Chores and Soda Fountains

Publisher: Todd Blair
Lead Editor: Karen Garvey
Design and Graphic Arts Editor: Karen Garvey and Laura Montgomery
Office Services Assistant: Laura Montgomery
Assistant Editors: Jodi Black, Greg Rutz, Monica Black, Heather Garvey, Lisa Hollar, Brianne Mai, Reashea Montgomery, and Tiffany Canaday

ISBN 978-1-940376-07-3
Copyright © 2013

Published by

Hometown Memories, LLC
2359 Highway 70 SE, Suite 350
Hickory, N. C. 28602
(877) 491-8802

Printed in the United States of America

Acknowledgements

To those The Texas Hill Country folks (and to those few who "ain't from around here") who took the trouble to write down your memories and mail them in to us, we offer our heartfelt thanks. And we're sure you're grateful to each other, because together, you have created a wonderful book.

To encourage participation, the publisher offered cash awards to the contributors of the most appealing stories. These awards were not based upon writing ability or historical knowledge, but rather upon subject matter and interest. The winners were: Peter Writer of New Braunfels, TX; Beverly White of New Braunfels, TX; Weldon Baker of Kerrville, TX; and Bob Lee of Fredericksburg, TX. We would also like to give honorable mention to the contributions from Judy Maersch of New Braunfels, TX and Austin Barber of New Braunfels, TX. The cash prizewinner for the book's cover photo goes to Zada Jahnsen of Bulverde, TX (you'll find their names and page numbers in the table of contents). Congratulations! It was extremely difficult to choose these winners because every story and picture in this book had its own special appeal.

Associate Editors

Edward Anderson
Weldon Dean Baker
Tommy Lee Barganier
Barbara C. Bird
Thelma Traveland Cardwell-Cale
Jack W. Clark
Lina M. Davis
John Friesen
Melvin Glenn, Jr.
Theron C. Hawkins
Wanda Holloway
Zada Jahnsen
Carol Johnson
Diana L. Johnson
Lowell Johnson
Joan Johson
Robert H. Kensing
Lanny Leinwebber
Adele Matthews
Lillian Mayer
Larry Edwin Mayfield
Mae Durden Nelson
Bill E. Seale
Richard G. Smith
Thomas Lou Roberds Whisenant
Beverly White
Linda Wiley

INTRODUCTION

We know that most folks don't bother to read introductions. But we do hope you (at least eventually) get around to reading this one. Here's why:

First, the creation of these books is in its fourth generation after we took over the responsibilities of Hometown Memories Publishing from its founders, Bob Lasley and Sallie Holt. After forty-nine books, they said goodbye to enjoy retirement, and each other. Bob and Sallie had a passion for saving these wonderful old tales from the good old days that we can only hope to match. We would love to hear your thoughts on how we are doing.

Second—and far more important—is the who, what, where, when, why and how of this book. Until you're aware of these, you won't fully enjoy and appreciate it.

This is a very unusual kind of history book. It was actually written by 177 Texas old-timers and not-so-old-timers who remember what life was really like back in the earlier years of the 20th century in The Texas Hill Country. These folks come from all walks of life, and by voluntarily sharing their memories (which often include their emotions, as well), they have captured the spirit and character of a time that will never be seen again.

Unlike most history books, this one was written from the viewpoint of people who actually experienced history. They're familiar with the tribulations of the Great Depression; the horrible taste of castor oil; "outdoor" plumbing; party line phones; and countless other experiences unknown to today's generation.

We advertised all over The Texas Hill Country to obtain these stories. We sought everyday folks, not experienced authors, and we asked them to simply jot down their memories. Our intention was by no means literary perfection. Most of these folks wrote the way they spoke, and that's exactly what we wanted. To preserve story authenticity, we tried to make only minimal changes to written contributions. We believe that an attempt at correction would damage the book's integrity.

We need to include a few disclaimers: first, many important names are missing in many stories. Several folks revealed the names of their teachers, neighbors, friends, even their pets and livestock, but the identities of parents or other important characters weren't given. Second, many contributors did not identify pictures or make corrections to their first draft copies. We're sure this resulted in many errors (and perhaps lost photographs) but we did the best we could. Third, each contributor accepts full responsibility for his or her submission and for our interpretation of requested changes. Fourth, because some of the submitted photographs were photocopied or "computer printed," their quality may be very poor. And finally, because there was never a charge, "fee," or any other obligation to contributors to have their material included in this book, we do not accept responsibility for any story or other material that was left out, either intentionally or accidentally.

We hope you enjoy this unique book as much as we enjoyed putting it together.

Todd Blair and Karen Garvey
August 2013

TABLE OF CONTENTS

The Table of Contents is listed in alphabetical order by the story contributor's last name.

To search for stories by the contributor's hometown or year of birth, see indexes beginning on page 264.

The Tales...

True stories intentionally left just as the contributor wrote them.

The Basement Dentist
By Peter Writer of New Braunfels, Texas
Born 1944

My wife and I live in New Braunfels, Texas and consider ourselves Texans. The incidents I speak of here occurred in the old family house in Nyack, New York. I grew up with my father and mother, two brothers, grandfather and grandmother, and Fuzzy, our Chow dog. These stories could have taken place anywhere, including the Texas Hill Country town of New Braunfels.

My grandfather built the house in the early 1900s. It had a cellar, two main stories, and a third story, which was an unfinished attic. My grandfather was a prominent figure in town and known to enjoy his scotch and whisky. Doctor Writer or Doc, as he was called, had been the first dentist in town and was liked and respected for doing pro bono dental work for people who couldn't afford to pay and there were lots of them in the early 1900s.

Doctor Writer's father, my great-grandfather, had owned a saloon before he died. My grandmother Ida Mae however was a strict Methodist and active in the Ladies Temperance Movement of the day. Mother Mae, as she was called, was also a member of the Anti-Saloon League, and her father was a fire and brimstone preaching Methodist minister and prohibitionist. The Reverend did not approve of his daughter's marriage to my grandfather and many others wondered why the daughter of a prohibition preaching Methodist minister would marry the son of a saloon owner.

When the 18th amendment passed and Prohibition came in the 1920s, my grandfather converted the cellar of his house into a speak-easy complete with billiard table, a wet bars, and cartoon murals on the walls. He even painted the windows black so nobody could see in. According to family gossip, there were some wild parties that happened in our speak-easy cellar during the "roaring twenties" before the 21st amendment ended the Prohibition Era.

My grandfather was determined to make sure none of his grandchildren had crooked

Peter's father is the baby, his grandmother, Ida Mae is laying down and his great-grandmother and great-grandfather Emma and Elcana at the ocean in 1908

15

Peter's grandparents, Ida Mae and Dr. George S. Writer (the dentist) in 1945

teeth and he worked incessantly trying to install braces on my brothers, cousins, and me. To everyone's horror, when he retired he moved the dental chair, the drill, and the rest of his equipment to the speak-easy decorated basement of our house. He continued working on our braces as well as other pro bono work on his old friends and patients. Grandpa could grab us at any time and take us down to the cellar and start drilling on our teeth. When I came home from school I always looked to see if grandpa was around and if he was I'd sneak out until it was safe to come home. One day he heard me come in and caught me, saying he needed to take some impressions for my braces. I couldn't escape so off we went to the cellar chair. The next thing I knew he had my mouth so filled with plaster gunk that I could barely breathe and thought I'd gag and choke to death. Then, unbelievably, he walked away to let the plaster dry and set up. Grandpa was a great tinkerer and he wondered over to his workbench and started working on some unfinished project while I sat gagging in the chair. Finally, he returned and tried to remove the solid plaster impression from my mouth, but to my dismay, he couldn't get it out. I knew he left it in for too long and it hardened like cement on my teeth. Cursing

the plaster, he held up a hammer and chisel and began banging away on the impression. At last, the plaster crumbled and he removed the ruined mess from my sore mouth. The last thing I heard him say as I ran away was, "This blankety-blank new-fangled plaster's not worth a tinker's damn." He later found me hiding and tried to get me back in the cellar to do another impression, but I wouldn't go.

When I was a young boy, I shared a small bedroom with my brothers. I wanted my own room and asked my father if I could move to the tiny room in the attic. He said he'd lived there as a boy and I could too if that's what I wanted. Happily, I moved up the 10 rickety steps to the musty attic and down the long creaky hall to my tiny room. There was just one bare bulb to light the outer part of the dark attic. Long strings with weights attached hung at both ends to pull the light on before walking up the stairs and off at my bedroom door at the end of the hall. There were holes in the old wooden floor planks and both sides of the hallway were filled with mysterious old family trunks and clutter. The secret treasures hidden in the dark corners and spaces under the eaves were reachable only by balancing

Peter's fater, Van and his friends in 1914

16

Peter's mother, Josephine VanNess and her brother, Johnny in 1918

on the bare floor joists. My sparse room had a small closet and dresser, a desk, a lamp, a bed, and best of all, my Emerson radio. At night, I liked to get in bed and listen to the old radio programs, *The Lone Ranger*, *Gunsmoke, Dragnet, Amos and Andy, Fibber Magee and Molly, Jack Benney*, and others I cannot even remember. My favorite was *The Voice in the Night*. The program came on at midnight with narrators reading scary stores like: *The Monkey's Paw, The Telltale Heart, The Pit, and The Pendulum* with realistic sound effects. I'd get under the covers and listen, too scared to move. I remember one story about a monster from outer space named Drill. The monster was coming to get a boy who was hiding in his bedroom alone at night. I listened, terrified, as Drill the monster, slowly walked down the creaky hall toward my bedroom. I cringed under my covers waiting for the slow, heavy footsteps to reach my door. I heard the monster breathing just outside my room and saw my doorknob turn. Did my door open? Was there a monster there? I'll never know because at that instant I sprang out of bed turning the radio off and

the light on. I spent the rest of the night hiding under my bed, too scared to open my door and see if anything was there. When morning dawned at last, I found the courage to open my door and walk downstairs. I don't think there was a monster there, but I couldn't be sure. I always wondered if Drill the monster was hiding among the family rubbish stored under the attic eaves. I never looked though.

We had running water in our old house but not in my attic room. I had a chamber pot that I was supposed to use and carry down to the bathroom every morning and empty. Soon I found it easier to open the window at night and relieve myself. After a few years of this procedure, my father noticed a tree that was growing up toward my window was dying. He asked me if I was doing anything to the tree and I said, "Just watering it at night dad." Smiling, he replied, "I did the same thing when I lived in that room as a boy."

In 1954, Hurricane Carol came and uprooted many trees and caused a lot of damage. During the storm, I called my neighbor friend and asked if he wanted to play a board game like monopoly. We decided that I'd walk over to his house with the game, without telling anyone. I got the game and started for my friend's house. As soon as I walked out the door the powerful wind blew the board game out of my hands and after a few more steps, it caught me and lifted me up and away. Luckily, there was an apple tree in the backyard and I managed to grab onto it before blowing off to Oz. I held on to the tree for dear life until my father finally saw me blowing in the wind and came out and saved me.

Fuzzy wuzzy was a bear, fuzzy wuzzy had no hair. Fuzzy wuzzy wasn't fuzzy, was he? Fuzzy was our family dog. He was a big red Chow and looked a lot meaner than he was. There was a dog ordinance in town so when Fuzzy was outside he had to be tied up. Rope didn't work because he'd snap it when

Fuzzy, Peter's dog and Donna in 1952

chasing after a cat or squirrel or most any other critter he saw. We secured him with a long ox chain and he'd usually just lie in the sun, but occasionally Fuzzy would take off like a shot after a squirrel. The squirrel would run up the butternut tree and Fuzzy would chase him until the chain jerked him up on his hind legs, barking and straining and trying to climb the tree in pursuit of the squirrel. It was a funny sight to see, three or four squirrels sitting safely in a row on the branch directly above Fuzzy, twittering and dropping butternuts on his head while he helplessly barked and tried to climb the tree after them.

Fuzzy would attack any male dog that infringed on his territory, but he was nice to his dog girlfriend, Donna. Donna was a brown Doberman Pinscher and she was equally mean to all other dogs, except Fuzzy who she would nuzzle and play with. Whenever Fuzzy escaped from the house, it was my job to go out and find him before the dogcatcher got him. I knew where Fuzzy liked to go and when I found him, I'd chuck rocks at him and he'd come to me with his head down and tail between his legs. Sometimes I'd hit him with the rocks, but usually I just had to pretend to throw and call him and he'd obey. If I didn't find him right away, I'd go to Donna's house

and he'd be there playing with her in the front yard. I'd pretend to chuck a rock at him and call him and he'd come to me. Donna wouldn't like it and she'd snarl and bare her teeth at me, but Fuzzy came anyway. Donna only liked Fuzzy and Fuzzy only liked Donna and me. I wondered if Fuzzy would protect me if Donna ever attacked.

My Hero, My Dad
By Beverly White of New Braunfels, Texas
Born 1936

When Franklin D. Roosevelt declared war on Japan in 1941 after the bombing of Pearl Harbor, I was five years old. My brother Buz got the name Buzzy doorbell because he was fast and buzzed around like a bee. We lived in the village of Evergreen Park. My father had volunteered to be a block captain, which meant he patrolled some of the streets in our neighborhood looking for any homes that had lights on. This was an air raid drill that took place about once a month. When the alarm whistle blew, all homes had to close their drapes so as to not allow any light to show on the outside of the house. This drill was intended to prepare us for a possible air attack. I remember my Dad running around the neighborhood dressed in black, wearing a helmet and having an armband identifying his post.

In 1943 Dad was drafted into the Army. Our government held off drafting fathers until the need was so great to fulfill the military positions that some fathers had to be drafted. Dad was 32 when he went off to boot camp at Fort Sheridan. After his initial training, he was stationed in Brownwood, Texas. When he left for Texas Mom, Buz and I accompanied him to the Chicago Railroad station. I was so devastated at his leaving that even today, as a 76-year-old woman; I feel the pain of his departure. I remember his holding me with my arms around his neck and I didn't want to let go. I cried and cried, not knowing if I'd ever see him again. I don't know how many months Dad spent in Texas, but I do remember his coming home over Christmas, hitch hiking all the way, buying coloring books and crayons for Buz and I for our Christmas gifts. Only thing was that Buz and I never got to see him. Dad came in late at night, spent the night with Mom, kissed his two children while they slept and he was off again hitching a ride back to Brownwood, Texas.

Next camp was in California, readying the soldiers for shipment overseas to Europe. Dad was in the 13th Artillery division under General George Patton. His division landed in Normandy and was involved in the Battle of the Bulge. I only learned much later, what my father did in the Artillery division. He was a

Beverly's dad, Alvin H. Senf in 1945

scout and reported back to the gunnery giving them their targets.

Back home in Evergreen Park, mom would receive her $100 monthly allotment check. This paid for our food and other essentials and I can't recall feeling deprived or lacking anything. We had a victory garden, as most people in our village had to grow vegetables. Various charitable people in our area would donate land for the use of gardens and my Mom accepted her parcel of land to grow tomatoes, beans, cucumbers, radishes, and other veggies. We loved it when the radishes were ready to be picked because one of our favorite sandwiches was a radish sandwich. It consisted of two slices of bread, buttered, and radishes sliced on top. We'd climb into bed with mom, prop up our pillows, and eat our sandwiches usually listening to the radio.

My mother and other families would save all kinds of grease from cooking and store it in cans to be taken to the butcher shop where they would send it to the factories that made ammunition. Many families did this as well as save tin cans, smash them and bundle them up for shipping. We even saved tin foil that was wrapped over gum or candy and made a big ball out of the tin foil. This too was used somehow for the war effort. I remember that it was my brother and my task to pull the wagon full of grease cans to the butcher shop about four blocks away. People were given food ration stamps for milk and margarine, which came in white sticks and a package of yellow dye that you mixed to make it appear like butter. Neighbors were so kind and supportive of each other sometimes giving others ration stamps that another family could use especially if there were quite a few children. Well, they all looked after each other, especially when the blue flag was showing in the window that indicated a member of the family was in the military and probably fighting the war in Europe or other places.

Finally, the war ended in 1945 and Dad

was one of the lucky or fortunate men to come home. Mom arranged for Aunt Charlotte to stay with us while she traveled to California to meet my dad as he got off the ship. We were so excited and happy to see him. It was two long years. Dad had some war stories to tell us, but I won't elaborate on any, just that he did his job for his country, was the most patriotic person I've even known, loved by his wife and his children. Eventually there were four children, two more girls born in 1946 and 1955. Dad died of a heart attack in 1990. My hero.

Weldon and his first horse, Blackie

The Nazis are Coming
By Weldon Baker of Kerrville, Texas
Born 1934

When I was a kid at a very small community school in the country, I was scared just like all of my schoolmates. We were told by our teacher and mom and dad that the Germans are coming to bomb and kill us by airplanes dropping bombs.

We were taught by Voluntary Air Raid Alert Teams and our teachers of how to react to the air raid sirens at school and at home. They had us to react to the sirens by crawling under our desks and covering our head with a book, as the teacher turned out the lights and pulled the shades down in all the windows. We had to stay on this alert until the sirens quit blowing.

This same alert was practiced at home by my mom and dad. We crawled under our bed and turned out all of the lights. We really thought the Nazis were coming! Most of these air raid siren warnings came at night. These were called blackouts, there were searchlights crisscrossing the skies almost every night searching for German planes. The search light bunkers were in our neighbors open fields and

manned by our US soldiers twenty-four hours a day, seven days a week.

To the best of my memory, these bunkers were in operation for approximately a year, before they were vacated and our soldiers left. The air raid blackouts were over.

We were asked by our teachers, radio, and special fliers in the mail, to collect and turn into the train station depot anything copper, brass, aluminum, or steel. Us kids would take two sacks (old burlap feed sacks) on our horses and go farm to farm and ask for any or all of these metals, as a donation for the war effort scrap drive.

This project was coordinated by our school and was the collection site. These were weighed and tracked by students, which we kids turned into a contest. When there was a load, which was a pick-up truck bed full, one of the farmers would take the load to the train station turn in area, which was seventeen miles from our little community.

Our community was very small, but close knit. Our post office was inside our Red and White store. We had no pavement, red lights, stop signs, law, or fire department. We did have a six-man football team with seven on the team. There was no industry in our community but we did have a blacksmith and farmers and ranchers. We all loved our state and nation.

During World War II, I remember many things being rationed, due to the war, and shortages of certain things, and the need to support and maintain our troops and equipment for them.

A coffee token for one pound of coffee

items. I still have a few of these tokens. If my memory serves me right, the dime size red tokens were to allow you to buy 1 pound of coffee and the blue token would allow you to buy 1 lb. of sugar. You had to turn these in to the store with your money. These tokens would come from the state of Texas office in Austin, Texas after you had made a one-time application. The amount of tokens you received was based on how many were in your household. Everything you needed was sold at the Red and White store including blocks of ice for our icebox.

Rationing of gasoline was controlled by lettered windshield stickers. Farmers and ranchers received a special lettered sticker and I believe it was a B sticker, which allowed us to buy more than the non-farmers and ranchers, who were a class A sticker. Gasoline was .28 cents a gallon then. Kerosene was .08 cents per gallon.

During the war, and rationing times and coming out of the great depression all of us country folks had a very large garden and mom and dad did a lot of canning of fruits and vegetables. Mom needed a lot of sugar to as she put it put-up and make a lot of jams, jellies, and whole fruit from our orchard. Our

Some of the things I can recall, as shortages, and therefore rationed to everyone was, coffee, sugar, gas, flour, corn meal, electrical wire, barbed wire, and lumber. Car, truck, and tractor tires were the hardest to get. We had to use our tires until they had no tread and slick. If we got a hole in our tires, we had to put in, what was called a boot inside the tire to cover the hole. The boot was glued in place and the tube patched and put back in. The tubeless tires were not developed yet. To get a new tire you had to turn in a slick, no tread, or heavily booted tire.

My mom and dad along with everyone else were issued tokens to be able to buy these

Weldon and his second horse, Danny in 1947

21

vegetable garden was called a victory garden.

The joke was on mom, due to not having enough sugar, one summer, to put-up our and our neighbor's crops, she got our Red and White storeowner to go to old Mexico and buy 50 lbs. of Mexican sugar. He went to Mexico and did buy her 50 lbs. of Mexican sugar for $3.00. Mom was so happy to get it and told all her church friends she would give them some, when we were finished with our canning. She did notice and showed dad and I that Mexican sugar was not as white as our sugar. The sugar from Mexico came in a 50 lb. burlap sack. Well, she ended up giving half of the sugar to her best church friends for their canning. The friends came to our farm a week later with the sack, unhappy but laughing, the bottom half of the sack was all white sand! Mom got the sugar and her friends got sand!

Some of my chores as a country farm kid was to milk three cows, feed (slop) two or three hogs, gather eggs, and every Monday morning I started a fire under mom's big wash pot. I had to do this every morning before I could go to school. After I fed my horse each school day, I saddled him and went to school. Our school F.F.A. and 4-H club members had built a corral for our horses. After school I would ride back home to repeat my chores of the morning. If I remember correctly there were about four of us kids that had horses to ride to school. We thought we were cool and tough cowboys; there was one cowgirl, tomboy that rode her paint horse to school sometimes.

In 1947, I finally got a bicycle and rode it to school. I remember that bicycle very well, since I saved up for it for 2-3 years! I didn't have an allowance, so I had to do special chores for a quarter. I hid my money in an old Prince Albert pipe tobacco can under our house in my secret place. When I saved up enough money, dad or mom took me to a western auto store in a town 17 miles away. I'll never forget as the new bicycle cost $14.50 and took all of my savings. My shirts and boxer shorts were homemade by mom up until 1948. When I went to the grocery store, which was also a feed store to buy hog feed; mom would send along a piece of the last feed sack to match up the print. Feed sacks were cotton white with different prints. I'll never forget my first store bought shirt. I was so proud of it; I wanted to wear it all the time. I was in the eighth grade.

The Schreiner store in Kerrville, Texas, they sold almost everything you needed: groceries, feed, clothes, shoes, boots, saddles, tack, horseshoes, and windmill parts. The store even had a Schreiner Bank branch inside. The feed store was in the back of the store by the windmill parts department. I remember my dad taking me with him to buy windmill parts for our windmill.

The train railroad tracks (SPUR) ran right by and up to the loading/unloading dock at the back of the store, at the feed store. I was always tickled when the train had stopped there, when we were there.

Where I was born and grew up, we didn't get to see a train very often. I remember going into the J.C. Penney store next door to the Schreiner store and was impressed by all the wire cables throughout the store. J.C. Penney store was on Water St. in Kerrville, in a two-story building. There were three checkout stations upstairs and one downstairs. When you paid for your purchase at the checkout station upstairs they would send the ticket (handwritten) with your money or check (no credit card) to the cashier downstairs by wire cables and carrier for processing. The cashier would send the carrier back to the proper station by pulling a handle and it was on its way. They sent the carrier up and down; this reminds me of today's zip line system. This cable carrier system was prior to the vacuum tube systems like today's drive-thru banks have.

The Bicycle
By Bob Lee of Fredericksburg, Texas
Born 1937

I have thought many times of an event with a bicycle that happened nearly sixty-five years ago. I was about ten years old and my brother was 6 years old. We had an old bicycle that we rode constantly. In those days, it was one speed that is as fast as you could peddle. I would ride on the seat and peddle, while my younger brother rode on the handlebars with his feet on each side of the front wheel.

On a hot summer day, we were riding as such on the main road in our little community, which was an "oil road." Yes, that's what it was. A tank truck with a rear sprayer would "oil down" the sandy road every few months, which created a hardened surface when mixed with sand. This concoction was similar to asphalt without stone, and during the hot summer months, the oil sometimes bubbled to the top, which was detrimental to our bare feet if you stepped in a puddle. The surface in itself was hot, but our feet had skin that was hardened from going barefooted most of the year, and we could tolerate the surface as long as you didn't stop for long.

We were making what I thought was

Bob's Grandfather Patterson, Uncle Billy Patterson, his father, Boyd Lee and mother, Catherine Lee, and Grandmother Patterson

excellent headway on the bike. I was peddling as fast as I could with my brother on the handlebars. We came upon a downhill grade and I really poured on the steam. My feet were flying on the peddles, the wind blowing in our face, happy with not a care in the world. That is until my little brother accidentally stuck his foot inside the spokes of the front wheel.

Well, as you can imagine, the front wheel came to an immediate and abrupt stop, and since the back wheel had no knowledge of what was happening, it continued forward, except up and over the top of us both, propelling us onto the hot oil road.

I cannot recall the exact extent of our injuries, but we both survived as apparent by our existence today.

I do recall that it was not in our best interests to lie in the middle of the hot oil, and despite our bruises and scrapes, we exited the middle of the road with extreme haste.

Were They Really "Good Old Days?"
By Judy Maersch of New Braunfels, Texas
Born 1942

Sometimes, especially in these times, we may yearn for "the good old days." Days when life was simpler, more peaceful, void of the latest technology. What was it really like?

Meet Doris, mother of three, grandmother of seven, and great-grandmother of three. She is eighty-two years old and a native of Texas. This is some of her story.

My twin sisters and I were born on my parent's farm in 1921. We were delivered by a neighbor in the same bed that my daddy was born in. Heck, in those days it was a luxury to have a doctor. Besides, the closest doctor was ten miles away, over roads that were more than bad!

When I was small, we didn't know we were poor. You didn't keep up with the

Jones's, because you rarely saw the Jones's. What was there to compare to?

There were five sisters in my family. During the harvest season, we picked cotton. It was hard work, very hard! The Depression made it worse. I remember a couple of seasons when we left with twenty-five dollars and came home with twenty-five dollars. The bottom had dropped out of everything.

We didn't go to school during harvest. In fact, we didn't get to school until after Thanksgiving. I still had to make up the work that I missed. That was plenty tough.

The schoolhouse had only two rooms. We had grades one through five in one room, and grades six and seven in another. We walked to school.

Daddy had two mules, but they weren't meant for riding, only plowing. There wasn't any such thing as a school bus, but that was okay. The walk was two and a half miles and was beautiful on good days. We took the "short-cut" over the hills and, then to the road.

Our closest neighbor had three BOYS. If we wanted to play with anyone else, they were our only choice. They were little devils who teased us relentlessly. Of course, we had to walk with them to school and we were taunted every day. However, we learned to play baseball like boys, so it wasn't so bad.

Our house was small. We had no plumbing or electricity. We enjoyed the house. Once a month we had dances there. The boys came over and emptied all the furniture out of the living room. We charged twenty-five cents for admission. Those who could pay, if only a dime or a nickel paid. The rest, who couldn't afford it, got in free. After all, none of us had much money.

The house was fun even though we had a well, an outhouse and it was lit with kerosene. I have fond memories of my days in that house. It burned down entirely when I was fifteen.

Would I like to go back to the good old days? In some ways, yes! You knew your neighbors from church and school. Friends helped you out with food and other things when you just couldn't make it. There was no such thing as "owing a favor." You appreciated the little things in life. There was no materialism to speak of. It was a simpler life.

Would I like to go back to pumping water, picking in the fields, using an outhouse, or cooking on a wood stove. Of course not, but I would like to go back to the beauty of that little farm, the friends that I had made and the caring people that I had known.

Now, I don't know my neighbors and wouldn't know who to call if I was in trouble. We have crime that was unknown when I was little. We rush around doing what?

Of course, it's nice to have a grocery store about a mile away, the convenience of air-conditioning and central heat, and the shopping malls. Would you like to go back to "the good old days?"

Outhouse "Annie"
By Austin Barber of New Braunfels, Texas
Born 1940

While growing up in San Marcos, Texas in the 1950s I developed a special friendship with a sweet 15-year-old girl. Her parents were wealthy, sweet, and generous folks. They were pillars of our town. This young lady reached her 16th birthday on a hot summer day in 1957. Some friends and I decided to give her a gift unlike any other. We quietly drove to a rather depressed part of our small town and secretly loaded a two-seater outhouse on the back of a friend's pick-up. We proceeded to place that big outhouse on the birthday girl's front yard. We proceeded to wrap it in toilet paper and a big card that said, "Happy Birthday to outhouse Annie." She still laughs about her special gift on her 16th birthday.

The Great Watermelon Snatch
In the mid-1950s three of us teenage boys

were standing around the small San Marcos Square bored and looking for excitement. Watching the bumpers rust on old cars was wearing thin! We noticed a large truck carrying a big load of watermelons pass carefully through town and proceed out a rough ol' country road. The melons were loaded on hay.

We loaded up in our old Ford sedan and slowly followed the "tasty load." When the truck slowed down to protect his cargo of layered melons I carefully sat on the front fender of my friend's Ford. We secretly turned off our lights and I proceeded to jump from the Ford up on to the back of the truck. Then I carefully chucked melon after melon down to my friend, who would catch the fat melons carefully laying them beside the road, and we proceeded to have a <u>great</u> line of numerous melons stacked.

Well this great plan worked perfectly until the truck driver heard our laughter and quickly stopped his decreased load. The truck driver quickly stepped out and began some ugly, ugly, language about our nearly perfect crime.

The driver of our "getaway" car took off leaving the "melon catcher" and myself to fight for ourselves. I cleared a barbed wire fence like an Olympic hurdler but "the melon catcher" caught his crotch on the top of the fence. We expected gunshots, but they never came. We laughed until we were nearly sick. We ate those tasty melons into the wee hours of the night, still laughing about the "Great Watermelon Snatch."

Learning to Spit
By Janet Beam Chase of Killeen, Texas
Born 1953

Snuff. That nasty, brown residue on men's shirts sleeves, leaking from the corners of their mouths. Totally disgusting. Why would anyone want such stuff in his

The Beam farmhouse

or her mouths? It must not be too tasty or they wouldn't be forever spitting it out. My grandpa was the champion spitter. I know because I'd observed him for years. Well several anyway. My childhood dream was to be like him, the next great "spitter."

My grandparent's farm was close to Grit, just 15 miles outside of Mason, Texas. It was commonly known as the farm, the ranch, or the Beam Place. Because my dad was in the Army, we didn't get to visit the farm as often as we would have liked to, so we looked forward to each visit with great expectation. We were city kids and life on the farm was so fascinating.

Grandpa and Grandma had large, handmade wooden rockers sitting across from each other in the sitting room. They spent many hours there, reading the paper, planning the next garden, snoozing, studying up on some problem, and visiting. I loved standing by grandpa's chair, watching him roll his own cigarettes. He smoked one after each meal. And since he was diabetic, I also thought it fascinating to watch him give himself a shot in the stomach several times a day, while sitting in that chair. I couldn't imagine how anyone could stick himself with a needle, on purpose. Right beside Grandpa's oversized rocker was his spittoon, strategically placed where he could lean slightly over the arm of the chair and with amazing accuracy, spit right into the narrow neck of the ceramic spittoon. Not once, did I ever see him miss. I did have a slight "contact" problem with this spittoon, though. There seemed to be a magnetic force surrounding it whenever I walked through the room, drawing me to it. With great regularity and predictability, I would either trip over it or step in it. Most of my memories are that I was barefoot. It was so disgusting to think what I was stepping in. To an eight year old, nothing could be grosser.

One hot, summer afternoon while visiting our grandparents, my older sister, and I could find nothing with which to occupy our time. There was no TV to watch, no one on the party line to listen in on, and we were tired of playing Murder, a board game my grandpa made. That's when the scathingly brilliant idea came to us. We would become master spitters like Grandpa. It looked so easy when he did it. Not only could he land the spit exactly where he wanted it, he could also spit great distances. There was no doubt in our minds that we could do it too.

On this monumental day in history, we armed ourselves with the Nestlé's Quick container and headed for the back door, leading out to the porch. We pulled our lower lips down, put a spoonful of the chocolaty powder in the proper place, and impatiently waited for saliva to build up in our mouths. Holding the screen door open and standing in the doorway we spit, each trying to be first to clear the porch. In our minds, it sailed over the large porch area and into the grass, exactly where we planned it to land. To our utter amazement, the gooey substance dribbled down our chins and onto the fronts of our clothes, some landing on the threshold. For sure, nothing landed in the grass. We didn't even make that few inches onto the porch. We lowered our expectations and tried again. Same results. For some reason, the thick substance would not easily pass between our teeth. We spent hours that day, just trying to get our spit to project a foot in front of us. Well, it seemed like hours to an eight and ten year old. We were determined to not quit until we could spit on the porch, not quite

the original goal, but success nonetheless.

I regret to say, our self-esteem suffered a huge blow that day. Occasionally, one of us would be mildly successful, but at the end of our lengthy, spitting session, all we had to show for our hard work were some clothes that even Tide couldn't get clean. Not to be outdone, we didn't concede to failure. On future visits to the farm, we'd spend vast amounts of time at the back door, loading and reloading our lips, only to find we never achieved the knack for spitting that Grandpa had. We continued this spitting practice for several years, whenever opportunity availed itself. We were dedicated and motivated but not naturally gifted in this area. It obviously was not an inherited trait, passed from one generation to the next.

I wish I could tell you that we eventually enjoyed much success as spitters, impressing all our friends and family, but we did not. In retrospect, I'm sure our parents were even secretly thrilled that we were not high achievers. But who knows? Someday soon, when I'm at the farm again, I may just give it another try. Is 60 too old for a lady to learn to spit?

The Battle of the Tennis Star and the Bumblebee
By Adele Matthews of Caldwell, Texas
Born 1940

This incident happened somewhere back in the 1950s when my class was in high school at RHS. "Bruzz" Smart was one of our tennis stars and also on our track team. I was at his house on day studying math problems. His Uncle Sam Hough lived next door. Uncle Sam's garage was facing Bruzz's house and we noticed bumblebees flying from under the garage, one at a time. Being tennis fans, we thought how much fun it would be to take our tennis rackets and swat the bumblebees

3rd grade in 1949-50

as they exited from under the garage. Things were going quite well until Bruzz, remember he's one of our tennis stars, missed one of the bees. This bee took great exception to what we were doing and proceeded to take in after us. We dropped our tennis rackets and started running around the house looking for a chance to get inside and away from this mad bee. Needless to say, I lapped Bruzz twice around that house, managed to get inside the door and was holding the door open for him, but when he slowed down to come inside, that bee "nailed" him right in the middle of his back. Bruzz could never understand after that why I wasn't on our track team!

The Bridge that Binds
By Rodger Cunningham of Atascosa, Texas
Born 1950

The bridge to my grandfather's ranch was solid, but old. Hand built by children older than their years, now adults with children of their own. In order to reach it from the house, you traveled down the dirt road bordered by a field of high native grasses and etched with shallow ruts from the Sunday trips into town to attend church. The trip was hot and dusty and just the thought of cool running water made the trek worthwhile.

The Sabinal River was flanked on both sides by tall cypress trees, which provided shade and filtered the light to cast shadows that gave the ripples a glistening glow that rivaled spun glass. The wood beams of the bridge that supported the travelers, friends, family or stranger alike, groaned and creaked whenever it was traveled. One could only wonder as they crossed when visiting whether it would be the last trip, but the bridge never failed.

The occasional floods the coursed from upriver and then uprooted trees that pummeled it would cut, nick and dent to add the character only nature can provide. It was at this crossing I recall that floating underneath the old bridge was a rite of passage for all who dared and I don't recall anyone who failed. Screams and giggles, as the youngsters would glide atop the moving Sabinal River under the bridge and amongst the grand daddy longlegs that danced and undulated with the water as it rippled atop the river rocks. Unprepared it would scare the bejesus out of you and I heard plenty of hollering before, during and after, but none failed to repeat the trip over and over. I never was certain which older cousin it was that reveled in the success of educating the younger clan in under the bridge cruising, but it proved a lesson worth remembering a lifetime.

Daddy Never Owned a New Car
By Joan Johnson of Brownwood, Texas
Born 1941

I was admiring my brand new Chevrolet Malibu; its sleek lines all of its bells and whistles available at my fingertips. I smiled. My dad would have loved this car. It was red. That was a plus.

In 1934 when daddy went to east Texas to marry my mom and bring her back to central Texas, he didn't own a car. He borrowed his brother's car for that trip. Two or three years later daddy bought his first car, a black model

27

T Ford.

I have a few memories of our Model T. It was a very simple car. No radio or heater, just plain vanilla. If something went wrong, daddy could tear it down, fix it, put it back together and we were good to go.

We would go visit my grandparents in east Texas once or twice a year. It was a long trip. I would lay up behind the seat. The space was just long and wide enough to fit me. When we started in the middle of the night, I usually got carsick. We'd have to stop by the side of the road. Sometimes we didn't stop soon enough.

We lived in the country, four miles from the little town of May. We did most of our shopping in Brownwood, 20 miles away. We didn't make the trip to Brownwood very often.

Joan's daddy's car a Model T in 1939

This was during the years when there weren't many Model T's left in our part of the country, but we knew of one. It looked very similar to ours, and it always passed us on the road. One day as we were going to Brownwood, daddy saw that car coming up behind us. He said he was going to see if he could keep up with it when it passed us. In a few minutes, the chase was on. Our car seemed to be straining and vibrating with everything it could put out, but the other car steadily pulled out of sight.

Daddy kept his model T until 1951. It was really getting in rag-tag condition, inside and out. By then I was conscious of the fact that we were extremely out of date, car-wise. I was ashamed for some of my friends to see me riding around in that car. I'd scrunch down and turn my head, hoping they wouldn't recognize me.

Daddy's next car was a 1941 maroon Ford Deluxe. Finally, I had a whole back seat to myself. Wow, what luxury! We were driving down the road one day while I was in the back seat, and I noticed one back door wasn't completely closed. Daddy slowed down. I didn't wait till he stopped. I opened the door and slammed it shut. The glass broke all the way across. It didn't shatter, but it stayed that way until daddy sold the car.

I think daddy was proud of his 1941 Ford. One day he was outside shining up a few places. He used a little shoeshine wax. A little bit looked good, so-o-o he went over the whole car with clear shoe polish/wax. Oh, did it shine! We took a trip to the city to visit relatives while it was sparkling. I don't remember now if it was weeks or months, but at some point that wax job went bad. Every little swipe he'd made began to show up and start peeling off. He had to go over the entire car again to get that stuff off. He never waxed it again.

I learned to drive in that Ford. It was twelve years old and so was I. One summer daddy was hauling hay from a field a couple of miles from our barn. He was using the car and trailer, instead of the tractor. On one trip after we'd unloaded and were about to return for another load, he asked me if I wanted to drive. I did. I drove from the barn to our house, which was probably a quarter of a mile or less. It was a short trip, but a very special one, because that was my debut behind the steering wheel.

Daddy kept his cars as long as they held together. In 1960, he finally traded off old red. This time he got a 1956 light green and white Ford. We went from a car that was 15 years old to one only 4 years old. It had turn signals. Great! No more holding your arm out the window to signal directions. In the next ten years, we put a lot of miles on that car. It was a pretty car. I took my driver's license test in it.

In 1970, one of daddy's sisters had a stroke and was in a Marlin, Texas hospital, some 130 miles away. She decided to give up her home in Bremond and move to a nursing home in Brownwood to be closer to us. Although she didn't drive, she had bought a new Plymouth Valiant in 1965. When she wanted to go somewhere, she hired a driver. The move meant giving up her car. She sold it to daddy for a token amount and the understanding he would see after her the rest of her life, which he did.

For a short while, we were a two-car family. Actually a three-car, because by that time I had my own car.

Daddy took turns driving each car to work. Mom didn't drive, so there was always one car left at home. Eventually the Ford lost its get-up-and-go. It would hardly run DOWN-hill, much less UP-hill. Finally, daddy had to put it "out to pasture." I wondered which part of the farm he would leave it on to slowly rust away. Maybe he'd pull it over to some forgotten corner of the pasture and let it die peacefully. But no, he pulled it around to a place where he had room to work, and began taking it apart piece by piece. He took a trailer load of parts to the junk yard and sold them. When only the stripped shell of the car was left, he took his ax and chopped that up into pieces he could handle, loaded them on the trailer and we took them to the backside of the pasture and threw them into a hole. Thus was the demise of the 1956 Ford.

The blue Plymouth was a faithful vehicle from 1970 to 1994. My parents and I took lots of trips in that car. It was another "plain Jane." It just had a radio and heater, but it served daddy's needs.

Daddy had three motors put in it, the first because it really needed it. The second and third motors because, he simply forgot to check the oil. He was never quite the same after mom died. They'd been married over 57 years. He was lost without her, but he grieved silently.

If something went wrong with the Plymouth, he couldn't rest until we got his mechanic to work on it so he could hit the road again. He loved to drive to Brownwood every day and get malt and French fries at the Sonic.

By this time daddy was 88 years old. He'd always been a good driver and a careful one. However, he was not quite as alert and his reflexes were a little slower than they used to be. I wondered how I was going to convince him he didn't need to be driving anymore. I needed some kind of scheme to lose his car keys or sabotage the battery. In the end, I think he, unknowingly, did it for me.

One evening in September of 1994 when I drove into our garage after a day at work, I immediately noticed a bad smell. Later daddy told me that he couldn't get his car started. I think he must have left the ignition switch on and it just burned up the battery, or ran down the battery…whatever it does to one. A few days later he said, "I don't know who to call to work on my car, do you?" His memory was getting bad too. I pretended to think very seriously about it. Finally, I said, "I don't know either."

He never drove again. The car remained in the garage. Daddy died in October 1995. Later I sold the Plymouth to a family in town. The last time I saw it, there was a teenager driving it.

29

Homemade Corn Dogs and Donuts

By Joyce Weatherby of New Braunfels,
Texas
Born 1951

My school days were wonderful! I had three sisters, no brothers! I was the only one out of my sisters that went to Pre-K. Back in 1956, you paid for kindergarten. I went half days, in the mornings. Kindergarten was held in a small beige brick church with dark stain glass windows. The class would go in the sanctuary part of the church to do our singing. The nursery part and one classroom were in the other part towards the back. The nursery had baby beds in it. I wanted to sleep in the baby beds! My kindergarten teacher was named Ms. Beehammer!

In the 9th grade, I took driver's education. It was offered through the school district. The cost was $15.00 for the classroom driver's education and $15.00 for behind the wheel instruction. I remember only one time did the driving instructor use the brake on his side of the car to stop me. Embarrassment! Two other classmates were in the vehicle also. I did learn to sew in home economics in high school. It was fun. I actually wore the clothes I made and they never came unraveled.

My mom would give us castor oil. I would have to put a clothespin on my nose just to get

Ronald, Grandma, Grandpa, and Uncle Alex

the oil down. Yek! We had a milkman come to our door at our home. It was neat to hear the glass milk bottles clink when he would set them on our porch. The milkman drove a white van with an emblem on the side of the van. The milkman wore a white shirt, white cap, and white trousers.

My mom had a wringer washing machine. It was white. It was a lot of work. We would hang out our clothes on our clothesline, a great smell, clothes drying outside! We did not own a clothes dryer. My parents divorced when I was 13. I babysat all summer when I was 13-16 years old. I saved enough to buy my first electric typewriter from Sears one summer. I enjoyed babysitting and never had any problems with the children or the parents.

My mom would make me do with the best she had after the divorce. My mom made the best homemade corn dogs I have ever eaten. She made the corn dogs with pancake batter that the wieners were dipped in and deep-fried. Also, homemade donuts, out of canned biscuits deep friend with the holes cut out. She would then put powdered sugar, cinnamon, etc. sprinkled on the donuts. Yum.

I was blessed to know both sets of my grandparents. My mom's parents lived in Lampasas, Texas on a 40-acre farm. They grew corn on the cob in the fields. They had a cow, chickens, cats, and my grandpa had a dog named Bobby. It was always fun to go visit. These grandparents were German. My mom and grandmother would speak German to each other; it was part of my heritage. My uncle would let us drive his Chevy pickup out in the fields, he would teach us to drive, talk about a great uncle! Also, the truck was standard transmission, he would let us steer while he worked the clutch and accelerator. My grandparents had a basement in their home, it's the only basement I have ever been in, grandma had her canned vegetables, potatoes, etc. stored there.

My dad's parents owned two businesses.

Joyce's mom's sisters

These were taverns. One tavern was located downtown, the other tavern at Surfside Beach. Everyone liked my granddaddy. He was a giving person. The tavern at the beach was orange and had a big porch out front. It was neat to see the ocean at night. These grandparents were Swedish. This granny used snuff. I remember her brown snuff jar. My mom said she swam the Guadalupe River to get to school, and then walked five miles to school. She went to school through the 8th grade and then helped the family. She picked cotton until her fingers bled.

The only time my dad whipped me was when my younger sister and I climbed up on the neighbor's roof. My sister and I tried to sneak in the back door of our house, but our dad was waiting for us. I remember my mom putting me in a tub of cool water after my whipping. I think my feelings were hurt more than my bottom, for I was daddy's girl.

One time I almost stepped on a tarantula. Our family was at a friend's house. I asked mom, "What kind of bug is this?" I was barefoot and went to touch the "bug" with my big toe. Mom screamed, "Joyce, that's a tarantula, get away!" Whew. Close call. I went to the movie theater with my dad. We went to see Hank Williams True Life Film. My dad and I were close; none of my other sisters went with us. My dad loved country music.

The reason I mention this is because my dad did not go to inside theaters. My first kiss was nice. My date had asked me out seven times before I would go out with him. We ended up going steady for one year when I was 16 years old.

Riding Wild Horses
By Verna M. Engel of Fredericksburg, Texas
Born 1936

Great Grandpa Joe and his friends & neighbors, in the Texas hill country, often got themselves in jams. They were mostly the boys who would eventually become his brothers-in-laws, seven in all. They were well known for a lot of foolishness that at times got them into various forms of trouble in the early

Great Grandpa Joe

31

Great Grandpa Joe feeding his hogs

1870s.

There was a certain trail down to Spring Creek that wild horses used to come down to drink. Two large boulders flanked the trail at the bank. A very large oak backed one boulder with a limb that extended over the trail. Great grandpa Joe and one of his friends decided to see how long they could stay on a wild horse. So, they went to the trail at Spring Creek and got on the limb, with their back to the trail, waiting for the horses to come down. The sound of horses coming got them ready, facing the stream. As the first horse got between the boulders, Grandpa Joe dropped onto the horses back. But, he was not alone! A Native American was on the horse holding onto the mane. Needless to say, immediately past the boulder, the Native American went off the horse one side and Grandpa Joe on the other and grandpa Joe ran for all he was worth to get away from there. His friend in the tree didn't see where the Native American went and he didn't wait to see if there were any others in the area either! He jumped out of the tree and ran for all he was worth.

Neither Grandpa Joe or his friend stopped until they got home. When they caught their breath enough to talk, they decide not to tell their families about this. And, they never told anyone, until they were grown-ups, with families of their own.

Lover's Leap at the Kyle Ranch
By Dorothy Callahan of Bandera, Texas
Born 1918

Bandera, Texas is the county seat of Bandera County. A beautiful limestone courthouse sits in the center of town. The county is made up of many small towns, Bandera being the largest, Medina the second largest, Pipe Creek, Lakehills, Tarpley, Utopia, Vanderpool, and others.

On a Sunday afternoon in about 1936, I was dating Calvin Callahan. We later married in 1944. We used to double date with other couples such as Irving "Puss" Billings and Theresa Dugosh and go for rides in the country. We went in a black Ford sedan. The boys wore their best suits, ties, and shoes to match. The girls dressed accordingly. About 10 miles from Bandera on Highway 16N to Medina was the Kyle Ranch, our destination. "Lover's Leap" was on that property. It is on Winan's Creek, a big cliff and a waterfall that falls into a deep, dark blue hole of water. There are lots of trees and many big boulders around.

At "Lover's Leap"

Calvin and Dorothy at Lover's Leap

If we didn't go swimming, we just walked around and enjoyed the beautiful scenery. Legend has it that an Indian maiden jumped off the cliff into the water below when she learned that her Indian Brave had been killed.

In an effort to find out more about the legend I called the Kyle Ranch and left a message. When I didn't hear from anyone in over two weeks, I suggested that my daughter go online and see what she could find. The result was amazing! She found then the Kyle Ranch had been divided among three heirs and Kim Mueller owned the part where Lover's Leap is. Kim was so gracious and told my daughter that she would be at the ranch on Saturday April 6 and for her to bring me out there to refresh my memory about the place.

To get to the Kyle Ranch, you go on Highway 16N about 10 miles toward Medina, where there is a grove of pecan trees. After turning left here off Highway 16 on to the ranch, you go through two gates and we found Kim's house. She immediately put us in her truck and we drove to Lover's Leap. At one point, I asked her if there was really a road or was she making one as we drove up and down through the pasture.

When we got to Lover's Leap, I found the exact boulder where our pictures had been taken in 1936. My daughter Patty took a lot more pictures. Mrs. Mueller said there used to be a ladder to get down the cliff, but a wooden stairway had been built. I don't recall how we got down to the water. Due to my age, we decided I shouldn't go down the stairs, so I stayed on top with Kim. Her version of the legend of Lover's Leap was that the Indian Brave, the lovesick boyfriend/husband, and the Indian maiden jumped off the cliff together into the deep, blue water below, both drowning.

Kim and her husband have built a beautiful new fieldstone house on a hill with two cottages and garages, plus a paved driveway. They are from Seguin and always hate to leave the place. They vowed they would never get rid of the property. I asked her how we ever knew about Lover's Leap. It really is a mystery, but she said her great-grandfather had bought the property in 1922 and she recalls then there were parties held and people were invited. It is not open to the public now.

It was such a beautiful afternoon, not a cloud in the sky, and I really enjoyed the view. The only difference I could see was that due to the drought in our area now, the waterfall wasn't as full as it was in 1936. I am forever thankful to Kim for being so gracious in accepting us and I thank Patty for all her help. Just look what I started, after about 77 years!

The Prophecy Tree
By Joy S. Hawkins, of Comfort, Texas

In the Texas Hill Country near Kerrville, Texas near IH 10, about 20 miles north is a nice little town called Harper, Texas. In the 1920s and the 1930s the Duderstadt family from Harper, Texas, owned and operated a ranch of about 5,000 acres in Gillespie and Kerr Counties. One very warm day in early summer of 1930 Mr. Duderstadt and his two teenage sons were rounding up momma cows and calves on the south 1200 acres, most of which was in Kerr, County. During the trek back to the home place, they all got hot and thirsty and Papa Duderstadt had to have a smoke and a rest in the shade. He picked a large oak tree and sat to roll his own smoke. "Rest your horses boys, I need a smoke." He rolled a "roll your own" and took a few puffs. "Boys, one of these days there is going to be a great big road come right through here not far from where we are sitting under this tree." The boys sort of chuckled and in fun asked him why he would ever think such a thing.

"Because, right through here is the straightest shot between San Antonio and El Paso." They chided him a bit and one remembered that incident and one day in the 1990s, we were driving that same road in a Ford V-8 and he related that story to my husband and me.

Sure enough, in the late 1950s and early 1960s, IH 10 was laid out and it passes about 75 yards south of that big oak tree. We have sat under that tree with the surviving older Duderstadt man, and I could not help but affectionately call that tree, "The Prophecy Tree." My husband and I, the physician of the now older Duderstadt, visited and we observed that his Dad must have never been lost in his lifetime and Mr. Duderstadt confirmed it with, "he knew right where he was upon retiring and again upon arising."

"He never was lost, ever."

A Visit to Granma's
By Claire Johnston of Lago Vista, Texas
Born 1946

A visit to my great-grandmother's in Valley Spring, Texas when I was little was so special. Granma always made you feel as though you were the most special, wonderful person imaginable. First of all, there was Granma herself, a tall, slightly stooped spare lady, with warm, dark brown eyes, a quiet, gentle voice, and a soft, warm chuckle. She wore her thinning white hair in a bun and usually wore long-sleeved, simple cotton dresses over which she frequently wore a pinafore apron. She wore 'old lady' lace up shoes with a heel and brown cotton stockings. Granma's little house was like the most wonderful cottage— very small, scrupulously clean and warm and inviting.

It had a step-down sleeping porch at the far side of the house with a wonderful feather bed that Granma would let you jump up and down on. And there was a step-down little dining room at the other end of the house with Granma's best dishes that she would let you hold tea parties with. And there was a wooden stove for heat and there was a large old wooden crank phone on the wall—which we especially loved! Sadly, we were forbidden to play with it, but sometimes we would 'forget' and crank it and then the operator, Lola, would come on the line. About that time, we would be discovered and gently scolded as Granma took the receiver and bent over the mouthpiece to explain to Lola that her great grandkids had been playing. She apologized to Lola and explained again that the phone was not a toy and we shouldn't waste Lola's valuable time.

Granma did all sorts of interesting things. Her small yard was hard-packed earth, which she swept each day with a broom. Not a blade of grass, much less a weed, would dare to sprout there, lest Granma attack it vigorously with her hoe, always close at hand. Wagon hoops outlined Granma's colorful flowerbeds, which she tended tenderly and often.

Granma drew her water from a well, which she hand-pumped herself. We loved this process. We would beg her to draw a bucket so we could watch this fascinating procedure. You had to prime the pump with water and pump the handle vigorously and finally the cool water would come with a gush. That was the best tasting water in the world.

Granma kept 'banty' (Bantam) chickens instead of the large Rhode Island Reds or White Leghorns we kept. We adored Granma's cute little chickens. She let us help her feed them (we hated having to feed our chickens at home—so boring) and help her gather their small eggs (another chore we disliked doing at home). We loved to eat the small eggs—they were special, not like ours.

Grandma had a whitewashed, amazingly clean outhouse, which we found interesting—during the day. Everything at Granma's was special. And if you could prevail upon Mother and Daddy to let you spend the night with Granma, not only did you get to sleep on one of her feather beds, but the next morning you had the most special breakfast in the world: little Banty fried eggs, thick-cut bacon, large hot biscuits served with lots of butter and Blackburn's syrup—and to top it all off, hot cocoa. It was just the greatest. And you got to eat it in Granma's small little kitchen (still warm from the cooking) at her small table. It was so cozy and nice.

Granma told the best stories—she knew that Great-aunt Nora's husband was a worthless gambler who was murdered with a shot to the back after a poker game (his murderer was never found), and she could sing (but only after much cajoling) the most wonderful, achingly sad cowboy ballads in the world. While she was telling her stories, she would discreetly and delicately dip snuff (after a warning to you that it was a bad habit and never take it up). I once sneaked a good look at it while she wasn't looking—it was a soft powdery gray and smelled sort of sweet—I didn't see any real fun to trying it. Besides, you had to keep spitting it out every once in a while—I thought that could get to be a nuisance.

Granma loved 'stick' candy and always kept a good supply, which she obtained, from one of the little stores in Valley Spring. She

would let you pick out the one you wanted. She was just the most perfect lady and best Granma ever.

And Valley Spring was fun, too. It was a tiny hamlet, with a few scattered small houses and a couple of tiny Mom and Pop stores—one sold a few groceries and soft drinks and acted as the village Post Office and a hangout for the elderly village gentlemen who daily played dominoes and whiled away the afternoons visiting. The other sold a few groceries and sweets and soft drinks and kept some cattle and horse feed for the local farmers and ranchers. The little village also boasted two small white-steepled churches, which filled up on Sunday mornings with their respective little congregations of local folks. The preachers were also just local ranchers who felt a 'calling' and were willing to take on the additional responsibility of presenting Bible lessons to their neighbors. Sometimes there would be 'dinner on the ground', which meant a wonderful potluck lunch with each family bringing something to share with their neighbors. Everybody knew everybody. And everybody knew and loved "Aunt Molly" as my great-Granma was called by her long-time friends and neighbors. I was shocked to learn years later that her name was Mary Belle, not Molly. But truly, by whatever name this dear and precious rose was known, she was a treasure and a trip to see her was so special.

Chicken Catchers
By Diana Ingram of Odessa, Texas
Born 1951

My great grandmother, Polly Anna Wood, lived in San Saba County, Texas. During the depression, it was hard for everyone. However, most people were pretty self-sufficient in those days. Everyone had a garden; they had to in order to have vegetables to eat. Everyone

Polly Anna Harkey Wood and Ovella Louise Wood Temples

also had chickens so they could have the eggs and the meat. Well, Polly and her husband Warren Wood had a lot of chickens and they sold the eggs to get a little spending money for the stuff they could not make.

If you have ever raised chickens, you know a garden and chickens don't mix. The chickens are born to "scratch" the ground looking for bugs, seeds, or anything else they can eat. My grandmother had a small fence around her garden to keep the chickens out, but those chickens were determined! They would find a way through the fence to damage her garden. So, she used good old American ingenuity to protect her garden. They also had some cows and those cows would go through the fence on occasion. Some were worse than others. Granddad would put a

metal "neck guard" around their necks that was shaped kind of like an egg. This didn't hurt the cow, but it just kept her out of trouble. On the top and bottom of this guard, which would be under their jaw and above their head, was about a 10-inch extension with a hook pointed the direction the cow was going. These "hooks" which were a part of the guard, would catch the fence wire and the cow could not get through the fence! I believe these were called "cow catchers"!

My grandmother handmade some of these same guards for her chickens to keep them out of her garden! Mom said when they were put on the chickens they would walk backwards for a time trying to get away from them. These guards would "seat" into their neck feathers and hold it in place. It didn't hurt the chickens and the garden was safe!

The Jury-rigged Go-cart
By Wendell Pool of Spring Branch, Texas
Born 1945

I am almost 68 years old. I was raised in Greenville, Texas, the county seat of Hunt County. Greenville's population was about 18,000 then. Hunt County was primarily a cotton farming and ranching area.

I was the family "engineer" from an early age (later went to Texas A & M and studied EE). I sorely wanted a motorized vehicle from about age 5 when my grandparents took me to a friend's house and I got to drive a slow "go-cart" like vehicle the owner had built for his grandkids. I was always scheming a way to motorize something. At about age 8, friend of Dad's gave me a 1 1/2 hp Briggs Stratton engine, but it really did not have the power without gearing (I was not there yet) to pull anything.

When I was about 12, another friend of Dad's gave me a partially operative 7 1/2 hp engine with an automatic clutch. Perfect,

I thought! We built a three-wheel "tricycle" like "go-cart" from 2 X 6's and plywood. The tiller was a piece of pipe that would have impaled us if we crashed. The wheels were cheap 1 1/2" tread with ball bearings. The rear axles were 5/8" bolts on each side. We found the motor side with the drive wheel too heavy for one wheel, so we got a longer bolt and put two wheels on that side. We bolted those wheels together with a 5" pulley also bolted to them. Our throttle was a piece of electrical wire from the engine over our shoulder we would pull to accelerate.

Oh yes, the "partially operative" part: the engine would not idle due to a crack in the intake manifold, so it was "all or none" with the throttle.

Well, time for a road test on our two blocks between stop signs. Mine, so I was first. Throttle wide open, buddy cranked the engine, then I laid 6 feet of rubber with those two drive wheels on the left side. One block down, at least 40 mph, I realized we had not engineered brakes. So, the next block was shoe heels for brakes to turn around before the stop sign. I did say it would not idle, so when I turned around, it indeed died. I started pushing it home while my "pit crew" was hurrying to meet me with the starting rope.

We all rode that day with no brakes; several pair of shoes were ruined, and several sets of parents were aghast at our story. We engineered brakes very crudely the next day.

I am still engineering and jury-rigging things, but am a bit more refined in my completed projects!

The White Dishtowel
By Theron C. Hawkins, MD of Comfort, Texas
Born 1930

We raised chickens and turkeys on our dry land farm in Castro, County, Texas. In the 1930's, during the dust bowl years when we were plowing the west side of the fields, when we saw the black duster approaching we knew to watch carefully for Mom to wave the white dishtowel as a sign for us to get back to the house in a hurry. Most days she would also see the black cloud of dust and would have already shooed all the chickens and turkeys into the chicken house where they would not suffocate in the thick dust. But occasionally, Mom would be busy and before she knew it, the poultry had also seen the black cloud, and thinking it was getting dark, they would have climbed up into the trees where the dust would suffocate them. It was our job to beat the cloud home and climb the trees to retrieve the fowl.

The Ubiquitous Hand Throttle on Pickups
We owned and used a 1938 Dodge three-quarter ton long wheel-based pickup. It had a hand choke and a hand throttle. We owned farms in central Castro, County, Texas about 11 miles apart and we often had to drive the very slow-moving Oliver Hart Parr tractor from one farm to the other. Sometimes we pulled some equipment but many times, it was just the tractor pulling the 1938 Dodge pickup. My two older brothers devised a clever plan to not spend so much time moving the tractor and pickup. The pickup had a Standard stick shift 4-speed transmission. This combination made for some fascinating experiences. They would hook up the pickup to the tractor drawbar, turn on the ignition key, put the transmission in 3rd gear, pull the throttle out about three-fourths of the way(when they got out of sight of Dad or other family members).They then climbed aboard the tractor and started off. The engine roared to life and pushed them at nearly 25 miles per hour down the road. They merely put on the tractor brakes to make turns or to stop they would just kill the truck engine. This beat the 7-8 miles an hour in the fastest gear the tractor had. They would arrive and have time for a nap before Dad would arrive

to help them with the project he had planned for them. My older brother denies ever having done this but I am sure he participated.

Half-Breed Indian Guide Buck

I had a delightful patient named Fred who had been what they called an Indian fighter and his trusted and talented half-breed Indian guide Buck. Buck was so skilled at his trade he could follow the trail of Indians at a full gallop on his horse. In those days, the Indians were stealing horses and it was Fred's job to track them down before they sold or ate the horses. Buck would find their campsite and by what he saw at that site could describe the party of Indians perfectly though he had never seen them. For instance according to Fred they were after this particular party of Indians and when Buck examined the campsite from that morning he said" there are 2 Indians in this party, a young Indian and an old Indian, they have a long haired black dog with a stubby tail, they are riding 2 horses, one black with a white mane and a chestnut with a dark mane." Fred couldn't believe he didn't get a peek at them. Buck said," here is where the dog sat and got something to eat, over here is where the horses rolled in the brush after the saddles or blankets were removed, all the while leaving traces of their hair for me to identify them." And here is how I could tell the ages of the Indians. Here is where the young Indian emptied his bladder this morning and the stream shoots way out there, and the older Indian stood here and the stream dropped almost between his feet. They caught up with them and he had described them perfectly. He did this same thing often on their jaunts to retrieve horses.

Remembering My Grand Mother's Stories
By Dean Kothmann of Leawood, Kansas
Born 1951

My grandmother, Alma Willmann Grosse was born in 1893. As a small girl, she picked cotton, which was loaded into a wagon and taken to the local cotton mill. The cotton was processed and left the county on a wagon for markets far beyond the Hill Country of Texas. As a teenager, I took her on Sunday drives. During those drives, she told stories of growing up in Mason County and the Hill Country of Texas.

When driving through Koochville (a suburb of Ft. Mason, Texas), she would point out Kooch's Store, a two story red stone building, and state it could tell many stories. The story usually went that a Christmas dance was held on the second floor in 1860 for the local citizens and Fort Mason soldiers. My grandmother related that her grandmother had danced with Robert E. Lee at that Christmas dance. She did not know what they talked about during the dance, but in January of 1861, Robert E. Lee wrote home from Ft. Mason that "I can anticipate no greater calamity for the country than a dissolution of the union. Secession is nothing but revolution." In March of 1861, Lee left Fort Mason, his last Union command.

With the Civil War over, Kooch's Store became a bank and last stop for supplies before taking long horn cattle to Kansas City. The cattle drivers would leave their gold and worldly possessions in a storeroom and safe in the back of the store. In the early morning, long horn cattle passed six abreast from day light to dark. The clattering of the long horns, one against the other, could be heard from long distances. She would smile and say, "Crossing the street was a real problem."

One Sunday we were on the James River Road (FM 2389), and she asked that I pull to the shoulder. She pointed to a small knoll to the South and said that was Tod Mountain and her mother had a story about the knoll. In December of 1865, the Tod family and their slave girl were going to town. A band of Comanche Indians riding horseback attacked the Tods. The young slave girl was killed instantly and Mrs. Tod received injuries and soon perished. The Tod's daughter was kidnapped. Mr. Tod and local men formed a posse and pursued the Indians, but the young girl was never found.

She loved the spring rides because it brought forth local wild flowers like the Blue Bonnet and the Indian Paint Brush. She would tell me how her brother had impacted the world. He worked for the Texas Highway Department. He changed the practice of cutting grass and weeds along the road's right of way from regular periods to waiting for the wild flowers to go to seed. With the expansion of fertile seeds, wild flower's flourish. In an interview in U.S. News and World Report, February 22, 1965, Lady Bird Johnson, President Johnson's wife, recognized his efforts by stating that "For about 30 years, we have had a wildflower-seed-planting program there which has really made it a glorious experience to drive across the State between about the middle of March and June. The roadsides are a carpet of color if there has been rain." She was proud her brother had created a wildflower-seed-planting program, which expanded to the highways of the world.

My favorite remembrance of my grandmother was her observation of how the world had changed during her life. In the early 1970s, I was a young engineering student in a prominent university. On her black and white TV, we were watching one of the moon landings. She looked at me and asked, "Do you think that is really happening?" I told her I did not understand her question. She asked again, "Do you think the moon landing we are watching is really happening? Now! As we watch!" I shared that this event was real. With still somewhat of a doubtful look, she gazed at me and said, "My! What a life! I have seen the world go from horse and buggy to the moon."

Pilot Training
By Chester Bagby of Lampasas, Texas
Born 1922

You don't see row crops on the Lampasas River anymore but in the '20s and '30s that's all you saw. The main crops being cotton, wheat, and maize. Cotton was the money crop and we had about 50 acres. As a very young boy I witnessed my dad plow under three acres of beautiful plants of cotton about knee high. I was too young to understand, but cotton was eight cents per pound and Hitler was causing trouble in Europe.

While picking cotton with my dad and older brother I recall times in the tall cotton with my sack full enough for a pillow. I would

Chester F. Bagby

lay back and watch the buzzards sail until my dad missed me and called my name. I didn't have a watch so I learned early on that I could tell how many hours until lunch by holding my hand just above the sun and coming up hand over hand until overhead. Each hand represented an hour. I did this often during the morning until mom waved a white cup towel from the front porch a mile away.

It seemed as though I went from the cotton patch to World War over night. I found myself in the Air Force pilot training program. My most harrowing and gut-wrenching experience during my pilot training came on a cold winter day over the wheat fields of Kansas. My instructor told me to take the plane up to 7,000 feet and practice some spins. This would be the first time for me to spin the plane solo. I suppose he said 7,000 feet just in case I didn't bring it out on the first attempt. I took the plane to 7,000 feet, put it in a steep climb, and cut the throttle. The weight of the engine broke through to the left and I kicked the left rudder in and pulled the stick back in my lap. My first thought at that time and moment was it seemed such a short time between that cotton patch and now. I was at 7,000 feet in an open cockpit plane. My instructor taught me to hold the stick all the way back, kick the opposite rudder, count to three and pop the stick forward and you would come out of the spin. He was right and I missed that wheat field by several hundred feet. Pilot training was dangerous, but so is war.

The Case of the Miss-Spelled Name
By Melba Simmons Shaw of New Braunfels, Texas

Epilog—Map wise, New Braunfels is over half way to Belton when one lives in Corpus Christi, Texas.

My mother could have been born anywhere; I'm glad it was Sparta, top of a hill and five miles north of Belton. It is so easy to drive north on I-35. One can view the Resthaven Cemetery by the road, three miles south of Belton. The Courthouse is on Main Street. Rita Sutton, Court Clerk, was Registrar of Agnes Woodson Chapter–NSDAR during the '80s. She knew exactly what I needed when I walked to the counter and asked. She went straight to the registry book where my Great-grandmother Marticia Shofner Walton was recorded, printed a copy, flipped it over, pressed a Texas state seal stamp, and signed her name. She grinned, telling me it would be a dollar, and said, "It's as good as gold! May have the wrong name on it, but Washington, DC office will understand!" You see, Marticia is recorded as "Martin Walton." (Martin is the name of my seventeen year old patriot who served in the American Revolution.) The rest of Marticia's script reads, "Female, 81, place of death: Sparta, cause of death: exhaustion," Her tombstone reads, "M. D. Walton, b Apr 14, 1828, d May 31, 1908, wife of Nelson Walton" It is the one place in history, her name is not misspelled!

My kinships are so accommodating for memory reasons. A good many of them died in June. Our first grandchild was born June 12, 1982 and our first great-grandchild was born January 12, 2000. Jill's great-great granny, my mother, passed away on Christmas Day, December 25, 2000.

Family history is a fun thing. Had I known more about it while I was growing up, I might have planned to be a high school history teacher! No doubt, I would also have been an old maid. All of the above script was written the morning after I wrote lines about "the good ole days." It will fill in bits and pieces, which I may have left out while writing about a part of my life.

Proud to be an American
Memorial Day, the time to think about patriotism. It is a strange mystery, how

my husband and I wound up living in New Braunfels, Texas. It surely was not a long range plan. We did talk about living in the Hill Country someday. All my life I had heard about a relative of my mother's who lived in CC, but she didn't know her name. She only knew the lady was her third or fourth cousin? Since we lived eleven miles away, mother never bothered to look her up. Meanwhile, by 1967, I was married, had three children, and was entering Del Mar Junior College in Corpus. The thought of looking that ancestor up, kept bugging me. One day I stepped out of class and picked up a phone book in the library. No luck! No way, I could imagine a name.

Fate is what happened! I overheard someone at church mention a lady who played the piano for the FAN Club. I decided to attend the Friends and Neighbors Club dinner at the next opportune moment or ask someone for the piano player's address. I looked her up, asked questions and she immediately knew my mother was her third cousin, twice removed. She could remember my grandfather's wagon passing their house in Sparta, TX with his son and two daughters. She said she could single out my mother because of her red hair.

Nettie Walton Watson Jones went on to tell me about herself. She related many things about Sparta, TX, getting a teacher's degree, two divorces, writing three poetry books, and her three children...one of whom died at age ten. She told me about entering National Daughters of the American Revolution in 1920 and her sister Pauline joined in 1919. Her story, interested me to the point, I borrowed her approved application form and documents, so I could print copies. She was reluctant to loan, but did so with the promise I would return them immediately. With the documentation on file, I continued visiting Nettie until she passed away in 1982. By that time, she had talked me into joining Byliners Club, a writer's guild that originated in 1939.

We attended meetings together and had lots of time to discuss family. Nettie continued to play the piano during the noon hour for every group in Corpus Christi who invited her.

Since I was attending classes to become a teacher, I was heavy into Children's Literature. One class instructor announced she did not give a test, "student's would write a book and turn it in as though it were published, illustrations and all." That surely stunned my imagination, but I managed to write, illustrate, and get a decent grade. The Book was also, what I leaned on to be a member of Byliners Club. The college professor had paid me a compliment by stating, someday I should think about publishing it. The club members would read each other's material and make genuine remarks about altering the wordage. Several participants already had published articles, poetry, cook books, and a romance novel.

In 1984, my husband retired and I was set to think about entering National Society Daughters of the American Revolution, but it didn't happen! He accepted a second career, and we moved to Florida. I carefully put all of my documents in a folder and filed. I continued to be a substitute teacher, so I had more time to be at home. Even so, it was such a busy life, I had no time for extra research, but I did join Eastern Star. They only met twice a month and my husband had been a Mason since he was eighteen. After two years in Florida, Bo decided to retire again. Even so, the company liked his work and asked where he was moving. They requested he move, and when he was settled, to please give them a call. They wanted him to keep on working.

The Christmas before we moved to Texas, my gift was a trip to the Holy Land. I was to pack for that and a week extra, so I could leave out of Jacksonville, FL and return on a Houston flight to Corpus Christi, where Bo would pick me up and we'd spend a weeks' vacation visiting friends, kin and traveling in the Hill Country.

We almost purchased a house in Corpus Christi, even though we had never planned to live there after retirement! We drove to visit friends in Odessa, and Kerrville; then came in late one evening to lodge in San Antonio. The next day we came to New Braunfels and looked around. We talked about a house there and checked with Century 21. The first home they showed us was the house we now own. We paid down on it, returned to Crawfordville, FL to wait for the approval, and then move. We moved to Mission Valley Estates, June 8, 1988.

We had wall to wall furniture and a maze of boxes for several weeks. Our children visited and picked up items they wanted. Even before it all smoothed out, we attended a homeowner's club meeting and got to know a few in the community.

It did not take long before my file folder was on the counter! I think Bo got the idea, "he would like to solve that mystery and get it out of the way." I asked around and no one I met knew much about NSDAR. Folks in N.B. were so friendly, especially about asking your skills, talents, and checking your volunteerism. I did accept a tennis match, NewComers Club, and teaching GED classes. Meanwhile, I kept asking and a friend advised me to call the secretary of the First United Methodist Church. Bobbie Allen was a fountain of information. She told me she knew nothing about DAR's, but she knew members, and she quickly named three or four. Turned out one lived within a mile of our house.

I attended DAR's first meeting in September, 1988. The registrar told me what I needed. I merely listened and asked questions, but was soon hooked on locating as many of my family ancestors as I could. Bo helped a lot. After a July Shaw Family Reunion on July 4, 1989, we packed our lunch and traveled to Belton, close to where my mother grew up. In one day, we visited the courthouse,

library, lunched in the park, and toured the cemeteries. Fortunately, all five of the Sparta Cemeteries were disinterred before it became Belton Lake. Resthaven Cemetery is where most of my Sparta folks are buried. With the library and courthouse directories, we could find most of the gravestones I was searching for, so I could get a clear photo of each.

All of the research gathered nicely, and I was able to complete my DAR form to submit in 1990. I was approved October 9th and by that time discovered there was also a NSCAR Children of the American Revolution. It did not take me long to fill out forms for three grandchildren. Since none of our three children were interested, the grand's didn't have much of a choice. However, I knew someday, in some way, all would be proud of the fact they were CAR members at ages eight, six, and nine months.

Wes, our "nine months" grandson, was 22 years old in 2012. He graduated from Houston Police Academy, Wharton, Texas, May 24, 2013. (A child of the American Revolution ages out of CAR on their twenty-second birthday. They are actually eligible to enter SAR or DAR when they are eighteen years old. For a short time, the member can enjoy a duo membership.)

I am proud to this day, of being able to spread the word around. Our NSDAR Motto is "God, Home, and Country." I am guilty of stretching it a wee bit, "education to the hilt, top History programs, prayers, and patriotism!" I became even prouder to know there are three American Revolution Chapters in New Braunfels, Texas Sons, Daughters, and Children of the American Revolution.

While residing in New Braunfels, it does not take long before one learns this town should have been named "Volunteer City." I continue to enjoy every minute of living here.

Sloan Community
By Jymmie Linzey of San Saba, Texas
Born 1928

I grew up in Sloan community about 15 miles southwest of San Saba, Texas. I was a Sloan by birth and I had one brother, Tom. We lived with our parents and stones throw from our Sloan grandparents. My dad was a rancher. We went to Sloan School until I was in the 8th grade. We had two outhouses – one for the boys and one for the girls. We had seesaws and we played "kick the can," "Anti Over," baseball and cowboys and Indians. The school was two rooms and we had two teachers.

In the summer, we helped on the ranch, riding all day doctoring wormies. We had a wonderful swimming hole. It was a spring, it was deep, and it was cold. We went swimming often and worked every afternoon. We played Monopoly and listened to the radio at night. I liked "Fibber McGee and Molly." We had an engine under the house that made our electricity until REA came along. My mother

Tom Sloan and his grandfather, Bob Johnson in the '60s

ironed with sad irons. They were heated on the stove.

My parents and two sets of grandparents were very special to me. We went to my Grandmother Sloan's after school for snacks. She was wonderful. We visited my Maxwell grandparents in the summer for about a week. They lived on a ranch east of Cherokee. It was fun. My grandmother was a good cook also and our granddad would go to Cherokee and always bought us back a bag of candy. My grandmother told wonderful stories that she made up.

My dad brought us to a town (San Saba) to the picture show. I loved Shirley Temple movies and we went to every one of her movies. Everyone went to town on Saturday and we kids would go to the picture show. The streets were full of people country folk. My brother and I had a dog. Mine was a Pekinese and his was just a dog. My dog's name was Ching and his dog's name was Pug. We also had several ranch dogs.

I was in high school in San Saba during WWII. We went to football games in cattle trucks because gas and tire rationing. We had a

Jymmie and Tom Sloan in 1932

43

place called Mrs. Malloy's where we hung out and ate lunch. Many things, such as Hershey bars were hard to get. Sugar was rationed. I rode the bus a long way to school. All of my friends came a long way on the bus also. We would spend the weekends with each other and we hung out with those that didn't live in town. We went to the midnight show with our dates.

Buzz Bombs
By Roy Kemp of New Braunfels, Texas
Born 1936

Some of my most early memorable years date back to 1940 - 1945. At this time, I was growing up in South East London, England, during the war years. I guess I was too young to comprehend the dangers but for a young child they were exciting times.

Getting woken up in the middle of the night to go down our "air raid shelter" while bombs rained down was a routine nightly affair. To drown out the noise my mother encouraged me to sing and my song of choice was "you are my sunshine, my only sunshine; you make me happy when skies are grey." My mother told me that I would get very upset if someone else joined in the song as I considered it my very own. To this day, I still break into song whenever I hear the tune.

In later years, the "buzz bombs" namely the V1 and V2 rockets started to appear. You didn't worry about them as long as you could hear the engines roaring but as soon as they stopped, you knew they were going to fall and had to look for cover. In school, this consisted of hiding under your desk. A lot of good that would have done if it fell on the school.

After a night of air raids, my friends and I would explore the newly bombed-out houses in the neighborhood looking for shrapnel. Metal pieces of the bombs that fell. An especially good find would have markings on it. As a child, we never considered the destruction and loss of life the bombs caused.

Many years later, I visited the British War Museum. One of the exhibits was a captured German map that showed areas of London that had been pre-selected for serious bombing. One area included our house as we were very close to a large port on the Thames River where ships delivered all kinds of materials for the war effort. Also, close by was a major rail terminal for trains carrying troops and supplies to the coast.

Ironically, my wife and I attended a dance recently and sat with some acquaintances of ours. Both the lady and her husband were originally from Germany. The lady and I spoke of our war experiences, which were remarkably similar in that we both lived in areas that suffered heavy bombings.

Beds all in a Row
By Irma Lange of New Braunfels, Texas

I went off to nursing school in "the good old days," a scared kid right out of high school. There was no nursing school in my hometown of Brownsville, Texas so three of my friends and I took off on the train to Galveston. In those days, Galveston was an open town with all the gambling, prostitution, and whatever so I still am surprised that my mom agreed to allow me to go. In the '50s, girls either went to college to become teachers, nurses, or secretaries, so there were not so many choices.

What I remember the most was the wards with at least 8 patients but mostly 12 to 15. Of course, there were private and semi-private rooms, but somehow I remember the wards with its beds all in a row. In those days, we only had penicillin and Ampicillin. They were the only antibiotics available and we considered them the wonder drugs. Ampicillin was very thick and hard to get out of the syringe, and was the only medication that was pre filled. Everything else that was given as an injection had to be drawn up in one of those syringes, which we sterilized in those funny sterilizers we had in each ward, those would never pass inspection by today's standards. I remember walking down the hall with a tray full of syringes every couple of hours. Not too many medications errors in those days as most patient's got the same thing.

I'll never forget walking into the psyche wards, which were locked, scared the first time the door was locked behind me and I was locked in with all the patients. In those days, we had one tranquilizing medication, which was "Thorazine," and it was very new, we gave very large doses and had to take blood pressures before and after. Of course, shock therapy and insulin therapy were the most common treatments for psychiatric patients, and we all had our turns in working in those units. What an experience for us 19 and 20 year olds. To see patients, one after another, being put into diabetic coma and then woken up with high doses of glucose. The glucose had to be drawn up in 50 cc syringes and was very thick, that was the hardest thing to do. Did this treatment work? I really don't know we just worked the treatment rooms and never really had the opportunity to see the patient outcomes in the long term, but for those very agitated patients, it did calm them down immediately following the treatments.

There was much fun to be had in Galveston by young girls in nursing school. The beach was always a place to go, day or night. Never mind that we had to go to work in the wards the next day in a starched white uniform while blistered from the sun. There were clubs all over the beach, which I would have hated to see my children frequenting in their younger days, but times were different then and we did not have to worry about the things that happen today. It was all pretty safe. Just good fun with music and dancing.

The first year in school, we were housed in a very old nurse's home. We were so excited because the new home was being built and we looked forward to not having to share the room with three other students. But what fun we had in that "old nurses home" I will never forget when we were being rowdy and we heard that old cage elevator coming up, knowing that the house mother was coming to check up on us. Someone would run and open the elevator door causing the elevator to stop wherever it was, in between floors. Poor Mrs. O'Neil, I can still hear her calling, "Girls, shut that door" but we made her stay in there until we were all in our own rooms with books open studying furiously. I know God gave her a special place in heaven, she deserved it. We could sneak out after curfew down the old fire escape. A wonder no one ever got into big trouble. But by our sophomore year, we went into our new nurse's home. No way to sneak out or get Mrs. O'Neil caught in the elevator between floors. She was always at the desk in the front lobby and knew exactly what time we got in.

By the late '50s, I found myself in the big city of Houston working in the Medical center. What an experience that was working with children who had had open-heart surgery and where the residents walked around with a sterile scalpel in their pockets as that was the only way to revive those little patients if they went into cardiac arrest. I guess you would not call that the "good old days" but that was what we had then. We did not have the marvels of Intensive care units, defibrillators, or pacemakers yet. Those good old days were yet to come.

Early Childhood Memories
By Carl D. Scott of New Braunfels, Texas

Preface—How do young children remember things and how do we as adults remember experiences of early childhood. How do we know that these memories are

45

accurate? Maybe it doesn't matter. Maybe the memory is more important than the event itself. This story shall be somewhat disjointed because there is not much of a story so much as there are impressions and images.

San Antonio—I was born and lived my first eight years in San Antonio. My mother was a homemaker and my father was a teller at the Frost National Bank. We lived in a two-bedroom one-bath house in southeast San Antonio on Steves Avenue. My paternal grandfather lived with us. He had the bedroom in the front of the house. My younger brother and I shared the back bedroom with my parents. I called my grandfather, "Grandfather." He lived with us until we moved to Corpus Christi in 1945 when I was eight years old— More about him in another story.

My mother's family was close-knit; and we lived not far from my mother's parents, whom I called Grancy and BoPo (pronounced "baw paw"). They lived on Highland Blvd. My grandfather was a furniture salesman at Stowers Furniture. My great grandmother, "Bobbie," lived with them. My mother was the eldest of three surviving daughters. Her older sister, Lorena May, had died at the age four of acute appendicitis. Not too far away, up the hill on Hicks Avenue lived my mother's younger sister Dorothy and her family. They had a nicer house than ours. Dorothy's husband, Roland, was the manager of the National Shirt Shop in downtown San Antonio. He had lived across the street from my grandparents with his single mother and his grandmother before marrying my aunt. My mother's other sister, Ruth, lived across town with her husband, Dean. Dean was in the army air corps during the war. I had just turned four when the Japanese attacked Pearl Harbor, and I vaguely remember hearing about it on the radio and hearing my family talk about it. I'll say more about memories of the war later.

My father wasn't as close to his side of the family. He had two sisters who lived in San Antonio, but we didn't see them very often, and even less after we moved to Corpus Christi. When I was very young, my father's sister, Mavis, and her husband, Arthur lived in San Antonio before moving to Austin. Arthur was a poor lawyer, who the family said, was too softhearted to make his clients pay their fee. I liked Uncle Arthur. I remember one time when they came over to our house, he picked me up and gave me a hug, and I remember feeling his whiskers against my cheek. Maybe he hadn't shaved that day. Not long after, he got a job in Austin in the Texas attorney general's office, which turned into a career. Mavis and Arthur had two children, Little Arthur, and Gina. Little Arthur had hemophilia and was in an out of the hospital until he died. When they visited us, we were warned that he would have to be very careful not to injure himself. We couldn't play rough with him. I felt sad when I heard that he had died. Gina, who is six years older than I, was very pretty and vivacious. She still lives in Austin.

Another of my father's three sisters, Katrina, lived in San Antonio with her husband, George, and my cousin, Mary Jane. George had a business of making ornamental iron. I can recall visiting their house and shop. The shop was downstairs, and the family lived upstairs. I was fascinated with the process of heating pieces of metal in the coal-fired forge, then pounding them into various shapes on an anvil like a blacksmith. I can still remember the odor of burning coal stoked by big hand pumped bellows.

The United States entered World War II just a few weeks after I turned four years old. Many of our neighbors had family members who joined the military or were drafted; and I recall a next-door neighbor worrying about their safe return. A number of them didn't return. My father failed the physical because of "flat feet" so wasn't drafted. He became an air raid warden instead. I rode to the neighborhood fire station with him where he was issued a gas mask and a flat metal helmet like the soldiers wore in WWI. It had the triangular civil defense insignia on it. He may have had some other items, too, like a big flash light. After picking up his items, we got into our old car, an Essex Terraplane, and rode or rolled down the hill to our house. I remember him turning off the motor and just coasting part of the way down the hill. Several years later, I played with the old gas mask. I imagined it to be a breathing apparatus for a space suit, like in the movie serial, "Rocket Man." That was even before we had a space program.

When we went to the grocery store, my mother would pull out some ration stamps to buy meat, coffee, and sugar. You couldn't get butter, so she bought oleomargarine and mixed some yellow coloring in it to make it look like butter.

Later in the war, San Antonio experienced blackouts. I remember lying in bed near my grandfather with the shades closed and the lights off. I could hear airplanes flying overhead and I felt scared that they might be enemy planes. Of course they weren't, he reassured me. San Antonio had several army air bases where they trained pilots.

Near the end of the war, probably on a Sunday afternoon, we drove up to Fort Sam Houston, where we could see all these men dressed in white behind a big wire mesh fence. They were German prisoners of war. I guess they were repatriated back to Germany after the war was over.

One Fourth-of-July, we went to a big show at Olmos Stadium that demonstrated some of the American weapons and battle enactments. Guns were fired, explosions set off, creating lots of smoke and noise. It was an exciting and awe inspiring show.

The war in Europe finally ended, and not many months later the war in Japan was also over. We heard about this terrible atomic bomb that had been dropped on Hiroshima and Nagasaki that brought Japan to surrender on my mother's birthday, August 15. Frankly, I don't remember any family celebrations, but we were all relieved that the war was over, and I'm sure there was great celebration around the town.

Cars—As I mentioned, my family owned an old Essex Terraplane, a four-door car with headlights mounted on the front bumpers. I used to stand on the running board. (Not when it was going.) It was the same kind of car that John Dillinger used as a getaway car, but ours was black. The spare tire was mounted just above the rear bumper. My younger brother and I rode in the back seat, and my mother rode in the front with my father, who drove. Sometimes my mother would take my father to work and pick him up from Frost National Bank, and later from W. T. Grant Co. After picking him up, we had to cross a railroad track near the old Southern Pacific Depot. Frequently, we would have to stop at the crossing and wait for a train to pass. It was awesome and almost frightening to see the giant steam locomotive with eight or ten big iron wheels pass close by the car puffing smoke, hissing steam, and with its bell ringing.

Of course, the car needed gas occasionally. When we went to Texaco gas station, the station attendant used a hand pump to pump gasoline up into a big glass cylinder to measure the amount of gas my dad wanted. Then he put the nozzle in the car and let the gas drain from the cylinder into the gas tank.

BoPo and Grancy owned a four door nineteen-thirties-something Dodge. After the war started, new cars were hard to get. This car also had fender-mounted headlights; and its back doors opened from the front of the car. (The hinges of the back doors were toward the rear, opposite of the way car doors are now hinged.) I used to ride with my grandfather to get watermelons, or with my grandmother go to the Piggly Wiggly grocery. My great grandmother had an old Chevrolet. She had a little wooden box that was covered with some fabric that we kids could sit on to see better when we rode with her. I guess we mostly just sat on the box seat and imagined riding with her. She didn't do much driving, as she was getting pretty old, I thought. But in the days when I lived in San Antonio, she probably wasn't as old as I am now.

Found a Wallet and Lost a Girlfriend
By Jim Godat of Del Rio, Texas
Born 1950

Back in the 1950s, when I was in the 4th grade I was always getting spankings. It did not take much of a reason to get one either. Like when your mother comes to school on parent day and the teacher finds your desk crammed full of papers. Her name was Mrs. Rucker and let's face it; she was an old biddy that should have retired years before. The worst trouble I got into that year was because of my little girlfriend at the time. She had found a wallet in an alley on her way to school and had me to keep it for her later that day. Of course, I got blamed for the whole thing when the principal found out. He even came to our house and gave my mother a hard time. I can still feel that spanking after all these years. It hurt. My mother found out later that the principal had a very shady past. After that incident, Melody was not my little girlfriend anymore. Her parents made sure of that.

Love is Like Peanut Butter
By Rebecca Mendoza of New Braunfels,
Texas
Born 1929

My parents were Lalo Morales, Sr., and Refugin Morales. There were 12 in the family,

seven girls, and five boys. My father supported his 12 children working at the W.P.A. When it was cold, they didn't work. He was a cook at the P.K. Restaurant on San Antonio Street near the closed bank. We didn't have our own home. My father had to rent the house Mr. Oscar Hass had. He was such a good man.

We had to work. My brother Lalo, Jr. and I use to plant onions for Mr. Oscar Hass. He had a place with lots of acres. We had to plant lots of roads of onions at $0.05 a row. We didn't mind at that time, everything was okay. Ten rows was a lot of work. We wanted to give our father 20 row, for a $1.00 so it was a lot. We didn't have an air conditioner and there was no heater. When it was cold, we had a wood heater. Our air conditioner was to go across the street to a river and we didn't have to pay. Now there are apartments down the river where we use to work raking leaves for Mr. Walter Zipple and Mr. Rice on corner of Zink and Market Street. Like I said, I wanted to help mother, so every $0.50 I made working I gave to my mother to help out. I just thank God for my father and mother. They showed us how to respect the value of the family and everybody else. My father and mother showed us right from wrong.

So you see I don't mind that we had to work to help out the family. It's a blessing that I did all of this for my father and mother and all the 12 children. We all got married young, but I got married years later. I started to work at textile mills at the age of 16. I was still helping my father and mother. Then I got married in 1948 with the late R. R. Mendoza. I started working as a volunteer for Red Cross and worked there for 21 years. Then I worked at the courthouse at the information desk as a volunteer also. I'm still helping others. Visiting the sick as long as I can I will help whoever needs help. I give help to people that need help. Right now, I help a couple that need help. I take food and what I can because the husband of this lady has cancer. I have been helping her with what I have. Believe me when I say when I see this lady I want to cry. I thought I had it bad when I was growing up, but I was wrong. I just want to close this letter with all the love that God gave me. Love does not cost anything. Love makes one happy. My father showed us to respect everybody. Love is like peanut butter you spread around. Right now, I am 80 years old, but I am still helping my daughter in law.

Tripping out on Geography
By Virginia Hammond of Burnet, Texas
Born 1934

When you're an eleven year old confined to a stuffy, second floor classroom when it's glorious spring outside, that's bad enough. It's even worse that there's no air conditioning, it's right after lunch, and it's time for your least favorite subject of all, geography. I just

Virginia's teacher, Mrs. Mason

had to figure out some way to get out of there. I thought I'd found the perfect reprieve, but I hadn't counted on the wisdom and intuition of my geography teacher.

Here was my plan: I would wait until Mrs. Mason was well into the geography lesson, and then I would quietly go up and ask to be excused to go the rest room. How could she possibly refuse such a request, especially when it came from one of her best students?

Now, in the mid- '40s in our region of rural central Texas, going to the rest room didn't mean a two minute trip outside the classroom and a few doors down to a clean, antiseptic looking and smelling room. With us, it was an excursion. Done properly, it could mean at least fifteen minutes' freedom, and I soon learned to make the most of it.

Here is what the trip involved: first, exit the classroom door at the back and pass through the cloakroom, which was divided into the boys' side and the girls' side. At this

Virginia Hammond

time of day, it usually held the remnants of lunches packed much earlier in the day, so there was always a musty, funky smell. Then, take a left to the head of the stairs. They were magnificent! Two flights of steps, each perhaps five feet across and perhaps a dozen steps per flight were connected by a large, delightful landing midway. This allowed for all sorts of imaginary adventures. Sometimes I was a queen standing on the landing surveying her subjects; sometimes I was a bride descending the stairs to her groom; but never once was I an eleven year old girl playing hooky from school. Once down the stairs, I still had the central hall of the bottom floor to navigate. The outside door was to the left, and beyond that, the huge concrete porch flowed right onto the sidewalk where the real adventure began. A long, winding sidewalk meandered what seemed a quarter of a mile, but most assuredly was much shorter, to what was the girls' restroom. It was a long, low building consisting of probably a dozen or so one-holers linked together. Each had an open front with a wall separating it from the next stall, which afforded a modicum of privacy. On two sides of the building was a wooden screen, which shielded the unit from curious eyes. The open pits allowed for quite a stench, and the lime that was added only seemed to make it worse. Flies swarmed around, inside and out. The whole thing was painted a yellowish brown. It was definitely not a thing of beauty. It was, instead, a thing of utility.

It was to this unlikely mecca that I made my way each afternoon around 2:00 or so. I don't recall how long the plan worked, but one day, after one of my lengthy absences, Mrs. Mason called me to her desk. "Virginia," she said, "Do you have a problem?" She waited for my answer as I stood there, wishing I could be anywhere else. I couldn't look at her. I knew my afternoon geography trips were over, and I recall the heat radiating from me, as I blushed crimson. "No ma'am,"

I answered, and returned to my seat as fast as I could. But she knew, and I knew, and I knew she knew, that I had a problem, all right, and it had nothing to do with my health: I, the shy A student, compliant, sweet little teacher's pet, had been found out! I had been tripping on geography time, and I had just taken my last trip!

I often wonder if Mrs. Mason didn't have the last laugh, though. I majored in social studies when I went to college.

Hard Work and Perseverance
By Tommy Barganier of New Braunfels,
Texas
Born 1937

New Braunfels, Texas has been my home for the past 73 years. I was two years old in 1939 when my parents, Aubrey and Snowye Barganier, and my younger brother, Howard Jr., moved to New Braunfels from Falls County, Texas in a Studebaker truck. Our first home was located on Academy Street across from the Sophienberg Museum. I remember playing in the yard at a very young age and being frightened when the 12 o'clock siren sounded.

My family lived in several different locations over the years, but the most memorable was on Faust Street in Mill Town. We shared a four-room, one bath, house with a screened-in porch. Dad and mom rented two of the rooms with primary access to the bathroom. A female renter and her daughter lived in an adjacent room, while Uncle Hub and Aunt Alice lived in the fourth room – eight people living in a four-room house.

The textile mill was the major employer in Comal County at that time. It was probably about half the size of the current facility. Mill Town had almost everything its residents needed on a daily basis: Froeleich's General

Store, Red and White Grocery Store, Calvary Baptist Church, barbershop, and even a beer joint. Almost everyone living in Mill Town was an employee of the mill and remained there most of their life. They often rented rooms in the stucco apartment house still standing today by the Faust Street Bridge. The mill eventually doubled in size and had its own outlet for selling the gingham material manufactured in the mill. Mom sewed for the public so she made frequent visits to the outlet. There were people from all areas of the U.S. buying the renowned cotton material. When homemade clothing became less popular, decreasing sales forced the outlet to close down completely. That was a sad event for mom because she spent many pleasant hours shopping for material to make our clothes as well as those for her customers.

My grandparents, Lee and Jetti Barganier, and Tom and Myrtle Bridgewater, as well as my dad worked in the textile mill. Dad took a radio repair correspondence course at the same time. Upon completion of the course, he landed a job in San Antonio at Kelly Air Force Base in the electronic repair shop. This was a major step up for a former tenant farmer. After about 25 years dad took a medical retirement from Kelly and continued living in New Braunfels until his death in 2002 at the age of 89 years. Grandpa and Granny Barganier lived next door to us. After work at the mill, grandpa cleaned up and took Howard and me to the Mill Town stores – Valley Fruit Stand, Green and White Grocery Store, and the Red and White Grocery Store to name a few. We were treated to a daily cup of ice cream, costing only a nickel.

My 1st grade in school was at Karl Schertz Elementary. The family lived briefly on West San Antonio Street, before returning to reside in Mill Town. Howard and I enrolled at Church Hill School, which housed nine grades in three rooms with something less than 100 students. There was no electricity and no indoor restrooms. Each student brought his or her own water because the well was contaminated. There were two or three grade levels in each of the classrooms, which allowed the younger students to learn from the older students while they were being taught. If weather allowed, our sack lunches were eaten outside on the ground. First and second grade students enjoyed playing on the swings and seesaws. The older kids played softball and volleyball. Today tours of the small stone building are an interesting feature of New Braunfels' history.

I remember one teacher being so concerned about our eyesight that on a cloudy day she would stand by the window and read to us from the Bobsy Twins. We students, of course, weren't above faking poor vision to have a story read to us. Younger students were dismissed from school about 15-20 minutes before the older students. That allowed us to walk home while escaping possible harassment from the older kids. My family lived on Oasis Street, about a mile from school. If the weather was bad and we were lucky enough to catch the delivery guy, Slim, at Froeleich's General Store, he would sometimes give us a ride to school in the mornings.

A wood burning stove, at home and school, provided warmth during cold weather. Air conditioning was unavailable, so we got lots of fresh air from open ventilation. It was only after WWII that air conditioning was first experienced in New Braunfels at the Brauntex Theater and National's Five and Ten Cent Store. Howard and I began riding our bicycles to school in the 2nd and 4th grades. On Saturday afternoons, we rode our bikes to the Brauntex Theater. I especially enjoyed Red Ryder westerns, and our tickets cost nine cents each. There was no money for treats once inside the theater.

It was an exciting event when dad and mom purchased the first television set in New Braunfels. It had a seven-inch screen and the black and white images were far from sharp. Nonetheless, for a while our home was packed with visitors who came to view our newest piece of furniture.

In those early years, New Braunfels was composed predominately of German descendants. My family didn't speak German and that proved to be a problem at times. Mom would have to wait in the grocery line until all German residents had been checked out. She didn't make a fuss in the store, but thought it was terribly rude and unfair. Time took care of that problem however. Our progressive little community has grown to almost 60,000 today and is a mixture of several nationalities.

After completing the 9th grade at Church Hill School, my education continued at New Braunfels High School. I was a bit small in those days, but managed to become a member of the high school football team. Though I never played a single down of varsity football, I relished those hours on the practice field, taking out-of-town bus trips with the guys, and rooting for the team while warming the bench. I learned a lot about hard work and perseverance from being on the football team.

After high school, I attended Texas A&M College and earned a degree in mechanical engineering. I enlisted in the U.S. Navy in 1960 and served two years on the aircraft carrier, "Saratoga." My Navy experience was followed by an engineering job at Kelly Air Force Base in San Antonio, which lasted 28 years before my retirement in 1992 on my 55th birthday.

In 1964, I had the good fortune of marrying my wife, Emma Harlene Lowery. We are blessed with two beautiful children, Nancy Barganier DeHaven and Brian Lee Barganier as well as five grandchildren who continue to make us proud.

Catching Up on the Latest Gossip
By Sonja Reeh Moore of New Braunfels, Texas
Born 1945

There are a lot of things I remember growing up in the '40s and '50s like no air-conditioning and only wood heaters to keep us warm. We always left our keys in the car and never locked the house when we went to town, which was 17 miles away. We were poor but we didn't know we were poor because we had each other (family). I guess one thing that really stands out is the Western Electric Old Wood Telephone. We were on a party line, meaning everyone on that line could pick up the phone and hear other conversations. Our telephone number (or ringtone) was two longs and two shorts. A long ring could be two turns of the ringer and a short could be one turn of the ringer. So, when we heard the phone ring, we listened for two longs and two shorts. Our neighbor's telephone number was two longs and one short so we had to listen carefully for that last short ring

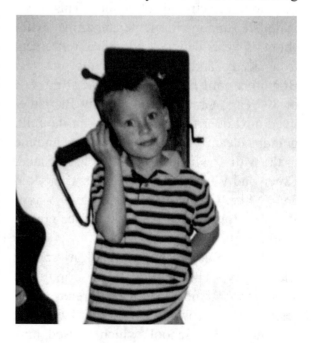

Sonja's grandson, William in her antique room

52

for our number. Of course, people listened in on each other's conversations to catch up on the latest gossip. Sometimes you would have to interrupt a lengthy conversation by breaking in and saying, "May I please have the line?" This caused an abrupt hang up.

Our Grandparent's Place and Saturday Trips to Town
By Mona Carol (Bates) Workman of Boerne, Texas
Born 1931

One of my fondest memories is when my cousins and I would spend time in the summer at our grandparent's house. They lived on a hilltop outside of the Central Texas town where I was born. We could look down and see all of town just beyond the railroad tracks. The trains ran many times a day, back in those days and it was exciting for us kids.

I loved going to the cow lot to watch the milking and gathering of the eggs. We all went bare-foot, so there was always stickers on the way to the barn. Because of the cows, chickens, pigs and the vegetable garden, we had everything we needed.

However, on Saturday everyone from far and near went to town. In those days all the cars parked in the middle of Main Street, all lined up. The men congregated all up and down the sidewalks of Main Street. They talked, whittled, and spit catching up on the latest farm prices and such. The women shopped in all the stores and visited. We kids went to the only 5 & 10 cent store in town to spend the change Papa had given us. Then, at 1:00 PM the only picture show in town opened up and for a dime and a nickel for popcorn, we saw two serials and a good shoot-m-up western. Those Saturdays were great times for me and my cousins and I shall treasure them always.

A Bitter Lesson, But a Life Saver
By Claudell Kercheville of Kerrville, Texas
Born 1936

We ranched north of Pumpville, Texas on 10 sections, raising sheep, Angora goats, and a small herd of Spanish goats. I was about 8 years old when my uncle Dave gave us a Border collie puppy, which we named Rip. Daddy wanted him for a sheep dog and told us not to play with him because that would ruin him for work.

My dad, a man of his time and upbringing, had strict ideas about animals, but considered them a valuable resource. He was kind and gentle to them and allowed no abuse. He once fired a horse wrangler for abusing a horse, but if animals broke the rules, they were put down. If a dog killed lambs, they were shot, if they got in the hen house, same punishment.

My brother, Jim, who was about 12 years old, saw Rip coming out of the chicken house early one morning. He waited until Mother and Daddy went to Pumpville to get the mail one day and told the rest of the kids. He got some eggs, punched a hole in them, and filled them with hot sauce. Then, we all went to the chicken house, Rip in tow, and gave him the eggs. He gobbled them down, but quickly spit them out, but Jim made him eat them. We was so scared Mother and Daddy would find out.

Years later, when we told the story, to my mother, after my father's death, she said he told her once that he suspected that Rip was getting in the hen house, but wasn't sure, and nothing ever came of it.

Lived Through the Bicycle Accident
By Ronnie Holloway of Pontotoc, Texas
Born 1947

Just before school was to start in the fall, my cousin, and I went to the swimming pool for one last fling on our bicycles. I was going

53

home and was running late. I was going too fast and hit a real low dip in the pavement. My bicycle broke and fell to the pavement on my head and face. The lady that lived by the street saw the wreck and called the ambulance and my mother. They took me to the hospital. I had a concussion, my teeth were knocked loose, and I was bleeding all over. My dad and mother stayed with me in the hospital and the doctor told them not to let me go to sleep. The dentist came in a few days and wired my teeth in, I was a sight. I couldn't eat any solid food. I stayed in the hospital several days and also at home. My mother and daddy and little sister were so worried about me. I lived through it all and went to Mortuary school and graduated and then got married. We have one son and he works with me, we both have our funeral directors and embalmers license and the business is going well. I now own three funeral homes and am very happy and thankful.

Beans, Beans, Beans
By Sandra Tarleton-Goll of New Braunfels, Texas
Born 1925

My family's diet in the 1930s consisted of beans, beans, beans, and beans. No meat in them, just beans. Beans on bread. Mashed beans. Bean soup. Since everybody that we knew was in the same boat, it never occurred to me that we were poor or deprived. In fact, we felt quite lucky and blessed. Our dad had a job. Granted, it was for only three days a week and only paid $3.00 a day, but $3.00 a day was more than millions of other Americans were making during the Great Depression. Dad supported nine people on that $3.00 a day: himself, my mother, six children, and our grandmother. How blessed we were to have a big company house, a car, and enough clothes. Shoes were a problem though. My dad had a

shoe repair kit for putting on new heels and half soles. Sometimes when he didn't have time to fix my shoes (I wore them out pretty fast with my rope jumping, hopscotch, and running.) I would have to cut out cardboard insoles every night for school the next day. Our diet of beans, lots of exercise and fresh air, was as healthy an existence to grow up in as could be had. I was so lucky and blessed.

Visiting the Grandparents
By Lo-Rena Scott of Tarpley, Texas
Born 1944

My maternal grandparents lived in rural Bandera County and we frequently drove up from San Antonio to visit them on weekends. My grandparents lived in a very old house with no indoor plumbing, which meant using an outhouse. At night, so as not to have to go outside to the outhouse, there was a chamber pot nearby. On Saturday night, we bathed in a large metal tub. The bath water was heated on a wood cook stove in the kitchen. The only other source of heat was a fireplace. My grandparent's water source was from a cistern and in dry spells; water was hauled to the home. The house had electricity but no refrigerator so an icebox was used. Telephone service was on a party line and I remember that the first telephone was a hand cranked wall phone. To make a call, you had to first call the operator and she would dial the number for you. Later, a rotary phone replaced the wall phone and you could then dial the number you wanted to call. My grandparents raised chickens and the feed usually came in patterned cloth sacks and I remember my younger sister and I wearing blouses made from the chicken feed sacks. My grandparents did not have a car, so my grandfather would ride his horse to town, which was several miles. I also remember riding with him in a wagon pulled by a team of horses. My mother's maiden name was Dugosh and she was a descendant of one of the original Polish families who settled in Bandera.

A Chilling Outhouse Experience
By Frank F. Ordener of Kerrville, Texas
Born 1930

In November of 1957, I went to work for the Texas Game and Fish Comm., now known as The Parks and Wildlife Department. I was sent to Kerr County as a game warden trainee. My headquarters was a one-room cinderblock cabin on the Marcus Auld Ranch near the intersection of Highways 83 and 41, by Gravin's Store. This camp had been used by game wardens and game warden trainees for a number of years, because of the distance to surrounding towns, so if a landowner had a game law violation, he had someone close by during the deer and turkey season.

This camp also had an outhouse. It was composed of four walls—no roof. The door had five large 45-caliber pistol holes in it. The story was told to me that one of the previous occupants was a ladies man and I don't recall if it was his wife or a girlfriend that had come to settle a score with him, armed with the 45. Not finding him in his car or cabin, she figured he was in the outhouse and fired away at it, but he apparently saw her coming and ran away and hid in the cedar and oak timbers. Now I will not attest to the validity of this story, but I will assure you of the truth of location and about the outhouse with no roof.

On rare occasions a freak snow storm will hit this part of the state, and one occurred during my three months at the camp, 19-20 inches of snow in one night, and of all times to have a virus, it was then! I was out there about every hour on the hour, many times with no time to brush off two inches of snow. You have heard of the "hot seat," well, this was the "cold" wet seat!

I am not a native of Kerr County, but I live in Kerrville now.

The "Round Trip Ticket" That Only Took Me One Way
By Robert Bell of Hunt, Texas
Born 1936

Our family moved from Houston to Kerrville in 1948. I was 13 years old.

During the summer of '49, my mother's cousin and wife came to visit us from Houston. My mother insisted that I ride back to Houston with them so I could visit my grandmother. She gave me a bus ticket that was good from Kerrville to Houston, and assured me the ticket could be used from Houston to Kerrville. She checked this out well. I went to Houston in good condition and spent a few days with my grandmother. She then took me to the bus station in Houston so I could get back to Kerrville, but the ticket agent would not honor my ticket, because it was from Kerrville and not to Kerrville. By then, my grandmother had left me, and I was alone.

I then, caught a local city bus to the Katy Highway. I walked about 100 yards, stopped, and started hitchhiking to Kerrville. The very first car to come along was a brand new Tan Cadillac Coupe Deville, and he stopped for me. The driver asked me how far I was going and I said, "Kerrville." He said, "That's fine, I'm going to Bandera." I said, "That was fine, you can let me off in San Antonio and I can hitch-hike into Kerrville."

About 30 minutes later, the driver said, "I'm going to go through Austin and let you off in Kerrville on my way to Bandera." I tried to talk him out of this, but he insisted, and did go through Austin and let me off in Kerrville at the bus station—two hours ahead of the bus, I was supposed to be on. I killed time for two hours and waited for the bus, but my father came early to pick me up and I got in his car and went home with him. Later, I cashed in the bus ticket and gave the money to my parents.

And that's the way it was in the '50s!

The Kindness of Neighbors
By Cynthia Engel of Fredericksburg, Texas
Born 1948

My favorite teacher was my 1st grade teacher, Mrs. Dora Meier. She taught the Rocky Hill country school. Her working day began by driving the school bus, picking up pupils from the Grapetown, Cain City, and Rocky Hill areas. She taught all the grades and played games with the children at recess and lunch. At the end of the school day, she again drove the school bus, delivering her charges home again. Then in the evenings, she graded the papers. There were no multiple choice in those days, in 1956. Her little daughter and I were the only 1st graders, so she also had a family to care for. When I hear teachers complain that they have too much to do, I admire her even more.

One of my favorite memories of childhood is of listening to the men tell their hunting stories, all in German, of course. I got great delight in hearing each little detail and breathless pause in sighting the deer and especially the tracking of a wounded deer with dogs. Everyone listened, spellbound, to the speaker.

In May of 1963, a bad storm came over our farm. Hail six inches thick covered the ground, destroying a beautiful crop of Sudan grass, which we would have made into silage for our dairy cows. A terrific wind tore all the shingles from the house roof. I was very touched the next day when a kind lady came to us with a box of groceries because she had heard that we experienced such a loss.

Settling in America
By Patricia Canellis of San Antonio, Texas
Born 1935

The fondness memories I have of my great-grandmother (Frances (Haiduk) Moravietz 1845-1946) was as she sat in her rocking chair by the wood heater in the rock house she helped build. She would be telling stories of her childhood in Poland. The lack of food, work, and cold weather. Her parents wanted a better life for their family, so they got on a boat headed to America. They made their way to Texas and then to Castroville with 15 other Polish families and then to the town of Bandera where they settled, just in time for her to celebrate her 10th birthday. The land of opportunity was a struggle, but everyone worked together and they tried to find work and survive in their new country.

She recalled the evening her father got shot and her mother removed the arrow with a kitchen knife and only a dim light and wrapped the wound with a white cloth. She also remembered the evening she was milking the cow when she was called to come to the house because it was late and dangerous to be outdoors after sun down. The next morning they found one of their calves missing and found the remains of the

Patricia's great-grandmother Frances (Haiduk) Moravietz

56

Frances Moravietz 100 year birthday

calf where the Indians had slaughtered it.

Everyone knew my great-grandmother as grandma or Aunt Fannie. I also remember grandma celebrating her 100th birthday. It was a Saturday morning at the ranch; everyone was busy setting up tables, chairs, and benches, and butchering one of the fattest lambs. Then Sunday morning all the cooking began before friends, neighbors, and relatives started to arrive with all kinds of food and gifts. There was so much food and people were everywhere. There were two birthday cakes, one was a coconut cake in the shape of a lamb, and the other was a big oblong cake with Happy Birthday on it. As everyone was leaving wishing grandma many more birthdays they were saying see you at your next birthday. As months went by and plans were in the making for her 101st birthday, which never happened, because five weeks before her birthday she suffered a stroke and one week later the second one left everyone in shock that this beautiful, warm, loving person was gone.

Sheep Herding and Indian Tales
By Lanny Leinweber of Mountain Home,
Texas
Born 1936

Back in the early '40s, I was a little boy, 8-10 years old. I am the only child, so I had to entertain myself.

My dad, Ernest Leinweber, was a rancher, as I am today. He had sheep, angora goats, cattle and a few Spanish goats for barbequing or just frying or baking. He needed help to handle or pen the goats and sheep.

So, he located a man, Mr. J. C. Hampton, who was the first man in Texas to have Border Collies for sale. My dad bought a pair and started raising and selling the pups. This made him the second man to raise these new kind of working sheep dogs. The gyps had pups nearly all the time, but one year he had four females that had pups all at once. There were 23 pups. I had a "red-rider" wagon that I pulled around. They all would not fit in my little wagon. So, I built a double deck and loaded them all, Sheep and pulled the pups "a many a mile".

We had a party telephone line to Leakey. When it rained or we had a heavy dew, we could not use the line, so when we wanted to "talk out" we would call Mrs. Maude Huffman, she was about half the way between our ranch and Leakey. We would ask her to ring "turn the crank" along with us and usually the operator in Leakey would place the call for us. There was a lady down the way that would nearly always pick up the phone when she heard it ring. We always knew pretty well it was her when we heard a click.

The more people on this party line, at one time, the less you could hear. One evening my dad couldn't hear very good, and he said loudly, "Effie, get off the phone!" Before she could think, she said, "I'm not on the phone."

One short story is when my great-grandmother was little, in about 1858. She saw some Indians come near their house down at the barn. Her dad told her not to make a sound. They all were quiet. The Indians took two of their horses. They considered themselves lucky to keep their lives.

The Good & the Bad From a True Vet Who Lived It
By Clarence Ray Lee of Ingram, Texas
Born 1932

I'm almost 81 years of age. My name is Clarence Ray Lee. I have a good memory of my childhood days. I never, ever used drugs or ever smoked. We had only radio to enjoy. The old non-violent funny radio shows including Amos and Andy, Jack Benny, plus mystery radio programs. Later, in the '50s, we had a small black & white TV with good family funny shows, unlike the violent ones now.

We could go to bed with unlocked doors even. Children could walk to school or the movies, unharmed. To help people, was a thing to do, as we were all poor people. Church on Sunday was a thing to do, maybe chicken for dinner.

Later, as I grew to the age of 17, my mother signed for me to enter our military. Respect was a must. Yes, sin was in us!

Boot camp in the Marines was tough. Later came Korea, the untold truth of this forgotten war of 1950-1953. (Not) to be revealed of very near, the number of deaths of this three-year war compared to the number of deaths over a10 year period while in Viet Nam, another pain staking, painful war. I earned eleven combat awards. Survival, our discipline, respect, and desire saved us.

I'm now in U.S. Veterans care and praise the V. A. care in San Antonio and Kerrville, Texas.

I feel most or our lawmakers should have had this experience. Most did not serve who make our laws.

In addition to my childhood days, our grandmothers were our doctors! To step on a nail, we soaked our foot in coal oil or better known as kerosene. To purify blood, grandmothers made tea out of a bark root called sassafras. When a doctor was really needed, few had money. Eggs, butter, ham, or bacon was given for doctor's fees. Grandmothers were wonderful! Mine was ½ Indian. She cooked her grandchildren fried pies from dried fruit. We had no car until I got out of the military. We were honest, but poor!

Read back on how President (Hoover) put America in worse shape than now. President Hoover, a republican along with his sassafras tea, all elderly will recall, came a tonic called "Hadacol." Go back in time, and do check, as songs about Hadacol also came out.

School buses were how kids far from school traveled, unlike kids now days with fancy vehicles.

When told to take garbage out, kids didn't say. "Awh, Mom!"

Gasoline for those with a vehicle was like 16 to 18 cents per gallon and wages like 30 cents per hour.

Yes, it was different then, but honor did exist and to help people did exist.

I Would Do it All Over Again
By Helen Deeds of Rochelle, Texas
Born 1930

I was born in 1930. As far back as my memory takes me, I can remember the Great Depression and the dust storms. I was born and raised near Fife, Texas in the northwestern part of McCulloch County. I started to school in Fife. I walked 2 ½ miles to school. The worst

Helen Deeds family, she is the baby

58

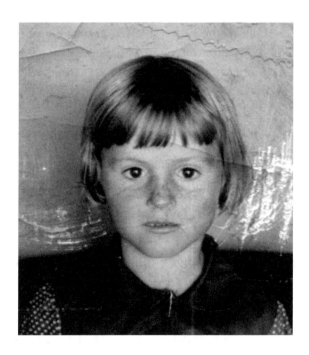

Helen Deeds in 1930

times in my life were every spring my mother gave me a dose of Castor Oil. That was the worst tasting thing I ever took. She thought we couldn't go into spring without it! My 1st grade though 4th grade teacher was Florence Whithead. I will always remember her.

My dad had several cows that he milked and sold the milk to a creamery in Brady, Texas. I wanted to learn how to milk, but that was the worst mistake I had made! We had a telephone that hung on the wall. Our number was two longs and a short. There were several people on our line and you could sure listen in and find out what was going on.

When I started to school, my parents told me if I got a spanking at school, I would get another one when I got home. I sure tried to be good. The most fun we had was the 4th of July jubilee in Brady, Texas. There was always a big carnival and horseracing. We didn't have much money to ride the carnival rides, but there were swings and slides that were free.

My dad would go to Brady, Texas every Saturday and at the time; my grandfather lived with us he would go too. They would let me go. My grandfather would give me a quarter and

I could get a hamburger and go to the movies. It was called the "pitcher show." My mother washed our clothes on a washboard. We had a creek that ran across our place. She had her wash pot there and boiled our clothes and rinsed them. She hung them on bushes until they were dry. She always had the whitest clothes.

My dad sold our place and bought another one in a sandy land farm in San Saba County. I cried because I had to leave all of my friends, but I spent my 11th and 12th grades in Richland Springs, Texas. I met a lot of friends there! I was almost 16 when I had my first date. I finally married him; I have had a wonderful life. We had three children and I now have grandchildren and great-grandchildren. My husband and I were married 63 years when he passed away four years ago. If I had this to do over, I think I would do this all again.

Catching Lawbreakers
By MiMi Hardwick of Rio Frio, Texas
Born 1932

A beautiful summer afternoon sitting on the Frio River running behind our summer place called Hi Vali. It was our annual family get together over the 4th of July week for our children and grandchildren. It can't be! I believe it is? Surely not! Total nakedness, yes! One? No! Three with sombreros strategically placed to conceal themselves when the right audience was not around. Maybe, to also avoid painful sunburn? Yes, I said when an audience was not around, because their purpose was to shock and gain sick, perverted attention. This desire to shock and gain attention was played out by three young men floating down the sparkling Frio naked. I froze for a brief minute to make a plan, as I was in shock and disbelief, and then I began to slowly pursue the culprits down the river. When they approached the bank on the east side of camp

Yeargan, they got out of their inner tubes to walk up to their cabin. I followed at a safe discreet distance, so they would not try to run away before being caught and questioned. I was in luck as I approached the Yeargan's office. There sat a D.P.L. car. The officer called the Sheriff's department and gave the report.

Exposing one's self to young children is a felony. We were having our annual family reunion with at least eight children under 10 years old on the river swimming and playing. There were soon numerous D.P.S. and Sheriff's department vehicles surrounding us! One of the D.P.S. Sheriff's cars had the three lawbreakers with them! The officers encouraged the young men to apologize and understand the laws pertaining to their conduct.

Our family is a family of schoolteachers, so we tried to instruct the young men about a better way to enjoy the Frio River.

My Dog Trixie, a Life Saver
By Michael Collins of New Braunfels, Texas
Born 1935

My brother and I were working in the field one day, when a faun jumped up. We caught her and decided she was an orphan. Not true, but we brought her to the house, got a baby bottle and fed her cow's milk. Of course, Mom did most of it, because we were in school. I named her "Mable" after my favorite teacher.

I was not a good student. The only things that interested me at all were history and literature. One day she gave us an IQ test. When she graded it, she called me in and said only one girl in the class made a higher score than I. She said no more C and D's for me. It didn't work, but she tried. This girl that had the higher score was a straight-A student. I think the only reason I scored so high was that I read so much.

Back to the little deer, Mom was the only one that could touch her. She would come and take a cookie out of us kid's hand. She loved gingersnaps, but she wouldn't let us handle her.

I hunted or fished nearly every day. Not hunting to kill something, normally I never had to kill for food. The main thing I would kill was rats and snakes. There were a lot of rattlesnakes in our area at that time. I only got bit one time, and I didn't tell Mom or Dad, because I was afraid they would take me to the doctor. Anyway, I didn't get sick. I know now it was what they call a "dry bite" with little or no venom injected. I still have those two puncture marks on my leg. I never did tell Mom or Dad, but I have shown them to my children. I'm not sure they believe me.

My dad brought home a small fox-terrier female one day. She was three or four years old. Her name was Trixie. He said she was a snake killing dog. No one but me knew how good she was. The first time we encountered a rattlesnake, her and I were going from the house to the river. The rattlesnake was off to the side of the road in some brush. He started rattling and she jumped right in there. I had my 410 shotgun and was screaming at her to get away. She paid no attention to me, and started shaking this snake. Some of the venom got on me, but it didn't hurt anything. Venom will not harm you unless it gets in an open wound. I heard you can even ingest venom and it won't hurt you. I never tried that. Trixie was my guardian from then on. She killed many snakes. I was always there with my 410 shotgun, but I mostly didn't interfere.

One day she found a rattlesnake in some low brush. I couldn't see the snake, or get very close. I heard her yelp and knew she was bit. She killed the snake, but there were two snakes there. I killed the other one finally, but Trixie was bitten behind her front leg in the rib cavity. It was hot and they were big snakes. I have heard people say a little snake is worse than a big one, but if I had a choice, I would rather get bit by a small one. Trixie died, and it still hurts me. Every boy should have a dog.

Not Two Pennies to Rub Together
By Alberta Elliott of Brady, Texas
Born 1932

I was born in 1932, amid the Great Depression. We lived on a farm. We had plenty of food. We had two riding horses, two mules to pull the plow, hogs, a cow, chickens and wild game to eat, plus our garden, fruit trees and beehives. What we didn't have, was even two pennies to rub together. We couldn't pay our taxes. The government decided to help us out. They would pay us for our extra animals. My father chose the two mules. He could still use the two horses to pull the plow with. They paid him for the mules then, they killed and buried them. Of course, they had paid for them. So we didn't get to keep them too. What a waste! At least we got our taxes paid.

When I was about twelve, my father started raising sheep. They would get worms and die sometimes. My father told me and my older sister, if we would pick the wool off the dead sheep and sell it, we could have the money. No one can even imagine how horrible a job that was. By the time we managed to find the sheep in a hundred acre pasture, they had been dead for quite a few days. We did it anyway, so we could buy material for mother to make us new dresses. We sold enough wool for us to start to school in new dresses and shoes.

We had chores after school every day. We were the oldest, so ours was to get wood. We had to get small sticks for the cook stove and larger wood for the heater in the living room. It always took us until dark. When we got in

from school, we would go by the stove for some left over cornbread and go by the garden for an onion. That would have to hold us until supper. After supper, we would have to start on our homework. We had to do this using a coal-oil lamp. It took my sister longer to do hers than it did me, so I got to stay up and read. We couldn't afford to waste the oil for the lamps. I could have stayed up and read all night on a good "Nancy Drew" book, or Judy Bolton. I felt too guilty for doing that, so I had to stop.

On Sundays, we could play our Edison Victrola player. You had to wind it up with a handle until it was tight. It had round records that slipped over a cone shaped steel cylinder about six inches long. We had about seventy records we could play. My favorites were, "She'll Be Coming Round the Mountain," "Listen to The Mocking Bird", "Mr. Jones," and many more. Of course, this was after church. We went to church every Sunday then, the rest of the day was spent visiting or doing what you wanted to do. We never worked on Sunday. It was a day of rest. Not any of the stores were open in town on a Sunday. No one worked. You either ate dinner with another family, or they ate with you.

Somewhere along the time of World War II, we had a ration book. Sugar, coffee, and tires were the things that hurt us the worst. I still have one ration book in my name. We were very vigilant and watched every bee that flew by. We would follow it, if we could, until it went back to its tree. Then we would smoke the bees out and get the honey. If you had honey, you didn't have to have sugar.

At about that same time we picked up old bones in the pasture and every piece of scrap iron that we could find. We sold it. It was used for the war. I don't know what it was used for.

I know a lot about all of your "memory joggers," but my three pages are filled. Sorry I couldn't get more of them in.

Life in Texas
By Winnie Scott of Kerrville, Texas
Born 1922

I was born in Bee County, Texas on March 3, 1922. I lived on a farm until I was 15. I rode horseback to school. We moved to Kendal County in the fall of '37. I lived five miles from Kendalia. I finished the 8th grade. I was married when I was 16. I moved to Kerr County to Kelly Creek area on a ranch for 12 years. I raised one child and remarried in 1949 and then raised four more children. I'm presently 91. I have a son in Easley, South Carolina. He will be 63 this year. My daughter lives in Puyallup, Washington; she is 59.

Leslie D. Scott and Winnie A. Scott

Stimulating the Senses
By Frances Schneider of Pleasanton, Texas
Born 1939

My mother in law, Maude Maltsberger Schneider, was born in 1894, and was 63 when her youngest son, Harvey and I were married in 1957. By then, doing the weekly laundry was not nearly the chore that it had been. I'm sure many can remember why laundry was done only once a week. Mom, as I called her, was a hard-working farm wife, who had a small outbuilding near the house, which was called the washhouse. There was a wide shelf along one side, which held a milk separator, but also had room for two large square zinc washtubs, which were placed side-by-side on the shelf, and filled with clean cold water on washday. The building also contained an old electric Maytag wringer washer.

The washer was placed next to the shelf beside the rinse tubs each washday. Before the electric model, mom told me, a gas-powered washer had been used. She told me that in the old days the water was heated in a large, old iron pot over a fire! In 1957, hot water was hauled from the house and cold water came from a garden hose. For obvious reasons, clothes were carefully sorted. Whites and light colors went into the washer first, ran through the wringer into the first tub and stirred by hand, then through the wringer again onto the final rinse. Colored clothes were washed next, and other loads progressed to the final load, the men's really dirty work clothes. In the old days, these were washed in a large iron kettle over the fire, stirred with long sticks and literally boiled clean. The powered washer was considered a giant leap forward.

I still remember the fresh smell of the bleach and bluing, and the feel of the progressively cooler water and the feeling of living on the edge as the clothes were put through that wringer from tub to tub. The clothes to be starched had to be treated separately after washing. The dry starch was dissolved in cold water, and then boiled. It took a sure eye, like mom's, to get the clothes starched just right. The clothes were then hung with clothespins onto long lines, raised in the middle as needed with long poles. One could wear a clothespin apron around the waist, or push a clothespin bag hung on a hanger along the line. I loved hanging the sheets and large items, but hated those socks and other small items. For obvious reasons, ironing was a chore reserved for the next day. And of course, rinse water was used to water the yard.

I can't remember exactly when we were able to have an automatic washer, but of course, we embraced progress. Then finally, I got a dryer, though I still hung clothes on a line for quite a while, as my children can remember that. Gone forever however, are the days when all the washing had to be done at one time. But I fondly recall the time we spent together getting to know and appreciate each other. And I remember vividly the senses that chore aroused in me. Incidentally, my sweet mother-in-law lived to be ninety-eight!

The Castor Oil Chaser
By Wanda Lancaster of Austin, Texas
Born 1923

Got off the school bus and walked/ran over a mile home to listen to the radio program, *Jack Armstrong, The All American Boy.* I was always told if l got a spanking at school, I'd get another at home. I carried water uphill from a spring. We had to clean the wooden frame around the spring to control the crawdads. There were no inside toilets, there were chamber pots at night and bushes in the daytime. At the grandparents two-holers we used and Sears and Roebuck catalogs were used as toilet paper.

At hog killing time we got to roast the "melt" over the coals and eat with salt and pepper! The grandmother would render the fat and we'd eat the cracklin. Then she would make lye soap in the black iron pot, cut it when it hardened and placed on a shelf made between mesquite branches. We had a three-room schoolhouse with the first three grades in one room, fourth and fifth in another, and sixth and seventh in another. There were no inside toilets in school.

When I left to watch the sister and twin brothers, I encountered a rattlesnake. I put a board on it and stood on it several hours until the parents came home. My dad was very storm conscious; his father's meat market had been blown away by a tornado at Zepayr, Texas. When they moved between San Saba and Richland Springs, Texas, grandpa built a storm cellar before he built a house. My mother was not bothered by approaching storms, so when dad was away on a job he would leave me with this comment, "Watch the sky for approaching storms, and take the kids to the storm cellar" about a mile away.

Our icebox had to be filled with blocks of ice. The drip pan had to be emptied often and we saved the "soft" water for shampoos. Parents thought it wise in the springtime to give us a "through of medicine" Calotabs followed by Epsom salts. Took a long time for me to enjoy orange juice as I associated it with Castor Oil "chaser." Farm chores were chopping cotton and corn, and then picking cotton, and the least favorite chore was heading maize. Oh yes, other chores were slopping the hogs and gathering eggs and feeding chickens. And a treat was going to the cotton gin with grandpa. He would harness the mules to the wagon, load it with freshly picked cotton and we'd head for the gin. On the return, he would circle by the grocery store for the few essentials they had to buy - coffee, flour, sugar, and he would add a bag of candy for me. The Watkins Dealer came by the house regularly with spices and flavorings and grandma would pay them in eggs and chickens. The Watkins man always had chewing gum for the children.

Weekly bathwater wasn't changed often (if ever) so you tried to be as close to the first as possible. We used old order catalogs to cut out paper dolls and made dollhouses out of apple crates. We used matchboxes for cars. Then outside we built playhouses under shade trees and outlined the rooms with rocks. I studied by kerosene lamplight and had to help keep chimneys cleaned and wicks trimmed. Experiences from growing up in the country have increased awareness of my environment. I belong to the Environmental Guild at our church and volunteer at the Wildflower Center using native plants in flower arrangements placed throughout the center.

River Bottom Campout
By Bob Wilson of Bertram, Texas
Born 1933

In early summer of 1939, it was agreed by a number of people to go fishing on the nearby Colorado River of Texas. These people were all closely related and were all surviving the Great Depression as well as they could. None had fared well financially, but all had plenty to eat due to their heritage of farming the river bottoms and ranching on the uplands that followed the Texas Colorado from its source on the high plains of West Texas to the Gulf of Mexico. World War II had not started and the government had not yet declared that giant reservoirs to control floods would be made in the peaceful valleys of Colorado. I was one of the people and since I was only six years old, I didn't know much of anything except that I loved my grampa and grandma and uncles and aunts as well as most of my cousins.

The river was only a half-mile away so the few trucks and cars that were still running in those lean years did the transfer of cooking and sleeping gear easily. They carried large tarpaulins for shelter and bed covers. They carried cast iron pots and skillets and fire blackened coffee pots. The essentials of lard, salt and pepper, and flour were not ignored. Nature and the river would provide the rest. There may have been a jug of mustang grape wine somewhere in the camp, but it caused no problem. In those days and

in that part of the country women and kids never touched alcohol except in the form of various patented medicines that contained enough alcohol to help you with your female problem or catarrh if either got out of hand.

It is not likely that in this century any child in a civilized country will enjoy such peace and harmony as existed in those river camp outs at that time. The only light was from fires and kerosene lanterns or the moon. There were no radios or televisions to belch forth obscenities, no telephones to jangle at 2:00 a.m. with a crank call, no sirens to indicate another death or injury to those who didn't survive another night in the city, and no roar of jetliners approaching or leaving a city sized airport. There was only the occasional owl hoot and the murmur of the river after women and kids were bedded down. Most of the men sat by the glowing coals of a dying fire and told stories and drank coffee. Tarpaulins were pegged tightly over a bed of small fragrant branches of the juniper trees that abounded. A 12x12 foot tarpaulin with quilts and blankets on it made a wonderful bed for a whole raft of kids or five or six adults. If rain threatened, another tarpaulin could quickly be rigged on poles driven into the ground to make a huge pup tent.

At various intervals during the night the sound of a tiny bell of the size often used on turkeys or geese would send the men to one or the other of the trotlines they had strung across the river or one of the creeks coming into the river. These bells were attached to a limber stake or an overhanging branch of a willow tree that was one end of the baited line. When the bells tinkled it almost always meant that a hungry catfish had sampled the bait on one of the hooks and was caught. That fish and others were only hours away from being part of a buffet that lasted through the campout. Bacon, beans, Dutch oven cornbread, fried fish, and the plentiful soft-shelled turtle is not haute cuisine, but I can smell and taste it these 74 years later. If there were families today that could gather to form such a camp out it would cost several thousand dollars and be fraught with many dangers – none of the dangers would be catfish or turtles.

A Rattlesnake Den and the Marvel of Electricity
By Larry W. Seiler of Blanco, Texas
Born 1944

When I was about eleven or twelve, my family took a short vacation trip through Central Texas. My parents and we kids along with my aunt and uncle were traveling together. A few miles north of Fredericksburg, Texas, is a giant granite monolith called, Enchanted Rock. At that time, Enchanted Rock and the surrounding area was on private property, but it still attracted many visitors. Today it is owned by the state of Texas and is a state park. Today it has become so popular that you must arrive early in the morning if you want to get into the park without waiting. Once the park reaches capacity, they will not let any additional visitors until someone leaves. This was not the case back in those days.

Enchanted Rock is a solid, pink granite rock that rises 425 feet above the surrounding terrain. The first thing that everyone wants to do when they arrive there is to hike to the top of the rock. This particular day was no exception. We, along with my aunt and uncle started hiking up the face of the granite. The trek is steep and fairly grueling. That did not faze my brother and I, but my parents and aunt and uncle being somewhat older, needed to stop and rest part way up the mountain. Mom stopped and sat down on a large granite boulder.

A few minutes later, Uncle Bill caught up with her and said, "Mildred, there are a bunch of rattlesnakes under that rock." Now, my uncle was a regular practical joker, always telling funny stories or playing jokes on people. He especially loved to kid my mother. Mom continued to sit on the large rock and swing her legs back and forth over the edge. "I'm sure there are," she said. "Sure," she said, rather nonchalantly. About that time, my dad and aunt caught up to them. "He's not kidding!" Exclaimed my dad. Suddenly there was fear in Mom's eyes. She quit swinging her legs. She quickly jumped off the rock in as big an arc as she could muster, and as far away from the rock as possible. She turned around and looked under the rock. Sure enough, there beneath the rock taking refuge from the sun was a den of rattlesnakes. Suddenly her legs got a little shaky.

We made camp that afternoon in Inks Lake State Park. After camp was set up, Dad and Bill went over to the camp headquarters, where they got to talking with one of the park rangers. He told them about a small peninsula that jutted out into the lake at one point. The ranger said that from that tip of land you could see both the Ink Lake Dam and the Lake Buchanan Dam. It was especially beautiful at night when the dams were lighted.

After dark that night, we all walked out to the end of the point to see the sights. After we were there a while, my uncle said, "Wow!" The ranger was right. You can see both damn lights from here."

When I first started staying with Grandma and Grandpa, they already had electricity, but not indoor plumbing. We had to use the outhouse out back. My dad used to tell the following story.

By the 1940s, most large American cities had electricity, but because of the cost involved in putting in power lines, most rural areas were still without power. This changed when Senator Lyndon Johnson helped push through the Rural Electrification Act. Almost overnight, power lines were being stretched all across rural America.

One da   y the power company notified Grandpa that they would be extending electricity to his farm within the next few weeks. Finally, the day arrived. The crew put in several utility poles and ran wiring all the way from the road to the farmhouse. They put an electric meter on the outside of the house and then ran a wire inside, around the wall, and up to the ceiling. From there they dangled a long wire with a socket on the end. They screwed in a light bulb, and when they pulled the chain, it lit up. Everybody marveled at the new-fangled light. All, Grandpa could say is, "I'm paying $3 a month for this?" Of course, over the next several months, they had lights in every room as well as electrical outlets.

Sometime later, my uncle and my dad got together and they bought Grandma and Grandpa a brand new 19 inch black and white television set. Color TVs did not yet exist. "What am I going to do with that?" Grandpa asked. "Watch TV," his sons replied. "There ain't nothin' on there I want to see," he proclaimed. "Why don't you just take that contraption with you?" Of course, they left it with him.

Several months later, my Uncle Floyd asked, "Dad, are you watching anything on that TV?" "Just the news, that's all. There's nothin' else worth watchin'," he stated. A short time later, everyone was sitting on the front porch, a favorite gathering place on the farm. Uncle Floyd, Uncle Bill, and my dad were talking about the latest episode of *I Love Lucy*. They would recall a particular scene and then really laugh. Finally Grandpa said, "Did you see it when…"—and he went on to describe a recent episode." I thought you only watched the news," said Uncle Floyd. "That's right," he said, "That's all I watch." Everyone chuckled.

I can also remember spending some time at the farm during the winter. The house had no insulation. In fact, the outside clapboard

was what you saw when you looked at the walls on the inside—just boards and 2 X 4's in front of them—no insulation whatsoever. The only heating was a wood stove and a pot-bellied heater in the kitchen. There might be a fire in the heater when they went to bed, but it would quickly burn out after everyone went to sleep.

Grandma and Grandpa slept in separate beds. They had old mattresses that sunk down in the middle so far that Grandpa's mattress was touching the floor. I would get in Grandma's bed, and I'd pull this thick feather comforter over my head. It would keep us warm until morning.

Grandma would always be the first one up, before sunup. She would fetch some wood and light the fire in both the stove and the heater. They had an old hand pump in the kitchen that pumped water into a washbasin that was kept on the cabinet next to the pump. There was an old metal dipper that hung on the wall. When you wanted a drink of water, you just grabbed the dipper and pumped a little water into it and drank. It always seemed to taste so good—nice and cold, even in the summer time.

I can remember on one occasion when it was really cold. I got up after Grandma had lit the stove and the heater. It was starting to warm up in the kitchen, but the water in the washbasin was still frozen solid.

Taking a bath at Grandma's was no fun, especially in the wintertime. She had a room off the kitchen where she kept fruit jars and other things. There was a big washtub in there that hung on the wall. When it was time for a bath, she would get the tub down, place it under the pump, and fill it half full of water. Then she'd take the tub out to that small room. Next, she would put a kettle of water on to boil. Once it was boiling, she would add the hot water to the bath water a little at a time until it was the right temperature. Then, we'd take off our clothes and jump in. It always seemed that you froze in the wintertime, even when the bath temperature was just right—it was always cold in that little room!

A Family of Pride, Living on the Guadalupe
By L.K. Walker of Canyon Lake, Texas
Born 1923

I am a ninety-year old great-great grandson of Wilhelm Martin Sattler,--one of the settlers of Texas. He was the son of a very prominent German family and came to Texas with Prince Carl-Solms in 1844. This group of German settlers chose the New Braunfels area and named it after Braunfels, Germany. My great-great grandfather was given city lots, but he chose to acquire rural acreage on the Guadalupe River instead. In about 1847, he

Caroline Bennie George

Wilhelm Martin Sallter

returned to Germany and brought his family (wife, two sons, and a daughter Caroline, who became my great-grandmother) to Texas and to live on that acreage.

More than six hundred acres are still owned and occupied by his descendants—my family (three sons and their families and myself and my wife) and a second cousin and his family.

The persons living on the acreage have changed down through the years, but one resident spent her entire life here. She was my grandmother's sister, my Aunt Carrie, who never married. She was a true pioneer who rejected modernization. When telephone service and electricity became available in the 1940s, she positively rejected them. When I became old enough, I started spending as much time as I could with Aunt Carrie and some of my fondest memories are from that time in my life.

There was a dug well on the property from which Aunt Carrie got water for household use, but not for drinking. That drinking water

Original Sattler Post Office

was toted by bucket from a spring along a creek below the house. Baths were taken in the creek in the summer and skipped (except for body "wipe-downs" from a basin) during the winter. Laundry was done erratically by putting a big iron pot over an outdoor fire to heat water. This heated water was put in a washtub and dirty items were scrubbed on a washboard until clean, wringing out and rinsed in a tub of cold water by hand and then hung on a line to dry. Some clothes had to be ironed. This was accomplished by heating "flat irons" on the wood burning kitchen stove. You had two irons and kept exchanging them as they cooled.

Aunt Carrie put in a huge garden, spading the soil by hand and planting the same way. To keep it growing in the Texas heat, she had to tote a bucket of water, and water each plant with a dipper as her garden plants ripened. She harvested them and cut them up and "canned" them in glass jars for winter use. This was time consuming, as these jars had to be processed (boiled in water) for sometimes hours, and then sealed tightly with lids and rubber sealing rings.

Meat on the table was not always available. It depended upon how good a "shot" Aunt

Carrie was, (and she was a good one). Deer, rabbits, and wild turkeys were available year round for the taking. She raised chickens for eggs and eating and she had milk cows. Calves were also available for butchering. The ranch lies on the Guadalupe River, so "seafood" was also available.

Mail service became available to the area during the 1860's, thanks to my great-great grandfather who applied for a permit and obtained one to carry the mail from the log cabin post office (still standing) on his acreage to other areas. Eventually the mail delivery was taken over by someone else who had a store about a mile away, but the name of "Sattler Post Office" remained.

Today there is a village of Sattler, named after my great-great grandfather.

By the time I was growing up, Aunt Carrie was riding her horse to get her mail at the "new" post office. She always had her 41-caliber Colt pistol on her hip. One evening her dog, "Wimpy" was barking outside the house, so Aunt Carrie opened the door to see what he was barking at. There was a big rattlesnake coiled up on a flat rock that served as her front step. She grabbed her 41-caliber Colt six-shooter and shot its head off. She would have been in her seventies at the time.

Aunt Carrie was a well-informed, self-educated individual. Her knowledge of astrology was remarkable, and when I was visiting, she would take me out at night and point out the Milky Way and other stars and astrological bodies.

I am extremely proud of my ancestors and have tried to pass that pride down to my children and grandchildren. There is no limit as to what they can do if they choose to. My great-great grandfather, Wilhelm spoke five languages and worked in the land office in Austin. My great-grandmother (his daughter Caroline) was a college graduate. They are proof that the sky is the limit, even this day and age.

Keep Looking Up, He's Coming Back
By Leon H. Sims of Kingsland, Texas
Born 1936

I was born in March 28, 1936, in a little place called Kirkland, Texas. This place is west of Vernon, Texas. I was the fifth child of a family of nine.

We had a cistern, water well. We caught our water from the roof of the house, homemade gutters down in the well. When it was dry and in the wintertime, we would go down to a frozen ground tank and cut ice and put it into the well. This would give us cold water for the warmer months ahead, and for them dry times it didn't rain.

My dad always worked for wages and it was on the farm or ranch. Time was very hard them years, but we always had food on the table. It was beans and taters during the week and chicken on weekends. We moved to a place called White Flat in the '40'. We lived in a grocery store that was the old Four Corner grocery store. My younger sister was born there in that old store. My mother put her in a potato bin that was built in the counter. That is where she slept. I started my first year of school there in White Flat. My dad was working on a farm there. This was the first time I got to drive an old regular Farmall tractor. It was on steel wheels with lugs so it would stay up on the beds. The cotton was planted in the bottom of the bed at that time.

We moved to Vernon, Texas in 1946. My dad went to work for the M.M. Tractor place at that time. M.M. put out the first combine, and I can remember riding in that big old hopper bin where the wheat came to. It was quite an experience for a ten year old boy. Then, we moved to Oklahoma in 1949, at Tillman County. We move down close to Red River, on a ranch and farmland. My dad made 100 dollars a month then, and got about 15 acres of cotton for his pay. We kids did all the hoeing and cotton pulling at that time.

I went to a school at Victory High School at that time and finished school there in 1956. When we weren't working, we were fishing on Red River; caught some good fish there. I moved to Wichita Falls in 56, I was going to get me a good city job and buy me a car. I saved my money up and which was 300.00 dollars. I always carried it with me. My friend, Jerry Robinson, which I graduated school with, moved with me to Wichita Falls. We also moved to a rent place together. One night when we were coming back from a picture show from down town, some young gangs pulled behind us and they started to get out of their car. One of these young men had a gun. They were going to rob us. I had this car money on me that I had worked so hard for. I told Jerry, "Let's run for it." Boy was we scared. We ran about 10 blocks and never looked back. I could have run another 10 blocks if I had to. They didn't rob us we got away from them. Anyway, I went down to a car lot and found me a 50 Chevy Club Coup, and bought it. I left Wichita Falls a year later. Went on a wheat harvest with my brother-in-law, Archie Clark. When we got through with the wheat harvest, we went to Plainview, Texas to cut maze that fall. When that was over, I needed to go to work, so Archie and I went out to a place called Green Machinery Company; this was a water well business. I started out on a drilling rig, and a man by the name of Bill Bloyce said that he was going to make a pump puller out of me. They dug up an old pump rig and I fixed it up so I could go to work on it. I didn't know an oil-lube pump, from a water-lube pump. So, I had to learn the hard way, by going out and working. I was with this company for 9 years. I spent two years in the Army. In this time that I was working at this place, I was working on the North Plains. I would go and leave at 4 o'clock in the morning and drive to Dumas, Texas. I would get there at about 8 o'clock that Monday morning at Dumas, Texas. My brother-in-law was working at this Green Machinery Co. there as a mechanic. They sold well engines for the pump to the farmers there. I was short- handed this Monday morning. It was in the winter time of the year. Archie Clark went out with me to Los Animas, Colo. This day we had a test pump to put in a hole there. We worked all day in the snow. It was cold there and the wind didn't help any. We started home and stopped in Boise City, Okla. for coffee. It was about 10 PM at night. We sat down there at the bar there in the café and was drinking our coffee when a man walked in from the street and sat down by Archie Clark. All of a sudden, I heard a popping sound 2 times. I thought it was some high school kids shooting off fire crackers. Then, I saw my brother-in-law fall off the stool. This man had put the gun to his head and shot two times. I stood up and cussed this man. He put the gun on me and then just backed up and sat down in a booth. He laid the gun on the table at this time. At this time, I didn't know the Lord Jesus. It was a miracle that he didn't shoot me. The Lord had a plan for this young man at this time. Praise the Lord.

Going back to 1962 is the year I got married to a young lady named Arlis L. Culp in July. About three years later, we had a baby girl that was born on my birthday. She was born with cerebral palsy. She was a very happy child, even though she could not walk. She had motor retardation. My dad-in-law and I built her a walker to get around the house. When she was almost 4 years, the Lord took her home. This is when I found Jesus as my savior. Arlis and I got in a church that was Northside Baptist Mission church. I was ordained as a Deacon in this church a few years later. We saw a lot of good things happen there in the 26 years that I was there. In 1972, we adopted a baby boy that was 11 months old. He never did go to a public school in his time in school. He was a good student in school. He got his first scholarship paid in full to go to Waylon

Baptist University then he was on the Dean's list for four years. In 1991, I had to take early retirement. Arlis and I had bought a 5th wheel trailer, so we started to go south in the winter time. We started coming to Kingsland in the winter time, so in 1999 we had a sale and moved to the hill country. Praise God, it was the best move we ever made. We looked for a church for about 1 ½ years before we joined Highlake Baptist church. This is where we are still at. The Lord hasn't moved us somewhere else. We built a new house in 2000. It took me 2 years to do the work. It is a Muller tin house. Some of the men at Highlake Baptist helped me put the roof on. A man by the name of Glyn Ash helped do a lot of the framing work inside. Going back a little, this is one of the best places in Texas that you can live in. Like West Texas, there are no dust storms and bad wind here like Plainview where the wind blows every day, and you have to put up with tornados there. When we built there, we put half of the house under the ground, two bedrooms, two baths and a Den with a fireplace there. It was a very quiet house during bad weather.

The Lord has been very good to us in these years. I will be 77 years old and Arlis is 73 years old. She is in fair health, but she broke her hip two times this year. I am her house keeper, nurse, and provider. She is getting around better these days, praise the Lord. I am looking for his coming to get us one of these days when he gets through with me.

Yes, I never have flown in an airplane, not that I am afraid of flying. There is a lot of Texas and parts of this U.S. I haven't seen. Keep looking up; he is coming back one day!

My Early Blanco Memories
By Dorothy Lee Howe Dillon of Blanco,
Texas
Born 1928

I was born January 21, 1928 in the old

70

Dorothy's parents, Annie Bessie (Corley) and Thomas Perry Howe

rock Harrison/Howe house on what is now known as 102, 6th Street. In September 1934, I entered 1st grade, Mrs. Zuma Wier, being my teacher. This was during the Depression years, with finances in our family being in very short supply. So my mom, Annie Bessie (Corley) Howe, sent me to the Red and White grocery store (located on the southeast corner of the square) to sell a dozen eggs. With the 15 cents derived there from, I was told to buy a small loaf of Butter Crust bread (9 cent) and the remaining six cents would buy a few slices of bologna for my lunch.

While Erna Weidner went to the back to candle the eggs to see if they were good, I waited in front of the candy counter. Gazing there at those wonderful bars of Baby-Ruth and Butter-Finger, I was overcome with a desire for those goodies, so when Erna returned and asked me what I wanted to buy, I told her, "One Baby-Ruth bar and one Butter-

Finger bar." When I got home my mom said, "Where are the bread and bologna?" I pointed to the two bars of candy. She said, "All right, young lady, you just find what you can for your lunch." I went out to the garden, but only found a couple of shallots, and back in the kitchen, I found one biscuit. With those items in hand, I ran off to school.

I usually had lunch with Vera and Lera Reeves, and Jean Evans; so at lunchtime I told them my tale of woe. Lera said, "I'll trade you a sandwich for the Baby-Ruth" and Vera said, "I'll trader you a sandwich for your Butter-Finger," so our exchange made everyone happy! I never told my mom about my good luck!

One day we were playing on a long "S" shaped, crooked oak log, vigorously seesawing up and down. I was on an end where a hole existed and my foot went straight through to the ground below. They continued to rock up and down on my foot, thinking I was laughing with glee until I finally convinced them I was crying out in pain. Forming a packsaddle, they carried me to our room. I don't remember

Dorothy's sister, Joanne Howe

71

how I got home that afternoon, but Dad went to work and made a crutch for me and he took me to school every day until I was able to walk again. (I never lost a day of school all eleven years, even going to school when I had a bad cold and should have been at home, not exposing others with my germs.)

One day during lunch, when we were in the first grade, we were outplaying near the back of the building when one of the girls said, "I wonder what it looks like down there inside the boys' restroom?" —a "six-holer" located on the east end of the campus towards Highway 281. (The girl's "six-holer" was on the west end near Mesquite Street.) I said, "I'll go ask Mrs. Weir if we can go down there and see!" Approaching her, I said, "Mrs. Weir, may we go down there and see what it looks like in the boys restroom?" I know it was all she could do to keep from laughing, but she merely said, "Little girls do not go into boy's restrooms."

When we got home from school, we had assigned duties; mine was to feed the one hog which Dad (Thomas Perry Howe) always fattened until it weighed 300 pounds. One day, with the bucket of slop in hand, I went out there to fill the trough, but the hog kept getting his head in the way, so that I could not empty the bucket. Thinking I could outrun him, with the bucket and its contents in hand, I ran in a big wide circle, dashing back to the trough, but blast him, he beat me back there. I just emptied the contents on him and into the trough too!

Another time, as there was a chicken brooder close to the outside fence, I got up on that stable metal roof and was able to safely pour the slop into the trough. However, as I jumped off the top of the brooder, I stepped on a block of wood, which had a rusty nail sticking out of it. Hobbling back to the house, Mom quickly made a cornmeal poultice. By reheating and applying this remedy many times, I didn't get lockjaw.

When I was six years old, my brother, Walter Eugene "Hoot" Howe, and I and my sister Joanne, a baby, all came down with chicken pox at the same time. Hoot and I had fever and wanted to scratch the sores all the time. Mom kept the blinds closed because she was afraid our eyesight would be damaged.

One day I asked Mom, "What is it like to die?" She then grew quite concerned about us, but since there was no medical doctor in Blanco that she could trust, she could only pray that the Good Lord would soon heal us- and He did.

In the late 1930s, the Depression ended and Dad got a job building a rock house for Lonnie Glasscock in Mathis, Texas. This was the first time he had ever worked away from Blanco, so Mom was very frightened. She wired the front gate closed; she wedged a bench against the back door and that night we all listened for any sounds of someone trying to gain entry into the house. Sometime around midnight she swore she heard someone trying to enter the back door. She whispered to me, "Go up to Goldwin Trainer's house and tell him to come down and see if someone is lurking around the outside of our house." Of course, since

Aunt Della Moe Corley

Dorothy Lee Howe Dillon 1943-44

the front gate was wired, it was necessary for me to climb over it, resulting in me landing with a loud thud on the other side. I ran all the way-two blocks-and awakened him, excitedly saying, "Come quickly, Mom thinks someone is trying to get in the house!" He came down and looked all around and of course, found nothing-no burglar. I heard them talking, and she later told me he propositioned her and she said, "Get out of this house immediately!" After that experience, she became braver and didn't send me again to seek someone's help.

When we walked to school, our "shortcut" took us through a wire fence between the Alexander property and our Howe land, then we climbed a four-foot rock fence next to Highway 281, and this resulted in rocks tumbling to the ground. One time to our disgust, the renters had wired the fence shut, but a kid from the house below us later cut those wires, leaving the sharp ends exposed. That afternoon when we headed home, Joanne was gingerly trying to crawl through the exposed wires and I, growing impatient with

her slow maneuvers, shoved her on through, causing her to receive bloody scratches and abrasions. Unfortunately, she still has the scars to show the results of that encounter.

It was Miss Olin who, in my senior year, had moved to Blanco because of her mother's health. She was a graduate of the University of Chicago, and was a wonderful English teacher. She encouraged me to study hard and to continue doing well in English. I was fortunate to have several other "favorite" teachers: Mrs. Zuma Wier in first and second grades, Miss Frances Brown in third grade, Miss Thelma Covington in the fifth grade, and Mrs. Elizabeth Burleson in high school typing and book keeping classes.

I spoke of Momma's chickens before, and how the eggs supplied us with grocery money. Well, each spring she would order 25 yellow Buff-Orpington baby chicks from a company in Missouri. You always knew when they had arrived at the local Post Office, because one could hear them the minute you entered the building. After bringing them home, she kept them warm by placing a lamp inside the big box. When they grew to the appropriate size, they were moved outside where they could search and scratch for most of their own food. Later, during the summer, when company suddenly arrived, she would go back, grab a two-pound pullet, ring off its neck, and after it stopped flopping around, she would bring it in, remove the feathers by dousing the whole chicken in boiling hot water. She then signed off the fine hairs by holding the bird over an open round burner on the old wood stove. Then came the part I hated; cutting the chicken into required pieces (I had a hard time finding the pulley bone.) The final step came by taking the grease found in a can located on the back corner of the old wood stove (this accumulation was from frying various things like bacon, steak, potatoes, etc.) This combination of greases made a great tasting liquid for frying the chicken. She had that final step down "pat." She knew exactly when the appropriate browning had occurred and it was time to remove those golden brown pieces of chicken from the pan.

Mom didn't sew, but her two sisters did, especially Aunt Della Mae. Just the other day one of my former high school classmates remarked, "I remember that beautiful bright blue dress your aunt made for you, it had white rabbit fur on the collar and on the two ties which extended from the neck."

When I was in the third grade, I only had two dresses. I wore one for a whole week and the other for the next week. Since all our clothes had to be washed on the rub-board and because Texas was experiencing a severe drought, water was at a premium. By-the-way, Dad would take a 55 gallon barrel and drive down to the river to a spring, fill it and return to the house with it sloshing all the way back. We did not have a well just a cistern-but since it had not rained in months, the bone-dry cistern was useless.

When a cold front blew in, it brought high winds filled with solid dust. I remember the wind blew for four straight days and the dust was so thick that we couldn't see across the road in front of the house. We would wet a washcloth and hold it over our nose and mouth until it became dirty with the collection of dust/dirt. What an unpleasant time.

This Harrison/Howe house is filled with two-foot thick rock walls which had cracks, wherein bedbugs would hide and additionally, the indentations in the mattress where places where bedbugs would also hide. It was a ritual and a chore each Saturday to bring a teakettle of boiling hot water and, with a strong rag, kill those pesky bedbugs by scalding and mashing them. We were so thrilled after WWII, when we were able to buy containers of DDT. This enabled us to eradicate those awful bugs forever. I know the environmentalist say DDT is horrible-not good for humans-but I say, "Thank God", that product allowed us to eliminate bedbugs-and we're still living!..

In 1951, Dad, being a rock mason, built an addition onto the old Harrison House, the latter having been built in 1859. At that time, I was living in San Antonio and took the bus home and was helping Mom tidy up the house after Dad's rockwork. He had flattened several big cardboard boxes and had stacked them on the floor in an area where he was not working. I decided it was time to sweep the floor in that area (Rock mortar makes lots of dust.) I picked up several of those boxes and was going to sweep underneath them, when to my surprise I saw a snake. Oh Harrows! I screamed and ran for the shotgun, and after loading it, I ran back and shot the snake. Since I could not tell if it was really dead, I went back and reloaded the gun and came back and shot the snake again. Still unsure if the snake was dead, I reloaded the gun and returned to the snake, but this time I concluded that it was really dead, so I returned to the counter and was in the process of trying to get the bullet out, when I somehow shot a hole in the cabinet door below the counter top, but the bullet penetrated the door and shattered some of the brand new dishes that I had stored down there.

I was so distraught! Mom had walked to the Post Office, so I ran up the road to meet her exclaiming, "I just shot a snake!" She said, "I hope you didn't kill my cat!"

Me & Momma's Cookie Baking Marathons
By Mae Durden-Nelson of Comfort, Texas
Born 1932

Every year in Momma's tiny farmhouse kitchen, the biggest and longest cookie-baking marathon happened weeks before Christmas—all produced by the use of our wood burning range. I shake my head in disbelief to realize that we had no oven thermometer. Momma just knew! It was her acquired and learned-from experience knowledge, knowing exactly how much wood was required in the fire chamber, so as not to overheat the cast iron or allow it to become too cool to bake a perfect batch of cookies. I still hear my mother's voice, "We cannot afford the waste of burned cookies!"

Throughout the 1930s Depression era, almost all ingredients were expensive and not easy to come by. Flour was purchased in large sacks, as was white sugar. Momma began to buy and squirrel away her cookie ingredients little by little throughout the year in anticipation of our cookie-making marathon. Items like coconut, dates, raisins, and candied fruit for fruitcake were on the list. Pecans were harvested from the huge tree in our yard. Daddy helped with those. He sat by the fireplace in the evenings, and with his

The Dixie cook stove

sharp pocketknife, he'd cut the tops, bottoms, and sides off the paper-shelled pecans. Then, the entire family got involved in the final, careful shelling. Momma stressed to us kids that it was important that the pecan halves, be clean, and whole-even though she later carefully cut up each kernel in neat slices. Momma also cut up her candied fruits early on, and then stored all in a cool place in the pantry.

The first Christmas baking began early in the fall-like October-with fruitcakes. She stored them away to "cure" after a good soaking with some of Daddy's homemade wine.

My earlier kitchen memories began after my older sister married and moved away. Since I was the middle child of the remaining three boy siblings-who were always outside with Daddy-I became my mother's constant shadow. While we were both big talkers, I was also taught how important it was *to listen.* As I look back, I realize that my momma had unbelievable patience with me-her eager, willing student-even when my lessons were not always painless. For instance, all mixing was done by hand with a large metal spoon. (It eventually became half worn away with use and age!)

To demonstrate the fortitude required of all cooks in those long ago farm kitchens, come with me on a 1939 experience-step by step-as Momma teaches me to mix and bake my first batch of cookies.

First step is lard-"Measure it into an aluminum-measuring cup out of the large crock of lard in our cellar." Lard was a by-product of a once-a-year weeklong winter butchering.

Those long grueling days began when a special fattened hog was slaughtered by a single shot to the head. Immediately my father stuck the hog in its juggler vein. The blood shot out in a steady stream into a large bowl that my momma was holding with one hand while she crouched down in the dirt beside the hog. She constantly stirred the blood with the other hand to prevent clotting. That would later become an ingredient in making blood sausage.

Since the selected "butcher hog" was a very large animal; using a block and tackle, the men tugged and tugged, lifting up the hog. Next, they lowered it into and sloshed back and forth, up and down, in a 60-gallon drum filled with boiling water.

After the hot bath was accomplished, they lifted the dead hog and then lowered it onto a low table. Immediately, several men went to work with a special sharp tool, totally shaving off all the bristles. Once clean shaven again, by the use of the block-and-tackle, the hog was lifted into a hanging position to accomplish the function of gutting and cleaning out the carcass. Some of the intestines were saved, washed and washed, then turned inside out, salted, and then stored on the warm end of the wood stove until needed for later venison and pork sausage casing. That too, was tricky, because if the casings got to hot, they would break in the latter sausage stuffing.

At this stage, the hog was split down the spine and the men carried the two sides inside the butchering room where it was divided into the various different cuttings. (The hog's head was usually boiled, for blood sausage ingredients, or it was taken into Fredericksburg to have tamales made by local Mexicans.)

Next, Daddy set aside parts of the hog for sugar-cured and smoked hams and bacon. The rest of the hog was then cut up into small pieces for grinding into sausage meat along with ground up venison. The white fat layer of the hog was also cut into short strips and ground. It was later rendered-that is-it was placed in an outdoor, large black cast iron kettle where a hot, hot fire underneath, melted it into a liquid state—lard. When it cooled, it solidified and was stored in a large crock in our cool cellar. That was our LARD supply for the entire coming year. It was a precious commodity.

Now, if I haven't lost you with all these details, let's get back to my cookies and the first ingredient; lard. To begin a batch of cookies—Momma walked with me to make the trip down into the cellar with a measuring cup and a spoon. It was a messy job! I hated it, because I could not get the lard into the cup without getting it all over my hands and-well-whatever! The next step was to get the lard out of the measuring cup and into our large mixing bowl, another messy job!

At last, the lard was placed in our large mixing bowl. The measuring cup then had to be washed with hot, soapy water and carefully dried-we had only one such cup. (It came to our kitchen from a box of Mother's Oats, my family's favorite oatmeal.)

"Measure and add the sugar", Momma instructed. "Now mix and stir, and mix and mix."

"Is this enough mixing, Momma?" I wish I had counted the "stirs." Momma continued; …"break an egg…one at a time…into a small bowl." Momma and I give each egg the "sniff test." If the smell is acceptable, "add each egg separately…one at a time…and mix, and mix and mix." "Is this enough mixing now Momma?"

The next step, sifting flour, was more fun. Momma always insisted that the flour had to be sifted *three times* before it could be correctly measured. I sifted it three times right back into the huge bag that stood against the wall in our pantry.

"Now, measure the three cups of flour back into the sifter, then, using a measuring spoon, add the salt, baking powder or baking soda, or spices…" (Momma purchased spices from the traveling salesman we called the "Watkins Man") "Now , with the sifter full of flour, salt, baking powder or baking soda and spices, you must sift three times again into a separate bowl to evenly distribute everything." "Can I mix it into the batter now, Momma?" "No, not yet, first we have to measure out the milk."

At last, with a tablespoon, we added the flour and milk-a little at a time-and finally we added the final ingredient was Watkins vanilla.

Again, we mix, and mix and mix. At the beginning, it was quite easy to stir. After the last flour was added, Momma had to complete the process, because my arms were tired, especially with the final additions of the pecans or whatever the recipe called for.

At last, we are ready to bake, that is, if Momma has added wood to the fire to have the temperature "just right." She generally lets a drop of water bounce off the stovetop. She seems to know when the oven is the correct temperature; amazing!

The aroma from baking cookies is one you will never forget! I also remember frequent swipes I sneaked out of the dough when Momma was not looking. The final reward for all this work—it was my privilege to "lick the bowl" clean after the last cookie dough was placed on the cookie sheet. There was always generous dough left in the bowl. It was, you see, the age before rubber spatulas.

You probably have concluded by now that all this was hard tedious work. That is indisputable! However, at that time I guess it was just accepted, and it was not lamented. Day after day, Momma and I made batch after batch of cookies. All those seemingly jillions of assorted cookies were then stored away in various glass and tin containers. Momma and I regarded our accomplishments with great pride and pleasure, and no one, I mean, NO ONE, was allowed a sample until Christmas Eve.

"Turning the Chickens"
By Charles Cale of Marion, Texas
Born 1929

My parents moved near New Braunfels, Texas in 1951 from Calallen, Texas. Dad sold his dairy and went into the stock cattle business. But then the notorious drought of the 1950s began and all his cattle had to be sold in 1956. I had served in the U.S. Army during the Korean War from 1950 to 1952 and returned to help dad with the cattle.

During the drought of the 1950s, around 1954, my dad Vernon, my brother Donald, and I went to work at Bud's Service station in New Braunfels, Texas. We put gasoline in people's cars, trying to make a living to pay bills in this place of hard times because of no rain for farmers and ranchers land. In 1960, a job was offered to me at an oil refinery. I worked rotating shifts, including the night shift.

One evening, as our work crew took a supper break, the conversation turned to "Growing up Days" back when we were children during the depression. The hard times of the depression and World War II days were remembered and retold. High on the list were the everyday chores that we did as children. Some recounted going barefoot and hoeing the garden. We saved our shoes for school. During World War II, you had to have a coupon to buy shoes. We got two coupons a year for shoes. Many kid's feet grew so fast that a pair of shoes wouldn't last the school year because of fast growth spurts. Besides some families couldn't get jobs and there wasn't enough money to go around to buy all their children's shoes.

Many families had gardens to supply food for everyone and when World War II started, we had Victory Gardens. Even in towns, Victory Gardens were in most backyards. Hoeing the garden was expected of all the children old enough to hold a hoe. Milking the cows was big on my list of chores. My dad had a 185-cow dairy and we started milking at 1:00 a.m., seven days a week. Feeding the pigs, plowing, and feeding the horses or mules, among other chores.

"My job was turning the chickens," said one man from the work crew. The crew looked at one another as he continued. "Well, back in the '30s and into the '40s, we never had screens on our windows! As darkness approached in the hot summertime, our chickens would find their roost on our windowsills. No window screens for us! Before we went to bed, it was my job to "Turn the Chickens." I had to make sure that their tails pointed to the outside with their heads on the inside. If I missed a chicken, there was a mess to clean up the next day on our house's floor." Turning the chickens was a topic long discussed by our crew group. Most of us had chickens, but our families had chicken coops where we made sure all the chickens were in before we locked the coops door each night.

Back then, air conditioning hadn't come to our part of Texas and we left our windows open to catch the night's breeze. We, my brother and I, slept many a night on a cot on the house's front porch. Window screens were one of the best inventions that came along, that is if your family had the money to buy them. On hot summer nights, there was no way we could sleep with the windows down. I wonder what we would do today, if we had no air conditioning and no window screens. Maybe our children would learn how to survive, as we might return to raising chickens in our backyards, and resorting back to nightly "Turning the Chickens."

Later, I returned to the "Back to the Soil Business" called Cale Greenhouses in 1964. For 46 years, starting with tomatoes and later in 1971 we grew flowering and foliage plants. As more greenhouses were added, we were able to plant and also grow 17,000 poinsettias at once in season, among other beautiful, colorful flowers. The Randolph Army Air Corp base near San Antonio bought our tomatoes for their commissary store along with other area retail stores and florists. We also sold to Fort San Houston Army base in San Antonio. I always said, "Only God can grow tomatoes and flowers. I can only help!"

China Creek Community
By Doris Craven of Helotes, Texas
Born 1929

My name is Doris Tyler Craven. I was born in Texas in San Saba County on July 2, 1929. I was the fourth child of Mack Tyler and Alice Outlaw Tyler. We were a family of seven children, four girls, and three boys. I was the typical "middle child". My dad was a farmer who worked several large farms through the years in two communities. Our lives were filled with hard work and many family pleasures through those years.

A favorite memory of mine is picking cotton beside Daddy at a very young age and being bragged upon for how much it weighed, then going to the cotton gin in town knowing that I helped. I started school in the China Creek Community School and enjoyed my first three years there. My teachers were Mrs. Knight and Mrs. Stroble. They had a big

Doris's parents, Alice and Mack Tyler in 1947

A Double Wedding
Doris T. and George W. Craven
Lillie Justis and N. Leon Craven in 1946

influence on my life. They taught me the fun of learning and doing well in my work. The school had two rooms. In the "big kids" room, the teacher was Clovis Ledbetter and was just as fun. My family and his were neighbors in the Cat Claw community where we moved to a farm there.

My first boyfriend attended the one-room school there. There were only six students until my younger brother, sister, and I made the total nine. I sat in an "old-time" desk made for two with my classmate, a boy. We were in the 5th grade at this time. It was strange, but I have to admit it was nice! I remember our dear teacher placed a candy bar in everyone's desk on April Fool's Day that year. Then we had a wiener roast in the woods nearby. It was such fun! The 12th grade was added that year to the school system and I skipped the 6th grade.

When my family moved back to the China Creek Community, my 7th and 8th grades were continued through grade school graduation. As luck would have it, my young 5th grade friend had moved there too, but we never acknowledged that we had liked each other. How strange! Our community had three-act plays, box suppers, and pie suppers. The box suppers were a fun thing. I would see my mother cook good things and decorate a box usually with crepe paper and place the goodies

inside. The men would bid on the box and the highest bidder would get to eat the supper with the lady who prepared it. It was very strange to eat with my mother and a man who was not her husband! My daddy would act in the play, which was always funny. Between acts, there were community musicians who played during intermission. It was so much fun! After grade school graduation, the big change was going to high school in town. It was hard for me, as I had to milk the cows, get ready for school, and walk a mile to catch the school bus to town. After a few months, World War II came and changed everything and everyone.

My dad and two of his brothers moved our families to California where the three of them worked in the shipyard doing defense work. The schools were crowded there and my younger brother, sister, and I went only half days. Daddy became ill there so we had to leave and come home to Texas. My older brother had joined the Navy and it was a time of much turmoil and sadness for everyone.

Back in Texas again, I attended high school, but due to illness and getting behind in my studies, I had to drop out of school in my sophomore year. Good teachers did try to encourage me. However, I felt I was needed very much at home. I still feel today that it was the right decision for me.

After the war was over, I met a wonderful returning veteran, a man born and reared in San Saba also. George Wiley Craven was the eldest of five children (three boys and two girls) born of Samuel H. Craven and Mary

A "foursome" in 1946 before the double wedding

Taff Craven. George and I were married in San Saba on June 29, 1946 at the home of Reverend White. We had three daughters and one son. They were all born in San Saba. When our youngest child was two years old, we moved to San Antonio, Texas where they all grew up, married and live today as I do in and around San Antonio. My favorite hobbies have been sewing for my family and writing poetry. I have been widowed for 11 years. George passed away in 2002 at age 86. Today I have eight grandchildren and 13 great-grandchildren.

I feel happy to share my story in this way as it helps me reflect on my many blessings. I'm happy to have had the years of growing up and living in a wonderful age, place and time; a time when life was simple, but challenging; a time to experience new and wonderful changes, but never letting go of the memories that make me appreciate a very full life.

The Town Kids Envied the Ranch Life
By Christine Anthony of Richland Spring, Texas
Born 1941

My Sister Sue is a little over two years younger than myself. We were raised on a large ranch 33 miles from Rocksprings, Texas. Our dad was ranch foreman for over 25 years with our mother by his side for all those years. We had a great up bringing far from town. No TV (too far from stations) or computers! We made our own fun. Looking back it seems like a great life. At the time, we really thought it was tough. We worked hard and learned a great many good life lessons. Sue and I and an occasional friend from school were anxious to learn to drive. After some lesson from our daddy, we thought we knew it all. We were allowed to practice out in the pastures in our old pick up with a stick shift. Daddy had

warned us about a new, big, black bull – stay away from him, as he seemed to be a fighter. So, as usual, we pushed our luck. On one of our driving forays, we found the bull and really tested his patience. We drove circles around him, yelling, and beating the pickup door. We felt safe – never realizing he could have easily turned the pickup and us upside down. A few days later, daddy came in and said, "I found some real odd circles out in the pasture – reckon what they are?" There was a great silence and it scared us to death. Needless to say, we tried to be very good for a while. We never could put much over on mother or daddy.

Now for the next unguided driving lesson, mother drove the school bus for years, since we were at the end of the line. The bus at this time was kept at our house. It was a van type and carried about 12 each day. It was extra-long. One day while mother and daddy were busy elsewhere on the ranch and we were old enough to drive, but not smart enough to think things through – we took the bus on a joy ride out in the pasture. We knew better than to ever get on the highway. There was a big, dry tank due to a prolonged drought with a fairly tall dam. We thought it would be fun to drive up on that dam and down the other side. The dirt dam and the length of that school bus matched perfectly! We got on top and high centered the bus. No wheels touching, just rocking back and forth on the under part of the bus. We tried our best to get it to rock and go on down the other side. Didn't happen! We had to walk home and tell mother and daddy what happened. They took another vehicle and pulled the bus off the dam. They didn't do to us what should have been done, such as beating us, but we were plenty scared and not allowed to drive for a while.

Another story about what a great life we had growing up in the country. We didn't think it was an easy life at the time – after all, our friends in town could run up and down the streets and run into stores and buy candy and stuff. Their life seemed exciting to us, but as we grew up, we discovered the town kids envied our exciting life!

We raised a baby deer on a bottle. Hunters had killed the mother and daddy brought it in. Pansy, as we named her, turned out to be an exceptional pet. We lived in a big, old ranch house – no carpet. The deer learned to sleep with Sue and I. One year we got a pretty new Chenille bedspread with flowers on it. Pansy decided the flowers looked good enough to eat! She unraveled most of that bedspread, all over the house. When Pansy was a couple of years old, she left us for a while and we thought she was gone forever. One day in the late spring, she showed back up with twin fawns. We were so happy to see her, we opened the screen door, and in she came with the little ones right behind her. We fed Pansy and she fed and raised her little ones in and out of the house. She continued doing this for at least four more years. We had a herd of cute pets. Usually the young ones wouldn't hang around much more than six to eight months and then take off. But some of the females would hang around with their young ones longer. Pansy did this until one time she didn't come back, actually, we could tell she was getting old by deer standards, but she always slept with us at the foot of the bed, except when she had young ones. We always fed and tried to keep the pets in a pasture close to the house. No hunting allowed in the pasture! We raised many other pets, deer, lambs, and goats as the years went by, but never like Pansy.

A very fond memory for us was when the ranch would get in a truckload of peanut hay. We would climb up on the hay and sit and eat the peanuts we could find. We lived too far from town to run to a store and buy a bag of peanuts. This is one of the ways we feel we were better off than the town kids. A great treat!

The Heart of the Hills
By Clarabelle Snodgrass of Kerrville, Texas
Born 1913

Look on a Texas map and find Kerr County where Kerrville is located on IH10, 65 miles northwest of San Antonio. The elevation is 1,650 feet and the climate is known internationally as the most ideal, year in and year out. Kerrville, known as the "Heart of the Hills" as the different ranges of hills along the Guadalupe River and other streams show off their beauty. The western edge of the county rises to a 2,200-foot elevation. Residents of the larger cities have constructed summer homes on the sides or tops of hills all over the county. Many people eventually reside here at all times of the year.

Also, along the upper Guadalupe River are numerous summer camps that thousands of youngsters have been attending for more than 60 years. There are three sessions each summer where the youth learn to swim, ride horses, and compete with campers from other area camps in lots of outdoor activities. It is a delight to see busloads of youngsters in Kerrville as they are supervised and accompanied by college-educated counselors. Third

Typical businessman on downtown street in the early 1900s

generation families now run some camps.

Kerrville is about halfway between Beaumont and El Paso east and west and also halfway between Brownsville and Amarillo north and south. The county was organized in 1856 and named for James Kerr, a surveyor from Kentucky, a friend of Joshua Brown, also of Kentucky. Families came and purchased lands near the Guadalupe River and established farms and ranches where cattle, sheep, goats, and horses were raised on many places that contained thousands of productive grazing lands. The town grew even though the Comanche Indians were still there. In 1841 the Battle of Bandera Pass about 15 miles south of Kerrville, was fought. Mexico approached from the south and the Indians were to the north of the natural low elevation in the rough hills. The Texas Rangers came from San Antonio into the Pass to help protect the neighboring residents. Lead by Colonel Jack Hays they killed the Indian Chief and the Comanche's buried their last man and left. Colonel Hays later moved to California and was elected the first Sheriff of San Francisco at age 25. After the end of the Civil War, more families began moving to the Hill Country. Some men were injured in the war and their wives were left with large families of children. It has been told many times of the courage and bravery of the women who protected their property and kept Indians away from their homes.

The Empty Cross

In the 1880s, the railroad built their lines from the Gulf Coast at Aransas Pass to San Antonio ending at Kerrville. This provided a way to ship cattle, sheep, goats, wool, and mohair to markets as far away as Boston and across the Gulf of Mexico onto the Eastern Seaboard. It was known as the S.A. and A.P. and called San Antonio and Aransas Pass Railroad. All of these activities helped develop Kerrville into a city of over 30,000 permanent residents and also brought a new multi-million dollar hospital, a 1,000 seat modern city auditorium, a popular University, one of the largest Veteran's hospitals in the state, a Mental Hospital, at least five theaters which have programs year round, a large membership Symphony Orchestra featuring talented professional musicians from surrounding towns, and in 2012 a local football player from Kerrville's Tivy High School received the Heisman Trophy as a freshman at Texas A&M University. Johnny Manziel or Johnny Football as he is called has made the entire

It took six horses to haul 3 wagons of wool from the ranches to the railroad in Kerrville

community proud to say "Go Johnny Go." The local radio broadcasting station of over 60 years connects the air with nationally known reporters namely Rush Limbaugh and others.

Another unique feature of this central Texas county is the abundance of white tail deer and wild turkey that have been a source of income for landowners nearly a hundred years. There is a fall hunting season that lasts eight weeks each year. Venison is a very good source of protein and the hunters lease a specified amount of land for hunting and come from all over the United States to camp out and hunt the deer or turkey. In 2010, a beautiful 77 foot 7 inch Cross was erected on a hilltop on IH10. Winding streets with Hill Country stonewalls are easy to ascend and look at the majestic Cross, against the beautiful blue Texas sky. People come from all over the world to pray in this beautiful garden and to see this 2 million dollar creation. This spot was chosen, as it is equal distance from the East Coast of the United States to the West. In the Sculpture Prayer Garden, a sculpture by Max Greiner Jr. was fashioned after he had a vision from the Holy Spirit. The Cross is at the same latitude as Israel. As we say in Texas, "You all come."

In the past 25 years, some large ranches have provided foreign game for hunting in Texas, which also has become a popular year-round sport. The largest ranch in Western Kerr County of over 60,000 acres of land has imported animals from all over the world and has hunting available all year long. An early newspaper publisher of a local newspaper in the late 1890s was the first one to photograph the beautiful surroundings around the Hill Country and trucked a load of his descriptive magazines to Chicago to advertise the benefits of living in and loving the "Heart of the Hills" in Kerr County. The boasting he did then is still prevalent today. So, come to enjoy the beauty God has bestowed. You may want to stay for the rest and best years of your life.

We Showed Our Love for Our Country
By Barbara Browning Young of Amarillo, Texas
Born 1934

Like most people, I tend to think that the years when I grew up were the best of all times. I was born in Lohn, Texas into a farming family after the depression, but before World War II. I was seven when Pearl Harbor was bombed and although I was too young to understand everything that was happening it affected every family as brothers, uncles, cousins, and friends enlisted or were drafted into service and deployed. Their welfare was of great concern to all of us. All mail going to and from the military was censored, so we had no way of knowing where they were or how they were fairing most of the time. Those were anxious times for everyone.

Americans, as always, rose to the occasion and were quickly initiated into the era of ration tires. Tire, coffee, sugar, and many other items, as all necessary supplies were diverted to the war effort. Young Americans today are deprived I think because this generation has never known a time when all of America was "true blue" patriotic to the core. I cannot even imagine the horror any of us would have felt back then if someone had burned an American flag or jumped up and down on it with contempt. Indeed, if anyone had any anti-American thoughts, they were kept well hidden! Patriotic slogans such as, "Uncle Sam wants you!" and "Loose Lips Sink Ships!" were everywhere. Not only did we love our country but also we showed it in every way we could. We said the Pledge of Allegiance to our flag each morning after the bell rang, sang the national anthem with gusto, our hands held over our hearts, and other songs of the time, such as "Over There", "When Those Caissons Go Rolling Along", and "God Bless America," to name a few.

Having lived through World War II, and

remembering the tremendous support we gave to our boys back then, I feel great sadness when I think of the troops in the Korean Conflict, Vietnam, and present wars who have been shortchanged in that area. There was no effort too great for our brave men! We planted Victory Gardens, scavenged our properties for scrap metal, saved tinfoil, and bought war bonds. Women, such as my Aunt Bill, left their household duties to work in airplane factories. Big name Hollywood stars made war themed movies and left their jobs to go to war and fight with our troops. As there was no television with continuing up to the minute broadcasts, we listened to radio newscasts daily, went to the movies, and watched the newsreels between features to find out everything we could about the war situation.

Summers were oppressively hot. There was no air conditioning or even an oscillating fan to temper the heat and humidity of those hot, sultry days and nights, so the adults sat out on the front porch in the dark after supper and talked of local and world events while we kids sat quietly and listened. Winters on the other hand were bitterly cold when those frigid Texas northers descended on us. It was too expensive to heat the whole house, so Daddy and Mothers room was the only rooms that were heated on a daily basis. How we dreaded going to bed in our cold room on winter nights! Our breaths steamed as we hurried into bed at night and out of bed and into Daddy and Mothers room to get dressed in the morning. We had so many quilts on our beds that we could hardly move, but even if we could, we didn't want to lose our warm place. We would lie in that one spot until cramped legs forced us to change positions.

Mother operated the café across the street from the school building when I was in the 4th grade. High school students came over for hamburgers and a soda while they listened to records on the jukebox. Over and over, they listened to Glenn Miller, the Dorsey Brothers, the Andrews Sisters, and other favorites. The red Coca Cola drink box was filled with Cokes, Dr. Peppers, and Nesbitt's orange and grape drinks. For me there was no drink as refreshing as the original R.C. Cola, which had enough zing in it back then to make one's eyes water with that first swallow.

Both of our general stores had wonderful arrays of goodies, but L.O. Marshall had such a variety that it was hard to make a choice. Walnettos, Double Bubble, or a caramel all day sucker? It was a treat just to look around that store! There was everything from dress materials, threads, and needles in wooden boxes to Dickies overalls, shoes, and fresh meats cut by L.O. himself wrapped in white butcher paper and tied with white string.

The radio was an integral part of our lives. Only something desperate could have prevent us from catching the latest episode of *Fibber McGee and Molly, Mystery Theater, Dr. Christian,* and other favorites. Censorship was in full swing, so a mixed group without embarrassment could watch any movie. In fact, movies and Broadway shows provided many of the popular songs that were part of our everyday life. They had lyrics, which could be understood and sung accompanied by beautiful music.

Dress styles were lovely, feminine, and modest, almost Victorian by today's standards. If a girl or young lady had appeared in a tank top and short shorts or a blouse with spaghetti straps back then, her father would have said, "Go back to your room and put on some clothes! You can't go out in public dressed like that!"

One of the things I miss most from my childhood was the quiet, peaceful nights back on the farm where I grew up. When the lights were turned out, you couldn't see your hand in front of your face. If you went outside on a moonless night, it was the same – not a pinpoint of light anywhere, total darkness. Quiet. The only sounds we heard as we lay there in the darkness drifting off to sleep was a random, gentle, lowing of a cow followed by a soft answer from her calf, the quiet bleating of a neighbor's sheep, or a drowsy bird cheeping sleepily as it settled in for the night in a tree nearby. Living on the high plains of Texas, we are never without lights around us at night!

We didn't have what would have been considered an enviable life growing up. We wore clothes made of flour and chicken feed sacks sewn on an old treadle sewing machine, we wasted nothing, used items long after today's generation would have thrown them out and counted every penny. By today's standards, we didn't have very much, but what we did have was love for God and each other, an appreciation for His blessings as well as love for our country, a sense of humor, and bedrock character. The saying, "We had everything but money," truly exemplified our generation, but few among us would have traded our priceless heritage for any other.

Gloria's parents, Bessie and Pete Duarte in 1940

Living in Fort McKavett
By Gloria Duarte of San Angelo, Texas
Born 1950

Fort McKavett, located on Farm-to-Market Road 864, 22 miles west of Menard, was established on March 14, 1852, and served as a vital role in frontier defense until its abandonment on June 30, 1883. The decision for deactivation was based on a decrease in Indian activity and the beginning of the Civil War. After the soldiers' departure, settlers moved into the area and adapted the fort's buildings to suit their needs. It was in the phase between the abandoned Army posts in 1883 to a historical site in 1968 that the Duarte family called Fort McKavett home.

Pedro (Pete) Duarte and Basilia (Bessie) Rangel Duarte arrived at the Morales Ranch, near Fort McKavett, late in 1937 after their marriage. Pete did some sharecropping at the

James Morales ranch, located seven miles from Fort McKavett, until about 1942. From 1942 through 1943, he worked as a ranch hand at several ranches in the Fort McKavett area, finally moving to the community of Fort McKavett on July 28, 1944. His main line of work was as a sheep shearer, working with Rito Hemandez's crew. Sheep shearers had to be willing to leave their families while they worked the circuit, endure a hard life with no benefits, and sleep in barns or outdoors for low pay. In addition, these men had to be in excellent physical condition as they wrestled 150+ pound ewes, dragged, and kept them down while they clipped the wool in the West Texas heat. Sheep shearing is a tradition that has slowly declined over the years.

Pete was also an excellent mechanic and often helped transients with their vehicles, which broke down in Fort McKavett. Pete and Bessie had six children and helped raise her half-brother Juan (John) Contreras who came to live with them in 1939 and an orphaned nephew, Antonio Molina, who came to live with them in 1950. By the time Bessie was 21,

Duarte residence in Ft. McKavett in 1959

she had three children that she was raising. Federico (Fred) was born at the Morales ranch on February 27, 1938. Minerva was also born at the Morales ranch on September 30, 1939, as was Marta on June 14, 1941. Gloria was born in Fort McKavett on January 30, 1950. Pedro (Pete) was also born in Fort McKavett on July 26, 1953. Dario, the youngest of the family, was born on August 13, 1959 in a hospital in Sonora, Texas, the only one of the Duartes to be delivered in a hospital.

Bessie worked very hard to help provide for her family. She worked doing housekeeping on the ranches around Fort McKavett where Pete worked. She also cleaned houses, washed dishes at various functions, such as those at the Mason Lodge and the Camp Sol Mayer Camp. On the side, she would wash and iron clothes for the Anglos in Fort McKavett for 15 and 25 cents apiece. The younger children wanted to deliver the ironed clothes to Callie Pullen, one of Bessie's several customers, collecting the money and of course, a tip! Washing clothes was very different from today. Bessie had a washing machine with a wringer outside the house in Fort McKavett and she would heat up the water using firewood in a big black "caso." Then she would prepare the starch with hot water heated on top of the wood stove and hang the clothes to dry on the line (laso). Washing clothes was a major endeavor, which took most of the day. Because she worked outside the home, she taught and expected her daughters to clean house and prepare supper

by the time she and Pete arrived in the evening. The wood stove required an ample supply of firewood, which was kept in an area behind the house. The wood had to be chopped in smaller proportions to fit the stove. Eventually, Milton Morales Jr., Pete's biological father, bought Bessie her first small butane stove.

Pete purchased their Fort McKavett home from Emma Moegelin Crump on June 3, 1954 for $350.00. The monthly payments were $25.00 with the first payment due on July 1, 1954. He had access to the water well but had to pay half of the expenses incurred for repairs of the windmill. Any time the windmill or the pipes needed repair or replacement, he paid for half of the cost. Pete and Bessie lived in Fort McKavett until 1967 when they moved to Menard, 22 miles east of Fort McKavett. They were forced to move when the state of Texas purchased the homes to turn the small community into a historical site. Because their house was part of the row of Officers' (no. 4) Quarters, it was restored as part of the project. After moving to Menard, both Bessie and Pete continued to work at different jobs with Bessie working in restaurants washing dishes and cleaning, and then finally working as a nurse's aide at the Menard Manor Nursing Home. Even at age 70, she would clean houses on the side, mow her own yard, and wash clothes for her favorite "viejitos" (elderly) from the nursing home.

Because Bessie did not have the opportunity to get an education, she insisted that her children attend school and not miss any classes. Even when she and Pete worked as migrant workers and traveled to Munday, Haskell, and even Kansas, she made sure they returned to Fort McKavett before school started so that her children could enroll at the beginning of the school year in the Menard school system. Other families stayed and worked until the season ended, and then their children would enroll late in the semester. When Bessie was school aged and attended school in Eden, Mexicans were discriminated against to such a degree that she would tell stories about the Anglo kids throwing rocks at them because they did not want them at school. The teachers as well did not care about teaching students who did not speak English. Her personal experience explains in part why she was so adamant that her children attend school and graduate. She succeeded in this goal - all her children graduated from high school. The one exception was Antonio Molina who refused to attend after age 16.

In addition to graduating from high school, Fred attended St. Mary's University in San Antonio and graduated with a Bachelor of Science degree in physics in 1962. He was commissioned and entered active duty in the Air Force in 1963 and retired from the Air Force in 1984 at the rank of Major. While in the Air Force, Fred received a Master of Science degree in Management from the University of Southern California in 1974. He also received an Associate in Science degree in Computer and Information Systems from San Diego Mesa College in 1989. Antonio Molina attended school in Fort McKavett and then in Menard. Minnie attended San Antonio Junior College for a year until she moved to Chicago to work. Marta enrolled in college classes after she moved from Chicago to California. Gloria graduated with a Bachelor's

The Duarte Family in 1968

degree in Spanish and minor in English from Southwest Texas State University in San Marcos, Texas in 1972. In 1976, she earned a Master of Arts in Teaching at Angelo State University. In 1985, she received a Ph. D. in English at Texas Tech University. Shortly after graduating from high school, Pete Jr. moved to Austin and began working as a dry wall contractor. Dario, the youngest of the family, earned a B.B.A. in general business from Angelo State University in 1982. He served in the Marines from August 25, 1983 to October 11, 1985. He died in June 2005 in Florida.

Although Bessie was not educated, she taught her children some valuable lessons. First, she taught them about hygiene. Although they had to carry water inside and heat it on the stove to take baths, she insisted they be clean and brush their teeth. For her, although they were poor, there was no excuse for being "sucios." She also taught them about proper behavior. They did not talk with food in their mouths and did not speak unless spoken to. One of her constant reminders when they left the house was "portense bien." Her reminding them about behaving each and every time they left the house carried on until they were older. Another piece of advice was "cuiden su trabajo." Whatever job they had, they were to do the best job they could and take care of that job. For her, taking care of one's job entailed such things as being not on time, but being early; being neatly dressed; and being on their best behavior. For someone who had maybe a 3rd grade education, she instilled in her children some good habits that have served them well in life.

Pete had his hand in disciplining the children; he did not believe in sparing the rod. For him, the faja (belt) or cuarta (whip), depending on the severity of the indiscretion, spoke louder than words. Time outs were spent kneeling in a corner on a rough, old wood floor of a room, facing the wall for a designated time. Afterwards, the perpetrator had to hug and kiss the victim, usually a brother or sister. While in current times, this type of punishment would have been considered child abuse in the 1950s and 1960s they were life lessons. When we were growing up, we lived in a very different world. We did not have electricity, running water, indoor plumbing, television, phone, toilet paper, Kleenex, paper towels, Christmas tree, fast food restaurants, and the list goes on. However, we survived without a hang up or a "poor me attitude" and are better off for the austere upbringing. Pete died at age 65 on December 2, 1979. Bessie lived long enough to see her children get an education, a source of great pride for her. She died at age 70 in 1990. They are both buried in the family plot in the Fort McKavett Cemetery.

Bee Cave
By Lowell Johnson of Bertram, Texas
Born 1937

Bee Cave is located 15-20 miles west of downtown Austin on the Eastern edge of the Texas hill country. Some publications refer to it as Bee Caves (plural) or Beecaves (one word). Both are incorrect. The few publications that I have seen indicate the name came from caves in the area inhabited with bees. This is what many people believe but is not true.

My name is Lowell W. Johnson (Dub)

The Trading Post before electricity in 1937

Lowell's father, Wiley Johnson in front of Johnson Bros. Trading Post

a Bee Cave native born in 1937. My father, Wiley W. Johnson a native of what is now Bee Cave was born in 1896. My grandfather, William Henry Johnson, a native of what is now Bee Cave was born 1871. My great grandfather, William Sampson Johnson was born in Ohio in 1818 and is buried along with my father and grandfather in the Bee Cave area. My grandfather, Will Johnson, lived there and is the source of the information about how Bee Cave really got its name.

In the late 1800s before Bee Cave had a name, the community was served by the post office in Oatmanville (now Oak Hill) a community just west of Austin. They wanted their mail moved from Oatmanville to their own community and arranged to get a post office. Two things were required: a building and a name. Carl Beck had a store, a gin, and a mill where my grandfather worked. It was located near where state highway 71 is now, and Hamilton Pool road. Located on the property was a one-room rock storehouse that would be used for the post office. It had a gabled roof and ceiling inside. Additionally, it had a beehive in the attic space and the bees entered through the gables. In those days, it was common to call a beehive in a place like that a "Bee Cave." Thus the name of the post office and the community was born.

This history of Bee Cave was told to me

88

by my grandfather. As a child growing up in my father's store, the "Trading Post," people from Austin out for an afternoon drive would often stop and ask, "Where is the Bee Cave?" My answer would be, "There is not any."

The Redheaded Woodpecker
By Edward Anderson of San Antonio, Texas
Born 1916

We lived on a farm in south San Antonio, Texas in the 1920s, and I attended the nearby Edgewood School, which had about a hundred students in grades one through eight. The school was a nice brick, three-story building. There were fire escape slides out the windows of the second and third floors. Twice yearly, we had a fire drill during which every child slid down the slides from the third story. There was a boy, who was the tallest student in our school, who sometimes got into trouble. On the day of the fire drill, he secretly brought a large piece of waxed paper to school. When it was his turn on the very warm slide, he sat on the waxed paper. No one had ever seen a person slide so fast. When he found the underlying cause of he became air born and landed in the gravel driveway. He had to go home due to cuts and bruises.

Once all the older boys were talking about a girl in school who had long curly red hair. I was younger but joined in the conversation saying, "She's as pretty as a redheaded woodpecker." I felt proud of myself for making the older boys laugh. The next morning as I walked into the schoolyard someone suddenly jumped out of the nearby bushes, ran up to me from behind, and kissed me on the cheek. I was in shock as I saw the cute redheaded girl running into the school. I was quiet about the incident as I was very shy and did not want anybody to know that I had been kissed. Well, I was almost afraid to go to school because the

redheaded woodpecker greeted me with a kiss nearly every morning for a month. I gradually got used to the idea and it really wasn't that bad after all.

There was going to be a school program and I was supposed to bring a dessert for refreshments. I asked my older sister to bake my favorite jam cake, an old time favorite family recipe. My sister baked the cake but the dark brown sugar icing was too thin and was running down the sides of the cake. It looked terrible. I was embarrassed but had to take the cake to school. When no one was looking, I quietly put the cake on the dessert table and then disappeared. At the end of the program, everyone ate the desserts. One of the teachers made an announcement, "Who made this dark brown sugar cake?" It is the best we have ever tasted and we would like the recipe!" I bowed my head looking at my feet and never, ever let anyone know that it was my cake.

When I was older, our neighbor had a very mean Brahma bull. The bull tore down fences and caused havoc with all the neighbor's cattle. Everyone was afraid because the bull was known to chase people and someone could have been hurt. The owner wanted to take the bull to the market but it was so wild he could not load it into his truck. We backed his truck up to the loading chute, but the bull would not go in. He ran around the pen butting the sides and pawing at the ground. I had been a track star in school and I came up with a plan to load the bull. We put some dirt in the truck bed and sprayed a little water on it to make it slippery. I carefully walked down the chute and teased the bull. He suddenly turned on me and began to charge. I ran up the chute into the truck and taunted him again. As the bull ran up the chute into the truck, he began to slip and slide as I leaped upon the top of the cab of the truck. I had almost a second to spare. My heart was pounding as the gate was closed behind the bull. That's one way to load a bull!

The Kitchen Rattlesnake
By Patricia Magerkurth of Marble Falls,
Texas
Born 1931

My husband bought a fireplace, and it sat in the front yard. We had many comments about it, but we said we were going to build in the front porch. That is where it would go.

All went well; we tore out the front wall of the living room after we had built in the front porch and placed the fireplace where it would sit when the construction was finished. They had to cut a small slice off of the front door. We figured that is how our rattler got into the house. He was not very big at the time. The floor was later covered with granite and made a beautiful room with my husband's church window from St. John's Lutheran Church in Illinois. It turned into a lovely room. Little did I know that it let in a rattlesnake? You never think about items like that unless they are in your sight. Well, all went well and we were pleased with the outcome.

That morning my husband was heading for south Texas to see his brother from Illinois. He was there with a seed corn company and watching how things were going for the company. I got up and dressed as usual in my shorts and barefoot. I had my coffee and breakfast when I remembered that I had an article to write for the sorority BSP. So I sat down at the desk in the kitchen and lifted up my portable typewriter and there sat the rattlesnake. He was just waking up, be he certainly knew how to rattle his tail. It really scared me. I am a country girl from Illinois and did not have to know how to get rid of that snake. No one was around me to get help. My neighbors had gone to work and no husband to call. Well, I had to figure this one out. The snake had me, but I was not going to let him win this contest.

I grabbed my broom and opened up the back door and propped open the screen door.

He was still rattling that tail. It was him or me. I flew around the kitchen table and hit him with the broom. Guess what? He did not go out the door as I had expected he would. He lay across the sill of the back door still rattling his tail. I moved quickly and hit him again. He flew all the way to the storage house. He may have been dazed, but he was gone that quick. I had him out of my kitchen and did I ever feel good about that.

Our Move to Marble Falls
My husband was always listening on the radio to LBJ and his beautiful Texas hill country. Well, we decided to take the kids on spring break and drive to Texas and see what he was talking about. Well, we found out. There was no drought at that time and the time was perfect for a trip. We were a farm family with four children. We had a girl and three boys. We were treated well in Marble Falls and enjoyed staying at Horsebay motel. We fished and played in the beautiful blue water around that area. Little did we dream that it would become our home?

We had a farm to sell and many items to auction off before we could move. Well it happened. We put our daughter at the University of Illinois and took our two young sons with us besides Joan's schnauzer. We sold hogs, machinery, household items, and junk. What a day!

The next day we got in our cars, a Cadillac and an Olds station wagon and headed for the great country of Texas. Our friends owned Buckhorn Lodge so that is where we stayed. We picked Marble Falls because they had the best track coach in Texas. My husband bought our house when we were in HSB at 11:30 at night with a flashlight. We owned a home and now starting a new life in Texas from near Moline, Illinois. What a life that my husband presented me. My resume got to the area before we did and I was hired as editor of the Marble Falls Messenger. Here I was in a house, 2 sons, one was 16 and the other boy was 7 in 3rd grade. Our middle son wanted to go to West Point or the Air Force Academy so I had some talking to do as well as run a newspaper, a household and a family. We were also worried about a pile of wood in the backyard that could have had snakes so my husband, Mage, hired a gentleman to un-pile and re-pile the wood. Come to find out later that he was from Moline, Illinois and married a hometown girl.

I got the boys registered in school and we joined the St. Peter's Lutheran Church. My husband said that he would shovel sidewalks if it snowed – guess what, in January it snowed several inches. All he had was a spade. That does not do well with snow. That is another story. Mage had been hired by NCRA and worked. I also did my jobs and enjoyed them. My news office was right next door to a real estate office so my Mage got with the realtor and bought Kampers Korner. The campground was for several people and trailers. It was fun running the campground, but it took a lot of bookwork and who did it- ME! The next thing in 2 years, he bought the Buckhorn Lodge in Marble Falls.

My daughter, Joan, graduated from the University of Illinois and moved to Texas, and the next thing her boyfriend followed her. Thank heavens that we had cabins as well as trailer spaces. We had room for them. My son, Mark, who had been in the Air Force also moved to Marble Falls. Now we had the whole family here. Many interesting stories went along with our life, but too many to tell. My middle son loved to play football, so we went to all the games and wrote about each one. We made many friends and I joined the VFW 10376 here in our little city. I have been a member for 40 years. I also joined Beta Sigma Phi Sorority in 75. Life was good and we worked hard to keep it that way. Our middle son got the appointment to Prep school and then West Point Military Academy. That was a sad day when we took him to Fort Hood and

Patricia and Brian Magerkurth in 1981

had to say good-bye to him. He was leaving me for New York. I also had to plan a wedding for my daughter, who wanted to get married in our home church. Thank heavens for Ladies Aid at St. John's Lutheran in Illinois. They helped me so much.

My husband built many boat docks at the campground as well as cleaned up the motel, which we also owned. During this whole time, we explored Texas and enjoyed it. We also sent the youngest son to West Point. We never had a dull moment. The Lord helped out all along the way. All of this took place in the 70's. Brian graduated in 1981 and Craig graduated in 1992. We were very proud parents.

God Bless Chrysler, Ford and GM:
Looking Back in my Rearview Mirror
By Larry Borchers of Kerrville, Texas
Born 1948

Intense rivalries between neighboring towns exist everywhere and in our little part of the world, this is no exception. I grew up in the Texas hill country town of Kerrville, about sixty-five miles northwest of San Antonio, off of I-10, and our main rival was and still is, Fredericksburg, only twenty-two miles north of us on Highway 16. We competed in everything: athletics, dating each other's girls, and drag racing. To say the least we didn't get along and still don't today.

This story starts during the spring-summer of my senior year in high school (1966). It was a Friday afternoon about 5:00 pm and two gentlemen from Fredericksburg show up at our local hangout, a drive-in called The Grove, and challenged us to a drag race, $100 per race taking on all comers. They knew they had us out-gunned therefore pretty brazen. One was driving a black 1964 327 cubic inch 375 horse power fuel-injected Corvette stingray coupe, and the other was driving a gold 1966 two-door Plymouth Satellite with a 426 cubic inch 425 horse power street hemi engine in it.

My buddy and I asked them to give us some time to round up our local talent, Kerrville had only three possible challengers at this time: A red 1965 GTO Pontiac, a 1966 white GTO Pontiac, and a 1966 blue SS 396 Chevelle Chevrolet. Both GTOs were 389 cubic inch 335 horsepower cars. The Chevelle Chevrolet was a 396 cubic inch 325 horsepower car. One guy was already out with his girlfriend and couldn't be found, one guy's car was in the shop, but the gentleman with the SS 396 was found and willing. He took his car immediately to a local Texaco station, where he worked, and gave his car a minor tune-up and also put on some cheater slicks for his back tires for better traction off the line. We asked the Fredericksburg boys to give us until 8:00 pm to get ready and they agreed.

Those guys were already licking their chops and counting the money they would win and it looked like Kerrville was only showing up to save face, and lose. O contraire mon amie- Kerrville has an ace up its sleeve and Fredericksburg knows nothing about it. We knew the odds weren't in our favor and they did too! My buddy had some friends with fast cars from Bandera, Texas, twenty-five

miles southeast of Kerrville, and they would side with us so he went to Bandera and lined them up but they didn't know if they could be ready by 8:00 pm but told us to hold on and they were coming over to Kerrville. Word of the race spread like wildfire among the local kids and by 8:00 pm several hundred kids had shown up and lined both sides of Highway 173 between Kerrville and Bandera, about five miles southeast of town. Out there was a rural nice and wide paved long straightaway. To the east of this strip of highway today there exists an exclusive residential subdivision called Comanche Trace. How the cops never got wind of this going down, I'll never know.

The racers show up, set the terms, place their bets, and proceed to get ready to race. The Kerrvillites didn't have $100 so we passed the hat around and got the money. The Fredericksburg gentlemen with the 426 Hemi said his car wasn't running good and bowed out, the truth of the matter was two-fold: dual four-barrel carburetors are hard to keep synchronized and his weren't, also having a big-heavy model car was a definite disadvantage. This leaves Fredericksburg represented by the "Vette." The guy driving the Corvette was a piece of work, he had on his racing jacket, leather shifting gloves and GTO shoes, supposedly allowed for better grip between clutch, accelerator and brake pedals.

The Vette and SS 396 Chevelle line up, the flag goes down, and they race a quarter mile. The Vette beat the Chevelle five links. Duh! No big surprise to anyone. When the racers got back to the line, the Fredericksburg guys were trying to line up another race! Easy money for them, but what they didn't know is we were stalling for Bandera to show up and Kerrville was beginning to worry if they will show up.

Well, well, well, the cavalry arrives to save the day and its show time! They come rolling in about 9:00 pm in a brand new gold

1966 389 cubic inch 360 horsepower Pontiac GTO with three deuces pulling a trailer and on the trailer is a black 1927 T-bucket Ford with a 327 cubic inch 350 horse power Corvette engine in it. Kerrville is now licking their chops and Fredericksburg is starting to get a little worried. Once again, the terms are set and bets placed.

The guys from Bandera are cool; they pull off to the side (shoulder) of the road, placed ramps on the back of the trailer and roll off the T-bucket. Remember how the gentleman from Fredericksburg was dressed, well; the Bandera guy was dressed like "the Fonz" from the TV series Happy Days. Blue jeans, T-shirt with "moon eyes" on it, work boots etc. Once the car was unloaded, they took out the windshield so a rock wouldn't fly up and break it while racing. Then the Bandera guy looked around and asked the crowd "Does anybody have some shades? I don't want to get any bugs in my eyes." Once that problem was solved, he climbed into his T-bucket and cranked it up. He was running an open exhaust so it was loud. I was standing next to it when he started it and the force from the exhaust came down with such force form the headers that gravel flew up and peppered my knees and lower legs. To warm up his car all he did was U-turn and pulled up beside the Vette, now he was facing south toward Bandera. Both are now ready to race, the flag drops and they're off. The T-bucket beat the Vette by seven links. The T-bucket did this feat missing third gear, thus only using 1st, 2nd, and 4th gears.

Once back to the line they begin talking about another third race. Fredericksburg wanted to redeem itself and save face but now faced the problem Kerrville had in the first race: they were now betting with their own money and were outmatched. They did it anyway. This time the T-bucket beat the Vette by nine links because he didn't miss any gears. Three hundred dollars exchanged

hands that night.

Poor Fredericksburg they go home once again with their tails tucked between their legs. Oh what a night! I'll never forget. Some were happy, others had their egos bruised, some wallets were lighter and others deeper, and all were thoroughly entertained. The rivalry continues today.

An example of how much Fredericksburg dislikes us is during the 2007 football season they printed up and wore T-shirts and it looked like you were looking through the scope of a high powered rifle with an antler (male buck deer) in its crosshairs, enough said. We are known as the Kerrville Tivy High Antlers. They beat us that year in football but overall we have the better winning record. Heavy hitters from both towns in past years have bet as much as $1,000 on the big game.

Also, one thing we have and Fredericksburg doesn't have, as a matter-of-fact most American cities and towns don't have, is the 2012 Heisman Trophy winner Johnny Manziel. Tivy fight never dies! (TFND).

The MoPac
By Arturo Alvarez of Converse, Texas
Born 1932

I was born in 1932 during the steam locomotive era. My dad was employed by the Missouri Pacific Railroad, and my mom was our stay at home mom, who administered spankings as needed, which was quite often, I am sorry to say. There was a generation gap among my older sister and two older brothers, so that we did not enjoy each other's social life too much. My next older brother and I did enjoy being closer and occasionally built homemade shoeshine boxes and went to make extra money to buy shaved ice cones by shining shoes in town.

Now 80, I have vivid childhood memories that I cherish and will remember as long as

I live. I had a passion for exploring, looking for neighborhood kids to play with, climbing monstrous trees, climbing roofs, watching square "gangster" autos pass by in front of grandma's front porch, playing with Sandy, our next door neighbors collie dog which got run over when he barked and chased a passing square car, watching tiny sleet pellets make tiny holes in the sandy ground in front of grandma's front porch during a storm, waiting for the older kids during the "tip the outhouse" incidents to come by on Halloween nights, a Halloween night custom, playing with toys of that era of the 1930s and 1940s. Toys like marbles, spin tops, kites, firecrackers, toy trucks and airplanes, Christmas morning four wheel wagons, tricycles, bicycles, homemade skates, homemade sling shots, and walking to the nearby railroad station to watch the steam locomotives pass by hissing steam and blowing their steam powered whistles. Later, rumors started that steam locomotives would be replaced by diesel engines, ending jobs there.

The most popular marbles game was where a small bowl shaped hole was dug in the ground, about four inches deep and about six inches in diameter and round. The object was to hold a handful of marbles in one hand, the number depending on how many marbles were being bet by two kids. Holding one's marble loaded hand about one foot plus above the hole, then lowering it, and unloading the marbles into the hole quickly. If an even number of the handful of marbles remained in the hole, you won the pot. But, if an odd number remained and the rest bounced out, you lost it. My older brother was expert at it and usually left the game with all pockets of his blue jeans suspenders pants loaded with all the marbles the other kids lost with him. The marbles were all the same size, except a few agates, which were a little larger. They were beautiful, some colored light blue like the sky, and some had swirls like white clouds inside. All the marbles had beautiful designs different from each other, some pure and clear, and of all colors of the rainbow. They were so lovely that our neighbor Lily asked me to bring her a few bags so she could have

Missouri Pacific Railroad employees in the 1940s -1950s
Kingsville Facility

a concrete sidewalk built and overlaid with many marbles for decoration. I did, I got them from my brother, and she had a mason do the sidewalk behind her house. The job was lovely and became the talk of our entire neighborhood that season. The sidewalk resembled like a diamond-studded belt, decorated with colored diamonds, rubies, emeralds, and pearls. Lily was so pleased with it she told my mother about it, and mom skipped a few overdue spankings I was due.

Quite often, my older brother would play marbles with our neighborhood kids while I watched. There would be about ten kids gathered at our neighbor's lot under the shade of three monstrous chinaberry trees at Alicia's house. Alicia Truan I believe, was related by her husband Charlie Truan to Mr. Carlos F. Truan, who grew up to become Senator Carlos F. Truan, chairman, Senate committee on International Relations Trade and Technology, Austin, Texas.

At the time I was much too young to go on vacations with dad and sister and two brothers. Dad had a "Free Pass" given to him by his employer the Missouri Pacific Railroad. One day I came home from playing in the neighborhood. My sister told me to wash and clean up so I would be more presentable. I did not know she was trying to make me look clean so perhaps dad would consider taking me on a Mexican vacation with his free railroad pass. Later that day, when I came home, I asked my mom where everybody was, and she said, "Promise me you will not cry if I tell you where they are." I was surprised. I said I promise, and she told me they were waiting for the MoPac train to go on a Mexican vacation, that they were going to Mexico on a free pass with dad. I almost passed out, I felt so double crossed. I remembered sis Hilda had suggested to me earlier in the day that I should "clean up but it did not occur to me why! Now I knew why she had told me that. I ran all the way to the railroad station and got

there just as the train was pulling out.

Anyway, as all the train had just about passed the railroad station, the caboose was passing by, as I watched it. I couldn't believe what I saw. Standing on the rear end of the caboose by the railing, was dad, sis and my two older brothers. Sis saw me staring at them, and she exclaimed, "Oh! Look! It's Arturito. Oh! No! He is crying!" I was crying and in hysterics as I saw them slowly disappear in the distance as the train slowly shoo-shood away south. I ran after the train, I was kicking the ground and crying inconsolably. It was the most heartbreaking feeling a kid can experience. But, a year or two later, dad did take me on vacation to New Orleans zoo, on his free pass the MoPac railroad had issued to him. MoPac railroad ceased operations in the 1950s.

In those days of the MoPac railroad, before it shut down, Kingsville seemed to be growing and growing. The Kingsville record newspaper ran an article one day, I read it. It said if appeared like there were two Main streets in Kingsville, competing for business, and that Richard Street was competing with the accepted Main Street of Kleberg Street. Richard Street was where hundreds of farm workers were unloaded from huge flatbed trucks after working in the outlying farms. While Kleberg Street had been always the shopping place to go to, Richard Street had developed into a grocery store, barbershop, butcher shop, and a beer joint metropolis, a new kid on the block.

Kleberg Street, long considered the main street featured upscale stores like Montgomery Ward's, Sears, JC Penney, three movie theatres, a large restaurant next to the Rialto Theater, hardware store, post office, and large bank, plus a nearby tourist hotel, the "Casa Richardo Hotel," where I imagine, a famous movie star was staying, by the name of Don Red Berry, with his wife. One day while I was walking towards the Rialto

Theater, Mr. Don Red Berry and his wife were walking towards me on the sidewalk. When I saw them about half block away, coming in my direction, I couldn't believe it. I was a fan of his cowboy western movies frequently seen at the Rex Theater on Kleberg Street. I tried not to look at them as they came near me, as they seemed to be having a family spat, so I just quietly passed by, while I kept my eyes towards the storefronts. As they passed by, I was elated, wow! They were on Kleberg our main street in Kingsville, Holy Moly! Well in contrast, the other near famous street Richard Street was also popular but only with a lower class. To me, Richard Street was my street. It was the Spanish street part of town. There, my older brother Lupe and I made more nickels shining shoes than on Kleberg.

During those years while dad's MoPac free pass lasted, my older female cousin used it many times with me. She borrowed it from mom Benilde and took me to the North Beach in Corpus Christi Texas. Sometimes Viola took me on the Greyhound or Trailways bus, which we boarded on Kleberg Street. North Beach was a wonderful place with a carnival and rides. We really enjoyed those trips.

My childhood ended at age 9 when Pearl Harbor was attacked. I got a job as a pin boy setting up pins in a bowling alley to help mom. I still have a souvenir war ration coupon book of those days.

A Dollar and a Drowned Cat
By Thelma Gutierrez of Del Rio, Texas
Born 1944

My name is Thelma Rodriguez Gutierrez and I am sixty eight years old. I want to tell my childhood memory, my true story; about the good old days when I was growing up. See, I come from a small town in the south of Texas, Del Rio. I come from a family of seven, four

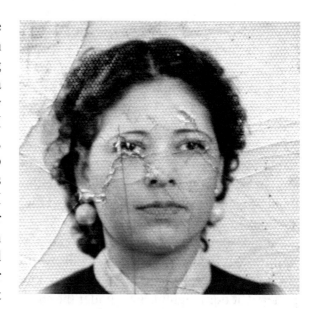

Thelma's mother, Eusebia Rodriguez Gutierrez

brothers and three sisters. My father's name was Pascual Gutierrez, and my mother's name was Eusebia Rodriguez Gutierrez. They are deceased now; my father was a good hard working man and a good father and worked all his life, and earned good money because he was a highway construction engineer and mother was a housewife, she never worked outside the home. So, my big brother's name was Pascual R. Gutierrez, Jr., his nickname was Nuno, he is deceased now. Then my second brother is Jose R. Gutierrez, and his nickname is JoJo, he lives in San Angelo, Texas about one hundred miles from here, so then is me, my name is Thelma R. Gutierrez and my nickname was Mami when I grew up, now they call me by my full name, Thelma only. So then, my brother next to me is Raul R. Gutierrez and we called him by Bule. Then my brother Leonel is next from Raul and we called him Vancho he is the baby of the boys, and he lives in Brady, Texas, so then my sister Estella and we called her Machi and I am ten years older than her. So, then is my sister Amelia and we called her Baby because she is the baby of the whole family. I was raised with my oldest brother, so I remember about my "Good Old Days" when we were growing up. I remember that we used to do things that my parents didn't know. My parents would go grocery shopping every time my father came in to town, because he was always working out of town and he would come only on weekends. So that's when he took my mother to the stores to do their shopping and they would leave us alone in the house. This was before Estella and Amelia were born, so we were only four of us, Nuno, JoJo, Me and Bule, but sometimes they would take Bule with them, and Vancho, so we would stay only the three of us, Nuno, JoJo and me, sometimes Bule would stay and I took care of him. So, mother would tell us, we are going to go grocery shopping I don't want you guys to go outside the house you stay inside the house, and we all say, "Yes, Popa" because we didn't call mom, mom we called her Popa, I never found out why we called her Popa, anyway, they would leave, and the moment they took off my big brother would tell us, "Come on let's go outside and play." One day I was looking for them, and I couldn't find them, so then I heard somebody coughing, my father had a tool shed so I went to look and sure enough there they were, my

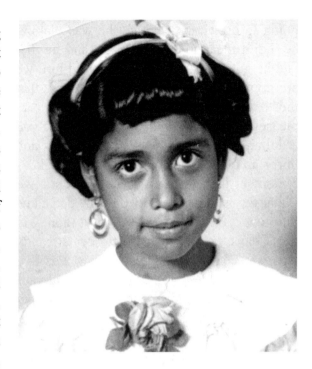

Thelma R. Gutierrez in 1951

Thelma and her father, Pascual Gutierrez in 1949

big brother and my other brother Nuno and JoJo and they were smoking cigarettes. I told them, "I am going to tell and you both are going to get a whipping" so then my big brother told me, "Please don't say nothing and I'll give you a dollar," and I said, "Ok, give me the dollar and I won't say anything." Then my brother told me, "Look sis, try it see how it feels to smoke," and I said, "No" and he keeps telling me, "Look just try a little puff," and the stupid thing is I did try it. Then my brother told me, "Ha ha I am not going to give you the dollar because if you tell on us, we will tell that you smoked too," so I said to myself there will be a next time. I knew my brother, so another time came up, and my parents went out again, and we stayed home again, and again the moment my parents went shopping there, we go outside. This time my brother and JoJo and me were playing and my mother used to have duck's and rabbits and she love cats. This time my brother Nuno got a cat and put the cat's head in the water of the duck pond, and I told him "stop it you are

97

going to drown the cat" and he was playing he didn't mean to drown the cat and he did, and he got so scared. JoJo and I told him we are going to tell mom because we knew that those were her cats, so then he told us "no please don't say anything, and I will give you a dollar," and we said, "Well, right now and hurry up before dad and mom come back." I remember that my mom used to give us two dollar for us to spend every time my dad came into town. Two dollars was a lot of money in those days, coke used to cost 5 cents, candy was two cents, and so two dollars was two dollars. My oldest brother would save always his money. He didn't spend it so I remember that he went to get his money out to pay us, because he used to dig a hole on the ground and put it in a jar. He got the jar out, and gave me and JoJo a dollar each so we went to the store and spent it. You know he never spent his money he liked to save his money. So I was always watching him what he did wrong so he could pay me for not telling, but after two or three days passed by I told my mom what he had done, because my mother was looking for her cat, and I went ahead and told her that Nuno had drowned the cat in the duck pond. My brother got a whipping for what he did, and then my brother told my mother he had paid us for us not to tell. Oh, my God my mother called me and JoJo and asked us if Nuno had paid us for not telling we said "Yes." So we got a whipping too.

I remember I had a friend that lived right next to our house, her name was Juana Martinez, and we called her Juanita. She used to come and play with me she was a little older than me. Me, Juanita, and my brother Bule were playing outside and one time we were playing in a car that belongs to my dad, and we were inside the car playing, and I was holding the door of the car, and Juanita closed the door of the car and got my fingers! I cried out loud and my mother came out of the house and asked me "what is it why are you crying,"

and instead of telling her what Juanita had done I blamed it on my brother Bule, that he had closed the car down and got my fingers so my brother Bule got a whipping. He never said that he didn't do it. The reason I said that he did it was because I knew that if I told my mother Juanita did it she was going to get mad and run her away, and she would never come back to play with me. My friend she has already passed away now.

This other time my mother gave us a bath and told us, "I am going to let you guys play outside for a little while ok but just don't get dirty ok and please don't cut the rose." She had a rose plant with only one rose. Well I just don't remember who got the rose; I know I did not cut it. The rose was cut and thrown on the ground and my mother looked out through the window and saw the rose and called us three. She asked us who did it and I remember that my brothers told her that they have not cut it, so I remember that one of them was lying because I was sure I didn't do it and we got a good whipping and until now, I never found out who did it. I think it was my big brother. Anyway, one time my dad and my brother Bule and I went with my father down town because he was going to get something. I don't remember what but he told me and Bule "you both stay in the car, I'll be back" so we stayed in the car. Then we saw this old lady crossing the main street when her panties fall down all the way to the floor and me and brother kept looking and said look her panties fall down and we said she was going to pick them up but no instead, she took them off in the middle of the street. I remember that she looked everywhere to see if somebody was looking at her but she never saw us in the car so we laughed so much me and my brother. These kinds of experiences were very entertaining for us. I remember that in those good old days we use to go to a theater that was a drive-in theater for one dollar a car load. I remember we used to get my dad's car without permission, and since he worked out of town. When he would come home, he would know that somebody had moved the car because the car was not parked the way he had parked it but we would tell him "nobody got your car dad" and my mother used to go with us too. So she would say "nobody got your car" and my father knew that we all were lying. So we never told him that was very fun for us. You know the car we had to push it in order for the car to start so we had to push the car to go to the movies and then push it again to come back. My father knew that the car didn't work, so he knew that we had to push it but anyway we never fooled him he knew we got it.

Something funny was we use to get up on the tree, a very big tree, and get some green little balls that the tree had and we use to throw those to people that passed walking. They would look around and see where they were coming from and never saw us on top of the tree. We use to play cowboys, and play dead when we got shot. Halloween was fun in those days. Christmas was Christmas in those days; I am talking about more than fifty years ago.

Blue Texas Norther
By Zada Jahnsen of Bulverde, Texas
Born 1935

A blue Texas norther rattled windowpanes, in the little farm house up on Honey Creek Hill, the night I entered the world. Earlier in the day, Benno, my father, had gone to the hall where the telephone hung on the wall. His call to the central switchboard at Specht's store about five miles away alerted Dr. Nooe from Boerne, about twenty miles away, about my impending arrival. The party line system assured that everyone in the community also got the message. My mother's parents Oma Selma and Opa Willie Weil had already

Zada with her father, Benno Bremer in 1936

arrived several days earlier from their home in New Braunfels twenty-five miles away. My mother, Wera, was an only child and, I, their first grandchild.

Benno, my father, had six siblings and was born and raised in Bulverde seven miles to the east of his beloved Honey Creek farm/ranch. They attended Ufnau School, a typical one-room schoolhouse with a small house for the teacher. Lessons were in German and English. Students walked several miles to school. Later, Benno's younger sisters had the privilege of riding a horse. Lunch was homemade, usually bread and smoked venison sausage. Martha, his youngest sister went on to attend college in Seguin to become a teacher. Benno was always so proud that he was able to help her with her college lesson assignments. Later, when I had algebra problems, he solved those too.

Most of the home place, first settled by Benno's maternal grandfather, George Werner Krause, was completely surrounded by rock fences, as were the fields, garden and cattle pens. Most of these rock fences are still standing today.

George Werner Krause had three daughters and only one son. One daughter, Emma, was my grandmother. The son, Walter, was killed by lightening at age 13 as he and his father stepped out on the porch to watch a thunderstorm in progress. The pants he was wearing at the time of the lightning strike are still in possession of the Krause family. His funeral was held at home with burial across the road in a neighbor's family cemetery. I now hold the deed to this Koch family cemetery, now a Historic Texas cemetery.

Photo albums attest to a very happy childhood for me. I was daddy's girl and where he went, I went, fishing, hay wagon, cow pen, anywhere and everywhere.

In 1940 when I was only five, a neighbor came to tell daddy that they had only three children enrolled in the little one room schoolhouse at Honey Creek, and five were needed to keep the school open. So, another neighbor's son and I suddenly found ourselves in first grade. Neither of us spoke any English since German was the language spoken by the whole community. The teacher was patient for a few weeks before the ultimatum "do not speak unless it is in English."

The students from the Honey Creek area attended classes at St. Joseph's Catholic School at Honey Creek. I was there for 3rd, 4th and part of the 5th grade before the new Bulverde School finally opened.

Weather permitting, I always walked the 2 ½ miles to the Catholic school. My mother could see the road from our home and checked on my progress as I came over the hills. These days no small child could be left to walk by herself like that.

By the 5th grade, we had moved to the Bremer Homestead, which was only ½ mile

Zada with her mother, Wera Weil Bremer

from the new school. This school was divided into two classrooms with two teachers, 1st through 5th grades and 6th through 10th grades. Any student who wanted to complete high school had to move in with relatives in town. I, of course moved in with Oma Selma and Opa Willie Weil.

Going to school wasn't the only change in my five year old life. Now I had to share my mamma and daddy with a baby brother. One day I was sent to a neighbor's home to spend the night. Daddy picked me up the next day and Oma Selma made a big deal of introducing me to the sleeping bundle on the bed. I was dark haired, brown eyed and I just didn't know what to make of this blond, fair skinned creature that didn't look anything like me. Now I realize that I am the exception because nearly all of our cousins are blue-eyed blondes.

Spending a few days and nights with Oma and Opa Weil in New Braunfels took a lot of pleading and planning. There was that 25 mile distance for delivery and pick up to work out. We lived in a different rural world, country all the way with wood stove, outhouse, kerosene lamps and no running water in the kitchen. Oma and Opa Weil lived in New Braunfels with electricity, gas stoves, nice large home and they frequented dances, movies, and restaurants. And, they ate beef roasts, steaks, and those wonderful beef meatballs instead of venison, squirrel, and rabbit that were usually on our dinner table.

Visiting with Oma and Opa Bremer, daddy's parents in Bulverde, was more like what I was used to, but sleeping with Oma, and "helping" her dust and cook were special times. And, Opa Bremer enjoyed teasing me and called me "stinkkatz" (skunk). He enjoyed sitting, almost reclining with a pillow, on a long bench on the porch. On Sunday mornings, he smoked a cigar there. I can still close my eyes and smell that Sunday morning cigar. The bench was surrounded by a trellis of

Zada with Oma Emma Bremer

Queen's Crown vines. Oak trees and a white fleshed honey peach tree also provided shade. This bench is where he chose to end his life at age 88.

Both grandmothers insisted on Monday as wash day unless weather or other circumstances cancelled it. Water was heated in a big iron pot outside and carried to the hand wringer machine and tubs, or simply put in tub with a washboard for hand scrubbing. Two other large tubs were filled with rinse water and the final rinse had to have bluing in it. Soap was homemade cooked in the big black pot outside with lard and lye. I always hated those gray homemade soap bars. Oma Weil's homemade soap bars were always snowy white. Hooray for Tide! Tablecloths, dresser scarves, pillow cases, shirts, etc. were starched before ironing. Irons were heated on the wood stove. Can you imagine a hot wood stove in Texas summers?

In the 1940s, when my daddy's youngest brother was drafted, leaving aging grandparents alone to manage 300 acres of farm/ranch, daddy's siblings decided that my dad was the one to move, and take over the Bremer homestead in Bulverde. Reluctantly,

he and mamma made the move from their beloved Honey Creek home to Bulverde, which is where their descendants still live today.

At least once or twice a year, daddy, and I would go fishing on the Guadalupe River. Daddy dropped baited throw lines from tree limbs and if we had a boat, he also put out long trot lines that we checked the next morning. If those fish lines were being jerked around, we knew we had a fish. If we caught a fish we rolled it in cornmeal and fried it. If we didn't catch anything we made bacon stew with bacon, potatoes, and onions that my mother had packed for us. At night we listened to the bull frogs croak and watched the lightening bugs. Unfortunately, lightening bugs seem to have vanished from this area now. Those solitary fishing trips also are no more. The Guadalupe River is now so full of people on tubes that fishing lines are out of the question.

Most old rural homes had cellars, usually underneath the house where canned goods were stored. These cellars usually just had wooden steps or a ladder and only a dirt floor. Cellars were dark and spooky. The cellar at our Honey Creek farm was much larger than most and had a porch over the stone steps leading down to the cellar. It also had a large wooden door; most only had trap doors that lifted up, that let in light when opened. This cellar was not spooky and I often played there. Cellars were also considered shelters from severe storms or tornados. When I recently had the opportunity to visit the place of my birth, I was so pleased to see the stone steps and the old wooden door to the cellar were just as I remembered them.

Sunday afternoons were for visiting. Oma Bremer always made sure there was fresh homemade bread, homemade cheese, smoked venison sausage, and her wonderful cinnamon coffee cake made with generous pats of butter and dollops of thick cream. When aunts, uncles, and cousins started arriving, the pot of strong black coffee was put on the wood stove. We children were required to shake hands and call all aunts and uncles by name, Aunt Hertha, Uncle Adoph etc.

I did my share of shucking corn, feeding chickens, cleaning hen houses, milking cows, butchering chickens, cutting corn tops, gathering eggs and cleaning them, etc., and I didn't like any of it. My mother enjoyed doing these things and much preferred working outside with my dad. She chose to ignore cooking, cleaning, laundry, ironing, etc. as long as she possibly could. So, by the time I was ten years old, I had found a way to get out of that field work. I loved cooking and baking and tried my best to duplicate the results that my grandmothers and aunts were able to achieve. Soon I was bringing home ribbons from the county fair, even while cooking on that old black wood stove. How I longed for a white, electric or gas stove. Now I have five stoves, seven refrigerators, and six freezers at my disposal when preparing meals for a dinner theatre.

I am a descendent of Heinrich Christian Bremer and wife Judith who came from Germany to New Braunfels with Prince Solms. Their daughter, Caroline was born at sea and was the first of the Verein colonists to be baptized in Texas in 1844 with Prince Solms as one of her godparents. One of Heinrich Christian's half-brothers, Fritz Goldbeck, wrote two books of poetry that are a wonderful source of history from the 1840s to 1890. A translation from the German language has been published by Ingrid M. Lingle, 651 Brand Road, Bulverde, Texas 78163. I have two copies of the original books published in German.

Another great source of historical information is found in the two massive books The Bremer Family in America and Germany. These books should be available at the University of Texas and New Braunfels libraries, written by Robert R. Robinson-

Zwahr, the great-great grandson of Caroline Bremer.

Opa Bremer was very tall, probably about 6'4", and Oma was less than 5 feet tall. Oma fell and broke her hip and spent the last five years of her life in bed. Opa had never lifted a finger with housework or kitchen duty. In fact, he was trouble for Oma who was absolutely determined to keep a neat and tidy house. I can still see him in earlier years defiantly propping his long legs with boots on his feet on a table that was placed in front of his day bed in the living room just daring Oma to say something. This table was always covered with a clean tablecloth in spite of the daily boot battles. A large glass basket in the center of the table held cards, letters, and pictures that arrived from the mail.

When Oma broke her hip, Opa insisted on taking over the cooking and cleaning. Soon he was baking bread, cooking oatmeal for Oma and even patiently feeding her. He also made molasses-pecan candy in a frying pan on the wood stove.

Vandals at the San Saba Courthouse
By Jack W. Clark of Rockdale, Texas
Born 1928

In the early days, they planted oak and pecan trees around the San Saba Courthouse. In a few years, they began to be crowded. The pecan trees were planted by San Saba's famous Englishman Mr. E.E. Risien, who grafted the first pecans in Texas.

One morning in about 1930, the city of San Saba woke up and every oak tree at the courthouse had been sawed down by vandals, they said. I don't know where the night watchman was. The vandals were never caught!

Mr. Risien was an Englishman by birth. He always sent the Queen of England some pecans every year. When I was in grammar school in San Saba, he always had his pecan trees thrashed and the first four grades in San Saba School went down to his home. We picked up the pecans and helped him celebrate his birthday. Mr. Risien had a ram's horn for a hearing aid. We would sing him "Happy Birthday" and eat cake. We all went home with a small paper sack of his paper shell pecans.

Happy days!

Corn Fatter
By Joe A. Moellendorf of Fredericksburg, Texas
Born 1938

I am seventy-four now, and I can remember my brother three years older than me. We would go to the fields to carry in corn fatter. My dad did not have a tractor, only horses, so we would go to the fields to carry the corn fatter home to feed the cows.

My dad, Theodore Moellendorf would take ten bundles of corn fatter, and he told my brother, Arthur "Addy" Moellendorf to carry at least four bundles. I was only eight at the time, so I could only carry two bundles, but my brother could bring more. My dad took his feed, and I got two bundles and followed my dad to the barn.

Well, when we got to the barn, my brother had not picked up any, and I can remember my dad took a corn stalk and whipped my brother because he had not brought any from the field. My brother took it like a man and did not say a word.

My father told my brother, "Now you go to the field by yourself and get some and bring them to the barn." My brother went to the field without hesitation and brought back six bundles of corn fatter.

That was life, and I never have figured why my brother did not pick up any corn fatter. I never asked him, and he never said why he did not bring any.

Growing Up in Fredericksburg
By Lorene Harmon of Fredericksburg, Texas
Born 1935

I remember a time when Main Street belonged to the locals. On Saturday nights, I remember getting together with a group of girlfriends, and one of the girls getting to use the family car. All of us would pool our nickels and dimes to put gas in the car, and then cruise Main Street. Back then, Main Street had two stoplights. One light uptown at the Kraus Bottling Works, and the other light was downtown at the Nimity Hotel.

After cruising Main Street for a couple of hours, we would go to Sunny Side Hut for our nickel Coke. There we would get to see other groups doing the same thing. Then after about an hour, we would go home.

Then on Sunday morning, I remember going to church. And after church, we would go to the La Mesa Café for our nickel doughnut and chocolate milk. Then on Sunday afternoon, we would either go back to the Palace Theater or go to the old fairground to watch the Fredericksburg Giants play baseball.

Then it was back home to wait for Monday morning to go back to school. Then came the weekend, when we would do the same thing over again, and we loved to do it. We had such a good childhood.

Other Memories
Other memories of growing up in the old Fredericksburg include Saturday night baths in the kitchen in a washtub by the kitchen stove to get as much heat as I could. It wasn't much, but I guess I got clean anyway.

I remember a very bad hailstorm. There

were hailstones as big as softballs. Everyone in Fredericksburg had to get new roofs.

All my clothes were homemade. They were made out of Daddy's feed sacks. But they were very pretty, and I was proud to wear them.

I remember going to the movies at the Palace Theater. It was always a good old western movie. I could spend all afternoon there. It cost nine cents to get in.

My favorite teacher was Sister Fedes. She had taught all my older brothers and sister. This was in the first grade.

One of my favorite games to play was marbles. I liked to play with the boys. I was good at it, too. Another game I liked to play was jacks.

A Place of Another Time
By Steven B. Kensing of San Antonio, Texas
Born 1953

Granny Surber was of another time even in 1958 in a small, rural town of Center Point, Texas. All one had to do was pass through the old wooden gate and gaze up at the weathered frame structure to know that the present was behind them, at least for a while.

I had never known the house to be painted. It needed no color beyond the palette provided by the flowers blooming in the spring. There were lilac bushes, with their intoxicating perfume and Queen's Crown, with its vining pink blossoms trailing to the top of the outside staircase.

In the yard to greet you was a tiny woman, even from a child's perspective. Granny Surber always wore a long dress with an apron and an old-fashioned sunbonnet with a wide brim, which concealed her entire face from the side. When one looked directly at her, one could see the deeply weathered skin with its years of wonderful patina and gentle eyes of one who

had known hardships but refused to become hardened by them. "Come in!" she would say.

The front room of the ancient house was sparsely furnished, making it seem larger than it really was, and it seemed dark. In one corner was a large iron bed with intricate detailing upon which sat a large antique doll with a china head. Over near the fireplace was a small armless rocker. That was where Granny Surber sat, and I can picture her there still.

It was with these memories coursing through my mind that I went there some ten odd years later when I heard the house was being torn down to make way for a new tennis court. I went there looking for some tangible aspect of those memories. All that I found left were nails, wonderful old square, hand-forged nails, probably made in a blacksmith shop right there in Center Point over a hundred years before. How appropriate, I thought, that the very thing that once held this old house secure was now the only thing left that I could hold in my hand as I contemplated my past.

I am grateful for those memories of that small rural community called Center Point and my wonderful Grandmother Lovewell who took me along when she went to visit those people of another time. Even today, I affectionately refer to those tennis courts as the "Surber Tennis Courts!"

Our Wood Heated Us Twice
By Dorothy Parker of Pearland, Texas
Born 1935

At this point, I guess I should say we didn't have much, money-wise. On this farm, we did have a good life. At times, we raised peanuts, cotton, corn, sweet potatoes, watermelons, Irish potatoes, several kinds of peas, beans, greens, onions, tomatoes, okra, peppers, eggplant, squash, radishes, cabbage, and cucumbers. We spent a lot of time canning.

There were the vegetables themselves, and then there were pickles, pepper sauces, kraut, and chow-chow. I remember washing the jars after we had emptied them from the year before. I guess we thought foods just stayed good for a year. We also raised cane and made syrup. We had peach trees, plum trees, several pear trees, and an apple tree. There were mulberries, grapes, muscadines, huckleberries, and dew and blackberries for us to eat. We made jams and jellies and cobblers. We had pecan trees and hickory nut trees, and I can tell you we ate our share of nuts, parched peanuts, and popcorn. We made candies and popcorn balls, and a few times a year, we made homemade ice cream. Food wise, we did great.

We raised guineas, geese, chickens, goats, cattle, and hogs. Hog killing day would be quite a workday. We had the smoked meat and sausage, salted meat in the meat box, canned meat, and we made cracklings for the lard to use for cooking. We ate the cracklings and used some of the lard to make lye soap.

Daddy loved to hunt and fish, so we had squirrel, deer, and fish, also. I remember in the summer, we would go to the river for a week. This was the time when the kids got to go. Mama would send two or three chickens so we would have something to eat before we caught the fish.

In the summer we would barbeque, goat most of the time. They would dig a hole in the ground for the fire and cover it with a screen.

We did not get Butane until 1947 or electricity until 1950, so Daddy would say we got heated twice by the wood we used. Once when we cut it and then when we burned it. We had a cistern by the corner of the house and a well near the barn for our water supply. We had cats, dogs, mules, horses, and a she-mule. Some of them were for pets and company, and some were for help.

What a good life we had!

Taking Andy to the Stock Show
By Guy Daugherty of Denison, Texas
Born 1929

Good old days growing up in Brunet, Texas. My folks on the Daugherty side were pioneers to Burnet County. They arrived in 1855 and had a home on the far eastern side of Burnet, across the street from where the Law Enforcement Center is now.

Our home was down the street on Live Oak. When I was about sixteen and in FFA, I had a calf named Andy. Mr. Heckman raised registered Angus cattle. He had six bulls and hired me to come every day to feed them. He also owned a café in town. When it came time to have an animal for FFA, Mr. Heckman sold Andy to me. He also let me take the mother cow home for about six months so the calf would have his mother's milk.

When Andy was about seven months old, my grandmother, Dee Kirk, wanted to pet him in the worst way. He would not allow her to pet him at all. She decided one day that she would too pet that calf. She opened the gate and got inside, where Andy promptly pinned her to the fence and started butting her, so she retreated out the gate. She decided right then that her interest in Andy was over! She never tried to pet him again.

I took Andy in a borrowed trailer hooked to my 1937 Ford car to the Houston Fat Stock Show. My friend, Thomas Hullum, and his calf, also in a trailer pulled by his 1935 Ford pickup, went along, too. We took off in the snow, with tarps over the trailers. Near Milano, close to Caldwell, we ran out of snow but it was bitter cold. Thomas got lost somewhere in Houston, where a policeman redirected him to the show. I got to the show before he did, where we both showed our animals.

I also had my Burnet Stock Show Grand Champion South Down cross Rambouillet sheep with my calf, Andy. I had fed Andy corn that the FFA boys had bought, a whole truckload. I bought 2,000 pounds and sold what I had left to Frank Humphries, who was a great friend and mentor to me.

For a sixteen year old, raising a calf, playing football, going to school, and working at the feed store for Frank Humphries, along with a part-time job at the Humble filling station, life was hard but full of opportunities and adventure. Now that I am eight-three, Thomas (the barber) and I remember those trips as a really fun time. They say it "takes a village." We sure had that in Burnet.

Early Times Marble Falls, Texas
By Leroy Trussell of Marble Falls, Texas

Roy, Barbara, and Leroy in 1949

Cedar Yards on both ends of Town.
Outhouses down the alleyways.
Had no red lights, an' no local Law.
Most Business shut down at dark, an' closed
on Sunday.
Johnny's Café an' Bus Stop, or The Blue
Bonnet Café.
Coffee was a nickel.
Up Town Picture Show uh' quarter, an'
popcorn uh' dime.

Started Marble Falls School in Fourth Grade.
In the Old Granite Building.
Mrs. Hit was my Teacher.
She was friendlier than her name.
School lunches were twenty-five cents.
Country Ladies that made good down home
cookin'.
Just across the street was Beacher's Store.
We walked to School, stop have uh' R.C.
Cola an' uh' Moon Pie.
Most remembered time, High school boys
went rabbit hunting.
The carrion was put down the School's stove
vents.
For weeks, windows were open, Teacher
spraying deodorant.

Cedar Chopper's, with his ax, uh'
independent lot.
But could make $35, uh' day.
Ranching was a hard life depend a lot on the
weather.
During drought, they would burn prickly
pear, or buy hay.
If times got real tough, take em' to the sale.
Mr. Jackson had two mules an' a wagon.
He an' a one arm man picked up the trash.
Pa open up a Humble Gas Station.
Gas was around twenty-five cents.
The first fast food place was Moonies Drive
through.

Bein' nine, walked, or' Muh' bicycle was
tuh' ride.
Summers were hot, was before air
conditioning.
In the river, We'd cool off.
SWUNG! From a fork of a big pecan tree,
an' dove off.

106

But she washed away, in the flood of 1975.
Some men floated logs from up river, built a
Scout Cabin.
At Scout meeting, We'd play Fox, an'
Hounds.
Then one night a drunk, burned it down.

Dad an' I use'ta fish the Trap, were a old dam
washed out.
Fishin' above the bridge, Blue Bonnet Hole,
an Bub's place.
With grass hoppers, shad, or' worms, usually
a string of catfish.
The flood of 1975, boats, fishing docks,
trailer houses, an' cows.
Went over the lower dam.

Sold coon hides, pecans, an' mustang grapes,
to
Old Man Challot.
He had a Store, on Main Street.
Cut a few cedar stays, an' peel tuh' bark, for
a little pocket money.
Swept, an' mopped Michel's Drug Store,
three days a week.

Old Timers met, an' to gossip.
In, an' in front of the Buckhorn Barber Shop.
Groceries were bought, at Brothers Market,
on Main St.
Own by the Giesecke Brotehrs.
The Ice House closed down.
The Volunteer Fire Dept. moved in.
A closed cotton mill, down by the bridge.
Was a Mathus Air Cond. Plant, then later
burn.

In 1950, construction started on the upper an'
lower dams.
Soon our river was a lake.
Now the School, an' the Town, started to
grow,
Marble falls became center of the Highland
Lakes.

New Post Office, widen the 281 bridge.
Widen 281 Highway to Burnet.
New 1431 Ranch Road to Kingsland.
H.E.B., new Store, an' Walmart came to
Town.
Real Estate was hot.
What was then, is now not.

Whittlin'
By Richard G. Smith of Hye, Texas
Born 1939

When my older brother and I were young,
we loved to make things out of wood. When
we could find time, we would go down under
the big live oak trees that grew around our
home not far from Bear Mountain north of
Fredericksburg, Texas. We would sharpen
our pocketknives, usually on a carborundum
stone. We tried to see who could get their knife
the sharpest. Gary, my brother, was usually the
best. We were always on the lookout for some
nice straight-grained white pine or sugar pine,
usually from apple box ends. We would start
whittling on a piece with no particular object
in mind. The things we made usually evolved
as we cut and studied the wood, letting nature
take its course. Sometimes the result was a
pile of shavings.

Our most common projects were boats
and airplanes. We loved airplanes. My brother
taught me how to carve a ball in a cage with
an attached chain from one stick of wood.
I had to be very careful and patient to keep
from splitting the wood, tuning the project
into a catastrophe.

Sometimes we would carve rifles and
pistols. Our favorite was the Army Colt .45
automatic pistol. Another favorite of mine
was a paddle wheel boat powered by a rubber
band or a sailboat. These projects would be
taken to the Palo Alto Creek to be tested.

During those years of my life, I developed

an appreciation for our native woods and their characteristics. Our favorite wood was white pine, because it was usually straight-grained and soft enough to carve but solid enough to hold details. Sometimes we would use harder, more dense woods such as walnut or hickory. Although they were certainly harder, they yielded some very pretty results. Our local juniper, which is referred to as cedar, was a very attractive wood but was prone to splitting with changes in temperature and humidity.

The secret to any woodworking endeavor is very sharp tools. The old adage, "You can cut yourself easier with a dull knife than with a sharp knife" is definitely true. We found that the common pocketknife was not the best for precise carving. It takes a knife with a large enough handle for good control and a small blade for intricate cuts. So when we needed to hog off a lot of wood for preliminary shaping, we used a strong, heavy blade that would not bend or break.

At first, our projects resulted in some pretty grotesque pieces of wood. But as we experimented and became more proficient, we learned to make things that were actually recognizable and useful. Eventually, our granddad would discover us wasting our time whittlin' and put us to work hoeing corn, hauling rock out of the field, or some other 'productive endeavor.'

How I Financed College
By George Seeburger of Rockport, Texas
Born 1935

College tuition is extremely high today, which forces many students to borrow money to pay for their college education. Student loans now exceed credit card debt nationwide, with some individuals exceeding $200,000.00 by graduation. Here is how one guy financed his education back in the '50s and '60s.

Upon graduation from Phillips High School in northern Wisconsin in 1953, I took a job at the Flambeau Feed Mill as a member of the "Bull Gang," responsible for loading boxcars and semitrailers with 90-pound bags of feed. Since I was only 17 years old at the time, I could legally only work 36 hours per week until I turned 18. Also, I worked the night shift for an additional premium of 10 cents an hour, which brought my hourly wage up to 90 cents. The purpose of this work was to save enough money for a year of school at Central State College, now U. W. Stevens Point, which was 120 miles away.

I had no car of my own and stayed at home with my parents and two younger brothers. My main entertainment was taking my girlfriend to a dance on Saturday night at the Bobcat Tavern on Highway 70, where a friend of mine played tuba in a polka band. I borrowed my dad's 1950 Studebaker Champion on these occasions. Needless to say, my expenses were low, and I managed to save most of my earnings.

When I registered for classes at Stevens Point, the tuition was under $40.00 per semester, including textbook rental.

Other summer jobs that helped me finance my schooling included highway construction, pulp cutting, and machine shop work. I wound up with a major in biology and would teach this subject at Wittenberg High School for three years.

Back then, beer was 10 cents a glass and 30 cents a quart, so I got along quite well. Not as well as the Korean Vets who received $110.00 per month from Uncle Sam.

While at the "Point," I met Nancy, the love of my life, who would become my wife and the mother of my two sons.

Three years of teaching high school biology qualified me for a National Science Foundation Academic Year Institute at the University of Georgia in 1960. I fell in love with the subjects of ichthyology, marine biology, mammalogy, bacteriology, statistics, entomology, and others, and earned an A+ grade in most of them (95 average or higher). It is amazing what doors can be opened by professors when you are the top student in their class. I was encouraged by them to apply for one of three National Defense Education Act Fellowships available. After scoring high on the Graduate Record Exam and other tests, I was awarded an NDEA Fellowship that covered three more years of graduate school plus all expenses and led to a Doctors degree.

Before I was thirty years old, I had my Doctorate and a job teaching biology at U.W. Whitewater in Wisconsin. I am now retired after a 27-year career at the same place.

Nancy and I have been putting money in a college fund for our only grandchild, Ashley, who starts school in the fall. Hopefully, she will not have to borrow too much to achieve her desired degree and a start in her chosen profession.

Sneaking to Smoke
By Linda Wiley of Burnet, Texas
Born 1946

Mischief I Got Into

We had a grocery store in our house in the '50s. I wanted to smoke. I was nine or ten years old. My mama put the cigarettes in a wooden box high up on a shelf she thought I couldn't reach. But I climbed up there, got me a package, went out to the car shed, sat on a bale of hay, and lit up. Shortly, Mama came out of the house to go to the well to get a bucket of water. Smoke was coming through cracks in the walls. She smelled smoke, looked around, and saw it was coming from the car shed. She came in there and said to me, "What do you think you are doing? Don't you know you could set the place on fire with this hay in here? Well, I'm not going to tell your

daddy when he gets home from work, but if I catch you doing it again, I will."

Encounters with Snakes or Critters

We had a house out back with a shelf that had baskets full of eggs we were selling to the hatchery. One day, we came out and the door wouldn't close. We looked up and a big old chicken snake was laying up there, full of eggs. We got the hoe off the fence and knocked him down. When we chopped into him, yellow egg went everywhere.

One night, we kept hearing something bumping in the smokehouse out back. It was a snake trying to swallow a gourd. He was hitting himself against the wall, trying to break the gourd so he could digest it.

We had an armadillo under the floor of our house one night. It was digging and it kept bumping the floor. We couldn't sleep. Daddy got up with his .22 rifle and put his overalls on. Mama went along to help. Daddy told her to turn the water hose on and shoot it under the house, and he would get on the other side of the house and shoot the armadillo when it came out. It wasn't long before it had too much water and came snorting out. Daddy shot and killed it.

School Days

I remember one day when I was in elementary school, in a three-room school. This was in the '50s. We had outdoor toilets, one for the boys and one for the girls. It had been raining for days and the ground was saturated and boggy. It was still raining hard on this day. The teacher said she would drive us in her car to the restroom. The car was a '54 Oldsmobile two door. All we kids who had to go loaded into the car. She pulled off the road up close to the toilet door and got stuck in the mud. We all had to get out and push the car back on the road. So we all got wet anyway.

I was seven years old and in first grade. A mare was having a colt in the pasture not far from the schoolhouse. The east side of the classroom was all glass windows so we didn't have much school that day. We were too busy getting up to see if the mare had had the colt. We wanted to watch. We had never seen anything like that. The teacher couldn't keep us seated to have our lessons. It took the mare all day to have the colt, but we got to see the colt stand up before school turned out.

Happy Times
By Marjorie Turner Wagner of San Saba, Texas
Born 1945

I was born to Dan and Mavis Turner in July of 1945 in Richland Springs, Texas. My grandparents lived in San Saba and my two sisters and three brothers stayed with my grandparents and a bachelor uncle, who we called Uncle Boog. His real name was Robert Nelson Turner. My two old maid aunts were Willie Dean Turner and Francis Elizabeth Turner. My grandmother married L.D. Kelly after her husband died at 29 years of age of pneumonia. So my dad was the baby at the time, and my aunts and uncle were not too old

Grandpa Kelly and Subilee the mule

Marjorie's uncle, Robert H. "Boog" Turner

either. Anyway, we only know Grandmother's second husband as our grandpa.

I don't know why we stayed so much at their home, but we loved it. There were cows and hogs and chickens and ducks and an old donkey named Jubilee. He was a mean old donkey. Grandpa would get anybody he could to ride that old donkey and they always wound up on the ground. I don't guess anybody every rode him.

Well, the best time was once a year. We would go camp on the San Saba River for two weeks by the old Richland Springs Bridge. That was before they built the other bridge out by Sloan at this highway that goes to Richland Springs. Anyway, we set up the best every camp. We had tents. I think they were Army tents.

My aunts and uncle would go to work every day in San Saba to their jobs, and when they got off work, they would to the house in town and milk the cows and gather the eggs and whatever else they had to do. Then they would come to the river and bring fresh milk and eggs. We had homemade biscuits cooked in a Dutch oven and gravy and whatever meat my grandmother cooked all day in a pot over the campfire.

At night, there were millions of lightning

Marjorie's Aunt Bill, Grandpa Kelly, and Uncle Merion in 1953

bugs. We would catch them in jars and use them to light up our tents. We had old lanterns, too, but the lightning bugs were fun. We spent our days, my sisters, brothers, and I, hunting treasures. We had so many rocks and driftwood.

Then my uncle and aunts were dead set on us learning to swim on that old San Saba River. We all did learn to swim. We would have to take soap and a washcloth at night and go close to the river to wash up, because we were going to be clean when we went to bed. We did not mind cleaning up in the river. It was a lot more fun that taking a bath at home.

We spent two wonderful weeks there for several years. I don't know if anybody owned that land or if my grandparents got the ok to go there. We loved it, and I am so thankful for that time in my life.

We would also go on little trips like to Goldthwait or Brownwood, and I think we just went and always at lunchtime. We would find a big shade tree and out would come the picnic basket. We had our lunch, always pork'n beans and lunchmeat and homemade cake. We did this often. My grandparents, aunts, and uncle really loved us a lot.

On Saturday, they would take us to town to get an ice cream cone, and we got to go to the little variety store to pick out one thing. Every Saturday night, my uncle would drag out the ice cream freezer and we had homemade ice cream. I always got to sit on top on the ice cream freezer while my Uncle Boog turned the crank. Boy was that ice cream good.

My dresses and pants were made out of really pretty flour sacks and the boys' shirts were, too. At the time, we were poor but did not know it because we had plenty of food and a lot of love.

I could write forever about our family. It was so different from today. However, I can say that the years we spent with our grandparents, Nancy Helen Turner Kelly and Ira Kelly, were the happiest days of our lives. I think we felt special because Dad was the only one who got married in the family, so we had our uncle and aunts to fuss over us all the time. They have all gone now, and I miss them all so much, but I will see them one day when we get to heaven.

Our Wonderful Adventure
By Robert D. Sevey of Center Point, Texas
Born 1949

Dad, Mom, my sister, two brothers, and I moved to Texas in May of 1963. It was hot and we drove all the way from El Cajon, California to Kerrville, Texas with no air conditioning in the 1958 Ford Fairlane station wagon. We drove in on State Highway 290 and turned right onto Highway 27 at Mountain Home, through Ingram and right down Main Street. There was no Interstate 10 at that time. When we got to Kerrville, we stayed in the only motel in town for about five days.

Dad and Mom found us a house to rent along the river where Broadway and Water Streets met. The man didn't want to rent to a family with four kids, but Dad and Mom

111

finally persuaded him, and we moved in that day. Our furniture had not arrived from California, so we slept on the floor. Mom cooked our meals on a single hot plate for several days.

That summer was hard on us all. I had left my first love in California. And at the age of thirteen, I thought the pain ran deep. Dad and Mom were busy trying to build our home in Center Point. My younger brother and sister stayed with Dad and Mom. But my other brother, Earl, just two years younger than me, and I were left to roam the town. I think Mom and Dad knew I needed some time to adjust to Texas. And so one day the adventure I will never forget began.

As was the family tradition, we all got up early. Mom fixed breakfast and us kids got dressed and made up our beds and straightened our rooms. Dad was off to check on the house being built in Center Point and Mom was taking care of my baby brother, Fred, and my sister, Cheryl. In those days after breakfast, Earl and I were outside as soon as we could be. But that day, Mom gave Earl and me a nickel each. And so we were off to town.

Down by the river was a deer trail we had scouted out earlier. It ran along the river up into town. The city of Kerrville is now putting in a new river trail. As we walked along the river, we found many "cool" rocks and sticks. The trail brought us up behind the icehouse, where we would stop and watch the men load large blocks of ice into trucks at the loading dock. The men were dressed in long, black rubber aprons, black rubber boots, and long, black rubber gloves. We thought it was a pretty great job to have in the hot summer. One of the men took out his icepick and broke off a shard of ice and pitched it out to Earl and me. What a treat! And we yelled a big, "Thank you!" and then headed back to the river and on up the trail.

Just a little ways up along the river was a small path up to Water Street, right by Reither

Chrysler Auto Shop. As Earl and I passed in front of the large glass front window, we saw Mrs. Reither at the desk behind one of the automobiles in the show room. She raised up her head and gave us a wave of her hand, and we waved back.

On up Water Street was the Blue Bonnet Hotel. The front doors to the large lobby were open, and Earl and I stepped in. Along the lobby wall was a shoeshine stand. A very large wooden chair raised up on an even larger wooden stand. In the chair sat a big man in a suit, with his pant legs stuffed inside the tops of his boots. In front of him, was a medium built black man wearing tan khaki pants and a white tee shirt with a brownish tan cloth apron around his neck and tied tight around his waist. I remember best the little AM radio over at the side of the shoeshine stand. It was tuned to the only station in Kerrville, KERV-1230. And the western music had a distinctive beat. We stood over at the side of the lobby as this fine man hummed along to the music and cleaned and shined the boots in front of him. But when he got out the buffing cloth and in time with the music, popped that cloth, and buffed those boots to a super shine, I thought the man was going to break into a song and dance at any minute. I thought, "What a wonderful talent this man has." But as quickly as he had started, he was through and the big man stepped down from the chair. Then it was time for Earl and me to travel on.

On up the street on the sidewalk, we came to Schreiner Bank, with its large glass window in front. We peeked in to see Mr. Schreiner seated behind a very large, wooden desk. And over his head, the largest Texas longhorn steer/cow we had ever seen was mounted on the wall. The horns from tip to tip must have been ten or twelve feet. Earl and I knew Mr. Schreiner, because this was our Dad and Mom's bank. This man stopped what he was doing and came to the door to shake our hands and say, "Good morning." It made me feel really grown up to have that moment, for Mr. Schreiner to take that time was very special for me.

But on up the street, we went past shops and the movie theater to the corner, where Pampell's Drug Store was, and it had the soda fountain! We waved hello to the ladies at the counter but did not stop in. They had customers from the bus station across the street. Earl and I had other places to go.

Down to the river and under the old suspension bridge and back to the river trail we went. Up along the river we went to the corner of Guadalupe and Hugo Street to the Phillips 66 Station – our goal at last. Now this was a very special place. Inside was a large tank with water bubbling and churning. A look inside the tank and we saw thousands of minnows swimming all over top of each other. What looked like a refrigerator lying on its back was filled with black-looking dirt. It was filled with worms, and if we stuck our hands in, we could not pull them out without a handful of the wiggly creatures. Of course, on the shelf next to that, in sealed containers, was the catfish stink bait. Four old men sat around a small square table, playing dominoes or moon. They paid no attention to Earl or me, but were more transfixed on the little white blocks.

In the back of the store was the prize we had traveled for–a chest-type cold drink machine. With the top open, we could see the water swirling around the bottles. They were lined up in rows with the outlet for the drinks at the front side. It was almost like a game, moving the drink bottles through the maze to the outlet. With my nickel in the slot, I grabbed the bottle by the neck and pulled hard. Out it came, the small, short Coke-a-Cola! Earl did the same. With a pop, the drinks were open.

We had to sit out front and drink our sodas, because there was a two-cent deposit on the bottles and we only had the money for the drink. As we finished our drinks, the man

at the counter said to us, "You boys be sure and rinse them bottles, because I don't want no bees around here." And Earl and I gave a quick, "Yes, sir," to him.

Outside the service station along the wall, was a water trough. They used it for checking tire inner tubes for holes to fix flats. The water was dirty brown but we plunged our bottles deep into the trough. Then we let the water run out of the bottles and back into the trough. Shaking them dry, we placed them in the wooden crate next to the soda machine.

As we turned to leave, the man behind the counter said to us, "You boys want to try out these new jaw breakers I got?" with the quickest, "Yes, sir," we darted up to the counter. The man lifted the lid on a large glass jar filled with what looked like hundreds of jawbreaker candies. Earl and I took turns reaching into the jar for one each and popped them into our mouths. They were almost too big to behold. With a slurping, "Thank you," we headed for the door. What a great treat a soda and a jawbreaker, what could be better! But the afternoon had come and Earl and I had to head for home. With another "Thank you, sir," we were on our way back down the river trail, headed for home.

In September of that year, we moved to our new home in Center Point. But I will never forget that wonderful one-day adventure in the summer of 1963.

Other Adventures in Center Point

I would be remiss if I didn't mention some of the adventures in Center Point, like putting pennies or nails on the train tracks behind Jimmy Lackey's house, or eating a homemade hamburger at Café 27 for 36 cents. I hauled hay for Lackey Brothers Feed Store. Really, I just drove the pick-up truck and the football boys did the loading and unloading. I also helped unload wood at Sallie's Lumber Yard.

I also visited with Mr. Curtis Buckner at the train depot.

I had really fun times with "Dink" Lackey

in that old 1954 Ford twin door coupe, out at "Beer gardens," spinning circles and throwing dirt everywhere.

I had great summers down at the Lions Club Park by the dam, swimming and swinging on the ropeway up in that Cyprus tree.

And of course, there were all the very pretty ladies who touched my heart and life as I grew into a young man, from 1963 to 1968. After that, I went into the service and things changed forever. But what great memories!

Folks Didn't Need Much Money in Those Days
By Melvin Glenn, Jr. of Llano, Texas
Born 1944

I was born in Lampasas, Texas, about seventy miles from Austin. I lived on Chestnut Street, on a hill about one mile from school. At the time, it was mostly dirt roads and a pasture behind the house. Highway 183 to Austin had not been built yet. If we wanted to go to Austin, we went on dirt roads or we went through Burnet, which was all right. Most often, people didn't have cars or gas as it was during World War II. My brother and I were raised by my grandma and grandpa.

We were very poor. We had a wood stove to cook and heat. We had a friend who gave us wood, but we had to cut it with an axe and drag it home. Sometimes we had to use coal oil lamps, because we didn't have electric some of the time. But everyone had gardens and chickens running in the yards and peach trees. If you didn't, you were told to cut a peach limbs and pull up your britches.

Mostly, we went barefooted during summer, because we would get one pair of shoes per year. I remember my grandma

making lye soap in an iron water pot, washing and ironing, and patching out clothes.

Everything tasted better because it was grown at home, made in the US, cooked with real lard, no chemicals, and not made in China. Water tasted good. It didn't have all the junk in it.

We always had fried chicken on Sundays. Meat and sugar were rationed. We all had fried liver and onions one day a week. It was about five cents a pound. Everyone ate salt pork a lot. We'd boil it in a frying pan in water, drain it, and then fry it.

Everyone put up food in jars. We all shared with each other.

We had real rubber, which was strong and red, and stretched. We used it to make toys and stuff. BBs were real and cheap. We had glass marbles, and the girls had dolls. Guys all had slingshots around our necks, which we made

Melvin's mother, Enda Glenn with her children

114

Melvin and his brother, James in 1948

with cedar limbs and rubber. We each had a yoyo in our pockets, too. Later on, we made bows and arrows with big cedar limbs and wire. We'd whittle down apple boxboards, put chicken feathers on one end and a 16-penny nail with the head filed off on the other. We used rubber to go around it. The arrows would go about two blocks.

Everyone had funny books. I had about a hundred or more. We would trade them with each other. We always went out and played with other kids until they called us to come in and eat.

There wasn't much crime then. There were rabbits, birds, horny toads, and quails everywhere. Soda pop was a nickel, candy was from three cents to five cents, and gas was a nickel a gallon.

To get to school, we had to walk down a hill and go across a creek on an old wooden chestnut bridge. Cars went across it, and there was a broad walkway on the side with some boards that had fallen out. There were no lights. Then we had to go about twelve blocks to school.

The creek was wide and deep at that time. It was full of big fish. It was before the flood of '57, when they built ten dams on it. We used to cut willow limbs for fishing poles or use cane poles, which cost 25 cents. Our grandparents would dig worms and meet us at the bridge most days to fish. We would take a screen wire and make a net for minnows and small perch. That was fun.

It was said they used to hang people in the pecan tree there by the bridge, and that a lady used to walk across the bridge at twelve every night, looking for her head, which had been cut off somehow. We never seen her, but it was always spooky there.

When I was real small, they had medicine shows on the creek. They would have a carnival show, show picture shows, have cotton candy, and sell something in a bottle that would cure everyone.

Later on, my mom and dad had three more kids, two boys, and a girl. They lived with them. My dad worked at the picture show, so we got in for free. They would show cowboy shows every Saturday, Tarzan and Jungle Jim, Buster Crabbe reels, short, funny cartoons, and stuff that was going on with the war.

Everyone was always hanging out on the creek, fishing and swimming, during the summer. One hole was called Wahoo Hole. It was a deep hole. We caught a lot of fish. We had a friend who would drive us to the Colorado River at the bend and let us out to fish. He would come back and get us after a day or two.

After the '57 flood, the creek was real deep under the 4th Street Bridge. I think it was called the Belton Highway Bridge. Some of us would jump off the top of the bridge into the creek. We would almost hit the bottom.

We also had a candy store and soda fountain. He made homemade candy and ice cream. They were real good to the kids.

We also had a swimming pool at the park. It had spring water that was real cold, 57 degrees all the time. They had a park on the creek where teams from other towns came to play baseball. I believe it was free.

Lampasas was a dry county. There were several bootleggers around. Some people who had a car and gas would drive around on Sundays.

I used to listen to the radio a lot with my grandpa. We listened to baseball, *The Lone Ranger*, *Amos and Andy*, *Fibber McGee and Molly*, *The Shadow*, *Abbot and Costello*, and *Burns and Allen*.

Also, during the war, they had a dance hall downtown where a lot of people went. I don't know if was a USO or what, as I as very small. There were a lot of Army and Navy people. There seems like they would buy a ticket for a nickel to dance.

We used to hitchhike to Austin most summers to spend time with kinfolks there. We would stay about two weeks. We had a lot of fun there.

About this time, our grandpa died. Our mom got killed, but our grandma raised us. While we didn't have much money, we had each other and love. Folks didn't need much money in those days. The air smelled good and fresh, the food tasted better, people shared what they had, people helped each other, we could buy something and it would be forever and not fall apart before we got home with it. Those really were the good old days.

Camping Out in Hill Country
By Shirley Wright of Marble Falls, Texas
Born 1937

Dad worked with Mr. Stroud at the roofing company and they became friends. He was probably the person who told Dad about the house for sale on Cottonwood Street.

The summer of 1943, the Stroud family took a trip to Devil's River to fish. Men, women, kids, cousins, friends, and a dog or two went along. There was a car caravan, and I could not count that high, but I know it was probably at least seven pickups and automobiles.

We spent the first night on pallets at the side of the road somewhere out of Sonora. The land was flat with sparse, low growth like sagebrush and scrub oak. I was taller than most everything growing on either side of the highway. I could see the horizon and there were no barbed wire fences in any direction.

I remember waking up to excited talking and laughing. Seems Mr. Stroud had been the first person up and went across the highway to explore, as men will do. He came upon a rattlesnake that had just eaten a nest of baby rabbits and could not move because the meal had not digested yet. He calmly walked back to camp, took a shovel from his camp stuff, strolled quietly back across the highway, and killed the snake. He thought it would be funny to coil the snake at the head of his brother's pallet, stand back, drink a cup of coffee, and wait for him to wake up. His brother was prompted in waking by some other early risers. His brother said the hair on the back of his neck stood up until he noticed the bashed in head of the snake. Then a lot of joking and laughing took place among the people already awake and those of us still asleep were awakened by the racket. It certainly made for a memorable first night on the trail.

We arrived and parked the cars and pickups atop a high rocky hill overlooking a one-mile hike down to the river. The men and boys carried tents, bedding, cookware, and groceries to the campsite. The largest tent was set up for the groceries. There were goats in the area, and we knew the goats would eat anything they could get a tooth into. After the first night, we found out other wild things were interested in our groceries. The raccoons had raided the bread supply and eaten or carried off a good part of it. Two of the men hiked out to the cars and drove to the nearest town to buy more bread. After that, we made sure the tent flaps were tied securely each night so the wild things could not steal our bread.

The campsite was in a grove of big, shady trees. We were on an upper shelf about twenty yards from the river. The slope was gradual and grassy and we enjoyed the play area close to camp. There had been campers there before us, and a ring of rocks for a fire were in place. There were Coleman stoves and lanterns brought by everyone. The women did most of the cooking, with some of the men helping out. I remember this being the first time I had ever eaten fried okra. We had great meals, but I never was one to care too much, about what we had to eat. I was always interested in exploring and seeing new things and new places.

We were cautioned to watch out for snakes and after the incident of the first night, we kids stayed close to camp. There were sheep pills everywhere. There were red berries everywhere and we girls decided we could make bracelets and necklaces out of the pretty red berries. We brought jars and bread wrappers full of red berries home with us. But nothing could penetrate the hard red berry. Mom finally put my collection outside and after a while, there were red berries all around in our yard.

After about the third day, women and kids were getting camp "fever." The men agreed to take us walking up the shallow part of the river and let those who wanted to fish a little. A lot of talk about what to wear occupied an hour of the morning. Swimsuits were the general attire for the women who brought one. I did not have a swimsuit so I wore my overalls without a shirt. I rolled the overalls legs up to the knee so I could wade easier.

The water was swift and clear, and some of us kids gathered shells and small rocks along the way. There were about twenty-five people in the group. There was much laughing and joking among the kinfolks and those of us new to the group enjoyed the banter. At least, I know I enjoyed the walk.

I do not know how long we were out walking in the shallow water, but when we arrived back at camp, there were a bunch of sunburned women and kids. Every remedy ever heard of was used that night and the next day to relieve sunburn. Some walked around zombie-like, with buttermilk on face, arms, and back. Some tried vinegar and brown paper bags. Some made a paste of cornstarch and water and smeared it on noses and upper arms. There was a lot of laughing and not much relief of sunburn.

That night, some of us decided to sleep on the lower level near the water. We thought the sound of the water rushing nearby would lull us to sleep. Some were tired of listening to us complain about our sunburns so we decided to find a cooler place to air our complaints. We spread our quilts and fluffed our pillows and laughed and joked and finally settled down to try to talk ourselves to sleep.

I was on my stomach with my chin on my hands when, in the darkness of a moonless night, I saw something light colored rear its head about three feet away from our pallet. My heart jumped to my throat and I whispered for Mom to look at what I saw. It had laid back down by the time Mom turned to look at what I saw, but someone else had picked up a flashlight and shined it in the direction I was looking. There on the ground was a big, white turkey feather. The wind had caught it just right and it stood on its quill and then settled gently to the ground when the wind settled. In the dark, I had imagined a snake coiled there just like the one on the first morning. We all laughed nervously, and the ones up the hill in camp wanted to know what we were finding so funny.

Growing Up at the Fish Hatchery
By Loretta Carney Treadwell of Kerrville,
Texas
Born 1933

I was born in Lubbock, Texas on January 6, 1933 to Donald Alvin Carney and Kate Robinson Carney, both now deceased. When I was 18 months old, my parents moved to Kerrville, Texas, in the hill country, to be near my mother's elderly parents, John Weldon Robinson and Minnie Lou Frazie Robinson. My brother was born in Kerrville in our home, with the doctor present, in 1938.

My granddad had retired from the railroad and chose to live in the hill country to enjoy the good climate. We lived next door to my grandparents. My folks saw the big flood of 1936. There was also the huge flood of 1934 just before we arrived.

In August, 1942 our house burned to the ground, destroying everything we owned. This happened during World War II and times were hard.

My dad was offered a job in Mt. Home, Texas, in the western part of Kerr County, to work for the Texas Game, Fish, and Oyster Commission, so we moved to the Fish Hatchery, as it was referred to. It was some 17 miles from Kerrville. There were three houses on the hatchery property. Grady Walker was the superintendent. He and his wife, Tootsie, and their young son, Billie Charles, lived in the first house. We lived in the second, and the Cadills, with their three sons, Ross, Wayne, and Wilbur, lived in the third house. All these houses were on the hatchery property.

In the early '40s, the fish hatchery had 32 ponds of water for raising fish. I remember the water moccasins lay around the ponds, waiting for a meal. At different times there got to be so many snakes that my dad would have to shoot them.

The purpose of the fish hatchery was to raise fish to supply and restock the Guadalupe River and its tributaries with young, healthy fish. By the way, the Guadalupe River flows through our town of Kerrville.

At times, my dad would let me ride along with him to dump young fish into the Guadalupe River. The fish were hauled in 50-gallon barrels on the back of a big truck to be poured into the river. My dad knew how excited I would become when he let me go along on his fish hauls.

This one time, he had a load of fish to deliver to San Angelo, Texas, about 120 miles away. Along about Eden, Texas, we were traveling along the highway next to a large cotton field. The cotton was mature and ready for picking. My dad stopped the truck. I got out and crawled under the fence and picked a boll of cotton. The next day, I took it to Sunset School. The teacher let me have a few minutes of Show and Tell. That was my first and last cotton to pick.

I also recall Louis Schreiner, a prominent Kerrville businessman, banker, and rancher, who helped settle Kerrville in the 1800s. He lived across the highway from the fish hatchery. On occasion, my dad and I would walk over to visit with Mr. Schreiner. While they were talking, I would sit out on the veranda and look out over his beautiful lake.

Alfred Ersch was the Schreiner's ranch caretaker. I remember he used to love to tease the superintendent and my dad about the buzzards lined up on the rock wall alongside of the hatchery near the fish ponds, looking for a meal. Mr. Ersch would say, "Looks like you fellows are also in the buzzard business."

All the water for the fishponds was channeled into the hatchery from Fessenden Springs, located at that time on the Ellebracht property, three-quarters of a mile away.

The fish hatchery was a great place to live as a kid. I got to learn some interesting things about fish, breathe fresh country air, see a lot of little wild animals moving about, and enjoy the beautiful hill country scenery all around me.

We kids from the hatchery and others from around the area attended Sunset School, located behind the fish hatchery. Just across the dirt road was the Sunset Cemetery. At that time, Sunset Country School had only one room. The redheaded, freckle-faced teacher, Ms. Bode, taught all the grades in the same room. She would spend one hour with the first graders, and then one hour with the second graders, and so on.

There were no indoor bathroom facilities, only his and hers outdoor toilets. On the play yard, I can remember one swing set with three swings, nothing else.

There were no drinking fountains. The schoolhouse had a small lean-to room at the back, where we students hung our coats and hats. Our lunch sacks and lunch boxes went on a shelf above. Each one of us had his or her own drinking glass with our name on it on a shelf in that room. The teacher put a gallon bucket full of water on the shelf with a big dipper in it. When we needed a drink, we dipped into the water bucket and poured it into our drinking glass.

As we came in the front door to the right sat a big, black, round, potbellied stove. Ms. Bode would have the boys fill it with sticks of oak wood. Then she would dash a little kerosene into the stove. She would then strike a big kitchen match and toss it into the stove. I was sure that the stove would blow up, but it never did. Needless to say, we all stayed warm.

One of the student's parents had a small grocery store in a rock building on the property where they lived facing the highway just up the hill from the fish hatchery. Once in a while, my brother and I got to walk up to the store and buy peppermint stick candy and a soda pop. The small rock building, empty now, remains today.

My girlfriend's parents owned a ranch not far from the school. It was really fun to go home with her on weekends. They had a colored maid who served all our meals, and we got to swim in the huge stock tank not far from the ranch house.

When I went into the seventh grade, my family had to move back to Kerrville, as Sunset School only went through the sixth grade.

The historical marker for the Sunset School states that the school closed in 1953. Today where the schoolhouse once stood proud are only beautiful, big oak trees and green grass.

As I said, across the dirt road from the school was the Sunset Cemetery. It looks somewhat different these days, with many more graves and much better kept grounds. It no longer looks dreary like I remember it looking when I was a kid. We kids liked to go after school and look at the Dowdy children's graves. They were killed by Indians. The graves had concrete on top, with a lot of different inlayed seashells.

As a family, we attended the Sunset Baptist Church just across the highway from the little rock grocery store mentioned. The church is

Sign for the Sunset Baptist Church

119

still active and has grown in membership. We also looked forward to going to the Cowboy Camp Meetings, held each summer for one week in August under a wooden open-air tabernacle a mile or two from the fish hatchery. The weather was always very hot; however, there were plenty of hand fans laid out on all the benches. On every Sunday, the men barbecued and the women made all the trimmings. We enjoyed socializing and dinner.

The fish hatchery continues to operate under the name of The Texas Parks and Wildlife. They study different species of fish and raise exotic fish.

Gee, how wonderful it was to be a kid with such happy memories. God has blessed me.

Runaway Tires and Yeast Bread
By Janice and G.L. Mays of London, Texas
Born 1939

In 1964, while living in our new home in Ingram, Texas, our land was on an incline. My husband had a truck he drove in his business. He had a blowout on one of the truck tires, so after changing the tire, he left it near our carport. I was six months pregnant at the time. After asking my husband several times to move the tire, I decided to move it myself, to an area where we burned trash. Well, being six months pregnant, I didn't travel so fast. So, while rolling the large tire on the incline of our land, the tire got away from me. An elderly neighbor man lived below us in a small Air-stream mobile home. The tire rolled into the screen door and on into his trailer. It hit the wall and rolled back out the door, where it had gone in. I was in shock and waited for the older neighbor man to come out of his trailer and confront me. No one appeared, so I got the tire and rolled it back up the hill to our land.

Several days later in the late evening, my husband and I were working in our garden. The elderly neighbor man came up and began visiting with my husband. I just kept on working in my garden. After visiting with my husband a while, the elderly neighbor man came over to me and asked how was I doing. Then he asked if I had been rolling any more tires. I was so embarrassed, and I told him I thought he was away from home. He said no, he was asleep in his trailer and when the tire hit and came into his trailer, it scared him so bad he thought a bomb had went off. I asked him why he didn't let me know he was inside the trailer. He said, "Lady, I thought you or someone had a gun. Also, I was scared ten years out of my life."

I had a newlywed neighbor. She was a city girl who had married a country boy. She was learning all about country living. As it was a ways into the city and she could not go there often to purchase groceries, she was trying to learn to cook country style. And this meant baking some kind of bread daily. I took sympathy on the new bride and taught her to bake biscuits and cornbread. I often had the newly married couple over for dinner and often gave her recipes and advice on cooking. I often baked yeast bread and yeast rolls and when they came for dinner, I often sent them home with a loaf of yeast bread.

One day, she asked me if I could teach her how to make yeast bread. I said yes so she came to my home, and I proceeded to show her how to make the yeast bread. She wrote down instructions and said she thought she would try making the bread. I encouraged her and told her she would do just fine.

Well, on the morning she decided to try the yeast bread recipe, it was cloudy and overcast. She made up her yeast bread, but with it being cloudy, it didn't rise. Her husband would be coming in from the field for lunch and as the yeast bread had not risen and time was getting close for lunch, she decided to made biscuits for lunch instead. She was embarrassed about the yeast bread not rising, so she decided to bury the un-risen yeast dough in a newly plowed garden area while waiting on her husband to come to lunch. The sun came out bright and clear and very warm.

The husband was late for lunch this day. As he walked in from the field, he walked past the garden area and the sun had made the yeast dough rise under the dirt where she had hidden it. He came on to the house for lunch and told his wife he had found the strangest thing he ever saw in their garden, some kind of unnatural growth. He said, "As soon as I eat my lunch, I want you to see this." She started crying and confessed it was her first attempt at yeast bread. They had a good laugh about it over their married years, and she became a wonderful cook.

Christmas, 1945

My first belief in God came at the young age of six years old. It was Christmas, 1945, during World War II. My faith was not Catholic, but since I had failed first grade my parents enrolled me in a Catholic school, thinking it would help me become stronger in my grades. My dad worked as a local truck driver and my mother worked at a wash-a-teria, washing other people's clothes. I had to be dropped off at school before school took up. Since I was early at school and could not be left alone, I had to go into the church each day before school started. Here I learned to bless myself with holy water and I learned to pray.

As Christmas grew close, in my prayers each night after blessing everyone in my family, I would pray that Santa would bring me this special baby doll in a bassinet. Money was hard to come by during the war, and my mother knew our Christmas would be slim. She thought since I was so young, I would not understand and I would lose faith if I did not receive the Christmas doll.

On Christmas Eve, my mother received a Christmas bonus of $20.00, so she rushed to the department store and there was one doll like I wanted left. The doll had been marked down half price to $5.00. Well, you can imagine what a happy little girl I was on Christmas morning of 1945.

I also remember receiving a long flannel gown and a robe made from feed sacks. We always had wonderful Christmas dinners with a lot of family and a lot of love. I was the baby of eight children so I had a lot of loving family.

In the 1940s, I was a child living in Kerrville, Texas. Feed sack clothes were a part of life. My mother would go with my father to the feed store so she could get the same print and have enough to make dresses and other clothing. My mother would sew four white feed sacks together to make bed sheets. She would make pillow cases out of small print feed sacks or white feed sacks and embroidery designs on them. I started first grade in 1945 and most all the country kids wore feed sack clothing. My mother was a talented seamstress, so she also took clothing people gave us and remodeled it or took it apart and made new clothing for her family. I loved all the homemade clothing my mother made for me, feed sack, or other material.

When I was a young girl, we lived in the country and had an outdoor toilet. At the time, my dad raised chickens and we had this mean old game rooster. He would always chase me, and I was afraid of him. I told my dad, "Kill that old, mean rooster. I don't like him." My dad said, "When you go outside to the toilet, don't run. But pick you up a stick or rock and throw it at the rooster." Well, this worked for a while, and then one day, I forgot my stick. Here comes that mean rooster after me. So I picked up a rock and threw it at him. Lo and behold, I hit him in the head with the rock and he fell over dead. I went and told my mom, and we got busy cleaning that old, mean rooster.

That night, we had chicken and dumplings for supper. My dad said, "Well, I guess that old, mean rooster got what he deserved, and he made us a good supper."

Riding the Logs in Our Birthday Suits
By Jerry L. Harkey of Bertram, Texas
Born 1936

I was born April 15, 1936 at home in Harkeyville, San Saba County, Texas, to Elvin and Cleo Harkey. My first memory is of living on Red McKee's place. In 1938, the San Saba River was on a rise that spread way beyond its banks. The floodwater got into our house, and we had to vacate our home. Our neighbor, Red McKee, helped us get out. He carried me while my dad carried my younger brother, Jimmie, and my mom held onto my older brother, Richard. They had to wade nearly a half-mile out of the river. We stayed in Red and Lilly's barn, along with other families who had been misplaced by the swollen river.

Jame's dad, Elvin Richard Harkey with Jerry, Jimmie and Richard

Jerry's mom, Cleo Harkey with Jerry in 1938

I am not certain how long we had to stay in the barn, but the McKees provided food for all of us during that time. We eventually cleaned up the debris from our home and moved back there. Not long after that, we moved into another small house on the hill and lived there until I began elementary school in San Saba.

My dad was a farmer who made about $600.00 a year from farming and another $600.00 from trapping in the winter. My brothers and I took turns going with my dad hunting. We took along our bulldog, Shorty, who was an expert hunter. When he treed the squirrel, the boy walked around the tree until my dad held up his hand. We stopped and he shot. I never saw him miss a shot.

Sometimes we hunted squirrel and rabbits and had fish from the San Saba River to supplement our meat supply. Other than that, everything that we ate was raised on our place. We had a huge garden and also

122

chickens, hogs, and cows. My mom canned all the excess fruit, vegetables, and beef. The pork was prepared and smoked in our own smokehouse. We helped neighbors do this and they in turn, helped us. In material goods, we were very poor, but we lived a good life.

Cooking was done on a wood stove or the fireplace, until a few years later when we got a kerosene cook stove. Then my job was to make sure that the kerosene jug was filled. A path led out back, where bathroom needs were taken care of in the outhouse. I could make that trip in record time when there was snow on the ground. Saturday night baths were attended to in a washtub in the kitchen, where everyone wanted to be first while the water was still clean and hot. Water was brought in from outside in buckets from the hand pump. There was no electricity in the house at that time. We relied on kerosene lamps until we moved to Algerita.

We kids had our share of chores. My job was keeping the chickens who had baby chicks, protected from varmints. My dad told me if anything happens to those chicks, then we won't have them to eat later on. That was pretty important for a little boy.

By the time I reached second grade, we bought a place in Algerita, still in San Saba County. I attended school in Algerita through the fourth grade, until the school burned down and my brothers and I went back to school in San Saba. The Algerita School consisted of three rooms, one of first through fourth grades and one for fifth through eighth grades. The third room served as a kitchen and cafeteria for all. I remained in San Saba schools until high school graduation.

Growing up, I can't remember having a care in the world. Our standard outfit was denim overalls that were handed down from brother to brother until there was nothing left to patch. Many of our days were spent on the San Saba River. Bud Roberts, one of our friends or "partner in crime," and my brothers

and I used to go to the river when it was on a big rise to ride the trees or logs down the river, and then get out and do it again and again.

One particular day, as we were doing this (in our birthday suits, of course) Bud saw a huge tree approaching and shouted that it was his. He swam out and jumped on, when suddenly the tree began to turn and he went out of sight. As we held our breaths, waiting to see him pop up, it seemed an eternity. Finally, he surfaced and swam back to shore. Not a one of us uttered a word, but rather, we put on our clothes and went back home, never to do that again. It took our near miss to show us the danger of what we were doing. Of course, our parents didn't hear this story until we were all grown up.

Another time, we were swimming in the river without benefits of swim apparel, when a group of girls showed up and proceeded to take our clothes from the bank. We all just hopped out and started chasing them. You never heard so much screaming and throwing of clothes. No more problems with those pesky girls.

A lot of nights were spent varmint hunting.

Jerry and his brother, Jimmy with Spud the dog in 1945

123

Sometimes, we would raid a local watermelon patch and just bust the melons open and eat the best part with our hands. I am quite sure that our neighbors would have just given us the melons, but it was so much more fun to do it in the dark of night.

I spent a lot of time with my grandparents, Taylor and Lura Harkey, in my growing up years. I was enthralled with the stories they told me of their younger years. They never owned a lock or key and never signed a contract. People shared what they had with others and your word was your bond.

They shared how it was back in the "mob days," which was later written about as the San Saba Mob. The mob was a group of self-appointed vigilantes who used their power to obtain the property and land of others. My grandparents said that our people stayed out on their farms and didn't talk about people for fear they might be talking about someone's relatives who were a part of the mob. Some people were told to vacate their property. I asked what happened if they wouldn't leave. My grandfather said that you either left or you would be killed.

My junior and senior years of high school were spent contracting work on people's homes or pouring concrete for storm cellars, etc. in my free time. I later worked full time as a carpenter for others in San Saba.

Dating in these years included riding through the pasture in a Jeep, rabbit hunting or just riding around town. We could do that for hours since gasoline was only 25 cents per gallon. Sometimes a carload of young people went to the local drive-in theatre since the whole carload could get in for a dollar. And if we were really having a good evening, we would drive over to the local drive-in restaurant and get some "gin fizzes," which was ginger ale with a maraschino cherry afloat. 11:00pm was curfew on weekends, and we were expected to be in church the next morning.

In 1959, I met the love of my life, Pat, on a blind date arranged by my younger brother. I walked up on her front porch, and when she answered the door, my first thoughts were, "This is the one, thank you, Lord!" We have been married nearly fifty-three years, and I thank God for each moment of that time. An interesting side note is that my brothers and I all married in San Saba in 1960, and we are all still married to those lovely ladies. I have seen hardships and many changes through the years, but I have so much to be thankful for.

Boots Was My Favorite Kitten
By Irene A. Scholz of San Antonio, Texas
Born 1928

Homemade Clothes: When I was a kid, all my clothes were homemade. I remember I did get a Shirley Temple dress when I was ten years old. It was bought at the J.C. Penny's Store. It was pretty, in pastel colors. I wore it to church on Easter Sunday. It was the only store bought dress I ever had until I was older and earned money.

Ice Box: My family had an icebox because no one had electricity. After church, my father would drive to the ice plant and pick up a block of ice. We made Jell-O and drank ice tea. Sometimes we made homemade iced cream with a crank type freezer.

Snakes: One day a snake was lying in the sun near our garage. It was a coral snake. "If red touches yellow, he's a dangerous fellow." I was scared. I was warned never to go near a snake, no matter what kind it was.

My family always had a garden: Fresh vegetables were plentiful, Cucumbers, tomatoes, green beans, corn, turnips, potatoes, and cabbage. We had a water-well, and could water with a bucket or a sprinkling can.

Christmas was very special: Cookies were baked such as Anise, Molasses, Ice Box,

124

Oatmeal, and Tutti Fruti Cake with dates and raisins.

Favorite Pets: I loved cats and the young kittens. Since we had cows, there was milk for the cats to drink. I would wrap the cats in a small blanket and carry them like a baby. I named the kittens. My favorite was Boots, because he was white with black paws. Our dog was named Rex, no particular breed.

The Little Store
By Deanie Smith of Bertram, Texas
Born 1934

I ponder to think how important this little store was to the community of Oxford, which is located ten miles south of Llano, Texas on Highway 16, founded in 1880 when a Confederate veteran came to Llano County and laid out the town site of Oxford. I remember the store was operated by a couple that lived nearby and they were open six days a week. The stock in the store was very limited to cold drinks, candy, peanuts, and tobacco products. Also, a big seller was gasoline, kerosene, and motor oil. Back then, kerosene was known as 'coal-oil', used to start a fire in the wood stove or if one cut a foot or hand the old timers would say, "Soak the foot in a pan of coal oil."

The little store served as a place to receive the mail, with the mailbox mounted in a long row of cedar post on the highway in front of the store. Neighbors would gather waiting for the rural mail carrier to arrive and visit about the everyday happenings. He would usually take a break, have a soda pop, and share any news he had gathered on his route, which took him all the way to Fredericksburg. Since the storeowner had no mode of transportation, the lady would go to Llano with the mail carrier as he came from Fredericksburg in the morning; do her shopping and return with him as he made his return trip.

The little store served as the rural school bus stop as this was the place designed to pick up children that lived as far away as two or three miles from the main highway. In the afternoon it was not uncommon, weather permitting, you walked home after getting off the school bus. In those days, the little store had no telephone, so there was no calling home asking for a ride. If there was no one there to get you, you knew just to start walking.

School—and Getting There
By J. C. Smith of Bertram, Texas
Born 1931

Starting to school in the year 1938, which was the last year that school was held at the Providence District in Burnet County, on the banks of Russell Gabriel Creek, I walked a mile each way, twice a day to school with the teacher who stayed in our home. The one room school was near the creek, so water to drink was taken from a spring. The older boys were responsible for pailing fresh water each morning. I'm sure we all drank out of the same dipper! There were two toilets, or outhouses so to speak, one for the girls and one for the boys.

In 1939, Providence School consolidated with Bertram, which was five miles away. This was a big change for the children of the community. Getting to school each day amounted to walking about a mile to meet the school bus, but it was not a big yellow bus that we see today. A flatbed truck with two sideboards and benches to set on was used. This mode of transportation was used for several years before buses were secured. By the time we arrived at school, the benches on the flatbed truck would have twelve to fifteen students. No matter what the weather conditions were, we still traveled to school in

125

the truck. As time passed, we had a school bus and this was a great improvement. When we went to Bertram, each grade had an individual room with fifteen to twenty students and the same teacher all day. We still carried our lunch and if you were lucky, you had a metal lunch box or used a tin syrup bucket. In a few years, the Providence school was taken down and the lumber was taken to Bertram to help to build a lunchroom.

The year I was a senior, I no longer walked, rode the truck or the big yellow school bus. My car was a two-door sedan, and I was the only classmate that had his own transportation! There were six boys and fifteen girls in the graduating class.

Combat Boots Saved the Day
By Roberta Smith Wallace of Victoria, Texas
Born 1937

Living in the country, we had to ride the bus to school. Going on dirt roads with gates; when the bus came to a gate one of the students got out, opened the gate and then waited for the bus to come back, closed the gate, got on and headed on down the road to school, maybe another gate or cattle guard before getting there.

Another time my brother, sister and me and some neighbor kids walking down to the bus one morning, messing around; missed the bus and we had to walk the whole five miles to school, getting in trouble when we missed some classes and then more trouble when we got home.

Sometimes riding the bus was pretty cool thing about Grandma's day of bread baking. When we got off the bus, we would start to run to see who would be the first one to get home and get the first slice of fresh hot homemade bread with fresh churned butter.

In the good ole' summertime, my brother, sister and I would look forward to going to the ole' swimming hole.

We lived in El Paso until our dad was killed in an automobile accident. We then, moved to Fredericksburg to live with our grandparents while our mom worked as a telephone operator in Austin. We had to do chores after school and in the summer, but when they were done, we had our own free time. We would head to the creek on those hot summer days. The pasture was full of those grass burrs. Because times were tough, we only had one pair of shoes each, and were not allowed to wear them for play. My brother advised a plan that would get us to the creek without pain. He had this pair of old clunky combat boots that he wore a little ways, then toss them to one of us. We would walk and toss to the next person. This continued until we were all, across the pasture and at our destination for that nice cooling swim.

My Life Was Full of Fives
By Cora Millett Coleman of New Braunfels, Texas
Born 1936

I was born fifth month, fifth day , weighed five lbs., was fifth child born in a family of one sister and five brothers. For over a decade, I have five generations in my family. I been married for 55 years.. When I was 5 years old, a book company gave my parents $5.00 for my birthday. They taking the money and bought groceries for a week. Back then, you could buy a loaf of bread for 10 cents, a 5 lb. bag of sugar sold for 25 cents! Dozen oranges cost 35 cents. A 16 oz. bottle of soda water was 5 cents.

My parents raised most all their food on the farm. They sold eggs on weekends and bought groceries for a week.

My childhood was full of wonderment

and discovery. We lived far out in the country at the Comal and Hays County line. For years, there was no electric. We boil water in a wash pot and used a scrub-board to wash clothes. We also had to boil water to take a bath in a tub. Our lights was kerosene lamps. No telephone, I walked 2 miles to school. I went to a one-room country school. It only went to the 8th grade.

In the late 40's, they close all country school, and bus us to town. So, I went 6 years in the country and 6 years in town. I went from a one-room school with one teacher to a 12-room school with over 12 teachers. Times have changed since I was a tot. We had no television to watch. We played lots of games. I had lots of fun growing up, playing cards, checkers, dominos, and monopoly. I always spent the weekend going to my grandparent's house. We used to tie a rope around an old car tie hang it up in a tree and make a swing.

I once hoed and picked cotton in the fields.

I graduated from 12 grade. Taken a 8 week course and became a certified nurse assistance. I worked 5 years in Nursing Homes and family homes. Later years, I worked in the hospital for 25 years where I retired. (I thank God for my life.)

Charlene Dickerson in 1948

A Special Visit From Santa
By Charlene Dickerson Heim of Haven, Kansas
Born 1943

It was a cold brisk day as my mother and I walked the 2 blocks to town. Excitement filled the air as we neared the town square, were Santa was to make his annual stop. Boys, girls and parents were everywhere trying to make it closer to the chair that was decorated for Santa.

Soon the siren on the City fire truck could be heard in the distance. The sound grew louder as the truck turned down Main Street bringing Santa to the reserved area where he would hand out the sacks of candy and talk to each child individually.

When it was finally my turn to talk to Santa, I was so excited that I forgot all about being cold. After telling Santa about the doll I wanted him to bring me, he handed me my sack, which had a big number 96 written on the outside of it.

This year, the city had helped supply the treats Santa handed out. In addition, they were giving three children a special treat. Santa would draw three numbers out of a box, read the numbers out loud, and three different children would receive extra prizes of $25 and $40, and first prize of $50.00. Everyone grew quiet as he called out the 3rd place prize for $25. It wasn't 96. The second place prize of $40 was drawn for. Not 96! Finally, Santa laughed his jolly laugh and drew out the final number to win the first place prize of $50. I said, "96, 96, 96" over and over again in my mind. When Santa said, "Boys and girls, the $50 goes to the person who is holding #96! I was so shocked and excited that I was afraid I hadn't heard correctly, except my mother was telling me to tell Santa I had the #96 sack. As

I was lifted up to receive the envelope from Santa, it was the happiest day ever.

I will remember that day just like it was yesterday. Every Christmas I think of that time long ago, when Santa's visit was extra special for me. I remember I bought my mother a pair of sparkly blue earrings and my father a pair of warm gloves. The balance of the money lasted me for a long time.

Too Cold For Comfort
By Dorthy Steadman of Burnet, Texas
Born 1932

In 1943, I was eleven years old and my brother, Joe Ed was eight. We lived with our parents in a little two-room house with a path. Yes, a path, not a bath!

We had a cow for milk, pigs for pork, chickens for eggs, coal oil for light and a woodpile for cooking and heat. Our water was hauled from my Granny Frazier's house, in fifty-five gallon drums and kept in a trailer at our back door.

All this was in my grandmother's front pasture in the community of Pebble Mound, a little north of Burnet, Texas. Burnet is in the Texas hill country.

While Daddy was in hand-to-hand combat with the wolf at the door, Momma was inside assuring us that we had it better than anyone else. We were blessed with enough to eat, a place to sleep, lots of chores and more than our share of love and fun. Sometimes we weren't so sure about all of that.

One thing that made us grumble was the one-half mile walk to the school bus stop. We were told it could be worse, didn't kids use to walk miles to school uphill both ways.

We didn't always have to walk. One very cold morning, Momma took us to the front gate where the mailman left the mail, and the bus driver stopped for us. We got out of the Model-A touring car and into the old coupe

car body, daddy had put there for just such a time as this. I guess we were not as mistreated as we thought. Mother told us she would pick us up that afternoon, and left us to wait for the bus.

Well, wait, we did, we waited, and waited, and waited some more. Was the bus really this late or had it come before we got there? Should we go home? Oh no! We had made that mistake before, and missed a bus that was running late. We weren't going to do that again. So, we waited some more. Only thing was that it felt colder and colder. We were shaking, our teeth were chattering and even though sat huddled together we were crying (that's a secret). How long, is long enough?

Suddenly we heard a wonderful sound! We now knew how long it had been since 7 AM. That beautiful sound gave us permission to fly home. It was five miles away, but it was clear as a bell! It was the noon whistle that was blown at Burnet every day at twelve o'clock.

Soon we were home by the wood fire sipping hot chocolate and receiving warm hugs from our momma. As it turned out— school had been canceled because of bad weather!!!

Party Line Phone
By Emma Jewel Goodwin of Bertram, Texas
Born 1934

Today we have cell phones, voice mail, texting, etc. That was not the case when I grew up. We had crank phones and party lines and "Miss Ella."

Most crank phones either hung on the wall or out on the table. There were no numbers on the phone, just the crank or handle. You just turned the crank when you wanted to place a call and the operator would complete the call.

A party line consisted of several phones on the same line. You called people by ringing the operator (Miss Ella) and asking for the person you wanted to speak to and she would plug your line into that line, and ring that person. It wasn't just one ring. You had such rings as a long and a short, two shorts, etc. When the phone rang everyone on that line could hear the ring. Everyone on that line could listen in on the conversation. That could be good or bad! There weren't many private conversations.

Now that you have some clue what a party line is like, let me tell you how the boys got a date on Saturday night in my little hometown in the 1950's. The big event was to go to the double feature at the "picture show." The boys never did anything in advance, so on Saturday afternoon they would go to the telephone office and call for a date from a small room inside the office. There were no pay phones, so the boys always made their calls at the office. They would crank the phone and tell Miss Ella to ring "so-in-so" and she would ring that number for the young men. On one occasion, the boy said, "Ring Jane Doe" and Miss Ella said, "Oh, Jane already has a date, but, Emma Jewel doesn't. Do you want me to call her?" You might say Miss Ella ran a dating service. She tried to make sure we all had a date on Saturday night.

When I went to college, I called "collect" when I called home. On one occasion, I called my parents and Miss Ella said, "Emma Jewel, your mother and dad are not at home. They are over at the Williams, playing 42. Do you want me to call over there?" Miss Ella was our answering service and voice mail, too!

I enjoy all the advantages of our modern phones, and I wouldn't want to go back to crank phones and party lines, but I am so thankful I had the opportunity to live in that era and to appreciate the progress we have made. I still miss "Miss Ella" and the personal interest she had in all of our lives. She actually did everything our "smart phones" do with a simple plug-in switchboard!

A Possum in Mother's Bathtub and The Horse Stole Grannie's Pie
By Joyce E. Scott of Llano, Texas

My mother was living in her home next door to us. Daddy had died 6 years ago. I called her every morning around 7:30 A.M. This particular morning I asked Mother, "How was your night?" She replied, "I didn't sleep good; at all." She went on to explain that when she got up during the night to go to the bathroom, she heard a noise coming from the bathtub. She moved the shower curtain back and there was a possum in the tub trying to crawl out, but his feet kept sliding. I got tickled as I asked her, "What Mother and Smiley the Possum did you do?" "Well" she said, "I wacked him with my cane." I said, giggling, "What did the possum do?" "Well" Mother said, "He showed me his teeth and I wacked him again." By then I was laughing, she went on to say, every time the possum smiled at her she wacked him with her cane. I asked her, "Do I need to come over and help you?" "No" she replied, "I went to the pantry and got those pick-up claw things you bought me to get things off the floors." She then added; that she went to the bathroom with the picker-uppers and got hold of the possum and he curled his tail around the picker-uppers. Mother walked to the door and opened it and shook the possum off into the flowerbed.

The next day our neighbor saw her mom's cat come home with a half grown possum in her mouth that was nearly dead. Sunday at church, I told our minister about it. He said that if that was him, after he got the possum on the picker-uppers he would have handed it over to his wife and fainted. Least to say, Mother never had another creature or critter to come inside for a visit, even if he smiled at her.

It was in early spring and as always, we had family gatherings and cooked Bar-B-Q. All the preparations took place, mowing grass, trimming trees, picking up odds and ends around the cooking sight, cutting wood for fire, also cleaning the old house up some. I had been real busy cleaning and later decided to rake around in the yard and outside the yard fence area. Picking up unwanted rocks and pulling weeds, as I went. Then, there was an area close to the yard gate that I wanted to get. There stood Kenner, our pet Bull. It was getting late in the evening and I was looking forward to completing my task. I tried to get Kenner to move, but being the Santa Gertrudis nature he was not going to budge. So, I held my rake up in the air and made a hissing sound as the rake shook---Huh, Oh, wrong idea—Kenner jumped straight up in the air with a loud fart and turned and looked at me and snorted. I threw the rake down and got inside the yard, closing the gate behind me, then went up on the back porch. From then on, he could stand anywhere he pleased!

Kenner the pet bull in 1987

When the day finally came for the Bar-B-Q, my mother-in-law had baked her famous Buttermilk pies. As we were helping her and my father-in-law unload the pickup, chairs, and ice chest, they had put the beans and pies close to the back of the cab. When we stepped out of the door on the back porch, Tangle Foot, the horse had his head inside the back of the pickup. He grabbed one of Grannie's

pies and ran off with it in his mouth. We heard Grannie call him names he had never been called before.

"As I Remember It"
By Lorine K. Metz of Mason, Texas
Born 1920

I was born in 1920; a Depression was on, but since we lived on our farm, no one really realized it since everyone was in the same boat. I was the oldest one, my brother and then my sister. I was the domesticated one. My brother and sister helped my dad, but Mother and I worked out in the fields when needed, like chopping weeds out of cotton fields and picking cotton, pulling corn, then, topping corn.

One early morning in the late fall my dad woke me and asked if I would like to ride in the wagon filled with cotton we had picked several days before. It was rather cold, but I wanted to go. It was 8 miles. Three hours later, we were at the gin. I enjoyed watching a flexible pipe suck the cotton up, then it went through a bunch of wire spikes taking the seeds away from the lint. Then it went to a press and was tied with metal straps into a big bale.

"Let's go to the drug store to get something to eat or drink," Dad said. When we got there, he asked, "What do you want?" I said, "A banana split." I was told, "That costs a quarter; take an ice cream." Well, to this day, I've never had a banana split.

Quite often we three kids went to the fields to work; Mother would make us lunch of molasses soaked corn bread and churned butter. Umm! I can just taster it now.

Neighbors helped one another. REA electric lines came through the farmlands, "Oh, happy day." There was a new radio and refrigerator!

Daddy farmed a beef exchange club

where four farmers who had a milk calf about the same size. One farmer would kill the oldest calf first, quarter it, and deliver to each member of the club ¼ of the calf. After three months, everyone had received a whole calf.

When I celebrated my thirteenth birthday, I was given a little Spanish pony and a new mid-sized saddle. By that time, all three of us could ride horses back to school. My sister hung on behind my brother on a plow horse and I rode my new horse and saddle.

Riding 4 miles from our house to school was lots of fun. On a corner fence post we placed a stick that was turned up in the fence on our way home from school, so the next morning, the first riders turned the stick down. That's when we would kick our horses in the side. Away we'd go, and then we'd have to see who had the fastest horse.

My mom planted a garden so she could sell her tomatoes, roasting ears, cucumbers, and okra. She gathered fresh eggs and churned the butter and put it in a pound press. Mother always made yeast cakes for bread making. This was her recipe.

"Buttermilk Yeast Cakes"—dissolve one yeast cake in one pint of warm water. Add 1 tablespoon full each of corn meal and sugar, and one teaspoon full of salt. Let stand overnight. In morning, boil one pint of buttermilk, have 1-cup flour, water-enough to mix a smooth stiff batter. Pour this into the boiling buttermilk and let it cook thoroughly, stirring it constantly. When cool, add to the yeast cake mixture; let it set in a warm place until it ferments. Then, work in cornmeal, enough to make a stiff dough. Mold into cakes (size of lg. egg) pressed flat and placed on a dry, clean plank in the shade until dry.

After she stopped making yeast cakes due to bakeries springing up, and no more yeast cakes were needed, but she still had calls for them.

When riding to school on our horses it was fun when we saw three or four school kids riding ahead of us. That's when we'd kick our horses in the side and catch up with them. Sometimes it turned into a race to see who had the fastest horse.

I had a boyfriend waiting for us to get to school. I tied my horse on an oak tree; he would unsaddle my horse while I took off my jeans from under my dress skirt, and in the winter I'd roll down my long cotton hose. I can just see those huge rolls around my ankles. I would dress for home and up would go my hose.

When we got home there would sometimes have a plate of cookies on the table and a note saying, "come to the back field to pick cotton." We were always busy—no time to get into mischief.

School was very different in those days. We had reading, writing, spelling, arithmetic, history, and geography. It was a three-room schoolhouse, three or four grades in one room. Our principal taught the senior grades, coached volleyball, tennis, and baseball, and he let us know our grades had to be good before we could play and he expected us to win, and we did!

I played tennis doubles with my girlfriend. We went to the State and won second. Instead of trophies, they gave us felt banners. Our volleyball team was best of all schools around.

I went to college in San Antonio, graduated, and worked for an insurance Co. The World War II was on, I joined the USO. It happened! I fell in love with a handsome Air Force man from Seattle. How great that was in many ways. No more milking cows, feeding chickens, shucking corn, picking cotton; I did miss my horseback riding.

For 63 years, we enjoyed traveling, cruising and working in Kellogg's Cereal Plant in California. A strawberry boss in Washington, in the spring my ladies sewing club was asked to help hoe the weeds out of the strawberries. It did help to be a farm girl, because this strawberry farmer saw my husband in a restaurant with his buddies. The farmer hit my husband on the shoulder and said, "Your little wife is the best hoer I have." That's the way I recall it!

Peter's Prairie School House is now a Community Hall. Camp Air had three gas stations and some groceries are closed and made into homes. Bethel Church is only used for funerals. The crank phones and party lines have been gone for many years. Cotton is a crop of the past. Fields of irrigation have been added causing lots of wells to go dry. Windmills are the things of the past.

This is the good ole days passed!

Down Memory Lane
By Loys Tippie of Burnet, Texas
Born 1923

It amazes me how often you hear, "I remember when," at family reunions, birthdays, dinners, or family holidays. Now that I'm 90 years old, I know why. If you would like to sit with me a spell, I'll tell you about my journey through the good old days.

I am Loys Hunziker Tippie. I have lived

L. B. Tippie and Loys Hunziker

Loys with her parents, Fred and Suzie Hunziker, Jr.

here all my life. My dad, Fred Hunziker, Jr. was the youngest of fourteen kids. When he got married, it was his lot to stay on with Grandpa and Grandma Hunziker. They lived on a farm at Council Creek, a country community in Northwest Burnett County. When I was five years old, my mother passed away. Nine months later, my grandparents passed away. That left my dad with three little girls, me being the eldest at six. Life on the farm was great, but after we moved to town, the bottom fell out. The Depression hit. People lost their jobs, their homes, banks failed and it was a battle to survive. We lived in a tent until Daddy got our little house built. We had an outhouse and storm cellar, no electricity, and no water. We carried water from three blocks away. We walked two miles to school, no mail delivery, and no lunchrooms at school. Sometimes, no lunches, period!

Oh, Yes, I know about bathing in a number 3 tub, penny post cards, 3-cent stamps, cedar pencils, Big Chief tablets, pickle barrels, 10-cent movies, 15-cent gas, Model-T cars and wash day. We washed on a rub board. The smell of lye soap still lingers. It usually took all day. Then, we had sad irons you heated on

132

the stove. It was a hot job, but no fans to keep you cool. We had a good town, all the stores we needed to shop. It's not that way now. Our hospitals are different. It's like a whole new world. In this fast moving world we live in now, it's no wonder everyone is stressed out. No privacy anymore. Internet and computers are destroying the good life. Cell phones; did you ever see anything like it? People running around with cell phones in their ears, it's like a disease. I don't want one! I don't have a computer, a credit card, I don't have a dishwasher, and I still hang out my clothes. I have a dryer, but I use it when I have to. I'm not against progress. I appreciate electricity and bathrooms, but to me the pushbutton age is ruining our world. You don't have to get up to do anything anymore. Just push the remote, Facebook, E-Mail, Google, Twitter; they have it all. People don't even talk to each other anymore. It's amazing to sit and watch them. You talk about history, Boy, is the world making it. People will think I'm crazy, but if I had to choose between the two worlds, I would

choose the good old days. People were happy back then. They didn't have the problems they have now. They worked hard and did without a lot of things, but when they went to bed at night, they went to sleep, no Tylenol PM's.

I've seen so much in my life. I feel I've been blessed. I had a wonderful husband, three great kids, Brenda, Sue and Darrel. I have five grandkids, eleven great-grandkids, and one great, great grandson. Don't pity me, I wouldn't trade lives with anybody. I hope I didn't bore you, but it's time we head out of here. Hope you enjoyed your journey. So long!

Mothers Driving Lessons Paid Off
By Vivian Hoover of Burnet, Texas
Born 1933

The farm and ranch I grew up on was bought in 1926 by my parents. It is about five miles south of Lake Victor, Texas. There was an old house on the place, with the date 1878. The house had dirt floors, three small windows and no window or door screens. The outside walls were one by twelve's nailed to a frame. A log cabin would have been warmer. My mother had heard that the two people who had lived in that house died of tuberculosis. My mother voted NO, to the idea of living in the old house.

In January 1927, my mother's brother drove a team of horses pulling a wagon to Lake Victor, Texas. He loaded up a load of lumber bought from "Boss Warner General Store," in Lake Victor to start a new house. A woman back in those days did not have to worry about cabinets, counter tops, bathroom fixtures, appliances, carpet, and light fixtures. You had four walls and a pine wood floor.

In the beginning, the ranch and farm had a lot of timber on it. One of the fields still had a patch of timber in the middle of it. Daddy hired two Spanish families to come and cut

Loys Tippie with her two daughters, Sue and Brenda

the trees down and dig out stumps to make the land fit for cultivating. They lived in tents just north of our house. One day I was in the house and I heard this arguing going on outside. Being three and a half years old, I ran out the screen door letting it slam hard. When I got closer, I could see the one called Charley had the axe drawn back ready to strike my dad. The distraction I made, gave my dad time to take command of the situation. Needless to say, they were paid off and told to roll up their tents and move out. The thicket stood there a long time before all of it was removed.

After Mother and Daddy married, he insisted that she learn how to drive a car. A lot of women of that time did not know how to drive a car. His teachings paid off. One day Daddy got the horses in the barnyard, put the harnesses on them, and walked them to the field. He hooked them up to the plow. They made a few rounds and the dirt was sticking to the plows. He kept a paddle with him to clean off the dirt that had built up on his plow. He took his pocketknife out to sharpen the edge of his paddle. The knife slipped, plunging it into his arm at the bend, and cutting the artery. God was with him; my mother was outside. He got her attention and told her to bring the car. When she got there, he told her not to look at him and get to the doctor as fast as she could. He put his thumb on the artery and applied pressure. The doctor said that was what saved his life. The danger now was the threat of infectious disease. There were several really bad ones; lock jaw, blood clot, blood poisoning and gangrene. The only defense available was Epsom salts and hot water combined. He had to soak his arm in the hottest water he could stand with the Epsom salts three times a day, for an hour each time. This had to have been a very anxious time, because there were no antibiotics or tetanus shots available. It all ended well.

One of my favorite things to do as a young child was when I heard my dad and the horses coming from the field. I would run out of the barn, climb up on the rail fence, and wait for them to get to the barn. Each horse would go in his stall. Daddy would take their harness off and hang it on the dividing wall between the horse's stalls. He would feed the horses some ears of corn. While they ate, he would comb their main and brush their hair. This was my time to tell him about my day. Then when he was through, he would pick me up off the rail fence and carry me to the house, what a special time!

My dad told the story how one day I crawled up on the rail fence and began saying, "Vivian, where is Doris, Vivian where is Doris?" I kept saying this until he came over and picked me up off the rail fence. Then I said, "that's how many times Mama has asked me, Vivian where is Doris" this morning. I was three years older than my sister; she followed me around like a puppy. Mother made me babysitter; I was not a happy camper.

The horses we had were just workhorses, around to pull plows, wagons, stumps, and heavy work. Even so, I loved to watch them kick up their heels, lie down, and roll around in the dirt after they were let out of the barnyard. A horse went missing one day, I asked my dad about him, his answer was; he jumped the fence and ran off.

Sometime later, my mother and I were driving the turkeys in. You had to pen them every night to keep the different varmints from eating them. We were in the back of the pasture and, Oh, My gosh, there was the skeleton of a horse. I realized then what had happened to the horse. I was so upset by the fate of my beloved horse. I had to mature some to realize the facts. The horse was old. No one wanted an old horse that couldn't work; as they age their teeth fall out, he took up room in the barn and what feed he did eat could feed a healthy animal. On a farm, lots of decisions must be made in business management attitude, not by your heart.

My mother made a decision one day about this old chicken hen that had been moping around for three or four days and didn't seem to be improving. Her decision was to hasten what seemed to be the old hen's destiny. So, a good knockout blow to the head should do it. She took the old hen up in the pasture and tossed her on a pile of brush. She set the brush pile on fire, came back to the house, and continued her day. Two or three days later she was out tending the chickens and noticed something coming up toward the chicken house. Holy cow! It was the old chicken hen. I guess the fires of hell revived her. She overcame and continued to live on.

Emelia and Marshall Smith in 1936

Farmers and ranchers had a vicious adversary that was everywhere just waiting to lay eggs on any animal with a scratch or wound. It was called a blowfly, and when its eggs hatched, you had the screwworm. Soon after hatching, it would begin eating away at the live animal's flesh. I can remember my dad putting a black tar looking thick goo on every goat or sheep that he nicked while shearing them. Then you took a survey of your stock, looking for one that was stomping its feet, shaking its head or moving around. Once they (screwworms) got a start, you couldn't stop them and it caused the animals death. In 1962, a program was started by treating the blowfly with radiation, rendering the fly sterile. Then the sterile flies were released into the atmosphere in boxes dropped from airplanes. This took twenty years or so to finally eradicate the devils.

The New Glass Eye
By Martha Smith Carlson of Center Point, Texas
Born 1941

When my grandfather, Marshall Smith, was 14 years old, he was helping an older brother butcher some hogs for winter meat for the family. His task was to hold the hog to keep it from swinging while his brother used the big knife to strip the hide off. It was very cold, and he was having a hard time holding it still and the knife slipped and stuck my grandfather in his right eye, blinding the eye for life.

I am not sure where he was taken for treatment, but the ending result was a poor fitting, lifeless looking false eye. It was uncomfortable, constantly watered and always looked straight ahead, causing him to be embarrassed by his appearance.

I was born in 1941, and the year that I was 5, my grandfather heard of an Eye Specialist in San Antonio who was making glass eyes that looked almost real and moved appropriately, matching the movements of your good eye.

It was mid-December, so they took me with them to San Antonio so I could see all the Christmas decorations downtown and see Santa at Joske's. We stayed at the Gunter Hotel, right across the street from The Majestic Theatre on Houston Street. WOW, I was so excited I can still remember every detail of that trip. It was also the only time that my grandfather spanked me.

After having made several trips on multiple days to the Dr.'s office for measurements and fittings, the big day finally arrived. He left my

Martha Nell Smith in 1946

it. I was just trying to see what his new eye would look like on me.

He very quietly came into the bathroom and took the eye out of my hand and placed it into a little glass bowl that was made to hold the eye when not being worn. He then proceeded to lecture me to never, never play with Granddad's eye, and gave several swats to my bottom so I would remember.

He told the story of how horrified he was when he woke up and saw me. "I just knew that I came very close to losing my brand new $500.00 glass eye."

When he passed away several years later, he was still wearing that same eye and it was still one of his most prized possessions.

grandmother and me at the hotel early one morning and went to get his new eye. It was everything he had hoped for. It fit perfectly; the color was a perfect match to his real eye and for the first time since he was 14 years old, it moved. Up, down, right, left, whichever way his real eye turned, so did the false eye. He was so proud of that brand new $500.00 glass eye.

We had lunch in the hotel and then went up to take a nap. This was to be our last night in San Antonio and we were leaving early the next morning to go home. We were going window-shopping that night to see the lights and hear the Christmas music one more time. My grandfather woke up to see me standing in the sink in the bathroom, trying to put his new glass eye into my right eye socket. He knew that if he yelled or hollered, I would drop the eye and it would go right down the open drain. Back then, the sinks did not have stoppers made as part of the sink and there were no traps built into the system. There was just a big hole and sometimes there was a rubber plug on a long chain to stop up the hole, but of course, I had not thought to use

My Heart Belongs In The Texas Hill Country
By Linda Carta of Llano, Texas
Born 1941

I was born during World War II. My oldest brother enlisted about a year after I was born. In a year or two, my dad was building ships in Vancouver, Washington. I still have post cards that he sent to me from Washington.

My parents had sold our family farm a year or two before I was born, to pay debts incurred during the Depression. I missed the years when my sisters had three outfits to wear one on, one being washed and one dirty.

I do remember the rationing of sugar during the Second World War. Everyone had sugar stamps that allotted them a certain amount. They may have rationed coffee too, but I didn't care about coffee then.

The year I started to school, all the little country schools in our county ceased to operate and everyone was bussed to our county seat, Llano, Texas. My sibling, just older than me, graduated in the spring, and I started to school in the fall. So I was reared, basically, as an only child.

My parents had an outhouse and we used chamber pots in the house at night until the year I graduated from high school and got married. That year they got an indoor bathroom and a TV set. I must have been expensive to rear. I hated the old outhouse. You don't know what cold is until you set there on a cold winter day with that part of you bare, and the backside of ours faced north.

I was three or four when electricity came to our little town. I remember watching the workers put up the poles and connect the wires. About all we used it for then, was the light in the ceiling in each room, and the plug that was between the socket and the light in case you wanted to plug up a fan or something. I think the first thing that Mother and Daddy purchased was a new Westinghouse refrigerator. It came with three covered bowls. I think one was red, one was green, and one was yellow. Years later, when I broke one of those bowels, my mother was pretty upset. Unlike my daddy, she took excellent care of everything and thought it should last forever.

Lina Reagor

We didn't have one of the old wind-up Victrolas, but a friend did, and it was fun to wind it up and listen to the records.

My parents always said that if I got a spanking at school, I would get another one when I got home. Mother said that no one in our family had ever gotten a spanking and I had better not be the first one. When I was in the fourth grade, I got my one and only lick for talking too much. (What can you do when you are an extrovert?) I never got around to telling my parents about that. Since I have been an adult, I have wondered if some of my siblings never got around to telling about theirs, either.

By the time I was in junior high school, I took a bath every night. My parents said I was going to wash all my skin off. It wasn't an easy feat. I had to pump the water into what they called a foot tub. The hand pump was on our back porch. Then I had to carry it to the bathtub. Then, go pump some more cold water into the foot tub to add to the bathtub water until it was just the right temperature. We always saved that water to pour on the flowers, later.

My second brother was the right age for the Korean War. He was a train dispatcher in Korea. While he was gone, my sister had a baby girl. She wanted to name her for my brother, but decided on a different name; one she said her mother-in-law liked. My sister-in-law had already given her baby son my brother's second name a couple of months earlier. When my brother got home from Korea, all the family got together and went to Inks Lake to picnic and swim for the day.

Every Monday was washday. Mother kept the wringer washer on the back porch. We pumped water for the washer and the two washtubs that sat on small tables next to where the clothes came out of the wringer. She put bluing in one of the tubs. That was to make the whites, whiter. She would wash the whites, then the other clothes and if there were really dirty work clothes, they came last. After the whites, we would run them through the wringer to let the suds fall back into the washer, then, she would put them in both tubs of water, then, run them back through the wringer to get the water out. Then we took them to the clothesline to hang them. (It almost makes me tired just to write about it now.)

My mother had grown up picking cotton and milking cows and when my parents had lived on the farm she canned lots of fruits and vegetables and had to draw water from a hand dug well for everything. She still canned quite a lot after they left the farm. She and dad always raised a large garden. She lived to be one hundred and one years old. Tell your kids that hard work won't kill them. Mother made many of our clothes on her old Singer treadle sewing machine. I started making some of my clothes around twelve or thirteen years old. For special occasions, I would design a dress that I wanted, and Mother could make

Linda's mother, Mary Carson with Joey and Richard

it. Two of my favorites were a red taffeta with a bolero, with rhinestones on it and a navy, velveteen with an inch wide strip or white rabbit fur, lining the scoop neck.

We raised some of our meat. Dad would get a hog and fatten it. We always raised chickens. Mother and dad always killed and took care of the meat themselves. I remember Mother making lye soap in our big old black wash pot once when I was small after we had killed a hog. They probably did a lot more of that kind of thing when they lived on the farm. I know that she said that they used to make their own hominy.

When I was small, we still had a milk cow. We weren't on the farm, so some member of the family would milk the cow in the morning and let her out in what we called the lane. It was just public property where she could graze during the day and someone in our family would put her back inside our small property and milk her in late evening and keep her fenced in until morning. You could do that in those days. Some of our neighbors did the same thing. At that time, the only milk that you could get at our small local grocery store was canned milk. So Mother and Daddy kept a cow for a few years until we could get pasteurized milk at the grocery store.

I had a bicycle and roller skates, but we still had fun with other things. At the filling station (gas station, now) we could get lube cans that we could stomp our shoes into and walk around in. Daddy made us stilts on which we learned to walk all over town. Back in those days, we played a lot of cowboys and Indians with cap guns. I think mostly, because that is what a lot of our movies were. Roy Rogers and Dale Evans, Gene Autry and the Lone Ranger were always after outlaws or Indians. Never once did we think it would be cool to shoot a cowboy or an Indian in real life. We knew it was all make believe. Nor, did we see blood splattered everywhere like you can on today's video games. We also went to church regularly and knew you were supposed to treat others well.

A friend had an old dirt tank that sometimes got pretty dirty, but when I was a teenager, a bunch of us and a few adults went there to swim in the summer. I learned to swim on my own. I took my first few strokes in a friend's concrete stock tank and finished learning in that dirt tank. I now love to swim and have a pool, but I have never had a swimming lesson.

My mother loved to read and she would read books to me at night. I read to my children a lot and they all love to read. My dad only went to third grade but he could work any math problem you gave him, in his head. He didn't know how to put it on paper, but he could give you the answer. For entertainment, he loved to read mysteries and play dominos or forty-two and he was hard to beat. He liked checkers too. Mother only went to eighth grade. That was as far as the little country schools went. Then you had to go by horse or horse drawn convenience to the county seat or further to school. Mother had an uncle that lived in the Texas Valley, that wanted her to come, stay with them, and go to high school, but her parents didn't want her to go. She didn't have science when she was in school and she read all of my Science books. She loved learning from my books. For entertainment, she liked traveling, movies and books. She wrote poetry, too.

I was in 4-H club from eighth grade until I graduated high school. I got a lot of experience with cooking, sewing, modeling, public speaking (still can't do that) and went to state on a rifle team sponsored by NRA.

When we were kids, we liked to play scrub (a baseball game that can be played with just four or five participants), Annie Over, Hide and Seek, Kick the Can, Volley Ball and Tennis. We spent many hours on our bicycles. Some of us that lived in our village would ride our bicycles occasionally to some of our friend's farms and take a picnic lunch with us and visit for an hour with our friends and share our picnic lunch. One thing we didn't do much of, was sit in the house. We liked to climb trees and be outdoors. Our parents worked hard and we had to help, but when they gave us free time, we took off. They didn't have time to keep very good tabs on us. We had a lot of freedom in between when we left, and we were told to be back home.

Spring is beautiful in Central Texas when we get rain. Bluebonnets, Indian Blankets, Indian Paint Brush and all kind of flowers are in abundance.

When I was a teenager, I ran the old country switchboard for the operator when she needed to be away. The old switchboard is now in the Llano County museum. At our house, we had an old wooden phone on the wall that rang with longs and shorts. That was the way I called people from the old switchboard, too.

I married a boy from my county, reared three children, lived in the Texas Hill Country most of my life, and love my family, my God and my Texas Hill Country.

A Smart Little Dog and Dad's 'Toot' for Mom
By Victoria Swanson of Wichita Falls, Texas
Born 1926

Before mail delivery in Fredericksburg, Texas in the early 1930s, at age 6 and 7, I was often allowed to go to the post office a distance of about 3 ½ blocks. On one occasion, a local businessman came with his terrier, who had a Sherlock Holmes type pipe in his mouth. There were several other larger dogs outside approaching the terrier and apparently wanted what he had in his mouth; perhaps thinking it was a bone. The terrier laid the pipe down, growled, and chased the dogs away, picked up his pipe and continued on his way with his master.

Days later, I saw the dog again, alone; the door was opened for him and the postmaster placed several letters in his mouth and opened the door. The dog left; I never saw him again.

My father owned a cotton gin in Fredericksburg, Texas, located at the end of what is now Pfeil Road. During ginning season, a noon whistle was blown, followed by a short and quick 'toot'. Many years later, I learned the quick toot was added in Dad's courting days to let Mama know he was thinking of her, and they continued into the 1930s, until the gin burned.

In Fredericksburg in the 1930s, one could visit any house on the block without having to walk in the street, as yards had gates between neighbors—just be sure to close the gates.

Inner Tube Floating on the Guadeloupe
By Bette Ann Geren of New Braunfels, Texas
Born 1935

Well, these stories go back to the '50s and forward. I was born and raised in Houston, Texas in the early '30s. Not a huge city then, and ended up taking trips to San Antonio to visit my brothers, who attended Peacock Military Academy for their high school years.

By the '60s and '70s, I was married and had a small daughter, Kerri Louise Geren. We would go to Wimberley and camp out and swim at 'Blue Hole' swimming area and also at Lisa Howell's camp and swim acreage. Then, we started coming to New Braunfels, to go down the river on inner tubes and swim at Linda Park. It was then a small, lovely town. Downtown had a drug store with a soda fountain and some shops. I would bring girlfriends and friends for my daughter's birthdays in August during the '70s and '80s. There was no water park then. We stayed at Camp Warnecke in Army huts and crossed the street to get inner tubes. We also got tubes to go down the Guadeloupe River. Such fun was had by all!

I also attended my freshman year of college in San Marcos at the Southwest Texas State Teachers College in '55-'56 years. I went to Wimberley a lot to stay at friend's houses and always went bobcat hunting in the hills and was so glad I never even saw one! Heat, never as bad as it is now and not a lot of air cond. We were living in Seguin and got flooded out in 98-flood and now in New Braunfels full time with many good friends and lots to do!

Four Children's Lives Changed Forever, in Just One Second
By Donald Bauer of Fredericksburg, Texas
Born 1930

This story is one that changed the life of four children in one second.

On a farm in Fredericksburg, on Tivydale Road, lightning struck and killed Robert and Louise Dannenburg.

Robert and Louise were the parents of four children; Adolph (fourteen), Christine (twelve), Lina (six) later became my mother, and Rolf-four.

Robert and Louise awoke to just another day of farm chores, not knowing it would be their last. After they tended the children, they hitched the mules to the wagon, loaded hoes and buckets and drove away to the vegetable garden.

Later, there was a bolt of lightning, a clap of thunder. The children looked toward the garden and saw the mules pulling the wagon, running back to the house. The children ran to the garden and found their mother and father lying dead. The bolt of lightning killed them both, the day, May 7, 1896. This left four children with no parents.

Adolph ended up in San Antonio; Christine in Dallas, Rolf went to live with the Kerchoff's, the Wolf Creek School Master.

Linda, my mother, went to Sisterdale to live with the Langbeins. The Langbean home is the big white house beside the dance hall now belonging to Wayne Wright.

My mother later married Charles Baver, a farmer. Charles had a farm on the Guadeloupe River, went to school, in the Rock School, at Sisterdale.

Because of poor farming conditions and Gaudeloupe flooding, they moved to Beevile, then, to League City, where I, Donald Beaver, was born. I married Betty Johnson and many times, we would visit Fredericksburg. Every visit, Betty would say, "Let's move to Fredericksburg." Well, in 1978, we did just that!

I think I was destined to live where my roots are.

We Both Got It with the Bridal Reins
By Audrey Perry of Kingsland, Texas
Born 1923

I was born on a farm in Texas on June 5, 1923. I had one older brother and 2 sisters. I was the middle girl. My father leased the land by the year. We had horses and cattle.

We lived in a three-room house with a screened in hall where my brother slept. We had a fireplace for heat.

My mother cooked our meals on a woodstove. We had no electricity, no fans, or telephone. We had no well; only a cistern that furnished us water.

In dry weather, we would run out of water, so we would load the wash pot and clothes in the wagon and go to the dirt tank. We would heat the water in the iron pot with lye soap. We would hang the clothes on the field fence. When the clothes were dry, we would take them off the fence and carry them to the house. We were a happy family and I never heard my mother complain.

We all worked in the fields, my dad farmed with mules.

My uncle had a gin where we would take our cotton. Me and my sister Wanda would go with my dad. We would play with our cousins until it was time to go home.

My uncle and aunt had 10 children. We liked to eat at their house. My aunt cooked beans and fried potatoes in big iron pots. We got to eat setting on a long bench. After the cotton was ginned, we would take the cottonseed home and store them in the barn. We played paper dolls in the cottonseed. We cut paper dolls out of the Sears catalogue.

My dad milked 2 cows. We drink the milk and Mom churned the cream and made butter. We were a happy family.

My mom and older sister sewed all our dresses on a treadle sewing machine. Mom would sew a lot at night by a kerosene lamp.

I remember getting one spanking. My dad sent me and my little sister to find the horses and bring them to the pen. We were gone longer than necessary. We were playing and forgot what we were supposed to be doing. When we heard our dad coming, we knew we were in trouble. We both got it with the bridal reins. Me; being the oldest got it first. After that, we always remembered what we were looking for and played later.

My dad would buy fresh meat from a meat peddler that came by our house every 2 weeks. Dad would put the meat in a flour sack and hang it on the porch. It kept until we eat it all.

Three Straw Hats, and a Bloody Nose
By Glen B. Bates of Burnet, Texas
Born 1929

When I was about nine, or ten years old, my dad leased a farm at Spicewood in Burnet County, Texas.

When I started to Spicewood School, I

Glen Bates in 1963

was an outsider, because nearly all the people in the community were related in one way or another. All the boys at school wanted to fight the newcomer. I wore a straw hat to school every day. When recess came, I put my straw hat on and went out to play. One of the boys ran by and grabbed my hat. When I tried to get my hat, he would sail it over my head to another boy, until they destroyed my hat. Daddy bought me another straw hat. The same thing happened to it. Daddy bought me another third hat, and he told me if I let those boys tear up that hat, he would tear up my rear end. I put my new hat on and went to school.

Recess came and I got my hat to go out and play. One of the big bullies ran by; grabbed my hat and sailed it across the schoolyard. I did not chase the hat. I went over to the bully. I got him down on the ground and I had his nose bleeding. His name was Max. The man teacher, Howard Adare, was up on the other end of the schoolyard playing volleyball with the girls. Someone ran up and told the teacher that Max and I were fighting. The teacher quit playing with the girls and he went by a big live oak tree and broke off some switches. He came down and told me and the other boy to go in the schoolhouse. When we got in the school building, he told both of us to bend over a desk and he gave us both a whipping

with the live oak limbs, and then he said, "Now you both kiss and apologize." I said, "You might as well whip me again, because I am not going to kiss that son-of-a-gun." But, he did not whip me again. I wore khaki pants and I had green stripes on the seat of my pants from the tree limbs.

My younger sister, Dee, ran home after school so she could tell on me for getting a whipping in school. Daddy always told me if misbehaved and got a whipping in school, I would get another one at home. When I told him what I got a whipping for, he did not give me another at home. A few days later Daddy happened to meet Mr. Adare, the teacher, on the road. He told the teacher that it was probably his fault that I was fighting in school, because he had told me not to let those boys tear up my hat.

I am now 84 years old and none of the people named in my story is still alive.

My Heart Melted
Along With the Chocolate Covered
Cherries
By Joe Morales of Del Rio, Texas

Back in the 1960s, I was in the 5th grade with Mr. Joe Sanchez in the old Stephen F. Austin School in Del Rio. There was this very pretty girl by the name of Mary B. Back, then she was the most wonderful, most beautiful girl in the class. It was early December, and Mr. Sanchez announced that we were going to pick names so we could exchange Christmas gifts. When I heard that, I said to myself, "I wish I could pick Mary's name." Well, God must have been listening. When the day came to draw the names, I was hoping no one would pick Mary's name. One by one the box went down the row of kids till it got to me; stuck my hand in and pulled out a name. It was Mary B's. I just smiled and looked at her, but she wasn't paying attention. I felt like; WOW, I got Mary B's name.

As soon as school was out that day, I asked my mother for a $1. I said to her, that we were going to exchange gifts at school and I needed to go get something. She gave me a dollar. Back in the early 60's, one dollar was a lot of money.

I went down town to Kress's 5 & 10 Store. I got me a box of chocolate covered cherries. Back in those days, cherries were the thing to give to your sweetheart. I got home; wrapped them up in white wrapping paper with a red bow!

The next day they were under the Christmas tree to Mary B. from Joe M. The other kids were like, wow, Mary already has her gift under the tree from Joe M. Later, as time went on, gifts would appear under the tree. I would go in early and move Mary's gift to the top of the pile. If you have ever lived in South Texas in December, it is still hot. The days are sunny temperatures in the '80s. I still would come in early and move Mary's gift to the top of the pile. The tree was in the middle of a picture window.

The day finally came to hand out the gifts. Mary's gift was on top, so she was one of the first to get her gift. Finally, all of the gifts were handed out. Mr. Sanchez tells everyone that they can open their gifts now. There I am setting three rows across from her. She opens up the box and quickly closes it. I can't understand; maybe she did not like them.

Well, the box sat in front of the window for three weeks; the sun was on them all day. The chocolate melted; the cherries were sitting on the white filling that is in the covered cherries. To make a long story short that is why my wife's name is Dolores, and not Mary, love you honey and I'm glad I married you!

This story took place back in the 1960s at the Stephen F. Austin School on Chapoy Street.

The Place I Love…
By J. Driana Redwood of San Antonia, Texas
Born 1941

What is that place I love and remember and still have a good feeling about? It is a place that gave me comfort, security, warmth, strength, courage, and freedom. Often, a smell, a sound, a feeling, or something that I see…triggers the embedded memories of yesteryear and place; and that place is simply "El Rancho."

"El Rancho" is that place in Central Texas where I was born more than 72 years ago.

In the early 1900s, my grandfather, Juan Perez Espinoza; my mother's father, bought land in McCulloch County, which consisted of wooded areas teeming with live oak trees, mesquite trees, algerita bushes (agritos) and cacti. Pecan, Black willow, and assorted elm trees grew along the banks of the creek that ran along the foot of the hills on the north side of the property. Some acreage was cultivated into rich farmland.

My grandfather built a two-story house on top of a hill from which one could see forever to the west and to the north. The front porch on the east side ran the width of the house and on the west side of the house, a screened back porch provided a place for potted plants and a place to sit and visit or play.

I associate smells, sounds, feelings and sights or images with the four seasons of the year as I remember them, living on "El Rancho."

In the springtime—The smell of new linoleum throughout the house. The smell of fresh paint, the smell of freshly tilled soil, the sight of the first tender, green sprout of new crops, the aroma of fresh homemade birthday cakes, the sight of newborn calves and the smell of fresh milk. After a hard and long rainstorm, the sight of uprooted trees and dead farm animals in the muddy, swollen creek as it rushed down stream, the feeling of freedom

143

when we shed the heavy winter clothes.

In the summertime—The smell of freshly washed laundry hanging on the clothesline and the smell of fresh, crisp, sundried white bed sheets and towels, the soft, cool summer morning breeze that came through the open windows along with the sound of the cicadas promising a hot, cloudless, sunny day, the sound of roosters crowing at the break of dawn, the sight of yellow wheat and oat fields triggers the memory of the sounds of combines, tractors and grain hauling trucks that produced a constant drone lasting late into the night, the aroma of Pan Dulce that was prepared on the big wood stove for the merienda, the aroma of the algerita berries being prepared by my mother to make jellies and jams, the sound of sheep bleating as they were headed to be sheared, the sound of the shears. The sight of large clouds with brilliant white tops and dark bases promised a thunderstorm with possible hail and high winds. To stand at the top of the hill and watch the magnificence of the approaching storm from the west was breath taking and at the same time, a frightening sight.

Oh, but after a summer rain, there is nothing like the smell of wet earth and the sight of the most beautiful green colors. I know the meaning of "God's Green Earth." The sound of the ancient Singer treadle sewing machine was constant, as my mother made our school dresses for the new school year. The scent of the honeysuckle that covered the front porch on all sides, providing a cool cave of green foliage and white flowers for anyone who was brave enough to take on the bees and the wasps and the feeling that the hot, cloudless summer days would never end.

In the autumn—the sight of the mountain of chopped wood for the huge cook stove and pot belly stove throughout the house, the smell of fallen and decaying leaves on cut wood and on the wet wool of sheep, the sight of the barren, leafless trees on the trees by the creek,

the anticipation of the coming Holidays; Thanksgiving and Christmas, the sound of the sewing machine as my mother made our holiday dresses, the sight of livestock being butchered, providing meat for the rest of the year, the early morning smell of barbecue that had been cooking all night and the noise that the long pole made as it hit the branches of the pecan trees, so the pecans would drop to the ground.

In the wintertime—The feeling of comfort and security as one snuggled in the warmth of big, downy homemade quilts and homemade pajamas, the smell of wood burning in the stove, the aroma of empanadas baking, the aroma of tamales cooking, and chicharones frying, the sound of bleating newborn lambs, the sight of the Christmas tree lit up in red and green Christmas lights, the warm feeling of coming in from the cold into a warm kitchen where the aroma of fresh coffee and hot chocolate greeted you and the cold living room.

"El Rancho" was the place that I loved and still remember with nostalgia. I miss the serenity, the peace, the comfort, and the warmth.

I Met My Husband While Swimming
By Barbara C. Bird of New Braunfels, Texas
Born 1937

My brother Archie and I had the unique opportunity of growing up in the neat little town of New Braunfels, Texas, a town with two rivers running through it at the edge of Texas Hill County. In the '40s and '50s it was a simple life and the area was beautiful.

Our parents, Archie and Gladys Culpepper, were good hard working people and managed to keep food on the table by working at the local textile mill.

By the time we were preschool age, they

144

Jim and Barbara Bird in 1967

took us swimming in the Guadalupe River, next to the mill. I remember vividly how they taught us to swim at ages four and five. We shared lots of laughter and fun in those early days of summer. On one of those days, we noticed a family with a cute red haired son who was our age. The reason we watched him, was his ability to dive from his dad's back, swim under water, and fast, truly awesome! Boy, did we learn from him. The family was Jim and Loleat Bird and the 5 year old, they called J.D.; later we knew him as Jim.

We got to know the family better as we attended a little Baptist Church and also went to high school with Jim. My brother Archie, and Jim became good friends.

Times were hard and since Jim's sister was sick and there wasn't extra money for college, he joined the Navy. He learned to be an electrician as he had the opportunity to serve and to learn his trade as well as his love for travel was realized.

We stayed close to their family and he and I were married in 1957. Jim and I raised four beautiful children together and I have many beautiful grand and great-grand's.

Jim went to be with the Lord in November 1983. He had a beautiful faith that glowed during his illness. I have been very blessed.

Country Life, We Made Do, With What We Had
By Hildegarde Gebert of Manor, Texas
Born 1924

I have seven children and they had to have clothes to wear. Luckily I could sew, so I sewed lots of homemade clothes. At that time, we bought feed for the animals that came in printed cotton material bags from which I made dresses and shirts and underwear for my husband and the boys. One time, when I was in high school, my mother made an orange and green flowered dress, which was nice, but she also made a red and black plaid jacket that I had to wear with it. I haven't forgotten that combination until this day.

I remember playing 'store' in an empty chicken house. We didn't have many bought can goods, but empty sardine and salmon cans, so we used them to 'sell'. The boys also used those cans as cars.

I was so young when I was introduced to chopping cotton, that when they told me to chop cotton, that's exactly what I did; chopped all of the cotton out, until someone set me straight. When the cotton was ready to be picked, the whole family went to the field to pick it into long sacks that had a strap at one end that you put over your shoulder so that the sack held the cotton behind you. Some people picked two hundred pounds in a day and others could pick four hundred pounds a day. When the corn was still green, we had to cut the tops off and put them on piles, and the next early morning we had to gather two or three piles and tie them together with twine and put them in shocks to dry. Later we would haul them home for feed for the cattle.

Red rover, red rover let so and so come over. Sometimes you broke through the line, which was formed by children holding hands with the next person. One night at a birthday party, we decided to catch lightning bugs and we trampled down my dad's field of growing hay. When he saw it the next morning, he was upset, to say the least.

We had a wooden icebox that held 100 lbs. of ice that was purchased at a country store and fit in a certain place in the icebox. A drip pan was put underneath to catch the melted ice water, which was used to water the flowers around the house. At first, my favorite dessert was Jell-O, made in the icebox. We could buy fresh meat from a butcher who delivered meat that he had just slaughtered. The meat would keep a few days in the icebox.

When it rained and the road was muddy, we rode our only horse (Bill) to the main road, turned him loose and he walked all the way back home on his own.

Our family had a two-hole outhouse about fifty yards from the house. It was supplied with corncobs and a Sears and Roebuck catalogue. When you wiped with a red cob and then a white cob, and it was still dirty, you would just use another cob to get the job done. You never used the slick pages from the catalogue.

To this day, I can't eat white corn syrup, because it reminds me of castor oil.

While the rest of the family took a nap at noon, I would listen to the Stella Dallas and Pepper Youngs' Family. I wouldn't waste any time, so I would embroider dresser scarves and tablecloths for my hope chest.

One time our party-line phone rang 42 times, so I picked it up and told the caller that they better check to see if the person was still alive. Later, it rang again, so I listened in and this lady (his girlfriend) accused him of having another woman in the house. (A city girl didn't know about party lines).

We didn't have bath rooms, so we carried a #3 tub and warm water into the pantry (the smallest room in the house) and the oldest bathed first until the youngest in the same water (you have to remember that we didn't have running water in the house). Thank goodness, that it was rainwater, because it was soft water and didn't leave soap scum. By the way, we never rinsed the soap off our bodies.

My husband and I were married and we had two children by the time he went into the Army. I saved the money that I got from the government, and later, when my husband returned from the service, we bought a farm. While my husband was in the Army, my mother cared for the children and I helped my father work in the field. Four of my five brothers were also in the military; some were away for five years.

Wringer washers were alright until the clothes started to wrap around the rollers, and you had to undo it all. One time I was almost electrocuted by standing on the wet floor next to the washing machine.

We would take eggs in a 12 dozen crate; and butter that was churned and made into one pound blocks, to town so we could buy groceries such as flour, coffee and sugar. We would eat in a restaurant, which was a treat for a country kid.

When the children were little we took them to a roller rink to watch some girls skate. The next morning, my son talked about the girls with the wheels on, which I thought was a cute observation.

My Prized Bantam Hen for a Pair of Sneakers
By Thomas Lou Whisenant of San Antonio, Texas
Born 1929

I am a woman, even though my name is Thomas. It was always given to the first-born. I'm the only female in the family with that

146

first name. I was born in Algerita, Texas, San Saba County, during the Depression, Feb. 1929. I was born at home; most people were then, because there was no hospital nearby.

Since I was named Thomas, I had a nickname (Corky) at a very early age. I attended elementary school in Algerita. It was a 3-room schoolhouse. I walked about 2 miles to school most of the time, but when weather was bad, my dad or my uncles took me. As I got older, I rode a horse, at times.

We had outhouses at school and I got a spanking from the principal after two other girls and I threw a tennis shoe in the toilet. The shoe belonged to my cousin (we didn't know) who was playing baseball at the time. I also received a spanking at home and my dad made me sell my prized Bantam chicken hen to buy my cousin a new pair of tennis shoes.

Thomas Lou "Corky" Whisenant in 1946

We had school plays and I usually got to be the star, not because of my ability, but because my mother was an excellent seamstress, and she made most of the costumes. We also had church in the schoolhouse and many singing conventions were held, usually on Sunday. It was all day affairs—like the old saying, "All day singing, and dinner on the ground."

I had to gather eggs and help with other chores. One time when I was gathering eggs, I put my hand in the nest, (it was a few feet off the ground), and there was a chicken snake in the nest. Needless to say, I was not too happy to gather eggs after that.

I always had pets, a pet goat, a pet pig, and always a dog. A preacher gave me a beautiful white dog and I named him "Preacher." He got a fishhook in his jaw; it became infected and he died. It broke my heart.

I can still remember when we heard on the radio on December 7, 1941—when President Roosevelt announced the attack on Pearl Harbor, starting WWII. I had several cousins and uncles to volunteer for different branches of the service.

We didn't have middle or junior high school then, so I went from Algerita Country School to high school in San Saba. I rode the school bus to school. During the war, gas was scarce, so we didn't have many activities away.

After graduation from high school, I went away to college for a while—I became homesick, much to my parent's chagrin. I returned home and I went to work at the Gas Co. After a couple of years, two girlfriends and I moved to the city (San Antonio). We lived with a lady that our families knew. I moved to the city, but I never forgot my roots and life in a small hill country town where everyone knew you and cared about you.

Freckles, the Orphaned Longhorn Steer
By Fred C. Anderson of San Antonio, Texas
Born 1917

This story is about old Freckles, the lead steer for the Longhorn herd at Comanche Creek Ranch. It all started during Christmas time 20 years ago, while Bonnie and her family were home for the holidays.

We rounded up a few Longhorns at the OK Corral and loaded them up to sell. Early the next morning Daisy, Bonnie, and I drove up to the corral, and lying next to the fence was a newborn Longhorn calf. When we saw the calf, we immediately realized the mother had been mistakenly sold.

The calf was named Freckles because of the red spots on his body. As we were debating what to do with our newborn calf, Kenneth Clary and his two children, Emily and Kyle, drove up. Kenneth, his father and brother ran the farm operation for us. Kenneth asked, "What do you plan to do with that calf?" My answer was, "I really don't know, possibly destroy him, since I don't have anyone to care for him." He said, "Can I have him and let my kids raise him?" We all enthusiastically agreed! This small newborn Longhorn weighed approximately 25 pounds and was gently picked up and was placed on the front seat of their truck. The fortunate baby Longhorn was raised on the bottle by Kenneth's children. He led a happy life with the Clary children until they grew up and lost interest.

Four years later, Kenneth approached me with this question, "What shall we do with the steer?" By that time Freckles was a beautiful, full-grown Longhorn steer. I told Kenneth that we had a 40-acre tract of land separated from the main ranch where we could pasture the steer. This 40-acre tract became the home for Freckles for the next 12 years.

During this time, Freckles had never seen any other cattle. I do believe that he actually forgot what he really was! He had no other friends except wild hogs and deer. During the stay, he and a baby wild hog, who apparently also lost his mother, became inseparably good friends. On jeep rides, we would drive up to the stock pond site where they spent a lot of their time. Freckles would be lying down, chewing his cud, and the small hog would be on his back. Occasionally, Freckles, with his long horns, would turn back his head and gently push the hog off his back. The hog would immediately climb back on Freckles. Freckles would turn his head the other way and gently push him off again. This was a game they often played and it was very amusing for us to watch their games.

Freckles and the hog lived together on the tract for over a decade until we decided, "Why not bring Freckles home!" So then, the question became, "How do we get him back home?" He was wild then. We decided the only way would be to trap him. We set up a cattle trailer on the tract where he lived. We opened the back gate of the trailer, putting alfalfa hay and corn in the trailer, then scattered it about 25 to 30 feet outside the trailer. Each

Freckles

day we would shorten the distance from the trailer until he finally was eating inside. While he was enjoying his lunch, we slipped up and closed the gate. Old Freckles said goodbye to his hog friend and we hauled old Freckles home. When we got back to the ranch and let him loose around the Longhorn herd, Freckles was definitely a confused steer. He could not remember ever seeing a Longhorn, and he stood in amazement watching the cows and calves running around. But this is all in the past.

Freckles, is now very much at home at Comanche Creek Ranch. He enjoys eating fresh hay with his new Longhorn family, but he will never forget his hog friend and his days at the stock pond.

Freckles, was the commander and chief of the Longhorn herd. He was respected by all the coyotes, bobcats, wild hogs, etc. and there was a reason. He was a steer with a beautiful set of large horns measuring 6' 2' from tip to tip. He was a gentle steer who would eat out of your hand. He was highly protective of the herd, especially the young calves. He would use his horns when necessary.

His life on the ranch was about the same for several years, but he finally reached the ripe old age of 30. His health began to fade. One day I arrived at the ranch and was told by Adam and Joe that Freckles was lying about 300 yards from the OK Corral. They had been trying unsuccessfully, to get him up to walk to the corral. So, I jumped in my golf cart and went to see Freckles. I drove up, got out, and said, "Freckles; get up!" It would be dangerous for him to stay there, because of the coyotes. He immediately got up and we herded him to the corral.

We put him in a pen, fed him alfalfa hay and grain he liked. He stayed in the pen where he had ample food and water. The rest of the Longhorn herd paid no attention. So, finally one day he got sick and laid down. The Longhorn cows outside the pen were bawling

and milling around. That night he died.

The next morning, the herd was still milling around the pen, moaning. Then, the steer's body was loaded on the front-end loader of the ranch's tractor. He was taken out in the woods to a nice spot and left. The Longhorn herd followed the tractor to the spot and formed a ring of about 8 or 9 Longhorns around his body. Every once in a while they would change shifts. They did this for approximately 18 or 20 days until his body was completely decomposed. During that time, they would not allow any buzzards or other scavengers to bother the remains until they were completely decomposed.

His beautiful horns were mounted, and now hang over the front door of the Comanche Creek Ranch headquarters. Old Freckles will be highly missed. He was a great asset to the ranch and we know he must be in Longhorn heaven.

Fred saw that Freckles beautiful Longhorns were mounted at ranch headquarters for his grandkids, great, and great-great, so the story of Freckles is passed on for generations.

Aunt Alice
By Helen T. Hahn of Mason, Texas
Born 1935

I was raised out in the country where neighbors usually lived several miles away; however, we had one lady who lived only a bit over a mile from us. She was not related, but because I stayed with her often for days at a time, I called her, 'Aunt Alice'. My brother was a Hemophiliac, and required hospitalization frequently. Her home became my second home over the years.

Aunt Alice never married, so my times spent with her were special since I could have all of her attention. In my younger years, she lived with and took care of her parents as they aged and became dependent on her, but she always made time for me. Staying with them was different, because there was no electricity or indoor plumbing, both of which I was accustomed to at home.

Taking a bath in a large galvanized washtub was an adventure. It was done outside in the summertime just before dark, so we could not be seen by people driving by, and in the kitchen in winter. The water was heated on the wood burning stove. Homework and playing cards were different too, doing them by the dim and flickering light of the coal oil (kerosene) lamp, though the lamplight had its own soothing effect. Going outside to the 'out-house' to use the bathroom made me appreciate more what I had at home.

Her house consisted of a larger room on either side of the hallway that led to the kitchen with the wood burning stove, table and chairs,

Aunt Alice in her garden

pie safe and cupboards. The ceilings were of painted gauze held up by lathing strips.

I recall one day when Mother and I stopped to visit on the way home from the country school. I went to the kitchen, and without asking permission, 'helped myself' to some leftover biscuits from the warming oven and Mama reprimanded me. Aunt Alice just said, "That's alright, she can make herself at home here any time." Mother was not terribly pleased.

When I was six or seven years old, on the way home after school, Mama told me that Aunt Alice's house had burned. What a terrifying sight to see the smoldering ruins! Thankfully, she and her father were safe, although he only escaped by crawling out just before the roof caved in. (Her mother had passed away a few years earlier and I can still visualize the casket in the room to the right of the hall. I recall also, the constant vigil family and friends kept until her burial). She and Grandpa Doyal were so independent that as soon as the neighbors could prepare living space in the wood frame garage, they lived there until a new house could be built. Daddy was instrumental in organizing the construction, and with the help of the neighbors, a new house was erected. Electricity and a bathroom were included, so the lamps and the 'out-house' became a memory.

She had a vegetable garden every summer, even in her 80's. It was more fun helping her pick her produce than to do the same thing at home. She was such a tease! Once, after we ate watermelon out in the yard, she put the rinds in the red wagon to pull them down to the barn for the cows to eat. I begged and begged for a ride. She told me I was too big, but I persisted, "Okay, but I'll turn you upside down," she said. I didn't believe her—but she was true to her word. About half way to the barn, in a nice sandy spot—over I went watermelon rinds and juice all over me. How I cried, and she laughed. Hmmm!

Aunt Alice with Kayla in 2004

Another watermelon story took place a few years later. We'd walked across the creek where big beautiful melons were growing in her field. We picked the best two and began carrying them home. Not far from the field, she 'accidently dropped' hers on a small rock. We dug in with our hands and ate the sweetest heart of a melon I've <u>ever</u> tasted. When we got back to the creek, dry and full of gravel, she started telling me how fast she could roll over. Well, I was skeptical, and she said she would show me. I was to start rolling, with her giving me a head start. My pride was crushed when she rolled right over me and kept rolling. That was an afternoon of special memories.

We went to the barn each evening where she milked the cow. I loved the taste of warm milk and couldn't resist dipping my fingers into the bucket where she was milking. She told me to squat near her and to open my mouth wide and close my eyes. She then proceeded to squirt milk from the teat into my mouth. What made it especially fun was that once or twice she purposely 'missed my mouth' and hit me in the eye! We laughed and laughed.

Her method of discipline was easy going. Of course, with no one with whom to get into trouble, it wasn't always necessary. One tactic she used traumatized me somewhat. She told me that the grader man would come and get me if I wasn't nice. (The grader was the operator of the gravel-road maintainer for the county). Once when I was making mud-pies out under the shade tree on the roadside of her house, I heard the machine coming. Believe me, I ran to her in the house crying for her to not let him get me. I don't remember her ever using that threat again. But for several years, my heart skipped a beat at the sound of the grader.

She was also like a Guardian Angel. One summer when I was eleven or twelve, a neighbor's Shetland pony wandered up to our barn. Daddy saddled it and let me ride before dinner. As usual, Mama and Daddy took their nap, afterward. I laid down on my bed, but the saddled pony tied to the yard fence just wouldn't let me rest. I snuck out of the house in bare feet, got on, and started to ride. He clopped along past the barn and up to the gate next to Aunt Alice's fence. There he stopped— and no matter how I pulled on his reins, and kicked him, he would not turn around toward home. WELL, I knew I was in trouble with a Big T! I got off into the hot sand and grass-burrs, turned him towards home, got back on, and he immediately turned the opposite direction. After repeating this several times, I began to cry. Exasperation, burning feet, and knowing full well that Daddy would spank me when he learned of my having disobeyed, added to the intensity of wailing. Aunt Alice heard me, phoned our house, and told Mama that I needed help. Minutes later, the pickup appeared on top of the hill. But just as Mama and Daddy got to me, Aunt Alice arrived, almost running from her house. With much difficulty, she persuaded Daddy that I'd learned a lesson—and I had!

It was a blessing to have had her in my life until she reached the age of 101. My children learned to know and came to love her almost as much as I. They each have special memories of spending nights with her when we visited Mother and Daddy.

Work Was Scarce and Pay Was Low
By Charles Crawford of Bellville, Texas
Born 1929

Old timers are always saying let me tell you a story that goes way back. That's what I'm saying now as my thoughts go back quite a while ago. I'm thinking back to a time when a huge building project was proposed. This project was the dam at that time called, Hamilton Dam. There was a quite important reason for this construction, and that was the need for controlling floods that plagued the lands and citizens along the Colorado River. Losses of property and life devastated the area, and this was something that would help relieve the situation. This was happening back in the days of the Great Depression. A well known fact during that time; is that jobs and ways of making a living were, putting it mildly, were very scarce. The project did get approval and got under way with the need of workers and machinery to get it completed.

A lot of people, including my family, were searching desperately for jobs and when there was a word of jobs anywhere came known, they quickly headed to that place. My daddy heard that there was a dam being built in Burnet and Llano Counties, so here we went, packing up our modest belongings hoping to find a job there. Travel was done in our old Model-T, pulling a trailer with all that we owned. Male members of our family thought that some of our possessions were not needed, and space on the trailer was limited. We hustled up a raggedy old spare tire and made sure that we had tube patches, a jack and hand air pump. Those days, you couldn't travel a hundred miles without having a flat. We were living in Meadow, Texas that meant we had many miles to go, with me, and the two year old baby of the family to care for.

After a few days and a few flats, we did finally arrive at the job site. I think that because our faces and bodies gave the image of hard

workers, my daddy and two oldest brothers after standing in line for many hours, were hired. We got settled down in a tent community like most all of the other workers. Even at my age, I do remember, and can visualize in my mind just what our tents looked like. We had one tent as a kitchen and another was for living in. Both tents were made from ducking we purchased, coated with melted paraffin, and hand sewn to their final shape. After the tents were up, we went to a creek and hauled back some nice clean pea-gravel and put it on the ground for a floor in our living tent. The other tent floor remained dirt, but was covered with an old piece of linoleum. The tents must have been well made, because they survived some strong windstorms.

Our community was known as Little Chicago, more than likely getting that name because the contractor building the dam was from Chicago. Work on the dam was very hard and the hours long, but the job was indescribably appreciated. There was a small area near the tents where people could gather and socialize whenever time permitted. We took part in these gatherings and got to know most everyone. I especially remember a guy known as Jack of Diamonds who thought of himself as the most handsome, smooth man and irresistible to the women. He felt he was God's gift to women. He seemed to be very interested in my sister, but for reasons of her own, she found him to be resistible and someone she wanted nothing to do with.

Work on the dam progressed with much hard work being done by the workers. For reasons unknown to me, the work on the dam shut down before completion and jobs were lost. The contractor abandoned the project, leaving behind a lot of machinery and equipment. What now? The end to Little Chicago!

Our family left the sight, ending up in Burnet where we were again looking for work and facing difficult living conditions. Work found in desperation ranged from cutting cedar, picking cotton, clothes washing and ironing for people, helping farmers, and anything else that might come up. At my young age, even I was working at such things as delivering grocery store circulars all over town, mowing lawns for the more wealthy people, digging troublesome Bermuda grass from gardens of people who felt sorry for me, and picking a little cotton. Work was scarce and the pay was low.

Two of my brothers got in the Civilian Conservation Corps., which we called the Tree Army. This program was for young men without work and needed help. The men received vocational training and did work to better the communities. One group worked in opening Longhorn Caverns and developing this natural resource into a tourist attraction. No one had really seen what was in that cavern. One brother was in a camp at Pflugerville, where he learned to cook. I remember when he was discharged and came home with a huge butcher knife he used in his training. The other brother worked around Blanco, doing rock work building rock walls.

As time went on the dam project re-opened as the Buchanan Dam with an added benefit, generation of electricity. This is where the Lower Colorado River Authority became involved. Here we go again, and jobs were found. This time we had a single tent set up near the Blufton store, and about two miles from the schoolhouse to try to get a little education. I was a skinny, seven year old kid in the second grade and walked to school, and as you've heard before, it was uphill both ways. Didn't carry many books because they were limited and studying by a kerosene lamp at night was difficult. The school house was a two room wood frame building where about thirty students studied. A temporary ball field was set up near our tent and was used on Sunday's. I became very jealous of a friend of mine, who after a game found a baseball glove on the outfield. You see, in those days every player didn't have a glove, so gloves were left at positions as the innings changed and the players on the field came in to take their turn at bat. This same guy got into our tent one time and stole some fruit. Couldn't really hold this against him, after all he needed it as bad as we did.

We lived at this location until the dam was finished. My mother and I were visiting my aunt and grandmother in Ft. Worth when the lake began filling, and very suddenly my daddy and sister were required to evacuate, barely getting across the old bridge before it washed out. We were still occupying the tent where we had lived during the work time. My sister carried, in her lap, a treasured heirloom; a milk-glass bowl, using all ways of protecting it because of the special care she knew it had received for all the time we had it in our possession. The bowl remains in our family, and is proudly used with memories of the past in our minds at holiday dinners for serving the usual treat, ambrosia.

There are memorable years in my life and great experiences, which amaze me in wonder how we endured the hardships and survived to reach our current place in this life. Live has been good with blessings beyond all expectations. Thanks be to God.

An Age of Innocence That No Longer Exists
By Mary Sue Fields of Brady, Texas
Born 1937

I was born in my aunt's house in Fredonia, Texas, in Mason County in the heart of Texas Hill Country. Fredonia was a very small town with maybe, 150 people. It had about half a dozen stores and a country doctor who was present at my birth. They didn't have a scale to weigh me, but estimated my weight as about the same as a five pound bag of sugar.

My mother said I fit in her arm and hand from the tip of her fingers to her elbow, so I was probably about 18 inches long.

This doctor was a big believer in the healing benefits of castor oil. As I got older, every time I had been sick, he would tell my mother to give me a dose of castor oil to clean the 'impurities' out of my body. One day when he told her to do this, I kept telling her I wasn't going to take the castor oil and she couldn't make me. I don't know how many times I told her this with my hands on my hips and my chin stuck out. Finally, she told me that I didn't have to worry about it anymore. She had put in some pineapple juice and I never knew I had taken it. For years, I wouldn't drink pineapple juice because I was afraid she would spike it again with castor oil!

My earliest memories occurred in the second home in which I lived. I was 2 ½ years old when we moved from there. I remember going to the creek to bath because the house did not have an indoor bathroom. It also did not have running water. We had to cross a creek to get water from a well in a bucket and carry it back to the house. I remember one night when we got home after dark and there was a rattlesnake in our yard. My dad ran over it with the car until he killed it. Another thing I

Mary's mother with Mary and her little brother

remember, is, I would gather up my dolls and some books and load them in my little wagon and go to the gate to wait for the school bus. I couldn't wait to start school.

By the time I did start school we had moved to my dad's family ranch home place. It was in the Fredonia School District, but the bus came closer to our gate from the Voca School District, so my parents transferred me to Voca, about 15 miles from where I was born. Mother drove a neighbor boy, who was a senior at Brady High School, and me to meet the bus every morning and picked us up every afternoon. This boy rode his horse from his house every morning, a ride of probably 5 miles. The horse waited patiently for him to come back every afternoon. Voca had 3 school buses. Each one had a route to pick up kids and then the three buses met in downtown Voca. The high school students got on the bus to take them to Brady and then the other two busses took the rest to the Voca School. In the afternoon, we met in Voca again and the procedure was reversed. Everyone went into a little grocery store to buy a soda, some candy, or a snack. I heard some of the other kids say, "charge it." I began doing the same thing. Since we did most of our business in Fredonia, my dad did not go to Voca often. One day he did and the storeowner told him about my bill I had there. Daddy paid it and then asked me that night if I had been charging at the store in Voca. I told him I had, because everybody did it. He said that was O.K. He just wanted to make sure I was doing it.

One rainy morning we went down a dirt lane (appropriately named Lost Creek Lane) to pick up two students. By the time we got them and got back on the road, the creek we had crossed was flooded. We had to sit there on the bus nearly all day before it ran down enough so that the bus could safely cross it. My parents didn't have a phone, so they didn't know about it until I got home. Of course, the driver didn't have a cell phone and I am not

154

Mary Sue Fields in 1941

sure how they found out why that particular bus did not arrive at school.

We had grades 1-5 in one room, and grades 6-8 in another. Grades 9-12 went to Brady. Each grade sat in a different row. It was amazing what we learned when the teacher was working with another grade while we were supposed to be doing our grade level assignments. The school had a gym with a stage and the cafeteria was under the stage. There were no indoor bathrooms. No matter what kind of weather, we had to make the trek outdoors to use the bathroom.

My early school years were during WWII. I remember we were driving to church one Sunday morning and they announced on the radio that Japan had attacked Pearl Harbor and the United States had declared war on Japan. I had one uncle that fought in the Army in Europe and one that was in the Navy in the Pacific. I remember the rationing. We were allowed only so many pounds of sugar

in a certain period of time, so many gallons of gas, and you could not buy anything made with rubber such as tires. This was a hardship for people living in the country. It took us an hour to get from the ranch to the nearest town Brady, which was about a 25-mile trip. The trip was all on a dirt road, so we couldn't drive very fast, but it was hard on tires that couldn't be replaced and we had to use more gas than city people. I remember they had rationing books to get sugar and gas to keep up when you got it, and if it was time for you to get some more.

I had nightmares almost every night about the Germans coming to bomb us. Since we had no television, our news came from the radio or newsreels at the movies. Brady had a big pilot training base called Curtis Field. We used to go watch the airplanes take off and land. Brady also had a Prisoner of War Camp for German prisoners. I remember my parents talking to someone about a prisoner who had escaped. They found him hiding in a hayloft in someone's barn. We had a hayloft. So I was sure an escaped prisoner would end up in ours.

My aunt, whose husband was in the Navy, lived in downtown Voca during the war. She had two daughters, one two years older and one two years younger than me. We spent many nights together in either their house or mine. It was more interesting to stay with them, because my aunt was the switchboard operator for Voca and the surrounding area. If anyone wanted to call someone, it had to go through the switchboard and my aunt connected the wires so the two parties could talk. One could listen in on their conversations. My cousins and I would do just that if my aunt happened to be out of the house. We thought it was great fun to eavesdrop.

When we would go to Brady to do our "big shopping" on Saturdays, everyone coming in from the country would park their cars on the square around the courthouse. People would visit, shop, go to the movies, or kids would just run and play on the lawn around the courthouse. My mother always did something special with me and my brother. She would always buy a small jar of Kraft pimento cheese spread and a loaf of bread at the grocery store. We would then go to Richards Park that had playground equipment. After we ate our sandwiches, my mother would get a quilt out of the car; lie down and take a nap. My brother and I played until she woke up.

The war finally ended and we moved to Brady. From 1945-1955, when I graduated from high school, were truly happy days. As I grew up, I became interested in boys. When I was in the fourth grade, a boy asked me to meet him at the movie on Saturday afternoon and sit by him. That was considered a date. I asked my mother if I could and she told me, "Absolutely not!" I thought my life was ruined and I would never have a boyfriend. If I had just kept my mouth shut and sat by him, she never would have known the difference.

The elementary years were carefree and fun. We had cousins, neighborhood kids, and friends from school over all the time. You have to remember that we didn't have computers, television, I-phones, or electronic games. We had to entertain ourselves. Outdoors, we played Hide and Seek, Kick the Can, King of the Hill, Red Rover, Tag, Red Light/Green, Croquet, Roller-skated or rode our bikes. Outdoors, at night, we caught lightning bugs and put them in a jar to watch. Indoors, we played board games like checkers, Chinese checkers, Parcheesi, card games and Monopoly. We kept the Monopoly game set up and when we got tired of playing it, we would leave everything in place and come back later to finish the game.

My brother and I read a lot. One friend and I had every Nancy Drew mystery book written between the two of us. She and I used to sneak off the playground during recess and hide behind a building on campus and read

Mary Sue Fields as the Head Majorette in 1954

our Nancy Drew books until the bell rang to go back inside.

I met my first love when I was in the 8th grade at the Episcopal Church in Brady, which had Square Dancing for teenagers every Friday night. We also learned to do dances like 'Cotton-Eye-Joe', 'Put Your Little Foot', 'Schottische', etc. He was in the tenth grade, and I remember the day he got a brand new Ford and brought it over to take me for a ride. He was so proud of the car. He was a lot of fun, a great dancer, my first steady boyfriend and broke my heart when he broke up with me. It took me a long time to find my next and last true love to whom I have been married 55 years. We started dating my junior year in high school and got married while we were in college.

When we were in high school, Sock Hops became the 'in thing' to do. We had one after every home football game and every occasion

156

that we possibly could. I used to have a bunch of friends over to my house. We would push the furniture back against the wall and dance in our sock feet. My mother never minded. We had hardwood floors, and she always said that was an easy way to get the floors polished.

We had many activities in which we were involved. Most of my friends were in band or played football. I was a twirler for two years in junior high school and three in high school. A lot of time was spent practicing with my baton. I started my career as a church organist at age 13, when I was in the 8th grade and played until I graduated from high school.

In spite of the modern conveniences we grew up without, we learned to keep ourselves busy and entertained in wholesome activities. I think, as a result, we developed close relationships that have lasted a lifetime. We were privileged to grow up in an age of innocence that no longer exists.

Christmas Memories
By Elizabeth Sieckmann Ellebracht of
Fredericksburg, Texas
Born 1940

As a young girl growing up on a farm in the Texas Hill Country during and after World War II, my fondest memories were at Christmastime. My Dad and one of his brothers emigrated from Germany to the United States in 1926. Dad came to Texas to work on a ranch and his brother settled in Buffalo, New York. During World War II and later, Mom, Dad, friends and neighbors would gather items of coffee, sugar, candies, soap and other necessities and put together care packages to send to Dad's extended family in Germany. In later years as Germany regained their economic status, the uncles and aunts would in turn mail small parcels of chocolates, hankies, and custom jewelry for our enjoyment at Christmas time. It was truly a

joy for us to receive those parcels, letters, and pictures. We would gather around the warmth of the wood stove on Christmas Eve and Dad would read and translate the letters. And the pictures? Oh, what pleasure it gave us to put faces to the names of our relatives! For him to hear news from his family was always a time to reflect back to stories of life as he lived it during the good times and also the struggles they had as a large family. Dad never returned to his Homeland but his traditions and way of life as he knew it growing up in Germany will be part of our heritage for future generations.

Once again, as we await the coming of the Holiday Season, we are hopeful that the one special letter and pictures will again be in our home on Christmas Eve. "Keeping in Touch" with a family in a faraway country is priceless!

With the Christ Child as the center of our church functions, gatherings and celebrations, Christmas is still my favorite Holiday. The family continues to carry on with some of the same Christian based traditions that evolved from our parents and grandparents.

Spirit Lady of Rio Frio
By Kathy Whitney of Victoria, Texas
Born 1942

The story I'm about to tell you will be a true story, but some will think I have lost my mind.

Leakey is my second home. I have been coming to the hill country since I was one and half years old. I love the area very much. There were many good times growing up and spending time at Garner and swimming in the good old Frio River. Along with all the good times, I heard tales of a mysterious lady in white that haunted the Rio Frio area. Of course, I thought it was a great ghost story. Little did I know that one day we would meet.

157

It all started when I was very young. We were traveling up to the Frio for our vacation and just after we passed through Concan, a car traveling in front of us hit a pony. The pony did not survive.

To make a long story short, we were traveling up many years later. I was married and had three sons. My middle son was driving the car and my husband and I were in the back seat. We entered into a conversation about the pony being struck by a car many years earlier. We also told him and his friend about the "lady in white." We all chuckled about that particular part of the story. Little did the four of us know that a few hours later we would eat our words. We were just rounding a curve when the car in front of us struck a deer and kept on going. The deer was killed instantly. It happened in the same spot the pony had been killed at many years earlier. This was just the beginning for us that night. We arrived at my parent's house around nine that same night. Around 11 o'clock, my parents retired for the night. My two sons and their friend stayed outside talking.

Around 12:00 midnight, they came running into the house very excited and all talking at one time. They told me they saw something outside by our neighbor's house. I thought they were teasing me at first, but they seemed so sincere. I went outside and in front of the neighbors outside light, I saw an image of a slender lady dressed in a long flowing dress. She seemed to float a few inches above the ground. You could see through her. Four of us witnessed this. It made a believer of all of us. We have heard many stories about her from local people. Some of the locals just laugh about her and think I made it all up, while others agree. Believe me she does exist. Maybe someday in the future on a clear summer night off in the distance the mysterious lady in white will reappear once again.

Natures Heating and Air-conditioning
By Joan R. Cielencki of New Braunfels,
Texas
Born 1942

In the '40s and '50 out in the country, we did not have central heating and air conditioning in our house.
In the winter, our father would get up and start a fire in the wood heater. Once the house warmed up, the children would get up and dressed for school or other daily activities.

In the summertime, we would let all the windows and doors open through the day and night to let the breeze go through the house and cool it off. If it was too hot to sleep in the house at night, we would make cots on the front lawn and sleep on them until it got cooler.

Saturday Night Date
By Diana L. Johnson of Bertram, Texas
Born 1941

I had been dating my husband to be for only a short while when his friend, who lived in Bee Cave, asked us to go on a double date. We decided to go to the picture show in Austin. There was a good movie showing downtown at the Paramount theatre on Congress Avenue. It was a Saturday night and we planned on going.

Little did I know when they picked me up his friend was barefooted! I noticed it when we were walking into the theatre. Who ever heard of someone going barefoot to the theatre in 1960. You know I was a "city" girl and boy was I embarrassed. Knowing friends might be there and see us really made me nervous.

We made it through the night. Thinking back it really was pretty uneventful, but never again did we double date! Truthfully, I don't know how his date and he married. I suppose he wore shoes the next time!

The Art of Sewing
By Joy Jenkins of Wickes, Arkansas
Born 1933

I lived the first 30 years of my life around Medina. 20 about 3/4 mile out Stringtown Road. 10 near Medina My Dad built homes on our 3/4 acre of land as the family grew. The first a large tent and the second a cedar pole house. The Medina River was our only source of water until I was around 13 or so. It was carried in buckets and later hauled in a barrel.

In those days, Medina was a thriving little town. The businesses as you came from south to north on Highway 16 on the right side near town was a handbag company where they designed, assembled and decorated various styles of handbags including the wooden box bag. In town there was doctor's office, where the present post office is, a mechanic and welding with a service station and the next corner also had a service station. The phone office was a little house behind the service station on Stringtown Road. Across the road a drug store, little dress shop, a pool hall, barber shop, hardware store and out a way a lumber yard.

As you crossed the highway and out a little farther a little motel. Heading back south in town a grocery store next to a locker plant. The infamous Live Oak cafe, a grocery store with feed behind it. Next, the old Hatfield house, the post office, a sewing factory, and the box manufacturing business, that made the wooden boxes sold to the handbag company.

There were several well-attended churches as well as other business endeavors around the little town and not all at the same time due to fires .closings and transfers. I have bits and pieces of memories of all of the businesses, including the pool hall and of course, the school, but my special memory is my first official job.

I was 19 at the time. The sewing factory

Joy and baby Hazell held by Grandma Edwards in 1935

specialized in little girl dresses. There were several older ladies employed there so they didn't need a girl full time, however they did need someone to work at home on one of their contracts. Doll dresses. They needed someone to make dresses for the 16-inch dolls, to match the little girl dresses. Well I borrowed a treadle sewing machine and proceeded to make around 50 doll dresses. It was tedious work but it was a job. I don't remember how long it took or what I earned but I do remember that every time I made a mistake all of the older women pointed it out to me, but they also gave me sewing tips that I still use today, 60 years later.

Blue Willow Plate or Designer Crystal Glass
By Elizabeth Bettle of Lampasas, Texas
Born 1942

Joe Faught was a master florist who also dabbled in antiques. So, among the floral magic he wrought, in his shop sat very fine Roseville pottery, Tiffany silver, and Waterford crystal, to mention a few. All in all, it was a very auspicious collection for a small, country town in the middle of Texas.

As one of his floral designers, I coveted much of the inventory in the shop. There was only one problem—my pocketbook could not cover very many of the pricey wares.

A couple who had been stationed in Germany came into the flower shop to see whether or not Joe would be interested in buying some crystal glasses they had. The story on the glasses was thus: the couple had not selected a crystal pattern when they married. When they arrived in Germany, they soon discovered that the village where they were living was well known for its glassmaking. They thought it would be just the time to pick out crystal. They ended up with Herr Schlining. He worked with them to customize an original design for their glasses. The plan was for the couple to get one glass per month until their set was completed.

An exquisite design indeed! The glasses were nine-and-a-half inches tall. An elaborate cut pattern of pave' diamonds and petals was rendered vertically. The stem had an hourglass shape, larger at top and bottom and more slender in the middle and was hexagon shaped. There were tiny notches down each of the six sides of the stem. The design on the round base was a wreath of small, uniform petals that went around the middle part of the base. The highlight of the entire pattern was a three-fourths-of-an-inch wide gold leaf rim around the top of each glass.

The couple was delighted with their choice and looked forward to having a beautiful set of glasses to take with them when they returned to the States. But alas! All did not go well. Having made just five glasses, Herr Schlining died. The outright edict was that when a glassmaker died, all of his patterns were burned, never to be copied or reproduced again.

Since the couple only had five glasses, they came to the conclusion that they would rather have some money than keep the glasses.

Joe leaped at the chance and promptly decided he had rather have those glasses than the money it was going to cost him to acquire them.

Their arrival in the shop, with just the proper light reflecting off the magnificent crystal glasses, definitely caught my attention. They sat there for quite a long time, then one day I came in to work and the glasses were gone! Joe reported that someone had bought them.

A few weeks later, my husband presented me with a beautifully wrapped birthday gift. Excitedly, I opened it, and thought he had lost his mind. Greeting me was a Blue Willow plate. I have an absolute aversion to Blue Willow dishes, and I really did not want this one for my birthday. Neither did I want to hurt my husband's feelings. I carefully unwrapped that less-than-desirable blue plate and removed it from the box. YEA, YEA, and HOORAY! Under that plate were those five glasses! Joe knew I was not fond of blue dishes, especially Blue Willow, so he connived with my husband to slip it in on me as a joke.

The glasses have been used in various wedding and anniversary toasts and for other special occasions by people in our community. They are exceptionably pretty, but the neatest thing about them is that there are only five of them in the whole world, and they're mine!

Seale Family Adventures
By Bill E. Seale of Rock Springs, Texas
Born 1930

In 1935, I was five years old when my family moved from Rocksprings to Brackettville, Texas. My dad had leased a ranch in Kinney County. Our house was about 200 yards from the riverbank on the West prong of the Nueces River.

My sister, Nadine, and I were feeding 97 Sancho lambs and kids. It started raining and we put them on our screened front porch thinking they would be safe when the river came down. It rained 18 inches that night. About dark, Mom and Dad carried Nadine,

160

The 3 little pests

myself and Kathy (my 2 yr. old sister) about 200 yards to the barn. The water was waist high then. They took our horse and went to the top of the hill behind the barn. The house lifted off the foundation and a little after daylight and the screen door came open and all our Sanchos fell in to the water. That was the last time we saw them. Our house lodged in some trees about 400 yards down the river.

Dad's little Pontiac was in the shearing barn. When we returned the next day, our car was covered with silt. We could only see 2 to 3 inches of the top. Dad dug it out of the mud, changed the water, gas and oil. Mother drove it about 60 miles to Rocksprings. Dad and I drove his stock to Rocksprings and turned them over to the bank where he had borrowed the money to buy them.

A lady that lived about a mile down the river from us had two $100 bills. In 1935, a hundred dollar bill was like a thousand now. She had placed her money under the floor covering for safekeeping but had forgotten them when she left her home due to rising water. When she returned, her home was gone but she found the two $100 bills hanging on the fence that had been around the house, just like they were left there to dry.

Another neighbor living up the river from us had been to Uvalde, Texas and bought some new boots. He took the new boots off when he returned home. When he left the house, he wore his old boots but found his new boots side by side under a pecan tree about two miles down the river.

The Bet Gone Wrong

Another funny story—On one of the ranches where we lived, my Dad was feeding a hog to fatten and kill. My Mother used a five-gallon bucket to put table scraps, clabber, potato peeling, and everything else in. Our fence around the yard was about 3 ft. tall and every day when I went to the house to get the milk bucket to milk the cows, I jumped over the fence. Our neighbor's son was smitten on my sister, Nadine. This day my sister was looking out the window of our breakfast nook and the boy knew she was watching. He bet me that he could jump the fence with the five-gallon bucket. He picked up the five-gallon scrap bucket, backed up, and started to jump the fence but his toe hung in the fence, falling with his head in the scrap bucket. He was a little bald headed and he came up with potato peelings and clabbered milk all over his head. Nadine had to leave the window because she was laughing so hard.

A Quest for Water

By Jane Ann Myers McBee of Rochelle,
Texas
Born 1939

I was born in 1939, the year my family returned to McCulloch County from New Mexico where they had proved up a homestead and had qualified for eight adjoining sections of land. The lure of more land wasn't strong enough to keep my parents in a place where daddy felt it necessary to be armed as he went about his work. He wore a shoulder holster for his pistol, a 38-40 on a 44 frame and carried a 38-40 rifle. This he did for protection from the two-legged varmints who didn't like homesteaders. Four years was enough. They sold their homestead for two thousand dollars, twice the going rate and returned to McCulloch County to family and friends. They purchased land that joined my grandfather's property, which was located in the Deep Creek area. There was a house of sorts that provided shelter until the new house could be built in 1940.

Water was difficult to get and often in short supply. Back then if you lived in the country your water came from a well if you were fortunate enough to have one, from a cistern that caught water from the roof when it rained, water hauled in barrels from some neighbor or an earthen pond or tank. We had a dirt tank that supplied our water. The tank was built at the bottom of the hill south of our house. It was higher than our house so gravity brought the water into our house.

Now a tank built in the dirt to hold the rainwater that runs off the hill if and when it rains may not seem like a good thing, but it is better than no water. The cows, sheep, and goats also like a drink now and again so they would go to the nearest supply. My parents built a fence around the tank to keep the livestock out. They dug a hole by hand behind the tank dam to make a seep well. They packed it with sand and it served as a simple filter for the water for our house.

In New Mexico dad built a water tank with horses and a frezeno, in Texas he had a dozer come in and do the work. Several times, we had a well drilling rig come in and drill for water only to have the heartbreak of all that hard earned money poured into yet another dry hole.

I remember a hand dug well that was also a dry hole. I thought it was a scary thing to peer over the edge and look down to where daddy, mom, or my brother was working. Using a pick and shovel the person in the hole would loosen dirt and rock; load it into a five gallon bucket to be hand cranked to the surface. That bucket was suspended by ropes attached to a

crank supported by strong post on each side of the hole. Someone up top would turn the handle to bring the bucket to the surface. There it would be emptied out and sent back down to be filled again. One time before the hole got very deep I got into the bucket and was let down into the hole. I wasn't afraid then for I knew my daddy wouldn't let anything happen to me. I remember the wonderful fresh smell of the soil. That was quiet a ride for that skinny little girl. Later as the hole grew deeper and was somewhat dark I was terrified of falling in and would only crawl up to the edge to peek over with mom always cautioning me to not get too close.

I don't know how deep that hole finally was when finding no water it had to be filled in to prevent someone or some animal from falling into it and being killed or injured. All of this work was done by hand. It never entered my mind the danger of a cave in or gas seeping in to suffocate them not to mention the extreme hard work that was being done by my parents in a quest for better water for our family.

In the early 1970s, a well was drilled and finally water was found. Daddy died in 1977. A short time before his death he said to me, "I am so glad we finally got a good well, it will make life easier for your mother when she is alone".

Today we walk to the sink and without giving it any thought turn the handle and clean, hot, or cold water comes out. It was not always so easy.

In the Service of my Country
By Gerald R. White of New Braunfels, Texas
Born 1937

My U S Army experience began in 1959 when I was drafted. This two-year stay would be a life changing for me, as I was a young 21 year old out of a small town just outside of

Chicago.

After a day of induction, we were all placed on a train destined for Fort Leonard Wood in Missouri wherever that was. There, I would have my basic training and having endured a battery of tests, the Army probably felt because of my size, I would make a good Military Policeman.

I was sent then to another place in Georgia in the middle of nowhere called Fort Gordon for specialized training. After my training was complete, I had high hopes of being sent somewhere near my Illinois home. Instead, I was flown to a place I had never heard of named Fort Sam Houston. The name gave me the idea that I would be going to Houston, Texas. But instead, this fort was located in the middle of San Antonio, which I knew nothing about.

San Antonio turned out to be a lovely and warm city for which I was glad. My duty for the next two years was to be an honor guard at a place named the "Quadrangle".

The Quadrangle was a block square in size housing a park inside with deer and peacocks. Offices along the inside perimeter housed the offices of high-ranking Army officers. I would soon discover that the Quadrangle had a lot of history behind it. In the 1800s an Indian

Gerald R. White in 1959

named Geronimo had been captured and he and his small band of renegades were held inside and fed deer meat. Deer were kept there ever since as a reminder. The peacocks were a different story. I never did find out why they were there. But they would periodically fly out over the low roof and we would get calls that our birds were out. The birds knew they had a safe place and would fly back before dark.

In San Antonio, there were two breweries. There was the Pearl Brewery and the Lone Star Brewery. Being that it was in the fifties, soldiers did not get paid very much, and money always seemed to run out before the end of the month. So several of us soldiers would take turns driving to the breweries. We liked Lone Star because they would give out several free beers were as Pearl would only give out one.

Sunday evening meals were always cold cuts and bread. But a local cafeteria called Luby's then offered all you could eat on Sunday evening for only $1.00. We thought this was a good deal and they really lost money on us soldiers.

These are but a few of the memories of my two years in the service of my country.

Quadrangle main entrance

163

The Great Texas Hill Country Canoe Race of 1962
By Jim Runge of Eldorado, Texas
Born 1943

In the Texas Hill Country in the 1950s and 60s there wasn't as much for teenagers to do as there is in today's world, so they had to fend for themselves. One organization that did provide us with lots of activities was the Boy Scouts. We had weekly meetings, Camporees and summer camps, and the lucky ones got to go to National and World Jamborees, Canadian Canoe Trips and the Philmont Scout Ranch. In the meantime, we could always work on various merit badges, delving into subjects that we didn't have access to in school. Every once in a while, a special scouting event would come around that caught everyone's attention whenever it came to pass.

Jim Runge

Just such an event took place in the summer of 1962 when the Region 9 division of BSA sponsored a one hundred mile canoe race and invited all scouts in Texas to participate. The race was to take place in the middle of the Texas Hill Country, right down the Highland Lakes chain. That year, Austin began a gigantic ten-day event highlighting eighty-five different water related activities in the area, calling it the Austin Aqua Festival or Aqua Fest for short. The canoe race was the first event and when the racers crossed the finish line in Austin, a cannon would be fired that would signal the beginning of the festival. There was to be a beauty contest, diving contests, drag boat races, fishing contests, sailing regattas, swimming races, water ski competitions, an illuminated water parade, etc. Art Linkletter was the headliner for the spectacular this first year.

The response for the canoe race was overwhelming from scouts all around the Hill Country, plus some form other parts of Texas. There were teams entered from Abilene, Austin, Blanco, Boerne, Brady, Burnet, Dallas, Del Rio, Eldorado, Farmers Branch, Fort Worth, Fredericksburg, Georgetown, Houston, Irving, Johnson City, Junction, Kerrville, Llano, Marble Falls, Mason, Menard, New Braunfels, Rocksprings, San Angelo, San Antonio, San Marcos, Uvalde, Waco, and Wichita Falls. There were eight different teams competing from Austin alone. As there often was in Texas, a drought occurred in 1962 and the race had to be shortened to eighty-seven miles because the water levels in some of the lakes were way below normal, and parts of it were not navigable.

The teams gathered at Black Rock Park on Lake Buchanan on Sunday, July 29, for the beginning of the race the next day. Each team consisted of three scouts and the race would be run in five stages, with the scouts camping out each night of the race. Each day's races would be timed and recorded with the winner being determined by the shortest total elapsed time for the five days. Because of the large size of the lakes and length of stages, there were not many portages involved. Generally speaking, the racers would paddle to the designated bivouac each day where their time would be recorded.

The evenings were spent rehashing the day's activities, making excuses for not winning and planning for the next day's race.

On the first race day, Monday, July 30, the teams left Black Rock Park at 7:30 AM with a shot from a starter's pistol and they paddled across Lake Buchanan. The canoes were portaged by trucks over Buchanan Dam to Inks Lake because of low water, and the race resumed on that very small lake. The scouts had to carry their canoes over Inks Dam, entered the waters of Lake Granite Shoals, and finished the day in the city park of Kingsland. At each stop, the local chambers of commerce and civic clubs would provide meals and entertainment for the oarsmen and the scouts would get to mix and mingle with the other teams. Many lasting friendships were forged at these stopovers, despite the competiveness of the event. The Eldorado team ended the day with about a two-minute lead.

Early Tuesday morning, July 31, the teams lined up again, the gun was fired, and the clock was started for the day's race. This day's final destination was Marble Falls just above Wirtz Dam. Initially, the Eldorado team was leading for the day, but due to a miscalculation on a poorly planned portage by the Eldorado team, the Wichita Falls team won the days' leg, and the Eldorado team only led in elapsed time by seventeen seconds, with every team still in the hunt for the winner's trophy. The scouts spent Tuesday night in the Marble Falls City Park and prepared for the longest trek of the week down Lake Travis on Wednesday.

The canoes had been brought several miles downstream by truck due to the low water level on Lake Travis. Then when all canoes were lined up, the starter's pistol fired and if was off again for the paddlers. Wednesday's race was another close one, with Wichita Falls winning by twelve seconds, thereby leaving the Eldorado team with only a slim five-second lead in elapsed time. The Austin team was in third place. Wednesday night was special

for the group because they were offered the luxury of staying in the Lake Travis Lodges. All the young boys were thankful for getting to take their first shower in three days.

The teams left early Thursday morning and headed for Mansfield Dam, which backed up Lake Travis, the largest of the Highland Lakes chain. At the dam, the canoes were portaged around by truck and placed in the water flowing out from underneath the dam, which was frigid since it came from the very bottom of the lake next to the dam. The teams were now on Lake Austin and finished the day's leg at Austin City Park. Today's race belonged to Eldorado as they regained most of their earlier lead and interest in the race began to build, not only in West Texas, but statewide and from the AP as well. The reason for the media interest was primarily because a team from the arid flatland of the Edwards Plateau was leading the race. That area of West Texas had no lakes or rivers and conjecture dealt with how in the world they could ever learn how to paddle a canoe and/or practice.

Lots of visiting took place Thursday night at the Austin City Park because the boys had become better acquainted with each other and they realized this would be their last night together. Many phone numbers and addresses were exchanged before the night was over. Friday's race began from the city park and the teams raced to Tom Miller dam for the first leg of the day, The final leg of the day, and the race, was to begin at the base of Tom Miller Dam on Town Lake, but the start had to be delayed in order for the teams to reach Festival Beach at the designated time for the Aqua Fest to begin. This was the most difficult start of the entire week, because water was being released from the dam so the current was gushing out, as the canoes were busy trying to get in a straight line. The slew was not wide enough to accommodate all canoes in a row, as had been the custom on the previous four days, so it was a hectic situation while the boys jockeyed for position waiting for the starter's gun. Added to that was the fact that this last sprint was only four miles in length so a good start was critical, and all factors were pivotal.

When the time came and the starter fired the pistol for the final time, the Austin team seemed to shoot out ahead miraculously, ahead of the Eldorado and Wichita Falls teams. At the same time, Tex Wright, who was the headman from the Aqua Fest in charge of the canoe race, was on the bank hollering to all the teams that there was to be an additional trophy for this sprint portion of the race.

This had not been announced previously. The other teams finally figured out that the Austin team knew where the fast current was emanating from the dam water release. Of course, the other teams got into the fast current as quickly as possible and it was a race to the finish. The Eldorado team ended up barely winning this final dash, and hence the overall race with a total elapsed time of fourteen hours, twenty-four minutes and 26 seconds. This was only four minutes and six seconds ahead of the second place team from Wichita Falls. The winning team averaged traveling at approximately six miles per hour. The Austin team finished third.

There was a huge crowd and celebration at Festival Park on Town Lake, and Cactus Pryor, who was emcee for the event, asked the Eldorado boys how a team from arid West Texas could win the race. They jokingly replied that they had practiced in the Schleicher County cotton fields and when they got in water, it was smooth sailing.

Today's readers may not recognize the names of some of the lakes and dams as they have been changed over the past fifty years. During the course of the race, some teams had to drop out as some of the paddlers had become ill from the scorching heat. Still other teams had to drop out because of an unusual malady. In 1962, the general population was just learning about fire ants and most of the boys were not aware of the danger of multiple bites, etc. Either during the time the canoes were in camp, or during portages or whenever the canoes got too close to the shorelines, these ants got into some of the canoes and bit the scouts. Several teams had to drop out of the race due to these multiple ant bites.

After arriving in Austin, some of the teams entered other water related events, but usually did not fare as well. The winning Eldorado team was feted at most of the other events. At one point, organizers asked the team if they had their tuxedos with them! This took the team by surprise until the organizers explained that they wanted the boys to be escorts for the beauty pageant! Unfortunately, the boys not only had not brought their tuxedos, most didn't even own a tuxedo! Some of the team members did spend several days in the Austin area afterward, camping out and taking in some of the functions and sights of the big city.

The 1962 canoe race was so much fun, that word got around and nearly one hundred teams entered in 1963. Even today, participants often see some of their fellow racers in various parts of the state in the most unexpected places and get to reminisce about the summer canoe race of 1962.

Thirty years later, one of the winning team members was at a function in a man's retreat in Abilene and noticed an Old Town Canoe hanging from the rafters. He was looking at it intently when the owner said, "I've always wanted a canoe like that because I once was in a canoe race down the Highland Lakes and the winning team had a canoe like that. The other man said, "I was in that canoe." The two had been friends for quite a while, but until then did not know about both being in the race together.

Forty years later the captain of the winning team was at a coffee table in a cafe in Eldorado, telling about the race. A nearby local coffee drinker member was listening and seemed to have a quizzical look on his face and the man said, "You don't believe me, do you?" The other man answered, "Yes, I do, because I too, was in that race!" He had been on the Llano team and they, too, did not know each other had been in the race until that point.

The Austin Aqua Festival continued until 1998, but was a victim of its own success, drawing 252,000 people, but the noise, traffic and parking issues overwhelmed the city, and protests shut the event down.

Daniel Woodson with two Vietnamese comrades in 1967

"The Whole Time," I had an Angel by my Side
By Daniel Woodson, Jr. of New Braunfels, Texas
Born 1948

I came out of Three Rivers Texas with my Father, Mother, and three Sisters and not to mention, we were the only Black Family living there.

My Sisters had to go to school an hour away from home because there were no schools for Blacks. My Father was a ranch hand and My Mother a housekeeper I was too young to go to school so I was shuffled between their jobs.

Eventually we moved to Pleasanton Texas, it wasn't long before Pleasanton became the first South Texas School to integrate, this just was one more unpleasant thing I did not care about Pleasanton. Back then, Blacks had to go to the back door of restaurants and clothing stores only allowed Blacks to buy flawed clothing.

I could not wait to turn eighteen and volunteer the draft I left Pleasanton so fast I didn't even tell my Mother. Fort Polk Louisiana, boot camp, We had six weeks of training from there to Washington State, more

training to ready us for QuiNhan Vietnam.

No soon as the wheels hit the runway, we were filling the gaps for the wounded or deceased. Bombs coming from everywhere, I thought this could not get any worse, but before those words settled in my head, there came Placoo. We camped among the Mountain Yards (Indians) these people were considered neutral, not for us nor the Vietnamese.

We slept during the day and patrolled at night, I must have kept myself numb, because fear did not set in, and survival was based on if I wanted to go home, the way I got here or in a body bag.

Here I was twenty years old, had all my

Daniel on Hailburton Platform in West Africa in 1980

167

limbs still attached seen a lot and done things not proud to mention, but yet I had considered myself lucky, going home, so long Vietnam and all its ugliness it brought.

Washington State, here I come but upon arrival, there was no Hero's welcome. Our very own people (Americans) were calling us baby killers, spitting at us, those cold words were the last thing I added to my already unsettled heart.

I got on that Greyhound bus, told the bus driver I was headed home, every stop that bus made I got off and drank a beer with the hope to numb myself one more time.

When I arrived in San Antonio, Texas, I was drunk the bus driver took pity on me and offered me a ride to the Continental Bus Station to switch buses, there he told that bus driver to make sure I got off in Pleasanton, Texas.

It was about 4:00am, I got off the bus threw my duffle bag over my shoulder and started walking. As I was crossing the Atacosa Bridge, my Uncle Henry recognized me and offered me a ride home. My Folks were still sleeping, so I pulled up a chair and went to sleep on the porch.

Seem like things never change, jobs were hard to get, especially for the ones, just back from the war. They felt we were unstable. Finally, Halliburton gave me a break. I spent twenty something years with them mostly overseas all of Europe and West Africa.

There was one moment in Mauritania, Africa that brought back a piece of Vietnam. They were having a coup (war) all Americans were ordered to evacuate, I was the only one from the company still at the hotel, as soon as everything quiet down, I got in my truck nonstop to the airport, seeing the plane had not left, my heart stopped racing, again I made it.

I've had a full life, retired from Halliburton, and opened a Gym for five years. Took on other jobs retired from those also. Now I'm enjoying each day with my wife Barbara Jean, but every now and then I can't help but tell myself I should have known, "The Whole Time," I had an Angel by my side.

Daniel Woodson in 2012

"Good Old Days" In the Texas Hill Country
By Paul Kane of Kerrville, Texas
Born 1951

I was born in Kerr County 1951, and been here over sixty years. Actually, I am the fifth generation from the Hill Country; both parents and both grandparents on both sides were here in the Hill Country and the cemeteries in Mountain Home, Harper, Ingram, Hunt, Comfort, and Kerrville are filled with over 5 generations of family. My great grandpa and great grandma were the first two people to have been married in Hunt Texas. I grew up on a ranch in Mountain Home Texas where my grandpa, (at the age of 9) planted apple trees and at one time in the 1950s was recorded as the largest apple orchard in the state of Texas.

In Rock Springs, a small town about fifty

miles from Kerrville is a hole in the ground called the Devil's Sinkhole and is a humongous cave at the bottom and hundreds of feet to the bottom. Back in the fifties, my dad G.W. had a wrench truck, which he used, a fifty-gallon barrel tied to a cable and would lower people in cave explorations down in this hole. Most people when arriving back to the top would be crying and some even kissed the ground and praise God for getting them out alive. Today, it is owned by the Texas Parks and Wildlife, and groups can go watch the bats come out in the evenings, but no longer, people can be lowered down into this magnificent cave.

The most memorial times of my youth was playing and swimming in one of the three lakes in front of our home. I remember only having an outhouse for using the restroom, as well as taking a bath in a large tub with water heated up from the wood burning stove in the kitchen. I still remember getting my hand caught in the ringer of my mom's washer when I was about 7 or 8 years old. In the days when there were no such thing as computers, video games, or cell phones, I remember playing cowboys and Indians with my younger brothers and sister and back then germs not meaning anything to us, we would pick up soft cow patties and splatter one another and of course our mom would make us go jump into the lake before we could come into the house. We weren't allowed to use the telephone for pleasure and when it was used; sometimes we would have to wait a spell because of the phone being on a party line. That's where neighbors were using the same line.

By the late '50s, we got ourselves a black and white television and were able to watch things like Lassie, Sky King, and Old Yeller. My dad had a reel-to-reel recorder which we kids were not to ever touch, but sure were impressed with recording voices and music on it. We had our tinker toys and learned to shoot a 22 riffle and got to go into town on Saturdays to do some grocery shopping in

our Studebaker. I remember once my dad was waiting for us to all get ready to go to the Drive-In movie so he was quick drawing with his 22 pistol and it went off before he cleared the holster and shot himself in the leg. Needless to say, we didn't make it to the movies that evening.

About 1964, our mom and dad went through a divorce and we moved to Kerrville. The city sure wasn't ready for this. Of course, we had to find homes for some of our animals. And we were a little on the wild side, the Police Dept. come to know us pretty well. At one time, my mom had to find another home for her potbelly pig. We lived right across from the playground of Tivy Elementary School and this Horney little pig with his basketball in the front yard just wasn't appropriate for sex education.

Some folks didn't see a lot of humor in being woke up by their doorbell only to find a sack on fire at their front door, especially when they realized it was full of crap, real crap!

Well, we made through the days of the hippy movement, smoking our weed, and all night partying, join the U.S Marine Corp for 4 years, came back to Kerrville and have had the Swap Shop now for over 25 years, with five wonderful children, a wonderful wife, and hold a bible study here in the Swap Shop weekly. Serving and learning the nature of our Heavenly Father is the most important aspect of my life.

Memories
By Olivia Valderaz Herrera of San Antonio, Texas
Born 1944

Some of the events that occurred during my life in Comfort, TX I was born in 1944.

My grandma, Maviana Valderaz was a midwife; she delivered four of us and other

Olivia Valderaz Herrera in 1947

births in the neighborhood. We were a family of seven children the younger three were born in Fredericksburg TX clinic, I guess grandma retired by then. To pay for the hospital bill my dad raised hogs and took them to market for extra money.

My parents, Simon Jr. and Felicia Valderaz had a monthly charge account at the grocery store. Also raised chickens, on occasion ate fish, rabbit and squirrel. I don't believe I could eat the rabbit and squirrel today.

My dad drove a Model A Ford, which needed a crank or two to get it going. It had a unique fun horn.

A photographer came to the door one day and I had my picture taken barefoot sitting on a black box wearing a dress my mom made from a couple of flour sacks. I was about 3yrs old.

Spent most of my time outside didn't have anyone to play with I created my own imaginary friends made mud pies played with roly-poly, caterpillars, light bugs that are no longer seen.

Dolls were fragile head, arms, legs were made of claylike material that was breakable it didn't last long. Paper dolls were popular.

Kites were fun to put together, made our own paste out of flour and water, cut newspaper to a triangle shape, couple of lightweight sticks and pieces of cloth tied together for its tail. It was successful when it would go up so high it could hardly be seen.

First grade was an experience of harsh discipline. A ruler was used to hit the palm of the hand, shaking of the shoulders, pulling an ear. It didn't happen to everyone but to the unruly. I guess we were the best-behaved group in the county. The older student was paddled with a board that could be heard throughout the building.

Majority of students were of German decent and could speak fluently, today's majority are Hispanics.

We had a soda machine at school the price was a nickel before the price kept climbing.

Walked to school most days, which was a thirty minute walk each way. Comfort celebrated 100 yrs. in 1954 with a parade.

By age 12, I had babysitting jobs, cleaning house on Saturday morning, later on restaurants. Today kids work when they are much older or not at all while in school.

Monday was usually wash day. My mom would make a fire and set a steel washtub with water to get it hot and carry it by the bucket full to the wringer washer and get it going. A

Olivia behind the soda fountain counter in 1964

170

scrub board was used for extra soiled clothes. It would be a full day's work since clothes needed to be hung out on the line and brought in after drying.

We had a wood stove for heating the home and cooking.

Before television, we would listen to stories on the radio and let our imagination do the rest. Country music was popular at our house.

Our entertainment was the comfort theater, a movie and news reel on the weekends. The area towns had the drive inn theater with a special price for a carload on Wednesday.

The first phone I used was a wooden wall phone with a handle to crank to reach the operator.

Family time was spent at my grandmas home, meals, and watermelon parties.

The evening before Thanksgiving my mom would start preparing her cornbread dressing made from scratch. The next morning she be up like 4am to stuff the turkey put in the oven and it would be ready by noon. Took it for granted back then, I still can't get that dressing right.

Christmas was my favorite holiday my dad go out and cut down a cedar tree, not many presents, but the excitement and the warmth of the holiday was home. Christmas is too commercial today.

Spent time at the STEVE dam, don't know if it still exists. Fishing, picnics, our favorite time was in the evening listening to the water running over the dam and the noise of the critters.

Worked for Krum's drugstore for 3 years '63-66. It was a good learning experience. The cash register was antique, keying to the nearest dollar amount on the sale. I had to voice back the change to the customer; today people working the register may not know about giving out change verbally if they had too. I have a picture of myself behind the soda fountain.

Left comfort in 1967 returned for visits and witness the growth of the population and down town turn into an antique tourist attraction.

Our senior class were 20+ students. Today that number has tripled. Our graduating class of 1963 will be celebrating 50 yr. reunion at the Comfort Meet Market April 20, 2013.

The Coming and Goings of Ranch Life
By Vickie J. Williams of Eldorado, Texas
Born 1951

I can remember as a child going to my great uncle's, Cleve T. Jones of Sutton County, ranch in the summer to prepare horses for sale. My daddy, Jack W. Jones of Schleicher County, and my older brother, Jim Kirk Jones, and Johnny Mayo and I would get up before daylight to be in Sonora by daylight to work on horses preparing them for sale. My daddy would ride and break horses in a round pen all day. My brother, Johnny, and I would gather horses to trim, groom, and brush them one by one. We worked on many horses for several days. At lunch each day, Aunt Jack,

Vickie's mother, Billie B. Jones, Vickie, Kirk, Roy,
and her grandmother, Blance "Bangi" Barney

Vickie's father, Jack Jones with Roy, Vickie, and Kirk in 1957

Uncle Cleve's wife, would feed all of us with huge meals and always homemade bread and butter. It was a feast for everyone who came and helped out. It was a family deal!

We did that same thing for my uncle, Jess Koy of Schleicher County. He bred and sold quarter horses and was very well known in the cutting horse world. I can remember traveling to Ft. Worth when the Green Oaks Motel was brand new to sell his horses at an auction. Some of them were barely green broke. Jess could not say his "r's." He told my daddy to let that little girl, me, ride them in the ring because the "hauses" would bring more if people thought a little kid could ride them. I was about 6-7 years old.

As a child, Foremost milk out of San Angelo would deliver dairy products to homes in Eldorado on Tuesdays and Saturdays. Our milk delivery man was Elmer Garlitz. He would knock and then come in your home straight to the refrigerator to restock supplies that you used-milk, butter, etc. He knew exactly what each family on his route used weekly. On special occasions, our mom would let Elmer get us some fudge cycles for treats. One Saturday Elmer was running very late. It

was lunch time and we were all at the table eating our lunch when he got to our home. When he came in my daddy said, "Elmer, you might as well sit and eat with us since it is lunchtime." And so he just came on over to the table and sat down to eat with us; then he proceeded on with his route deliveries!

Footnote: Later Elmer Garlitz moved his entire family to Eldorado.

Before our church, First Presbyterian Church of Eldorado, got air conditioning, our windows would all be open in the summer. We would sit during church service watching wasps flying around. And when one would land in someone's hair or on their shoulder, etc., someone else would shoo them away or swat them.

Our favorite swimming hole was the big cement stock tank at the ranch house of my grandfather. It had old huge live oak trees around it. We always threw inner tubes into the tank and would climb up in the live oak trees to swing out on ropes into the tank to try to land on an inner tubes .There would be so many cousins there in the tank it was a wonder no one was landed on.

I remember watching at the drive in theater Disney's "Old Yeller." We all cried then fell asleep in the back of our station wagon.

During cotton season, the cotton gin would have a very large pile of the cotton seeds. As a teenager, my friends and I would always go play in the cotton seeds. We would crawl/walk up to the top of the pile and then just roll down the pile-sometimes knocking down someone who was trying to get back to the top. As we got older, we would dig holes up at the top to hide in when the local sheriff's department would drive by and shine spotlights up in the cotton seeds. They would holler, "You kids get out of the cotton seeds!" We would remain hidden and quite until they gave up and drove away. Then we would giggle and roll down again.

I always had a critter of some kind that I

would take in to raise. Raccoons, ring tails, rabbits, possums, red fox, garden snakes; you name it! At that time, our local pharmacist would vaccinate our dogs for rabies. I would carry my pet raccoons into the back of the drug store for our pharmacist to give each one their rabies shot. Each time, Eldon Calk would say, "Don't let that thing bite me!" One of daddy's friends always called me "Ellie May" from the Beverly Hillbilly's because of all of my pets. Everyone knew I could keep any orphan varmint alive. I had a baby cotton tail rabbit that I kept in my dresser drawer until my mother found it. I had taught it to stand on its hind legs to eat blades of fresh grass. One summer I had two raccoon babies, a brother, and a sister. They each had little collars with bells on them. I left them in the yard for a couple of hours one afternoon and had trouble finding them. Daddy came out to help me. He thought they were gone for sure but he went around one side of the house and I went around the other. Both of us were calling them by name, just like you would call your dog! Pretty soon, here they came from across the way just running to me. Daddy said he didn't think he had ever seen anything like that before. They all loved to crawl into half of a watermelon to eat it!

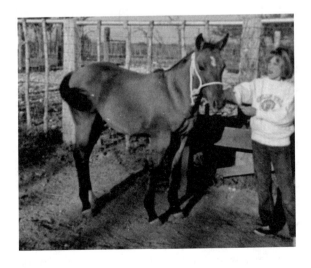

Vickie Jones with a colt named, Poco J. Chico

In the summer, all the kids in the neighborhood would play "Kick the can" and we would run and hide til we could come in to kick the can safely. Sometime we would play til very late and forget where clotheslines were in neighbor's yards. Someone was always getting the breath knocked out of them by running into a clothes line.

I don't ever remember going to the doctor for injuries. My grandmother, Blanche just sewed us up with a half-moon needle. She never deadened the area. But I don't ever remember it hurting either. One day my two brothers and I were playing army in our neighbor's vacant lot, digging holes like trenches to hide in. My younger brother threw a dirt clod at my older brother that hit him above the eye and it started bleeding. Kirk went running in the house crying with his hand over his eye bleeding telling them what Roy had done. I just kept digging with my hoe. Mama was having trouble finding out just exactly what happened so she hollered at me to come in. I had been digging a long time before she called me and my trench was really deep and big. When I was trying to climb out of my deep hole, I just pushed the hoe back but it came back down hitting me in the top of the head. And so I went running in to the house crying and with blood spurting out of the top of my head. My older brother was sitting on the commode with my grandmother sewing up his head above his eye. I was told to sit on the side of the bathtub because I was next at being stitched up. And my little brother was in a lot of trouble in his room for throwing dirt clods at anybody.

The Fort
By Larry Edwin Mayfield of San Antonio, Texas
Born 1954

Every young boy has or should have had a fort. A place of privacy, where many secrets

173

are shared. Many a battle plan contrived and defense strategies discussed and implemented. Just such a place existed for me, my brothers, and cousins. This was not your ordinary city lot fort, but a fort on the mighty Medina River. We of course constructed this imputable fortress off the beaten path of any unwary or occasional wandering fisherman or town kid. This was a place tucked against an old cypress tree off of an ancient feeder creek that we were sure no civilized man had ever laid eyes on. Forts, as every kid knows can be either a U.S. Calvary fort posted in hostile Indian Territory for reasons of eliminating, or it can in the instant required, become an Indian camp where raiding parties organized to attack and steal back from the white man what has been stolen from them. Now, we had our BB guns and our Popguns for raiding or defending but we needed something with a little more realistic battle sound. BB guns, popguns, and slingshots don't make the required battle sounds we learned about from all the westerns we had watched.

We couldn't afford nor were allowed to have firecrackers so we had to come up with a plan to make the earth shaking explosions we fell in love with from the T. V. I told the boys that I knew where Grandpa kept some 22 shells and I knew that dad had some shot gun shells in the closet at home. The plan as discussed and voted on as to how to obtain this much needed commodity for continuing our campaign against the settlers or the Indians as we saw fit. I, once again because of my wild and daring nature, was given the task of commandeering the coveted ordinance. The 22 shells were no problem. Grandpa had a box on a dusty old shelf in the wash house that hadn't been touched in years. He would never miss them (or so I thought) because I wasn't even sure, he had a rifle to put them in. At least, I had never seen one. Dad's shotgun shells were going to be tricky. You see, the closet where he kept them was across the hall

from his and mom's bedroom and the risk of trying to get to them while mom and dad were asleep made the visions of beatings and torture come alive in my mind if I got caught. I had to get them before Saturday morning because we were going back to grandma and grandpa's like we did almost every weekend during the summer.

David and I came up with a "Fail Proof" plan that would require a manly sacrifice, namely a whipping! You see the plan was for David to tease little brother Sammy, when Sammy started crying to the point Momma couldn't stand it anymore, (especially since it was interrupting her stories). This was to take place in the backyard thus, leaving me alone in the house to make the heist. David's screams caused by the switching was my cue to grab the ammo and hide it in our dresser. Success was ours and visions of exploding artillery around our fort were just a day away.

The cousins and the brothers met as planned that Saturday morning to create what we knew would be the "History in the making." I had a box full of 22 shells and about half a box of 12 gauge shot gun shells. Now came the problem of how to make these things go off. I had a good idea about how to make the shotgun shells go off, that was easy. I took my little pocket knife and opened the end of the shell and poured all the bb's out. The good Lord must have given me that idea because it was only slightly safer for the next step in my engineering plan. I then placed the now safer shell on the end of my bb gun, pointing straight up in the air when I pulled the trigger. The BB hit the primer and the shell went off making the sweetest of sounds. We had our explosion and smoke and a way of defending our beloved fort from all comers. Now, what to do with the 22 shells? We couldn't take the bullet off to get to the powder without a pair of pliers. We sat around our fire contemplating the situation and then it happened. The problem of how to explode these little bullets was solved. My brother David, not the brightest crayon in the box threw the whole box of fifty bullets into the fire.

Our next course of action wasn't planned but plainly, our tribal knowledge or maybe just instinct but, everyone immediately yelled RUN! And run we did. We ran, we dove for cover and we hid behind trees. But mostly we yelled our brand new war cry, which was, "David, you idiot your gonna kill us all". The shells exploded and zinging bullets went everywhere for what seemed like a very long time when things calmed down.

Everyone was afraid to approach the fire because there was no way to count the little explosions to make sure all fifty had gone off. Naturally, I was the first to reach the fire. Crawling on my belly, I was soon close enough to the burning coals to poke around and make sure there were no live rounds left. I didn't see anything suspicious so, I stood up to give the all clear when

The Mayfield Boys
Larry, David, Oscar, Bill, and Sammy

I heard a pop and felt a sharp sting on my belly. "I've been shot," I yelled. Brothers and cousins came running to me to probably watch me die and thinking about their whippins they would get for killing me. When I pulled up my shirt to see my exposed guts all that was there was a small red whelp where the casing from the bullet had hit me. Everyone pretty much agreed how cool this was, and they were all grateful I wasn't dead. Even though having a dead soldier or Indian in the fort would really have been cool.

Now, anyone would think by now that this is a happy ending to a story that could have

been a disaster for all of us brainless young boys. But, no, there's more. Completely out of ammo, we still craved explosions and smoke and here is where the genius of my cousin Oscar comes to play. He remembered that when Uncle Brice would burn trash in the backyard burn barrel now and then, sometimes an aerosol can would accidentally get in the barrel and make a beautiful explosion that sent ashes and smoke billowing into the sky! YEA! That's it everyone agreed. So, off we went looking for spent cans. There were a lot of burning barrels in town, and folks would always set their aerosol cans to the side to carry off to the dump. No one liked to blow up their burn barrels. We snuck around town and collected 30 or 40 cans. Some of them still had some of their contents and this made for an even more violent explosion! Armed with our bombs we made our way back to our fort and built a huge fire. We decided to place five cans in the fire at a time and hide behind whatever cover was available, logs, trees, bushes and my favorite a ditch that provided the type of cover I needed. I still had a nasty whelp on my belly and didn't need another war wound that day. The cans in the fire and us under cover the explosions began the—BIG, BEAUTIFUL EXPLOSIONS! Explosions that sent smoke and fire vibrating through the woods. We were in "Little boy fort heaven" what stories we would have to tell to our buddies at school. How jealous they would be when we told them how our plan had worked and how we never got caught! Lovely, Glorious, little boy thoughts that came to a screeching halt when "IT" happened. And it always happens, that one little incident that can turn the perfect adventure into a Malay of whippins, lectures, shame, and admonishment. My brother David, the same idiot that threw the bullets into the fire decided to climb a tree just above the fire to watch the exploding cans. This is where, I now know, that little boy's luck always runs out so they can and will get caught. David caught a piece of shrapnel in the forehead from one of the exploding cans and gave out a cry of pain and fear that made the rest of us want to run away from home, so as not to have to attend his funeral. Of course, even small head wounds produce lots of blood so everyone was scared.

I don't remember too much of what happened after that. I am sure a shrink would say that "I have blocked a horrible memory of beatings and torture out of my mind" But I do remember that "Fort Mayfield" was dismantled and to return to it was strictly forbidden by parental government. But, with any great battlefields such as the Little Big Horn, Gettysburg, or Valley Forge, history was made and recorded and remembered. Time cannot change that. Thanks for the memories boys. Love you all and am glad no one was killed!

The Best Christmas Present I Ever Had
By Leona McDaniel of Burnet, Texas
Born 1932

Early in the morning of December 24, 1945, my oldest brother, Stanton, called his wife Louise to meet him at Fort Sam Houston in San Antonio. He was coming home. He had been in New Guinea and the Philippines in the Pacific.

While they were gone, my daddy and I went to my aunt's in Lake Victor to get a turkey for Christmas dinner, and while we were gone, my other brother Charlie called his wife Mildred from Waco to meet him in Georgetown at the train station. He had been serving in England for almost three years.

We didn't know where they were, as we had not heard from them in about 2 months or longer.

We didn't have Christmas that night of the 24th as the brothers wanted to get presents of their own and everyone was so happy to have them home. They both came home the same day. It was the best Christmas present I ever had. What a day. This is a true story of 1945.

Back in the 1940s, everything was tight. We didn't have money for so many things. My daddy would take the car battery and hook it up to the radio in the house so he could hear the news about the war every day.

Making Mother's Famous Cook Cheese
By Gertrude J. Klein of Fredericksburg,
Texas
Born 1935

When I was a child, my parents and I lived on the outskirts of town, practically in the country. This is now definitely no longer in the country. My parents had a milk cow, and chickens, which meant milk, cream, butter, cheese, eggs, and homemade bread. Even though this has been many years ago, some people still remember coming to my mother's house to buy cheese, butter, and cream. She had quite a number of customers!

When the milk was brought in, my mother would pour it into large bowls to cool. As it cooled, the cream rose to the top and she would skim the cream off and keep it cold. The cream was sold and the remainder soured and then was churned into butter. The fluid that separated from the butter was buttermilk. My father liked to drink buttermilk and sometimes my mother made buttermilk pie!

A cream separator

The skimmed milk was let to turn sour and turn into clabber. She would then put it into a cloth bag and hang it so the whey (fluid) would drip out. What was left was cottage cheese. Some people liked it that way with sweet cream on top.

She also made cook cheese (Koch Kase). She would press the bag of cottage cheese between two boards until all the whey or fluid had been squeezed out. She would then crumple the dried cheese, add salt and soda, and set it in a warm place to age. After several days, it turned yellow and had a strong, distinct smell to it. (My children did not like that smell!) She would then cook it over low heat slowly, adding butter and salt as necessary. The result is cook cheese, which is delicious and does not smell at all like it does during the aging process. Another name for this cheese was "Krimmel Kase" because of the crumbling of the dried cheese.

After a number of years, my parents bought a cream separator. This machine, as if by magic, was able to separate the cream from the warm, fresh milk. This separator had a crank, which you turned at a certain speed to regulate the correct balance of heavy cream and milk. This really shortened the whole process and helped a whole lot. Some of my children remember enjoying watching the cream and milk come out of the different spouts.

This happened in the late 1930s until the early 1960s. I really miss the taste of the warm cook cheese on homemade bread.

Snakes in the Yard, Snakes in the Bathtub
By Barbara Touchstone of New Braunfels, Texas
Born 1941

After reading your list of subjects on Texas Hill Country memories, several rushed through my mind. The most significant revolves around my summers when I was about 5 or 6. My grandmother used to take me and my 4 girl cousins to Waring, Texas, for the summer. She rented an old house near the abandoned mansion in the center of town. The house did not have a bathroom so we used an outhouse and as children do, I waited too long to go use it. So as I ran along the path to the outhouse, I stepped on a black fuzzy caterpillar that stung me and as you can guess, I no longer needed the outhouse...

Grandma sewed our clothes from flowered feed sacks so the 5 of us were always dressed alike. The older 3 girls made fairy clothes from the scraps and left them at the base of a big tree. Early in the morning, my other cousin (we were the youngest) and I would rush to the tree to see if the fairies had picked up their wardrobe.

If we were good all week, Grandma would walk us down to the river to swim. She made the older girls wear swimsuits, but since we were so young we could swim in our underpants.

I do not remember having any toys but my young cousin and I used to build a house for ourselves by lining out the rooms with rocks. Then we could play house. We did have rag dolls that Grandma made for us.

On Saturday night, we got a bath in a big tub in the kitchen. And, of course, being the youngest, we were the last ones to use the water in the tub. Ugh!

As time progressed and I grew older and found boys, other memories prevail, including a party line telephone that we shared with a neighbor two doors down. I was always afraid that she listened in when my boyfriend called. My first kiss was at an 8th grade graduation party in the casa at the Arneson River Theater in San Antonio, Texas.

Marriage and children led to more memories: telling my 12 year old son to go out and mow the grass when I had just encountered a garden snake, and finding another garden snake in my bathtub after everyone had gone to school or work. Did I mention that we were living in the country? City people don't know what they are missing! Trying to turn off the water to my kitchen sink without success and asking the milkman to help me (my hero!).

These are just a few of the memories that I treasure. I hope that others find them interesting and/or amusing.

The Best Use for a Tub with No Bottom
By Charles H. Bierschwale of Kerrville, Texas
Born 1941

Drenching for the Public: One of my favorite stories occurred in the early 1940s when my parents, Charlie and Nell Bierschwale lived on the Fairview Ranch between Garvin Store and Rocksprings. Our family had recently moved to the Fairview as another brother, Clarence, and his family also lived at the older ranch house about a mile away.

Mom often helped Dad shed the Angora goats after spring shearing, as rain or extreme cold on fresh-sheared goats would kill them. In those days, people did what they had to, to make a living. Dad often "drenched for the public." Stomach worms were a problem in sheep and goats and at that time, the only viable treatment was phenothrozine drench, which came as a powder and was mixed with water, then administered with a drench gun. Drench was mixed in and drawn from a bucket, 2 oz. at a time, by a drench gun, then administered down the throat to each sheep or goat. This process was repeated as needed, often several times each spring/summer as the animals showed signs of stress.

Well, as a man of impunity, and seeking a better way to mix the powder with water, and with Uncle Lonnie as his accomplice, they decided Mother's old wringer washing machine could do the job. This was a gas motor-powered agitator washer, of course. There was no electricity in that area for another 8-10 years, and yes, we had "coal oil lamps" and wood stoves for heat and cooking.

Anyway, Dad and Lonnie, without telling Mom, decided they could speed up the mixing process in the washer. It worked pretty good, too, however, all the powder failed to dissolve and we wore pink and green clothes for several weeks (the powder is green turns pink when mixed). It irritated the skin and pretty much ruined everything. And Dad really caught heck for years to come.

Sheep Starter: This incident took place on the Fairview Ranch also. My dad was very good to me, always, but this particular incident took place when I was very young. Each year we on the rancher would have "dogies" (animals that lost their mama: lambs, goats, deer) that we would feed and care for. Dad used to bring these dogies home for my sister Jo Ann and I to mother and to care for. He milked a Jersey cow, or two at times, and we bottle fed the animals. I was pretty young at the time and Dad accused me of letting the lambs suck a while, then sucking on the bottle myself. I know that couldn't be true!

As I got older, I would accumulate a few lambs each year, and later fed 15-20/year. Long story short, by the time I graduated from high school, I had 200 ewes, and a good sheep program. These ewes helped pay for my college education and I still had a herd of 50 when I graduated. I would have had more but my first year in college Dad said half of mine died. He just "repo'd" them for the college funds.

Practicing Veterinarian: Back in the '50s and '60s there were only 2 vets in Kerrville: Dr. Nunn and Dr. Russell Thomas. Dr. Nunn took care of most of the dogs and cats and Dr. Thomas was mostly large animals. We traded with (knew) both vets as needs dictated and about 1967 a mare was scared by a neighbor visiting us. The mare had a white blaze on her face, eye to eye and forehead to nose, and she hit the fence and cut and tore the stripe on her face.

I called Dr. Thomas. It was late evening and he said he would be right out. I later found out he had been talking to a man with a colicky mare in Medina and didn't go, but just told him what to do on the phone. I felt privileged that he came to my place.

He sewed the mare up, 50-60 stitches across her whole face, and cleaned up. Then he sat down to visit. He told me a story of when he was a young vet in Kerrville.

A Divide area rancher, between Garvin Store and Leakey, named Marcus Auld, called Doc to come work cattle one day. Now, this was before chutes and calf tables and such, and he had a bunch of cattle. The cattle needed to be treated for pink eye, horn problems, or other ailments. The rancher roped them and threw them, and then the vet dehorned them, castrated them, vaccinated them, ear notched them, and branded them. Doc Thomas arrived

at dawn, worked all day, and still wasn't through, so they turned on the truck lights and worked a little longer. Finally finished, Doc started to his truck, and began hand writing a bill. Marcus wandered over and inquired if the Doc was a practicing vet. Doc said, well yes, he guessed he was. Marcus replied, "Well, come back when you learn how, and I'll pay you."

While this was just a little joke on the Doc, in reality it was probably a while till he got paid as ranchers in that day had a habit of paying bills only a couple times a year, when they sold their calves, lambs, or wool.

Kerrville in the '50s and '60s: Although we lived on the Divide (between Garvin Store and Rocksprings) and considered Rocksprings our hometown, we often traded (shopped) in Kerrville. Most of our clothes came from Kerrville and Dad came often to the livestock auction here to purchase cars and trucks, or to have them worked on at the Peterson Auto Co. on Water Street and Sidney Baker.

I was with them often and got to know many of the old timers (not old then) about town. Mom and Dad shopped at Schreiners, Harris', and Wolfmueller's, and we often ate lunch at 5 Points, the Chatterbox, and Mrs. Mac's in Ingram.

At any rate, I was fortunate to know at a young age many Kerrville natives, Red Guthrie, Otis Newman, Bob Stovall, Street Hamilton, and many many others in Kerrville and most of the ranchers in the area.

In 1965, after starving to death for a year at the ranch at Rocksprings, I took a high-paying teaching job (first contract that year was $4200, that's $350/month less taxes and dues). We moved to Kerrville and moving my checking account from People State Bank in Rocksprings to Scheiner Bank. Dad took me in to meet the president of the bank, a district, Judge, and friend, Jim Weatherby. Like I said, Dad knew just about everybody here.

I shook his hand, sat down, made small

talk, and told him I wanted to open an account. He was eager to help. I was impressed. Mr. Aime Schreiner was sitting in the front office window of the bank and the president was helping me.

He cautioned me that as a young fellow, I would probably overdraw my account, and when I did, he would call me. I assured him that would never happen.

A few months later, the phone rang, and who but Jim Weatherby was on the line. Overdrawn. I sweated blood. I had to go see him and I did. But I was really careful from that time on.

Now, that's personal service when the bank president does stuff like that.

Jo Ann: Another story at the ranch. As I said, times were hard in the '40s. Often livestock died, and then they needed to be dragged away from the pens.

Dad did his own auto repair work in those days and had the car jacked up and was working under it fixing something. My sister Jo Ann, about 8 years old, was playing in the car opening and slamming the doors.

Dad said to Jo Ann, "Jo Ann, don't play in the car. What would you do if the car fell and killed old Daddy?"

Jo Ann said, "Well, I guess we'd just have to drag him off."

Snake Stories: Once when on horseback rounding up the east pasture, I came upon a fairly large snake, 5 feet, or so. I tied my horse a safe distance away and proceeded to locate the snake. He was under a low cedar bush and I fought him for 10-15 minutes around rocks and stumps. I finally got a good lick on him and killed him. I pulled him out to make sure he was dead and headed back toward my horse. As I turned around, right behind me was his mate, there all the time! The hair on the back of my neck stood up, a chill ran down my back, and I headed straight for my horse.

Another time at the ranch, me and another wetback were pulling bitterweed (a spring season weed in that area, poison to sheep), that we found along the fence, as the neighbors did not control it. We would pull the weeds and put them in a sack, or if we were near the fence, throw them back on the other side where they came from. I reached down and pulled a large weed by the stalk, and when I did, I exposed beneath it a small rattlesnake maybe 15 inches long. My hand must have brushed it when pulling the plant. We disposed of that little rattler and were very vigilant and a few minutes later found 2 more.

Gene Lock was a rancher who raised good Quarter horses near Midway, halfway to Junction. I had heard this story for many years and asked Gene in his later years and he confirmed that it was true.

Many hill country ranches have oil/gas pipelines running through them with rocks scattered on top with small voids under and around them: snake heaven. Gene loved to show off his good Quarter horses, so when a friend stopped by one day he had to show his horses to him. Being in a small pasture, they went footback (on foot) down the pipeline in search of the horses. On the way, they came up on a rattlesnake and killed it, then went on to look at the horses. On the way, back they saw the snake partially under a rock. Gene said he had a nice set of rattles. He put his foot on the snake, cut off the rattles, and went on their way. A short way later, they came upon the dead snake. Yes, he cut the rattles off a live snake!

Uncle Albert's Embarrassing Story: My great uncle Albert Bierschwale was the head of the Agriculture Department at Sul Ross College (now University) in the '50s and '60s. While in college at Southwest Texas State (now Texas State) in the early '60s, I signed up for a soils course I needed for my Ag. Ed. degree. The professor teaching this course was Dr. Cecil Gregg. He asked if I was kin to his old friend Albert, and I confirmed that I was. He then told this story.

When they were young men around 1900 and living somewhere in the Harper Junction area, it was common practice in those days to take baths in rivers or in ponds when available. Well, Albert was enjoying such a bath when along came young Gregg riding horseback with some young ladies, possibly a Sunday evening outing.

What to do? Albert was trapped and his friends wouldn't leave. They stayed and stayed and stayed.

A few days later Albert saw Gregg and confronted him.

"I sure was embarrassed. You and those girls wouldn't leave. Luckily I found that old tub to hold in front of me so I could get out (of the water and to my clothes)."

Gregg retorted, "Not nearly as embarrassed as if you had known that tub didn't have a bottom on it!"

The Last Cattle Drive Through Austin
By Lucille H. Hough of Bertram, Texas
Born 1923

In 1931, I was nine years old and living with my family on a combination farm and ranch just south of Austin. The Great Depression was just beginning when my father, Colvin Cloud, decided to sell part of his herd of longhorn cattle to bring in some ready cash. The North was hungry for Texas beef and we had cattle to spare.

My father had struck a bargain with a buyer to deliver the cattle to the depot in Liberty Hill for shipment to Kansas City and had made arrangements with a trucker to deliver the steers when things went wrong. For whatever reason, the trucker could not move the cattle and this put my father in a difficult position. He was born near Blanco in 1889 and was an honorable man and had sealed his promise to deliver the cattle with

a handshake. This meant the cattle had to be delivered on time. My father was a skilled horseman and had been trained by his father and uncles to manage cattle on the trail, so he put those skills to use and decided to form a crew from his sons to drive the steers to Liberty Hill.

The crew consisted of my father, two half-brothers Sam and Roy, and my brother Alfred who would be driving a team of mules pulling a wagon with all the supplies. I had always thought of myself, as my father's pet so I was crushed when he told me that I could not come along for the drive. It was one of the biggest disappointments of my life.

My father wasn't daunted by the task of managing the herd but there was one obstacle that had to be overcome: the Colorado River. The Colorado of 1931 is not the river we know today. There was no chain of dams to tame the river and it had to be crossed. With such a small crew, Dad knew he could not swim the herd and the few ferries on the river were not suitable for moving cattle. He needed a bridge, and the only one on the way to Liberty Hill was the Congress Avenue Bridge in Austin. And crossing that bridge meant driving his cattle through what was then downtown Austin.

My brother Alfred told the *Austin AmericanStatesman* newspaper the story of

Lucille's father, Colvin Cloud

181

Lucille caring for her father's cattle

what happened on what I believe was the last cattle drive through Austin. You can find the whole story, which is quite entertaining, in their archives. Here is the gist of it:

My father wanted a permit from the city to drive the cattle, but they could not do that. Apparently, though, he was told that if no one saw it, it wasn't an issue. They went down Congress Avenue at 3 AM and only saw one policeman, who just watched. Later, near the old Seton Hospital, a streetcar rang its bell and spooked a steer to run away. That steer later rejoined the herd on its own.

If you are wondering how my brother's story ended... Yes, they did bring the herd into Liberty Hill on time.

A Lasting Impression
By Joel Ayala, Sr., of Kerrville, Texas
Born 1929

During the mid-1930s and '40s, my family lived and worked at the YO Ranch, in Mountain Home, Texas.

We lived at a section of the ranch named the Niedam where we were responsible for working that section of the main ranch. At approximately 3 o'clock in the morning of March the 23rd, 1943, we were awakened as a car drove up to our house. It was Clarence Hyde, the foreman of the ranch, informing us that an aircraft had crashed in the vicinity and that we should saddle our horses and start a search of the crash site.

We saddled up and began our search by splitting into two groups. My father, Ralph Sr., my brother Sil, and I headed to a hill about a mile east of our house. When we reached the top of the hill, we spotted a fire burning about a mile to the west from where we were.

We headed towards the site of the fire and when we arrived there, we saw the downed aircraft and met my brothers Ralph Jr. and Robert there. They had arrived at the scene minutes earlier.

The aircraft was a twin-engine type that was used in training at the Navigational Training School based at Hondo Airfield in Hondo, Texas. It carried a crew of five, which consisted of the pilot, copilot, engineer, and two students.

The plane had hit a copse of live oak trees about 6 to 8 inches in diameter, demolishing the whole forward section of the fuselage, the cockpit, and the wings. The two engines had been flung several yards forward from their mounts. The pilot was dead, still strapped to his safety belt. The copilot was also dead, buried under the foliage of the trees and part of the fuselage. The half rear section of the plane was mostly intact, resulting in the survival of the remaining crewmen. Two of these crewmen were severely injured and had been carried and laid by the fire and covered with their parachutes by the one crewman that had escaped injuries. He made them as comfortable as he could and left to seek aid. I believe his name was Lt. Caldwell.

Later he related that he walked back in the direction from which they had been heading and came to a wagon road a short distance from the crash site. He said he had an idea as to where they were, since they frequently flew over the area. Therefore he started walking south on this road and eventually arrived at a location of the ranch called the Gilmore. This place consisted of a shack windmill and feeding pens, where during the winter months we rounded up cattle from different pastures and drove them in to feed. He said he remembered seeing the penned cattle when they flew over the area.

He went to the windmill and climbed it and called out for help in the hope that someone might be living nearby and would hear him. My great uncle Nick Ayala did live in the shack but being unaware of what had occurred, he was a bit uneasy and did not respond to his calls. So he continued walking eastward and shortly came to a road. This road led from the entrance to the ranch on Highway 41. Luckily, he turned right and eventually after walking a mile or so he came up to the Warren Cline ranch, which happened to have a telephone, and from there contacted the airfield and reported the incident.

In the meanwhile, we remained at the crash site all morning and circled the area on horseback as we had heard possible predators nearby.

Later that day, personnel from the airfield arrived with ambulances to remove the victims and a flatbed vehicle to haul away the aircraft. We heard that the crash was caused from flying too low and was caught by an air pocket. A few weeks later, some of the crewmen and their parents returned to the site and met with some of us that had participated in the search to express their gratitude for our part in the search.

As I was but a youngster at that time, I couldn't help but get an eerie feeling whenever I rode near the crash site while working with livestock in that pasture. This incident that happened that night left a lasting impression in my mind.

Ranch Raising: Parental Guidance of the '50s
By Carolyn L. (Weegie) Cottle of
Rocksprings, Texas
Born 1950

April's Fool: My dad (Howard Cottle) and myself always had lots of fun on April Fool's Day. When I was in high school, he called me about 4 AM to come to the kitchen quickly. So I did.

There he stood with a broom, broom straws up, and the handle down where he could stab something. Then he told me to raise the plastic dishpan up real slow because there was a snake under it.

So, still half asleep, I grabbed it very carefully with just my thumb and forefinger. I got it raised out of the sink and I said, "Dad, I don't see a snake," and he laughed and said, "April Fool! Now go back to bed."

So about 5 years later on March 31st, I lived in Fredericksburg, Texas, and Dad and my cousin (Gary Reichenau) put up a carport

Carolyn's dad, Howard Cottle

Carolyn with her parents, Howard and Louise Cottle

at my mobile home. They finished just as a dark and really bad–looking storm cloud was coming up in the north. Dad, Mom, and Gary left to go home. I was so proud of my carport for my vehicle, so I went to bed so thankful I didn't have to take my car to a car wash and wait for the storm to pass to protect my car!

So I went to bed and it hit me: tomorrow is April Fool. So my head went to spinning trying to think of what I could pull on my dad over the phone! Oh, yes! It came to me.

I got up about 5:30 AM and I called my dad. He probably got to bed around 1-2 AM, after he got home and fed the dogs and milked our cow. He answered the phone pretty groggy: not enough sleep and he wasn't a spring chicken.

I said, "Dad, that cloud that was coming up as y'all left yesterday evening turned out to be a really bad storm—high winds, hail, and a hard rain—and it blew my new carport completely away. " There was total silence for a little bit and then he said, "The hell you say."

Then I laughed and I said, "April Fool! Now, go back to bed." I knew he would have killed me if I had been close enough. Ha Ha!

We always had fun, and especially enjoyed April Fool's Day.

Mind Says Go, Body Says No: I lived in Rocksprings, where there's not much to do, and on Saturday nights the highlight was going to Crider's at Hunt, Texas, for the rodeo and open air dance floor. Jack Rich and the Continental Cowboys played there a lot.

On Saturday morning real early my dad woke me up and said, "We are going to haul that hay that I bought on Highway 41 out of that old barn." So I got up and went to eat breakfast (peanut butter and Karo Syrup) and I reminded my dad that this was Saturday and Crider's. He said, "OK" with a smile. So I got my old clothes on. Even though I was a girl, he worked me like the son he never had. Believe me, none of it hurt me at all at that time, but I am sure paying for it now, about 35-40 years later with bad shoulders, back, and hips.

We got to the old barn and Dad put me in there to throw the bales off the stack that was stacked to the roof of the barn. Things were going well until I ran into a bumblebee nest in the hay. Dad took care of them by siphoning gas out of the pickup and throwing it on them. So we continued.

Well, we hauled two pickup and trailer loads and I was going up on top of the rooms to Dad out of the pickup and trailer and he was stacking it. I had to lift each bale to my shoulders and then over my head for Dad to reach it since I was so short. Believe me, after two big loads I was too tired to move.

Well, I told Dad "I don't want to go to Crider's tonight after all." My dad being the cutup and true to his word that he was (if he had told you something he would do he would bust a gut or get it done. Very honest and true to his word), said, "Oh no, we are going to Crider's. That's the first thing I heard this morning and we're going so run on to the house and get cleaned up and ready while I feed the dogs and milk the cow."

So I dragged myself to the house and I told Mom we were going to Crider's and she said, "Aren't you too tired?" I said, "Yes, but Dad said we were going because I had reminded him about that as he woke me up this morning." So we all got ready and pulled out for Crider's.

We got there just as the dancing started and I sat down on the bench around the floor by the fence. I sat there all night and Mom and Dad didn't miss a set.

Lesson learned. I didn't mention Crider's as soon as Dad woke me up until I saw what was on the agenda for that day. Also, if the kids had to work as hard as we did there wouldn't be near as much meanness in this old world. They would be too tired to get unto stuff. Believe me!

True Blue Horse: Dad had broken a little sorrel horse with black mane and tail, a really beautiful little horse, for me. Our big 4th of July rodeo was coming up. Mom and Dad were really having hard times and Dad decided to sell my little horse to get some most-needed money. He wanted me to ride him in the parade that morning so maybe Mr. Gleason would buy him. Mr. Gleason had a ranch and my dad and his brother worked for him. Dad had been telling Mr. Gleason what a good horse Star was. Dad brought Star to town every night for about a week so I could get him used to traffic and the lights at the arena where the rodeos were. Everything went great until the morning of the parade. We rode around the square and my cousin Bobby Cottle was also on a horse, Buckshot that my horse was used to being around. After riding around the square and waving to the crowd, we struck out to the fairgrounds and arena. Well, right as we got to the football field, which had tin by the main road so people couldn't see the

Carolyn (Weegie) Cottle in 1968

game from the road, my horse shied from the tin and I went across the main road sideways, right in front of the cars. I had no control of Star at all. Yes, I went across in front of Mr. Gleason, the prominent buyer, and his wife.

I kind of got Star settled and I crossed back across the road beyond the football field where Bobby was waiting on me. We started to lope our horses going onto the fairgrounds and Bobby's horse Buckshot shied from a float with fringe blowing in the breeze. Buckshot planted his feet into the ground and Bobby went off over his head, landing flat on his back, but he held onto the reins so Buckshot wouldn't run off.

Bobby got up and I said, "Get back on, quick." Bobby said, "No, I am leading him the rest of the way."

Lo and behold, when we got to the trailer where Daddy and Uncle Carol were waiting on us and Dad knew nothing of how Star had acted by the football field, Dad asked Mr. Gleason what he thought about Star.

Mr. Gleason said with a raised voice, "I wouldn't buy that crazy horse on a bet!"

Then I told Dad what had happened when Star saw the sun shining on that tin by the football field.

So there went Dad's horse sale and Dad shook his head and said, "That's my luck." And me and my horse had many more happy years together!

Rodeo Queen and Duchess: I was Duchess to our Rodeo Queen my junior year the summer before my senior year. I was riding my same faithful horse, Star. We had all practiced how to come into the arena and where to stop our horses. I had ridden horses since I was knee high to a grasshopper, in other words, it was no new challenge for me. I helped on the ranch with rounding up and Dad had opened the gate for the ropers at the rodeo for years and I had seen all kinds of riders, believe me.

Dad had told me I was not to use the saddle horn coming in or out of the arena or at any time. So before the Grand Entry at the night performance we were all out in the arena warming our horses up along with ropers, barrel racers, or anyone else, and one of the calf ropers went by me running his horse and Star wanted to go, too!

I held him up and about that time he lowered his head and went to bucking with me. I was pulling on my reins with both hands as hard as I could but the air was getting thinner and thinner between me and my saddle.

Well, Charles Sweeten, a rancher here in Rocksprings, was the announcer and on the loudspeaker he said, "Boys, we have a REAL rodeo going on in the arena with our famous well-known Weegie Cottle riding!" Thank God, I got Star pulled up just before he bucked me off.

I rode up to my dad and Billy Seale and Billy asked me what that saddle horn was for. I told him not to catch or hold on to, if you wanted to ride in the Grand Entry in front of everyone!

Billy laughed and told Dad he was going to put him out there on a bucking horse and see what he grabbed hold of. We all laughed and Dad patted me on the back and said, "Sug, you did a great job."

So the end of my story is, I loved my dad dearly and had many good everlasting times with him.

If you did not know Howard Cottle, you missed one of the most amazing, hard-working, and the #1 ranchman in his time. He was an awesome man, true to his word. I can't put him high enough on a pedestal. I'm glad to call him my daddy.

My Mom's Recipe to a New Wife: I had gotten married and my husband, being of German background, wanted cornbread from scratch. This was about 40 years ago.

So I called my mom, Louise Cottle, because I thought she had the "best recipe" ever. So she told me she would write it down and get it in the mail that day. I couldn't wait to get that letter!

I got it out of my mailbox the next day, opened it, and there was my recipe: a pinch of salt, a dash of flour, ½ a cup of clabber or you could use cow's milk, a shake of baking powder and 2 eggs beaten, and that was it. So I called her and I said, "Mom, I got your cornbread recipe, but it has nothing about corn meal."

She laughed and laughed and finally said, "Good God child, you know you have to have corn meal," and my reply was "How much?"

She said, "Just pour it until it is the right consistency and pour it into your hot greased pan."

So I had red beans and cornbread for supper and my husband bragged and loved my mother's homemade cornbread. Thanks Mom, good job!

Home Delivery by the Butterkrust Man
By Regina Caulk of Kerrville, Texas
Born 1954

My family lived in Kerrville, Kerr County, Texas, from 1938 to the present. My mother still lives in Kerrville. She is 91 years old.

There were 5 children in our family with our father and mother. We lived a very simple life. My father was the breadwinner until my mother starting working when the youngest was in their teen years. We always ate our meals at home every day. I even walked home from school at lunch to eat and walked back to school.

On Sundays after church, sometimes we would take a car ride into the country. We would go to other small towns in the area. On these trips, we were treated with a Coca-Cola. It was a real treat to get to drink a Coke, which was something we did not have at home.

My brothers, sister, and I were always outside playing, chasing snakes, and horny (horned) toads. These horned toads are now extinct in that area. We would dig up doodlebugs and play in the creek a few blocks away. We would only watch TV after our homework and after the dishes were done after dinner.

One of my fondest memories was of the Butterkrust man. He would come around in his panel truck and hand out small loaves of Butterkrust in these tiny little bread sacks. He would go door to door.

Flour used to come in pretty cotton sacks, and Mom would make us girls clothes out of them. My sister and I would then make clothes for our dolls out of the scraps.

Milk was delivered on back porch stoops in glass bottles. One morning I dropped one of those bottles on my bare foot, cutting it wide open. My mom called Dr. Dyer, who came by the house and patched me up. Dr. Dyer made several home visits to our home in the early '60s.

Our yards used to be mowed with pushing mowers. My brother would sometimes give me a ride on the mower. The last time he gave me a ride, I stuck my hand under and into the blades, cutting my finger open. I had to go to the hospital for stitches. My brother got his britches warmed up that day.

I don't ever remember getting spanked, but I do remember my father always having a hard time getting me out of bed to go to school in my teen years. When he had had enough, he would come into my room with his belt. When I heard the rattle of the buckle that would be

enough to get me up and get ready for school.

I still remember my first grade teacher, Mrs. Clay at Tiry Elementary School. It was 1960, she was a very sweet teacher, and I learned a lot in her classroom. I had a crush on a boy named Bobby, but I never told him. We both went to the same schools all through our school years.

This is a story about my mother who lived in Bee County, Texas.

Winnie Young was born in 1922. Winnie only went through the 8th grade. Every day she rode her cutting horse to school. His name was Billie. She lived on a farm 5 miles from school.

When she was around 11 years old and coming home from school a neighbor boy on an old gray mare told her what he was going to do to her (it was not pleasant). He took the reins from her, but just as fast as him taking the reins, she jerked them out of his hands and with her heels kicked Billie in the flanks and off they ran and left that old gray mare in his dust.

Billie ran all the way home. He was winded and foaming by the time they got home. She got in trouble for riding her horse that hard, but never told her parents what had happened. Winnie was afraid her father would have hurt the boy, as well as his father would have hurt him or worse. She did finally tell her father when he was on his deathbed years later.

My mother had to quit school when she was roughly 14 years old. She had to help with the chores around the farm: feeding animals, cooking meals, cleaning, and taking care of her sick brother and mother. Her mother eventually had to have surgery. Billie, the cutting horse, had to be sold to help with expenses, breaking my mother's heart.

Winnie Young's great uncle was George Washington "Bonaparte" Young. He was the World Champion Bronc Rider in the 101 Wild West Show, as well as his wife (maiden name Goodnight) who was the women's World

Champion Bronc Rider. I am not sure what years they held their champion titles.

The neighborhood "Gang"

Can You Smell the Popcorn?
By Victor Ammann of Ingram, Texas
Born 1933

Saturday movies, wow. I haven't thought about those for years. Thinking back about them gives me the "warm fuzzies." I guess I was fortunate to live in what I now call the "Golden Age" of Saturday movies.

The earliest Saturday movies I can remember, was when my mother took me and my sister to the little theater four of blocks down the street. The theater was converted from a storefront amoung the other business. It was just about twice the size of the garage in my house now. Anyway, the Saturday movies there were great and after getting hooked on the serial that was shown, I didn't want to miss one. The serial was with Gene Autry and it was about an underground factory where the bad guys were making something and they

had built mechanical men to do their work. Needless to say, I could hardly wait until the next Saturday to find out what happened next. That Saturday's chapter always ended in a suspenseful scene.

I was in the third grade when the Japanese bombed Pearl Harbor and WWII was started. I didn't know much about it, except what I saw on the newsreels at the Saturday movies. I was old enough now to go to the Saturday movies by myself but only if my friend down the block could go with me. My hometown was small and the theater we went to was about six blocks away but we had to cross the railroad tracks. If a train blocked the tracks for a while, we were always afraid we would miss the start of the movie. The Saturday movies at this theater started at one o'clock in the afternoon. So a double feature, a serial, a cartoon, a newsreel, and the next week's previews took most of the afternoon.

The first feature was always a "cowboy" movie with maybe Gene Autry, Hop Along Cassidy, Roy Rogers, Lash La-Rue, the Lone Ranger, or one of our many more favorites. And the good guys always won, and rode off into the sunset. They didn't kiss the girls. The second feature was always a comedy, maybe Bob Hope and Bing Crosby, something always not complicated. Nothing scary. But this was great entertainment especially for the price. For us "little" guys the admission was

Victor Ammann

only a nickel (hard to imagine now). So with two nickels I had a big time.

With the other nickel, I could get a big, and I mean big, bag of popcorn. The theater was small for they didn't have a lobby and did not serve drinks (that would have only cost me more money). The only room they had for the popcorn machine was out on the sidewalk next to the ticket booth. Folks passing by could buy the popcorn, and many did for the smell was great and traveled far. But our two nickels for the Saturday movies were greatly "shrunken" when the theater raised the admission price to nine cents. There went the popcorn. But we could enjoy the smell going in the theater and leaving.

But with the penny "burning a hole in our pockets", we would stop by the five and dime store on the way home and spend the penny. I usually bought a penny top, for a game us guys at the grammar school played at recess. I won't take the time to explain that game, for in those days the rules at school were pretty slack. We also played marbles and a game with our pocketknives, (yes, most boys carried pocketknives, even to school). So after the Saturday movies we had lots of options to "use up" the rest of the afternoon. But it sure was "hard" to give up the popcorn. Thinking about it, I can almost smell it now. I think I will go see if there is any popcorn in the kitchen pantry.

The Lizards of Texas
By Penny Pennington of Brady, Texas
Born 1924

Your list has 33 subjects to choose from; I can write about all of them but three. I'm 89 since this past January, and my mind is still capable of writing. I've written for 22 years: 16 country western songs, 9 full-length books, 30 or more short stories, and over 2000 poems. I refer to myself as "The Nature Poet."

I've never had anything published as a book, just in a magazine, etc. I've written for AA here, funerals, weddings, and birthdays. I used to read poems and short stories for three nursing homes here in Brady and Mason, which is 20 miles south of Brady. I can just study a picture and sit down and write a poem that tells a story.

I know everything there is to know about the Depression days and country living, all true. My first full-length book is Journey to the Rainbow, naturally a book for children.

I wake up at night with verses running through my mind. I'm perfectly sane, alert, and imaginary. When I go on a trip to Colorado, I come back with all kinds of stories and poems. To me, Colorado is the next best thing to heaven. I love tall mountains, seashores, and nature in general. I have an upstairs redwood deck 14 x 22. That is where I hang out day or night. I erected freestanding bookshelves and added a marble coffee table and a wrought iron round table with 4 chairs. All are loaded down with shells and geodes sliced open. Some have lavender crystals in them. I bought a more or less fish net with star-shaped shells with lights inserted inside, with light bulbs inside, which hangs on the wall going into my 6th bedroom. People stop by to show their friends my wonderful collection. I have fool's gold rocks from Mason and fairy stones (ones with tunnels running through them like little caverns) that all look like bone.

I cannot write a short letter or poem. My mind just keeps describing what I'm thinking. This first book I've written was stolen by a full-blooded Indian who lives in Oklahoma back in 1995-96, who took my book and $850 cash. My book was printed and illustrated in color. I even had an oil painted picture for the cover. I had paid $4 per sheet to have it typed. Because he was a full-blooded Indian, the local law there would do nothing about it. I learned my lesson. At least I still have my original for the book.

I have 6 grown grandchildren, 2 great-grandkids, and 3 sons who I worship. I do Reflexology and Reiki. I have ESP, too, and can see events before they happen. I have witnesses to prove it.

The Lizard Family Tree

All cute little lizards are still friends of mine, except the old Mountain Boomer, who is green. When I was small, we lived in a settlement known as Long Valley. We never had electricity or piped in water. Our natural spring and a stream from it furnished our Saturday night bath in a #3 wash tub. Washing was done in an old aluminum Maytag gasoline-powered washing machine.

When I was 5 years old, I daily carried 2 buckets of water from our spring, crossing my creek, and had to watch out for 2 mountain boomers who loved to chase me. When I started back with my water they made a drumming sound as they bowed up with long tail held straight out their back and legs all bowed up with large jaws open. They were fierce! I'd jump on rocks to get across the water. They were good runners and mean. I'd splash cold spring water down my bare legs as they came after me. I could outrun all the kids in Long Valley. They sunned themselves on a large flat rock and lay in wait for me. We were told they were poisonous, but I don't know to this day if it was true. I took their word for it. This went on for years. I never found their young ones or eggs.

Next comes more of their family tree, the Rusty Lizard. He was passive, stayed on old oak trees, and his or her eggs would bounce like a rubber ball and were about the size of a marble, which were white and had a rough texture on them.

Lizards never sat on their eggs to hatch them. They lay them in leafy places on the ground and let the sun do their setting. When they hatched out, she showed up to teach and find bugs for them.

Next are the striped ones about 6 to 8 inches long and with a skinny tail, which they can really grow a new one when needed. Their eggs are peach colored and wider at one end. They are harmless and cute. Cats catch them for food for her kittens, including birds and small snakes.

Next on our tree is the Chameleon Lizard, who has magic! When they are just fooling around or resting, the color is pale peach. They are slender cute little things. When in danger they rush into green underbrush and quickly absorb its color to blend with grass, leaves, and other fauna. Whatever they lay next to, they become the same color. I never saw a nest of them.

Next is the Salamander. They are black and white, brindled, I guess you would say. They are lazy, good natured, and usually live under old carpets of dead leaves. There are a lot of them in Colorado. They have a soft, nearly fat, body. I never saw a baby one.

Last but not least I have numerous 1 ½ inch long ones that look like a small cousin to the Rusty Lizard. When I find one I catch it and let it crawl on my arm or lap. They are always that same small size. I'd like to find their eggs. I don't know what color they'd be.

All these four-legged creatures are harmless except for my Mountain Boomer. I'd call the old horned frog a lizard too. They have two painted hollow horns, a flat body, big mouth, and rather short tails and live on red ants only. My cousin and I used to hitch a twine string around his horns and hook him up to an empty kitchen match box with the string. Add a few small rocks to the box to keep it from capsizing over, mark off 2 lines in the dirt, and turn them loose and see which one will run faster from our starting line. They actually can and do spit blood out of their horns at you. We never killed any of them. They were our entertainment.

Twist the Tail
By Clinton B. Solbrig of Amarillo, Texas
Born 1927

My school days started when I was 7 years old and I started to school with my right wrist broken. I was naturally left-handed, but as soon as my right hand was healed, the teacher would not let me write left-handed any more. My mom said I had to start to write right-handed which I did. But as my luck would have it, I broke my right wrist in the 8th grade and at my final test; I had to take it with my left hand again.

We rode horses to school. We lived 3 miles from school but in the country. Later on, we walked to school.

Yes, we did have outhouses, 1 for boys, and 1 for girls.

We didn't have a radio until 1940. My oldest brother worked for a neighbor and he took that money and ordered a Silvertone battery-operated radio. Then we fixed us a wind charger to keep the battery up. We listened to "High Ho, Silver!" with Roy

Clinton and Ada Solbrig in 1956

Rogers and many other westerns.

Yes, we did use castor oil and it didn't taste good.

We did have a 13 party telephone which was hand cranked, and whenever the phone rang other people would listen in. So everybody knew what was going on.

We didn't do much drag racing, but we did have racing. We raced our '35 Plymouth one night from town against a neighbor boy, who had a '37 Ford coupe. We could outrun him. But when we split up we had a flat tire 2 miles from home and our spare was flat too. So then we had to walk 2 miles home to get the pickup and go back to fix the tire and it was by then 6 AM and we were supposed to shear our granddad's sheep. So we went and sheared all the sheep, and then went home to get some sleep for the next day.

We had a windup record player that we listened to and some of the older people danced to that.

As for spanking at school I did get a spanking. But there was one day that everybody got spanked all at one time. It was for some bad words they used against another boy. I did get my hair pulled against the grain by my teacher because I told him to hit the ball in German and we weren't to talk German on the school grounds.

Yes, Saturday night was bath night in a #3 tin tub. We had to heat the water on the old wood stove and it did have a vat on the back end to heat water and we would bathe 2-3 persons in the same water.

I had 2 uncles that served in World War I and then in World War II I and 4 brothers served. My eldest brother had enlisted in 1941 and had to repeat enlistment the 7th of December when it was declared. He was in the Panama Canal. The 2nd brother got drafted and served in the Air Force for 35 months. He didn't have to go overseas. The 3rd brother didn't pass his physical and I had to go as soon as I turned 18. I served until discharge in

1946. I served in Japan for 11 months.

As far as wringer clothes washers, I did crank those and turned the wringer to get the water out and then hung them on a wire line.

As far as movies went we didn't see many. Once in a while to get to town to see western movies, we were too poor to spend much more than that. I think they cost 15 or 20 cents to see.

The Depression years were hard because we didn't have any money. What little we had, had to go to the government. We lived 18 miles out of town in the country where we raised most of our needs for food. We had wild game and sheep and goats, cows we milked, and hogs for sausage. We found juicy wild plums and blackberries and made our jelly and jam. We milked our cows for the cream and milk, which we used to make butter and cheese.

We worked for our neighbors in the fields a while. We small boys got 50 cents a day and Dad got 75 cents a day and as we got older we'd get 75 cents, $1, $1.25, $1.50, $1.75, $2, and finally we got $2.25 a day. So when I got out of the army in '46 and '47, me and a friend came to the Texas panhandle to make the wheat harvest and we were in high cotton: $11 and board and room. We also learned to shear sheep and goats. This was in and around Fredericksburg. We got 7 cents for each goat and 12 cents for each sheep. Last sheep I sheared I got 15 cents a head and goats 11 cents a head. I got to where I could shear 100 head of sheep in a day and 140-150 head of goats.

We had homemade clothes. Some of our shirts were made of flour sackcloth, which was different colors: red, black, green, and white. Us boys got our work clothes from Sears and Roebuck through mail order, and the girls had dresses made out of flour sacks too. One didn't have shoes in summer. We went barefoot. Usually we had a pair of dress and a pair of work shoes for in winter.

Charles Hartman was my favorite teacher.

He was tough on us, but she could be real nice, too. We had one big room school and then they divided it into two rooms. Grades 1-3 were in one end and 4-8 were in the big room. We did have a pail of drinking water. Our water was provided by windmill. We played sock hop with rags where we would hop around, and have races.

I remember the car with the rumble seat, which I did ride in once in a while.

The blizzard we had in 1940 gave us 30 inches of snow and it drifted up to the gates and fences. We couldn't ride our horses to school because the gates were covered with snow on top. We walked to school and had to climb over the gates. It was several days before we could get our car out and then the black dirt roads would be where you had to push the car to get through one snow bank.

My pet was a little rat terrier. My dad picked him up on the highway coming home from town and that dog would follow me everywhere. I went possum hunting one time and it was cold and wet. We were out in the pasture and when we got home it was past lunchtime. Anyway I got to eat and when I got

Clinton B. "Pete" Solbrig

192

through I always took a snack of some kind to feed him. Well, I went out to the porch to feed him and I passed out on the porch and when Mom looked out I was lying on the porch passed out and my dog was all over me, licking my face. Well, Mom and Dad took me in the house, put me on the bed, and it was quite a while before I came to again. They rubbed on my chest and got me back to life.

I had encounters with snakes several times but never got bit. We used to gather chicken eggs sometimes at night and you'd reach in the nest to get the egg and you'd feel something cold and it would be a chicken snake in there and it had eaten all the eggs. But that snake didn't eat any more because we would kill it.

We didn't make homemade toys except we'd take a spool and string and get a rubber band through the hole and put a little wood on one side and an onger one on the other side. The spool was notched on the same side each side. Then we'd twist the rubber band and string tight and we put it on the floor and it would roll until it got unwound. We'd roll old tires around and have a race, too.

Our farm chores included shucking corn, feeding hogs and cows and horses and tending to sheep and goats. We'd milk cows and tend to chickens and turkeys.

We didn't have any swimming holes except the water trough that the animals drank out of.

My dad told us about him and one of his friends playing a trick on one of their friends who was dating a girl they liked. They knew when he was going on a date with this girl and he and his friend left early to get to this friend's house, so they'd be there to see what he'd do. They didn't want to date her, just wanted to make him feel like they were going for her, too.

My grandparents, uncle, and aunt were in my life a lot. I spent more time with them than my brothers and sisters. There were three of us boys that if Mom or Dad were gone we'd get the milk calves and we'd ride them. I rode one and it pitched me off and stepped on my stomach and I quit riding after that.

There was one day it had rained. Me and my next 2 older brothers decided to go riding, and caught one of the bigger calves and put a saddle on it. The older brother was going to ride it. Well, he got on it and it wouldn't pitch, so he told me, the youngest, to twist its tail to make it go. Well, it did go a few steps and the saddle began to slide. He landed in the mud. Dad came down to the pen to see what was going on. We didn't see him. But at the dinner table Dad said, "Twist its tail" so then we knew that he had seen all of it.

The games we played most with our neighbor kids were baseball, toss, stall, tag, dodge ball, jump rope, dominoes, cards, and pickup sticks.

We didn't make many trips to town.

We didn't have an icebox until about '47-'48.

We didn't have a milkman; we milked our own cows and separated the milk with a hand-cranked separator. Cream came out one spout and milk in another. This was done every morning and evening.

Family time was playing cards and dominoes, and talking about what we had to do around the farm. We went to church once in a while.

Rotary phones didn't come along until in the late '30s or '40s.

The Travelin' Bureau
By Thelma Traveland Cardwell-Cale of
Marion, Texas
Born 1932

When I was seven in 1939, we still used horses and wagons, but cars were becoming more available in Texas, and everyone wished for one. "The Travelin' Bureau" is an almost-forgotten name now, but it was in use back then. People would put an ad in the newspaper or tack up a note in the grocery store that read, "Going to West Texas" or Dallas, etc. "I Need Riders."

I remember my mother, Margaret McDonald Traveland, called one man, and told him, "We want to visit my mother in Silver Valley, Texas, near Santa Anna." He replied, "Yes, Ma'am! I'm going that way. I can drop you off."

My mother, my younger brother, sister, and I rode in his car's backseat and another man rode up front with the owner. Mother paid, as did the other man, to help pay for the gasoline.

It was like hitch hiking, but you had to pay. It was a "one time deal" when someone would make a trip, needing help on the gas or someone to help drive.

We left about 4:30 am and it was dark! We had a long trip. Cars were slower back then. I was so excited that my stomach hurt. I remember later at daybreak, when we passed farm and ranch houses, their lights were suddenly coming on.

The dark countryside with the twinkling lights was like magic! I could even see the farmer and rancher's lantern swaying as they walked to their barn. Electricity was just coming to some of the country people. The Great Depression was still with us and men struggled to find work and feed their families.

We lived in a wooden shanty. It was a 2-room house with a lean-to for a kitchen. The rent was $5 a month. My mother "took in washing" to pay the rent. We lived in a tent before then. Hand washing other people's clothes on a rub board scrubber was hard work. She also had to hand pump the water up from the well. Jobs were hard to come by, and Daddy was always searching for work. Sometimes he could make $1 a day.

I remember the hoboes who came to our house. In the 1930s, they were the men who rode the rails in train boxcars looking for work.

The train tracks were near our house, across a sugar cane field. Hoboes would knock on our door looking for work. They cut firewood for mother for our wood-burning cook stove. They didn't want charity, only food and other work. We only had food and we shared.

If the cow was giving milk, they drank milk. If the hens were laying, Mother fixed them eggs. They also ate oatmeal because we did. Oatmeal was very cheap. We ate oatmeal a lot if we had money to buy it. One year, we only had oatmeal for Christmas dinner because it was all we had in our house to eat. Times were hard!

We had a garden but had to wait until the vegetables grew big enough to eat. All vegetables were eaten only in their own season and that was usually only once a year when they ripened.

When we didn't have much to eat, Mother would make cornbread and sometimes she was able to buy a jar of peanut butter. She would take us three children out to find a tree with shade and we would have a picnic with cornbread and peanut butter.

She taught us to look up at the clouds and find shapes in them. She would find the shape of George Washington, our first President, and told my brother Louis, who was 4 at the time, that he could become President someday. Today he is going on 80 and he did become president of 2 successful companies that he started.

Mother always taught us to obey "the Golden Rule," "Be Honest," to "Work Hard," "Love One Another," and to "Be Positive." And that we wouldn't be poor forever!

When I was about 4, our mother bought a piggy bank for each of her three children at that time. Each time that she was paid for taking in washing, a penny for each child was put in the piggy banks. It was the beginning of our Going to College funds. She planted a seed in each child's mind. All 5 of her children, 1 boy and 4 girls, did go to college beginning in

1951.

Today, I can tell and help teach our grandchildren about "How to Survive." I was born during the Great Depression in the 1930s and I was 9 years old when World War II broke out.

We were taught to save, to take care of all our things, and to be respectful to others and their things. We were taught to "make do, do over, and do without."

In 2010, I was asked to teach as a guest teacher for all the 5th grade classes in an elementary school a few miles from our home. The students were studying the Great Depression in America.

In the 1930s, a package of gum cost a nickel, a whole 5 cents. When we got gum, we saved the cellophane cover to be used at Christmas time. We usually got Juicy Fruit gum and the cellophane cover would hold 3 marbles. Tied with a string, it could be used as a Christmas tree decoration on the tree Daddy cut from the woods behind our house. My brother was happy to use his marbles for our tree. You couldn't buy a roll of cellophane plastic back then. It wasn't around.

We also took (to show the students) our hand-turned butter churn. It was made like a large clear glass bowl turned upside down with a large metal lid screwed on top that had a hand crank to turn in a sideways circle. That turned the paddle that was down in the jar full of cream. Some of the churns were called "Daisy Churns."

Families that couldn't afford a churn could use a quart jar with cream in it and shake it back and forth to make the butter come. We always sang a little song during the Depression and World War II as we made butter this way:
"Come Butter Come
Johnny's at the gate
Waiting for his Golden Butter Cake."
We sang it over and over again and never tired of this song. It was fun to watch the small pieces of butter beginning to form. We made

butter and then got to drink buttermilk after the butter was dipped out.

The students loved the churn and they all wanted a turn at turning the handle that turned the paddle around and around.

During the Great Depression (I always wondered why they called it "Great"), they used everyday words like "patched clothes", "hand me downs" (sometimes called "pass ons"), and "feed sacks" that had flower prints on them so mothers, sisters, and grandmothers could make dresses, shirts, and underwear out of the material after the cows ate the feed.

Diapers were made out of cup towels that were made out of "broadcloth" from cotton. They were washed every day!

We had "Elsie" the Borden's cow and everyone loved little Shirley Temple, the movie star with the bouncy curls. We got to visit Elsie at the Borden's Milk Company and put a daisy flower wreath around her neck. I was in the 1st grade. We looked forward to seeing Shirley's movies.

At night, after we said our prayers on our knees, we looked out to see the moon. If it was up yet, we said,
"I see the moon
The moon sees me.
God bless the moon
And God bless me."

There will be Trials
By Jerry D. Blalock of Leakey, Texas
Born 1940

You may wonder just what steel bars and a weed have in common. This story will enlighten you on the subject.

When we decided to build the great room onto our ranch house, we turned to Claude Haby, a longtime resident, customer, and building contractor in Real County to build it. We had concerns about using just wire mesh in

Jerry, Kevin, and Debbie Blalock

the slab with as much Saltillo tile and rock as we were planning, so we decided to use rebar (1/2 to 3/4 inch steel rods that came in 20-foot long pieces) instead. I had begun to prepare the soil to build the concrete slab on three years earlier by bringing dirt and limestone base to the footprint, spreading and applying water and packing it with my ranch Case 480 tractor.

When Claude showed up at our home site to start work, he brought tools and a full kitchen and chairs to eat and rest on during breaks. I knew when I saw these items that we were getting serious about getting this job done. We lived 28 miles from the nearest Coke machine and so meals had to be prepared every day for as many as 5 people.

Claude and his crew began to move more dirt around and using boards to construct the forms to receive the concrete and rebar. I started to pile the necessary rebar up in Leakey at the lumberyard for transport to the ranch when Claude ordered it. One day the call came. "Jerry, bring that rebar home with you tonight" was Claude's order.

That afternoon, using the forklift, I loaded 3/4, 1/2, and 5/8 rebar onto the 18-foot trailer that we had hooked to my Chevy Z71 pickup. The Z71 package had four-wheel drive, so I felt I could get up the steep hill at the ranch without any other assistance. We also had a refrigerator already loaded and lashed to the

headache rack for the trip to the ranch.

That evening, after work, Debbie and I loaded up in the truck and headed up 336 to our ranch. This doesn't sound bad if you say it real fast. However, 336 to where we lived was very mountainous and in many cases, 15 MPH with 90 degree curves on the narrow paved road. People riding motorcycles come from all over Texas just to ride this one section of the three roads that make up what is called the twisted sisters. The elevation drop from our home site to Leakey is about 1000 feet.

When we drove past Sonny Sansom's ranch house and made the curve where it turns left in a 90-degree angle along the west prong of the Frio River, I happened to glance in my rearview mirror to check to see that the trailer and tires were doing ok, when I saw lots of smoke. Ouch, this was not good. I kept going for about 100 yards across the cattle guard before pulling off onto the shoulder where there was room to make any adjustments that I suspected would need to be made. Every tire on the trailer was flat and smoking but one. Obviously, the steel bars weighed much more than the brand new 15-inch wheels could handle. This had been poor judgment on my part to say the least, it pains me to say.

I unhooked the trailer and drove back to the lumberyard. There we had our delivery truck we could use that would surely do the

Jerry Blalock and Real Building Supply delivery truck

196

job. When I got back to where Debbie and the trailer were waiting, it was already dark. I pulled the truck up alongside and even with the trailer. Using what gloves we had handy and in our clean not so dirty work clothes we began the arduous task of taking the rebar off the trailer and lifting it up to and onto the bed of the delivery truck, about three feet. Some of the rebar was so heavy it took both of us just to lift one 20-foot section.

Loaded and heading home, when we got to Hwy 3235 where we turned left the road was filled with vehicles (about 15) and people. I had no idea what was going on. I stopped and checked my load just to make sure we were ok, and without being obvious, try to see who and what might be happening, and if we had a chance of making it on home. I could see no problem but we sure got the eye from those 30 or more suspicious people.

When we reached the house on the ranch, I let Debbie go on and start supper while I rolled the rebar off the side of the truck. It was dark and I was dog tired and filthy with dirt and rust so I just let it fall wherever it would as I pulled it off. The next morning we left before daylight and I had no idea what shape it was in. Later that morning I called Claude and apologized for the shape the rebar might be in. To which he just casually replied "Jerry, there will be trials."

Meanwhile, I began to wonder what was going on up at and around Neal and Vannettes with all those people and cars the night before. So, I called their house and the story they had to tell! One of their neighbors was an individual who had purchased 100 acres of raw land about 2 miles past them down a dirt road that went west off 3235. On the 100 acres, the owner had planted marijuana plants and put in an irrigation system because he was an absentee owner and could not keep it watered. He had a partner helping him in the plan, until the partner felt like he was getting taken advantage of, and ratted him out. The

next time the *Leakey Star* came out, there was the story on the front page showing Sheriff James Earl Brice with a double armload, piling it onto a fire.

You Never Forget the Sound of a Rattlesnake
By Lillian Mayer of Bulverde, Texas
Born 1928

I am going down the list of memory joggers, as printed in the form.

The outhouse was a must, but never close to the house and no toilet paper. We used newspaper and Sears catalogs. Rain, cold, or shine that was the way it was.

We had to take Castor oil on a regular basis. No fun. Mom thought we had to be cleaned on a regular basis.

We had no old radio programs. We had no electricity until 1942. That was the biggest thing and time in our time. From then to now it is hard to believe, with all the new electronics.

Party line telephones were wonderful. Our ring was 1 short, 1 long, and 1 short. You had to be careful what was said because usually someone would be listening. Of course, this communication was good. In order to talk with my sister, my call went through 2 switchboards. So we did not call each other very often, and then our conversations were short.

I remember one old car Dad had. It was a Chevy with no windows. In the summer, it was natural AC. In the winter, we had to put windows on made like curtains. And then when we went somewhere and it was cold we had feather covers to cover with. It was so cozy.

We had a windup record player but did not get to use it often and then it was German music. I still have some of these records.

We had Saturday night baths in large

Lillian's grandmother

washtubs in the kitchen next to the wood stove. My older sister went first, then me, and then my brother, all in the same water. We had a large rainwater cistern. We had to hand pump the water into buckets. To drink we had a wooden bucket with a large dipper and that was our drinking water. We made do. We did not know any different.

Once a year my dad and mom, us kids, and another family went fishing and camping at the Medina River. The men put out trout lines and the moms and kids stayed at camp. We got to play in the water and slept in the back of the old truck. At midnight the men checked the lines, and in the morning. They did catch catfish. We later had a fish fry.

I could go into long detail about WWII. These were hard times. Gas was rationed with stamps, there were sugar stamps, and many other items were hard to get. There were so many sacrifices. The government bought my dad's farm and we had to move. This was so hard.

We had a wringer washer and we had to boil our water in black kettles and bucket-carry it to our washing machine once a week. The white clothes were washed first, then colored clothes and jeans and heavy cloths last, all in the same hot water. We had double rinse tubs and no dryers: the clothes were hung on clotheslines to dry.

During the Depression years, we had very little. Money was short and we did without. But everyone else was in the same shape. As kids, we didn't know any different.

All our clothes for school and Sunday clothes were homemade. Mom sewed our clothes and made most of them. She also made clothes for my daughter.

My first 8 years were in a one-room school, with one teacher for all grades. We had a wood stove for heat and an outside lunchroom and outside outhouse. We played baseball and had swings and see saws. There were 3 students in my class. We had a Christmas program and a program at the end of the school year.

We had bad storms. When it rained a lot, we had a hard time getting from our house to the county road. Our road was mud. Often the car got stuck. Then Dad had to pull it out with horses. Dad would say when it rained he could not fix the road and when it was dry he did not have to. Sometimes we did not get to school.

There were many encounters with snakes. One I remember was when I went to the barn to get some corn. After I got into the room, I heard a rattlesnake in the room. There was one

Eric with his car

Lillian and her sister Evelyn in 1928

way in and one way out, so I decided to run for it. I got Dad and a flashlight and a hoe. We got the snake and I had to go right by it on my way out. There were other snake stories, but that was the closest I ever got. Rattlesnakes were very common on the farm. Once you heard them rattle, you never forgot that sound.

One time at night, our cats made their screaming sound. They had a rattlesnake charmed, the snake in the center and the 3 cats all around it. That sound I never forgot, either. Dad got the snake.

There were many farm chores. We had to milk cows, feed pigs, feed chickens, pick up eggs, wash eggs, bring in wood, and whatever needed to be done at the time. In the summer, we helped with field work: chop cotton, pick cotton, cut corn tops, and whatever else was to be done.

My first love turned out to be my husband. We were married 61 years when he passed on. We had so many good times and some not so good. We always worked together. On the ranch, there wasn't anything I did not help with. This was a real partnership. I would do it all over again.

The most memorable people of my life were my parents and my grandmother. I lived with my grandmother when I was in high school. I learned to cook, bake, sew, can, and so much more from my mother and grandmother. I hope I passed this off to my daughter and grandchildren. Family means so much, and I do have a good one.

We did not get to take trips to town often. Dad went to town once a week to sell eggs and butter. Mom and us kids got to go once in a while. We each got 25 cents to spend on whatever we wanted. That was a real treat. We got to get new shoes: 1 pair for school, 1 for winter, and 1 for summer, which was actually Sunday shoes for church and when we went somewhere. In the summer at home, we went barefooted. Our trips to town were seldom.

We had ice boxes. Dad brought ice home once a week. It would melt sometimes long before he got to town again. Our first electric refrigerator was in 1942. What a great improvement.

As kids before 1942, in the evenings and in the summer time, we would sit or lay on quilts on the porch, look at the stars, and talk and catch lightning bugs. In the winter, we sat in the kitchen where it was warm. We would do homework, play games, and tell stories. There wasn't much to do and we had no electricity. It was kerosene lamps. On Sunday, we went to church and sometimes visited uncles and aunts or someone would come visit us.

Those were good times and hard times, nothing like today. I am so glad we had those times: a lot of memories.

Throwing Snakes and Swimming Hole Mischief
By Shirley A. Barbe of San Antonio, Texas
Born 1939

I was born in an old wood frame house. When I was about 2 years old, my dad built a big rock house. We didn't have electricity or indoor plumbing in the house at first, but the Saturday night bath was something else.

I was about 4 years old when we took a bath in a big round tub. We got indoor plumbing and my sister Nadine was told to give me a bath in our new tub. She took a wet washcloth and placed it on top of my head. I thought she was trying to drown me! But then it was over. She dried me off, gave me a big hug, and I knew she loved me.

I was about 7 or 8 years old when we got electricity. We had a radio sitting in the bedroom where Mom and Dad slept. We were listening to the Screeching Door. I was leaning up against the window in an old cane-bottom chair. My brother-in-law Cotton Frizzell took his fingernails and scratched on the glass. It scared me so bad the chair fell and I landed on the floor.

My school was from the 1st grade through the 8th grade. I got in trouble a lot. Mrs. Smith was my 1st grade teacher.

I was out on the merry-go-round eating a piece of hard candy when my front tooth came out. I was 6 years old. Mrs. Smith heard me say a bad word. She took a bar of soap and put it on my tongue and then told me to go wash it off. She told me to go home and tell my mom and dad what she had done and why, but that meant another spanking at home. I just took all the spanking that they were going to give me.

In the 7th grade, I said, "I can't" too many times to Mr. Palmer. He had a flat board with 3 holes in it. He didn't give me but 3 licks.

Miss Edith Lidstone, my 4th grade teacher, was my pet. She was the best teacher in San Saba County. She failed me on the report card, which I still have. I made all Ds and two Fs. Mrs. Davenport was my second 4th grade teacher.

That brings up the mischief I got into. My dad, Chris Hibler, was a good rock mason. He had made the lunchroom from the ground up. I thought in my mind, since my dad made the building I could write on the windowsills. Nell Spears and I, Shirley, left our names on every windowsill: "Nell loves So and So" and "Shirley loves Whimpy," a boyfriend I had.

Mr. Lane, the principal, made Nell and I

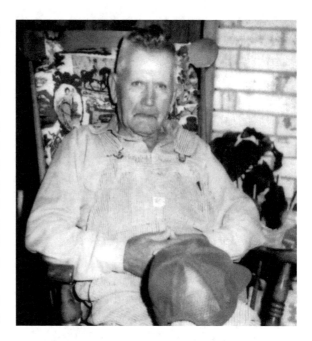

Shirley's father, Chris Hibler

wash every windowsill. It's a good thing we used a Number Two pencil. It came right off with soap and water.

My homemade dress was made of a flour sack. My mom was a great cook and used a lot of flour. She was also good with an old-fashioned Singer sewing machine. I was about 10 years old and the dress fit well, but it was too low in the V-neck. Mama crocheted a roll of shells at the top of the V. I loved that dress. When it got too small, Mama gave it away to a rummage sale. It sold to a little girl named Molly Hunt for a dime. To her it was a new dress and she wore it to school. She had no shoes on, but she loved that dress just like I did.

I had a school project. I had to get different kinds of leaves. The encounter with the snake was very short. I reached up to get a cottonwood leaf and a water moccasin came out of the tree and hit the water. By that time, I was back at the house already about 300 feet from the tank.

The second encounter was when Mom told us, my brother Hunter, and I, to pick up all the rocks and sticks and put them over the back fence. It looked like a long black burnt stick. I grabbed it and it moved in my hand. I threw it over the back fence real fast.

Mama said it was a black chicken snake, but it sure scared me.

My first kiss was from a boy named Lloyd Smith. He also got me my first box of Valentine's candy. I am 73 years old but have never forgotten it.

The trips to town I will never forget. My brother Hunter and I were sitting in the back of a Datsun pickup. I was sitting on the fender inside the pickup bed on the driver's side. My mom talked a lot and my dad listened and shook his head left and right to answer her. Dad dipped Garrett snuff and it was not in spit form but leaned his face out the window.

I was enjoying the wind in my face, leaning on the side of the pickup bed, when the snuff hit me full in the face, nose, and mouth. It was there until we got to town 15 minutes later. I know to this day if anyone comes around that dips snuff. I know what kind it is. The smell never left my nose.

I started going to swimming holes with

Shirley Hibler and her boyfriend, Jimmie Alexander in 1953

my boyfriend, Jimmie Alexander, when I was 14 years old in 1953. It was on the San Saba River at Risen Park. His dad, J. R. Alexander, owned a car lot on Highway 16, right across the street from Golding Motors. He owned a wrecking yard coming down the hill from Llano, Texas.

Jim and Jerry, his brother, got a piece of cable off a brand new cable truck they had. They took it down to the river and took a steering wheel of a wrecked car up on the hill around 1949 or 1950. Jerry, the brother, is still alive and I talked to him. He said they got into a lot of trouble for that.

The wheel has probably been changed. I don't know who is claiming to have put up the cable, but the tree tells the story. The cable was put up by Jimmie and Jerry Alexander about 53 years ago, and the cable is grown inside the trunk. It really is a good place to swim. I don't think anyone has ever drowned there. I lived in San Saba County from 1939 to 1956. I moved to San Antonio, Texas, where I now live.

Shirley's children Jimmie and Nelda in 1962

Beyond the Judge Roy Bean Story
By Leo Cardenas of Denver, Colorado
Born 1935

The large sign atop of the roof of the small office shouted: Judge Roy Bean, Law West of the Pecos.

No one could miss the large black and white sign at 904 Chapoy Street in Del Rio. I grew up across the street at 907 Chapoy in the 1940s and ran errands for the owner of the sign, Gonzalo (G. G.) Velasco. The authentic sign and saloon—the one that to this day makes tourists take a detour off U.S. Highway 90—is some 62 miles northwest at

Leo Cardenas in front of the Jersey Lilly

Langtry where the site of original saloon, the Jersey Lilly, continues to attract history buffs and folks who have seen some of the cable television shows of the famed justice of the peace.

So, what's with the sign?

All you had to do was ask Velasco as I made the mistake of doing, on more than one occasion. And to hear the answer, you had better have some time on your hand. As far as Velasco was concerned, those stories of the famed justice of the peace hanging outlaws and meting his own style of justice, well, that stuff was for the movies, and later television,

as far as he was concerned.

Velasco-born Gonzalo Gutierres, but everyone simply called him G.G., was fascinated with Judge Roy Bean. So much so, that he wrote a 28-page book that was published in the early 1940s and today finds space in libraries of colleges like the University of Texas in Austin and Baylor University at Waco.

While researching Velasco's life story, I was surprised to learn—from Google, of course—that Velasco had written the book. Since then, I have learned from Velasco's son, Dr. Gonzalo Pena (G.P.) Velasco, an 86-year-old retired chiropractor living in Los Angeles that his father's connection to Judge Bean was through his family. G.G.s sister, Manuela Velasco, was married to Judge Bean's son, Sam. A saloonkeeper and a deputy sheriff, Sam Bean was stabbed to death in 1907 in Del Rio where he and his famous father are buried at the Whitehead Memorial Museum. Judge Bean's death certificate, signed by Velasco even though he didn't witness the death, is also on display.

Judge Bean died in 1903 in Langtry. Velasco was 15 years old at that time, so he never got to meet the judge. That didn't stop him from taking advantage of his sister's

G.G. with his sister in 1948

202

marriage. He was always one of the orators at the *Cinco de Mayo* and *Diez y Seis de Septiembre* celebrations at the historic Brown Plaza where he would start out by asking the large crowd "Do you know who I am? I am G.G. Velasco, brother-in-law of Sam Bean, son of Judge Roy Bean, the Law west of the Pecos." He would then follow with a boisterous "Yeh-hey" that would bring cheers and laughter. He then would sneak in "I am your funeral director and notary public."

For the people living in the San Felipe neighborhood of the city, seeing the sign simply brought a chuckle and seldom questioned him about the judge. For them, Velasco was someone in the barrio who was fluent in English, a rarity for Mexican-Americans in the 1920s and 1930s, and, therefore could represent or help them with their legal matters under the guise of his notary public business. Few people knew that Velasco only had a third grade education, but who through perseverance and determination, had learned English mostly from 78-rpm records in his dusty record player in his office.

The same catalog firm provided him with the discs, including details and instructions on how to become a mortician. He augmented the discs with books and learned enough to become a licensed mortician after passing the grueling examination in San Antonio. He then served an apprenticeship at Doran Funeral Home, the only funeral home in Del Rio at the time.

After the people in the San Felipe neighborhood fought and won a legal battle to create their own independent school district on July 27, 1927, Velasco was elected to the school board in the early 1930s.

By the late 1930s, Velasco, the businessman, had saved enough cash to buy a used hearse and funeral preparation equipment to open his own funeral home. He added a back room to his small office and a garage for the shiny black hearse. By

then he also had seen too many of his fellow neighbors buried in paupers' graves for lack of money. So, along with the funeral home, he started an insurance firm with emphasis on burial insurance that people could afford.

The typing of legal papers and his notary signature brought a whole twenty-five cents. But, together with the funeral home, it was sufficient for his growing family that included his wife, Clotilde Pena Viesca, a widow from Brownsville, and their two sons. An accomplished pianist, Clotilde brought in extra cash by teaching piano lessons at home.

One of his most important contributions, however, was never planned and was taken for granted by those who visited his office out of need. His office had the only telephone for blocks around, so when people in the San Felipe neighborhood needed to call a physician, an employer, or a relative in another city, the neighbors went to *la oficina del Senor Velasco*. In time, the use of the telephone became second nature: drop a nickel in the glass jar on the desk for routine calls or wait for the monthly bill to pay for the long distance calls. If the call was of a personal nature, the caller would simply ask Velasco *por favor* (please) and he would leave the office to go the funeral home room.

Early in his adult life, Velasco had found that dealing with the public demanded a certain kind of personality if folks were going to become return customers or refer his services. He developed an ever-present smile that went with a strong greeting of *¡Ay Caramba!* and followed it with overexcited laughter that invited a similar laugh in return. That was for the Notary Public side of the business, which once seated in the only other chair in the small office, required tact and diplomacy to determine the best way to handle the customer's delicate matters. In some cases, this required for Velasco to put on a lawyer's hat even though he did not have formal legal training. This training came from his bookshelves, the discs, and his ability to manage his trusty manual typewriter, one finger at a time from each hand.

For the day to day business, he usually wore a pair of worn dress slacks and dress shirt with sleeves rolled up and an open collar to handle the hot weather in the border town. Some folks often talked, away from his presence, of course, about the need for newer and cleaner attire.

This type of talk would go away when all of a sudden there was a need for the mortuary side of the business. The need would come from a child with the simple explanation that *se murio mi abuelito* (my grandfather just died), or a sobbing wife or husband burping out *Ay, Senor Velasco, ya paso.* (Mr. Velasco, it has happened). By the time the hearse arrived at these homes to pick up the body, the driver, Velasco, was dressed in a spotless black suit in a clean pressed white shirt and a gray tie. Days later, I would be delivering *esquelas* (funeral notices) door to door.

When the funeral had been completed and a second visit to discuss payment was in order, it was Velasco who would say, much to his wife's chagrin, that "You can pay me when you can" when the burial insurance had expired or worse, there were no burial funds in the family's budget.

All of these neighborly business niceties came back to pay in handsome dividends to the Velasco family. One dark day on the tenth of October in 1942, a U.S. military officer came to 904 Chapoy Street to inform them that their son, Second Lieutenant Jerry Viesca, had been killed. A navigator, Lt. Viesca was on a fortress bomber named *The Judge Bean* when the plane went down in North Africa during World War II. Neighbors and even people beyond the immediate barrio poured out for the funeral services in Del Rio for Lt. Viesca, who is buried in Fort Sam Houston Cemetery in San Antonio.

Water Development Made It Possible to Enjoy the "Good Old Days"
By Robert H. Kensing of Menard, Texas
Born 1925

My parents, Ed and Annie Kensing, bought an unimproved property in the Reservation community in West Kerr County in 1920 for $8 an acre, no money down, 10% interest. This was in the Hill Country on the Edwards Plateau. The ranch now joins I-10 at the 488 marker. They moved there with my 3 older siblings. I was born in 1925.

Unimproved meant no fences to retain the livestock, no home to live in or outbuildings, pens, or even a water well. They built the barn and lived in it, or possibly drilled a well for water and put up a windmill, first. Gradually, they built a 4-room bungalow-style home with a front porch and back screen porch: no running water indoors, bathroom, or electricity. They fenced the property, built pens, another barn, chicken house, blacksmith shop, wash house/smoke house combination, dug a spot for a garden, fenced a yard, and

Robert's father, Ed Kensing

204

Robert's mother, Annie Kensing

plowed 20 acres of land for dry land farming.

As is the present situation in many parts of Texas, water was necessary and precious. In addition to the underground well, gutters were put on the roof of their home to catch rainwater when it rained. This water was stored in a hand dug underground cistern.

A hole for the cistern was dug about 7 or 8 feet deep and 5 feet in diameter. The bottom and sides were plastered with cement so it would hold water. Wire was used to hold the plaster to the dirt. When I was a 125-pound teen, we cleaned the inside. It was my job to be inside. Probably I fit best. I scraped the bottom and sides with a steel brush and put the loose dirt and cement in a bucket to be lifted out. We'd had a dry spell with no rain, so there wasn't any water in the cistern at that time.

Bolted to the lid of the cistern was a tin contraption about 4 feet high with a spout on the front and a handle to pump on the side. Inside the cistern was a chain connected with cups, approximately 20 feet long, that would bring the water from the cistern and out the spout as the handle was turned.

The pipe carrying the water from the gutters when it rained went into a box approximately 4 feet by 4 feet by 16 inches tall that was filled with gravel and homemade charcoal to clean and purify the water. Before it rained, the pipe was turned to allow the water that had cleaned the dust off the roof to run on the ground before going through the box of charcoal and into the cistern. After it rained a bit to clean the roof, it was my job to turn the pipe to let the water go through the box and into the cistern. It was an exciting time when the rain came with thunder and lightning. It made a little boy anxious.

Most homes in the community had a similar means of catching and using rainwater. Reservation School had gutters on the school building, the same as family homes, except with the big roof it didn't take as much rain to fill the cistern and it came down the pipe much faster. Therefore the lid and pump system was raised much higher above ground to make sure the water from the ground didn't run into the cistern. This was the only water available for teachers who lived in the teacherage. They had to carry in the water with buckets.

The water for the school kids was put in a 5-gallon container with a spigot and put on a bench on the front porch of the school. When the Taylors came to teach at Reservation they explained this only one cup used by everybody was unsanitary. Thereafter, each child was encouraged to provide his private cup. Mr. Taylor put hangers on the wall for the cups. The Marschall kids had tin cups that folded up, to the envy of us all. You could drink all the water you wanted, but do not waste any by playing, spitting on a friend, or throwing it away. It wasn't important to wash your hands at school. Water was too precious.

Rainwater was nice soft water where the well water had minerals. I didn't like to drink rainwater, no taste! When we had lots of rain, Mama really liked to use it for washing clothes.

Robert H. Kensing

The wash pot was filled with rainwater, a fire built under it to boil the water, with cut up homemade lye soap. Most of the time we used well water the same way. With either the well or rainwater there wasn't much suds. She always used well water in the rinse tubs, along with stuff called bluing. She had pretty, bright white clothes by using the lye soap, bluing, and hanging the white clothes on the line in the sunshine: her own method to bleach to whiten.

Mama liked to use rainwater to wash her hair and made it soft. Pa liked to drink it.

After the wash, the soapy water was used to clean the porch and the rinse water to water the garden or trees. It was valuable water.

Underground water in this part of Texas was and still is in streams. A douser or a person who could witch water was used to locate the streams. But it wasn't always successful as only 3 of the 8 wells drilled on my parents' property had enough water to warrant putting a windmill. The well drilled for the house water was more than 200 feet deep to reach water. There are complicated, boring details to explain how the windmills were used. Here is the short, simple version: Over 200 feet of 2 inch galvanized pipe was put in the hole that was drilled. At the bottom of the well was a cylinder with a bottom and top valve connected to the rods that brought up the water as the windmill fan turned.

The Aeromotor brand windmill was used at that time. There was a need for good wrenches, a block and tackle, ropes, and chains to repair the well and get it pumping again. Often several neighbors shared this work. It was very common in our community to share work that required several men.

The size and depth of the windmill needed was determined by the depth of the hole. Ours was 35 feet tall. Extra power was needed to bring water from a deep hole. The wind provided the power to turn the fan. Hot still summer days were not good! No wind, no water, and no bath either.

The "Good Old Days" bring memories of a good many wonderful days and times. I do not wish living with a water shortage. One of the best ones from that time for a country boy was watching the well driller. It usually took about a week to drill the well. The rotary drill was not available at that time.

One thought comes to mind about water use. We have many more people who use more water than really necessary. The "old timers" lived a hard life however, water development made it possible to enjoy the "good old days." This certainly makes me grateful and I appreciate being able to turn the handle of our faucets and get hot, cold, or lukewarm water in my home.

Gully Washer Escape
By Gary A. Smith of Visalia, California
Born 1934

Mom (Winnie Mae Hagee Smith), brother, Richard, sisters (Lorna, Roberta, and Betty) and I, Gary, lived in El Paso, Texas, in late 1920s. Our dad (Arden) had died in an automobile accident in 1945. Mom's oldest brother, (Ralph Hagee), and his family lived a few miles from us.

Mom's youngest brother, R L Hagee, had purchased a quarter section of land north of Fredericksburg, Texas, just south of Uncle

206

Gary's sister, Betty, his mom, Winnie Mae Hagee Smith, and his brother, Richard

Ralph who had moved there earlier from EI Paso. He was a career man in the U.S. Navy and was still serving. He moved their parents, George Washington and Bertha Mae Hagee, into a house on their property. In 1948, Ralph called our mom and told her that Fredericksburg was a good place to raise children. She moved my brother, two sisters, and I to Fredericksburg to live with our grandparents. She and our older sister, Lorna, stayed in EI Paso where work was available for them. The only trade Mom knew was being a telephone operator. She inquired about work in Fredericksburg but their rate of payment for salaries was far less than what she had been receiving. She eventually went to work for South Western Bell in Austin. She would travel almost every weekend to Fredericksburg to be with us. She had no car so her nearly weekly travels were by bus. Uncle Ralph would pick her up to and from the bus station.

We attended Rusk Elementary in EI Paso and Fredericksburg High School. Our home place was a mile from the school bus stop but we had to walk to and from there regardless of the weather conditions.

Uncle Ralph and Aunt Myrtis and their family had moved from EI Paso and lived about a mile north of us. They had to drive past our home to go town. She was the pianist in the little Presbyterian Church, which was on the north side of Fredericksburg. I had been raised in a Baptist church in EI Paso but soon became Presbyterian. We went to church every Sunday with Aunt Myrtis who was the church pianist, which we enjoyed.

I don't recall listening to the radio in Fredericksburg but do remember the local radio station was KNAF. The first time I watched television was at Dr. Springall's home. He and his family were members of the Presbyterian Church and they invited us over on numerous occasions to watch television with them. The television was so small and of course the pictures were all in black and white but we didn't mind. There were only two channels available. One was from San Antonio and the other from Austin.

We were fortunate in having a telephone, which was on a party line. It was a wooden box, which hung on the wall with a crank on the right side. Our ring was one long and two shorts and, should we be so inclined, we could hear the conversations between other party line members.

Our bathtub was quite unique. It was a hand fabricated, galvanized sheet metal tub over a wooden frame. Since the water was heated by a tub in the firebox of Grandma's cook stove in the kitchen, it was rare that any of us took a bath and drained the tub. Even more unusual was to bathe in fresh water.

In the summer between my junior and senior year I bought my first car. It was a 1934

Gary's first car and his first girlfriend, Vivian Kelso

Gary's dog, Jerry

Dodge for $75; made in the same year I was born. My plan was to have a car during my senior year... but my plan was short lived.

My dog, Jerry, was my constant companion and would eat anything we ate. I really loved little Jerry. One day Granddad found one of his sheep with a ripped throat and he assumed that Jerry had done it. He told me that once a dog tasted sheep he would kill again. Then he told me to take Jerry out into the woods and shoot him. Jerry would always follow me when I took my 22 rifle out hunting but this was one of those times, which I could not get my rifle and go to the woods. I just could not shoot little Jerry so Granddad told me to get in my car and go to town. I did and never saw Jerry again. My cousin, Clyde, and I often went coon hunting with successful results most times; but it was never the same without my buddy Jerry.

Clyde and I worked for Ruben Meier on the Morris Ranch. Clyde's car was in the shop and he wanted to go to his in-law's home to get his wife. We decided to go in my car and take a route that would cross Live Oak Creek. There had been no rain in our area but obviously, there had been a "gully washer" north of the head of the creek. We were to cross using a concrete culvert. Water was already flowing across the culvert although it didn't look to be of concern so I started to drive across.

The distributor on the car was mounted on the lower engine block where the pan joins the block. The water splashed up and shorted the ignition. IT STOPPED US COLD!

Clyde had been riding along beside me in the front seat. His nephew, Marshall, was riding in the back seat. I looked out the driver's window and saw the water rising on the side of the door. I yelled to the guys and told them to get out because the water pressure was going to shove us off the culvert. All of us had to leave from the right side of the car and I was the last one out. I had on tight Levis and combat boots, very poor swimming attire! Even though I was a pretty good swimmer, Clyde had to help me out of the rushing water. Just as I reached the bank, I turned in time to see my car being washed off the culvert and become totally submerged in the creek. Since the car was totally under water, we felt there was nothing else we could do and finally hitched a ride to Kelsos, Clyde's in-laws, who were also my girlfriend's parents. The next day, Sunday, we took a large tractor over to Live Oak Creek with the hopes of towing my car back to Kelsos. I had high hopes of cleaning and repairing it, but no such luck! When I opened the door and hood, everything was filled with mud and muddy water. I eventually sold it to the owner of the local junk yard for fifteen dollars.

My cousin Russell who was visiting from El Paso and I decided we wanted some fireworks for the 4th of July celebration. There was no one to take us into town so we walked. It was quite a walk but well worth it. Everyone enjoyed our mini fireworks show that evening.

Throughout my high school years, I lived 7 miles north of Fredericksburg. After graduation in 1952, I moved to Austin to live with Mom again. I found a job at a local service station where I worked until I joined the

Navy. My enlistment physical was completed in Houston. A very short time afterward, I was flown to San Diego in a DC3, my first flight, for boot camp! I retired from the U.S. Navy twenty- two years later and will treasure the countless, wonderful adventures of my enlistment for a lifetime... but my memories of living in Fredericksburg with my extended family will always remain my favorites.

New Challenges in Education Must Be Met
By Elmer Wahrmund of Fredericksburg, Texas
Born 1929

When the first settlers came to Fredericksburg, the construction of a church, the so-called community church. It was also used as a schoolhouse. The building began in the fall of 1846 and was completed in the summer of 1847. As the population of Gillespie County grew and more people were living out in the country, the one-room school was very important to the rural people. They built schoolhouses near their home. The children learned the 3 R's: reading, writing, and arithmetic. The structure of the one-room school was basically all the same. They were big enough for about 25 students; a wood stove in a sand box in the center of the room was the only source of heat. Some had kerosene lamps for light. The school that I went to did not have kerosene lamps. The only source of light was five windows on the south side and three on the west. The teacher's desk and a chair and a bench were in the front of the classroom. The teacher had a bell on the desk to summon students to class. There was a blackboard also some maps and a globe and usually the United States flag. There was a table or small closet in the back where students put their lunch buckets and dippers for drinking

water. All the students had to bring their own lunch. The dippers were used for dipping water out of a water bucket. Other students used their water dippers to go outside to get a drink out of a well or a cistern. There was an outdoor toilet about 60 yards from the school.

In September of 1936, I started my first day of school in a one-room schoolhouse in the Tivydale community. I remember very well that first morning my dad took me to school in his Model T Ford truck. I was seven years old and just a little bit scared. I kept looking at a globe of the world that was hanging in front of the room. I wondered if I would learn all the geography of the earth. I kept wishing to already be grown up like my dad. I guess I felt like a prisoner or something. I was beginning to think from then on I would have to spend a good part of my time in that building. We did have a few celebrations. At Christmas time, the students would put on a program and Santa Claus would be there. The school closing in May was a bigger celebration sometimes with beer for the adults and soda water and lemonade for the kids. The days are gone. The 21st century is upon us. New challenges in education have to be met.

Back to the Restaurants
By Ken Odiorne of Bertram, Texas
Born 1936

In the winter of 1949 on January 31st, the temperature in Burnet, Texas dropped to -6°F. I was 12 years old. I lived with my parents and two sisters, ages six and four at the time. We had done well during the end of the depression between 1938 and 1946 in New Braunfels, Texas. At the end of the war, my dad figured that New Braunfels would dry up so we moved to Dallas where he did well until the recession of 1947. After another unsuccessful restaurant fry in Wheaton, Texas, we moved to Burnet County, our birth county where our home ranch was. We were doing fairly well at ranching with a fairly large heard of 60 hogs and even more sheep.

One day in late 1948, one hog was found dead. The veterinarian was called and the first disaster struck, pink spots on the liver, Cholera! All the hogs had to be destroyed and incinerated before the quarantine was lifted. Then came that awful day on January 30, 1946. It began with rain then sleet, then that awful -6°F; the record low in Burnet (-3°F in Austin and is still the record). I am not sure what total number of new lambs we had but I pulled 22 out from within and under the barn. I know I cried and I would bet my dad did too. We all gathered around the potbellied wood heater. My dad said that this was it, we are moving back to Austin and we did. Back into the restaurant business we went.

Selling Cows
By Richard Clark of Rockdale, Texas
Born 1949

My Grandfather Howard was 90 years old in 1995. He liked to sit in his rocking chair and tell me stories about the good old days. He and Grandmother Vivian had been married four years in 1932 and had two children, Jack who was four years old and Nell who was three years old. These were in the Great Depression years, 1928 through 1939. Franklin Roosevelt was President and he got a bill passed in Congress to help thousands of starving farmers. The government would pay the farmer $8.00 a head for a cow. Grandfather had three cows and he drove them to a receiving center. The land where the receiving center was belonged to a man named Buddy Smith. The government employee would issue a check for $8.00 a head. They would kill the cows, skin them, and a bulldozer would push the carcass in a ditch and they would bury it. They would ship the hides to a tanning

factory and tan them to use in the leather industry. My grandfather told me he could take the $24.00 and buy a year's supply of groceries consisting of flour, meal, sugar, salt, coffee, pinto beans, bacon, lard, and syrup. The rest of our food came out of the garden. Grandfather worked for a large landowner, building a fence about, two weeks of the month for one dollar a day in the summer time. Grandfather said he felt blessed to be able to feed his family when people in New York City were selling apples and begging on the streets. There was no work, no jobs to be had.

Dealing with a Claustrophobic Horse
By Hazel Castonguay of Fredericksburg, Texas
Born 1944

I grew up in Crockett County on a ranch 40 miles from Ozona, Texas and 12 miles from Pandale, Texas. We had a lot of horses that my brother, daddy, and myself rode around the ranch. There were 32 sections on the ranch so we had a lot of riding area. My mother and dad did not own the ranch, but my dad was the ranch foreman. The owner lived in San Angelo, Texas and would usually visit my family on Sunday for lunch and discuss what was going on with the ranch hands and different seasons. When the lambs were born in the early spring, when it was time to round up the sheep and shear them.

My brother Jim was two years older than I and we enjoyed each other in school events like football, track, and cheerleading. My parents were very supportive. We both joined in the junior rodeos and our daddy would help us load the horses and we joined the parade and events in the rodeo. I was a contestant for rodeo queen one year. My brother and cousins joined in the goat-pulling contest and roping. One horse had washed away in a flood of 1954 and had claustrophobic problems when he got in a tight place. One day I was riding Aejo and he got in a lot of bush and close to the wire fence. He had a claustrophobic attack and started shaking and sweating all over and suddenly jumped over the fence. We were close and I grabbed the saddle horn and managed to cling to him as he jumped the fence, but when he hit the ground on the other side, I fell to the ground and landed on my back. The fall slammed the back of my head and back to the ground. I was the recipient of a long mesquite thorn in the middle of my back, 1-½ inches to the right of my spine.

My brother rode his horse over and helped me up. The horse stood there and calmed down that I was riding. My brother Jim said he would ride the 10 miles to the house where we lived and bring the truck to drive me home. My mother called our family doctor and he advised her to leave the thorn in my back for a couple of days until it festered and she could get it out with a needle and tweezers. This was in the early 1960s and my mother was always a good nurse when things like this happened. I was very uncomfortable, but she followed the doctor's instructions and managed to get the mesquite thorn out and put peroxide in to clean out the wound. I felt like Paul in the Holy Scriptures when he talked about a thorn in his side, but I was healed.

Escaping the Flood
By Lavon Clark of Rockdale, Texas
Born 1927

It started raining on July 12, 1938 and rained for over a week. The San Saba River was running full bank and at that time, we were sharecroppers on the U.M. Sanderson farm. The radio warned all residents that were in the flood zone to move to higher ground immediately. There were five of us in our family, my dad, my mother, my

two sisters and myself; I was nine years old. Dad loaded the wagon with some food and bedding, clothing and some cookware. He hooked two horses to the wagon. Dad saddled a horse for me to drive our three milk cows out and we were off to high ground.

It was a mile out of the bottom to high ground and we had to cross a slough bridge on the way out. The cows would not cross the bridge, so I forced them into the water and they swam across. The horse I was riding was blind in her right eye and when I rode her on the bridge, she shied to her blind side and I slid off and led her across the bridge. Dad followed in the wagon, it was about ¼ mile to our destination. The property belonged to Frank Allison; he had a nice two-story house and a big drive through barn.

The Leslie Jones family also lived in the Sanderson farm bottom. Mr. Jones, his wife, and two boys were already in the barn. As soon as dad got us situated in the barn, he and Mr. Jones loaded up and went back in the bottom to take care of the chicken, hogs, and horses. The floodwater got three feet deep in the house and the house was on the highest ground on the farm. Dad and Mr. Jones had to climb into the attic to escape the rising water. They had to cook over a kerosene lamp. They cut a hole in the roof, which exited to the porch roof to have an escape route in case the house was washed off its foundation. Dad took a rope and swam over to a large oak tree, close to the house and tied it to a big branch in the oak tree and secured it to the house so if the water moved the house they could escape to safety of the large oak tree.

The hogs and chickens all washed away! After they were in the attic for five days, a man named Elvis Brown had a motorboat and he came in and rescued them. It was about a mile you had to cross the slough, which was the main current when the river reached flood stage to get to the house they were in, which was so close to the river that

211

I could throw a rock in the river from our backyard. Mr. Brown and Mr. Ballow rescued dad and Mr. Jones and we all rejoiced because we had not heard from them in five days.

Babysitting the Turkeys
By Wanda Holloway of Llano, Texas
Born 1926

We lived in the country and this was before we got electricity. I would walk about a mile to our neighbor's house. They were an elderly couple and no children, so I was their grandchild. They bought a new kerosene refrigerator and she made homemade ice cream in the ice trays and boy was it good. She would also give us a jar of ice for tea at supper. They were wonderful people. She also gave me a birthday party for my 10th birthday and invited my schoolmates. She played the piano and on Sunday nights would have a singing for the community. After she got older, she gave me the piano and I still have it. My sister and I would go to Sunday school with them and ride in the rumble seat of their car. This was in the '30s before we got electricity. I had a very happy childhood.

I was the youngest of four children in my family. I didn't start to school until I was seven years old. We had to walk five or six miles along the edge of Brisco Mountain to school. My sister was three years older than me. We had to climb fences as we went through

Wanda, her sister, Audrey, and a playmate, Allen

several pastures. Sometimes we would take a different route. There was always little mountain streams flowing and we could gather wild onions and lettuce. One day as we were walking home from school, we found a big rattlesnake and it got in a bush pile. I carried the rocks and my sister was trying to kill it, but the rocks were bouncing off. We thought we had killed it, but the next morning it was gone. We just had it covered up. It was quite an experience, but all the other children walked. We lived farther than the others from school.

My grandfather was the great grandson of Daniel and Rebecca Bryan Boone. His grandmother was the daughter of the well-known frontiersman. He used to tell us stories about the Indians and panthers. This is a true story. He had a sow and pigs in the pen, when a panther attacked them. He grabbed his gun and rushed out to save his hogs, but had only one shell in it. So he shot the panther and wounded it, then jumped on it with his

Wanda's parents, Lonnie and Myrtle

pocketknife and with the help of his dogs and killed it. He lost one dog in the battle. He was a small man, but lived a great life. He died at the age of 93 years sitting in his rocking chair.

We were raised on a farm and ranch in Llano County and liked to get out and walk. My sister was three years older than I and we would walk in the pasture where there was mesquite trees and hunt for mesquite wax. The part we didn't eat we made glue out of it. This was in the early 1930s. We also hunted fox cactus, the kind that grew flat on the ground. They bloom first then have little red cactus. Sometimes we would find a lot of them and mother would make a pie out of them. We thought this was really good and was at the time. My mother raised turkeys and my sister and I would follow them around so snakes and hawks wouldn't catch them. Then we brought them home at night. We enjoyed doing this, as there wasn't much else to do after school was out in the summertime. I don't know how we survived without getting bit by a snake. When you grow up in the country, you are aware of this all the time.

My Grandmother, Big Mama
By Lina M. Davis of Seguin, Texas
Born 1951

I was born to a family of seven children, I was the third born. Two of my sisters died when they were babies and I never knew them. My parents had to leave us most of the time with our grandmother to work in the fields. My grandmother was one of the best ladies I've even known. She had a large family of her own, with one child that was hit by a car on his first day of school. She didn't mind keeping us at all, my grandmother was mom and grandma, to anyone's children, it didn't matter what race they were; they were always welcome in her home.

Everyone knew my grandmother as Mrs. White or Big Mama. My grandmother taught me and everyone else that wanted to learn how to cook, sew, and keep house. I remember everything she taught me up until this day, and I try and walk in her footsteps because she was one great lady. When I think of Big Mama, I cry and I get in my car and I drive to New Braunfels, Texas, where her house use to be. It looks so different, but yet it still takes me back to the days where I grew up and it makes me feel good to remember the days where I grew up at and the times I spent with my grandmother. I can't bring them back but I can remember them and share them with my daughter and my grandchildren, as much as I can. I want them to know as much about my life as my grandma wanted me to know about her life and adventures. I feel everyone should know about his or her family history and to keep it alive. This is the thanks that I will always give to my grandma and I'm glad to have had such a wonderful grandma. As long as I'm alive, I will remember her and will keep the memories alive. There was never a dull moment or anything too great for her to conquer, well maybe one thing. Her son got burned in a car wreck, coming home one night, all over his body from head to toe. Big Mama dealt with that also. My mom went to where her brother was in Galveston. My grandma kept us because at the time her other son that could not walk needed her also, since he was her youngest son. My mom came back after a while then my grandmother went to Galveston to her son where she stayed a while. My uncle was a fighter and with the blessings of God he came home to recover and Big Mama nursed him back to health. Everyone could see this was one great lady indeed. All the kids around the neighborhood and other friends started calling her Big Mama; she was Big Mama indeed.

I sit and think of her often and when I look at my mom, I think of my Big Mama because she looks just like her mom. Born in

New Braunfels, I will never forget my history and where I came from. I remember the day I received the call about my grandma; I was at work. My grandma took her last breath five minutes before I got there. I hated to see my grandmother go, but I just said my grandmother doesn't have to be busy anymore. God gave her to us and God took her home to rest and she can now be free with no more worries.

Take a Deep Breath and Go!
By Shirlene Rogers of Llano, Texas
Born 1943

We were poor when I was growing up, but it took me a while to realize that. Our house had no bathroom and no indoor plumbing until I was about 10 years old, so of course we had a horrible outdoor toilet. I always hated to visit that thing! The odor was atrocious and the Montgomery Ward catalog wasn't soft. Needing the bathroom after dark wasn't pleasant either. When bath time came, mother would heat pans of water and pour them into a round galvanized tub that had been placed beside the kitchen stove. Everyone took turns taking a bath, in the same water, and I'm sure I wasn't the only one who never enjoyed that. On nights that we didn't bathe, we took spit baths, which just involved wetting a washcloth, soaping up, and washing off.

Cold weather used to be colder in Central Texas and it was much colder in our house. We had one coal oil heater for the whole house and we would take turns standing as close as possible. At night, mother would pile homemade quilts on until I could barely turn over. She also hung quilts over our windows and when the wind blew, the quilts moved.

My grandparents and great grandparents were an important part of my life. Grandma Beulah used her treadle sewing machine to make some of my clothes. When I outgrew a dress, she would rip the seams, use the dress for a guide, and cut a pattern from a newspaper. Then she would cut out a dress from a cotton flour sack. Flour came in sacks of different colors and patterns. Sometimes she took me to the store and let me pick out the flour sack that I wanted to use for a dress. The dresses I outgrew got cut into squares and she used them to make quilts. The rest of my wardrobe was ordered every year before school started from Montgomery Ward. Mother would turn to the Economy Page where they had a selection of maybe six or seven of the cheapest dresses and my little sister and I got to choose three dresses each.

I had the croup a lot when I was young. One of my parents' home remedies was to warm some coal oil, mix some with a spoonful of sugar, and give me a dose. They would also dip a cloth into hot coal oil and put it on my chest. I'm not sure if any of this helped the croup, but it did make me feel taken care of and loved.

My best friend, Linda, and I lay outside almost all day, every day. We would pack a picnic lunch; go exploring in the pastures, and climb trees. One day as we played in the sandy bed of a nearby creek, we saw two red ants that looked like they were fighting. That gave us an idea. We decided if we got two red ants form different ant beds and put them together, they would probably fight. So we built a boxing ring out of sand, split up and each looked for ant beds. Each of us brought a red ant back to the ring and we watched to see which one would win. Unfortunately, our theory didn't prove true, but we tried several times.

I'm not sure why we went barefooted, but it wasn't always fun. Many times, we would come to a big sticker patch and there was nothing to do but go through it. We learned the best thing to do was stand on the edge, prepare yourself, take a deep breath, and go! If you stopped in the middle, it was worse, because there was nowhere to sit and pull stickers out. Run fast and get to the other side and then feel the pain and pull stickers. Those good old days of my childhood are fond memories now. Then again, maybe some are not so fond.

Escaping Vietnam
By Ralph Hatchell of Fort Stockton, Texas
Born 1947

A little town in the back woods of Texas, about 30 miles from Fort Hood, Texas, one of the largest military posts in the Army. A town of hills, valleys, rivers, also a place for hunting, fishing, sports, and many other activities. There were so many friendly people willing to step out and help other people. There used to be a drive in movie there in 1975 also at one time a bowling alley. Before television came in there were old radio shows like *Fibber McGee and Molly, The Lone Ranger, The Shadow, Lassie, Jackie Gleason*, and many more. There was the five and ten-cent stores, soda fountains before all the fast food restaurants came in. Oh, the joy of the black and white televisions when they came in, as then you could set in your own home with family watching love shows and many other shows without going to a movie.

Myself, I can remember all of them things, the good times I call them, but we also had bad times while growing up. We had girlfriends and girls had boyfriends. Driving around double dating parking somewhere to be alone. Then there was Halloween trick or treat, but was a lot safer back then than it is now. Yes, so many good times to tell your children about, as you remember back on them. Yes, there were a lot of bad times friends and family getting killed in some way, wars, and hurts that stay with people for the rest of their life, but most of the time good times outweigh the bad.

The first time I came to Texas was in 1960 with my brother Charles Monroe Hatchell. My mother, Catherine Proctor Ragle, and my stepfather, James William Ragle, and I was 13 years old at that time. My full name is Ralph Wayne Hatchell and I went by the name of Wayne until I joined the Army on

August 1965. I was in the Army station at Coleman Barracks in a part of Mannheim, Germany living in Schonau, Germany with my wife, Waltraud Hatchell, who everyone calls Traudel. When my father was killed in August of 1967 that was my stepfather, as I only met my real father January of 1968, along with my wife Traudel and our first son Wayne James Josef Hatchell. He was a baby and my father Carl Monroe Hatchell first got to see his first grandson and held him why I played my guitar and sung songs for him for the first time and though we made plans to see each other again, it would be the last time we saw him alive, as he died in December of 1968.

It had been a good time seeing him and my stepmother and stepbrother David, my stepmother I can't remember her named. We moved to Fort Hood, Texas and lived in a little one-room house at Killeen, Texas close to Killeen Post Office. While I was stationed at Fort Hood, I was called into my unit to go and escort the body of my friend home to his family and wife. His name was Bellamie and he had been killed in Vietnam, also I was to have gone with him, but my stepfather got to Vietnam and they took me off orders to go and I was sent to Fort Hood, Texas.

It was after I got back from escort duty that I again came down and was ordered to go to Ford Louis, Washington to train and go to Vietnam, leaving my wife and little

Ralph and his wife, Waltraud Hatchell

215

son with a baby on the way at Fort Hood and Killeen, Texas. Again, I got out of going to Vietnam as my brother Charles who was in the Air Force was going to get out and who he worked for wanted him to stay in so he said he would stay in if they took me off of orders going to Vietnam and he would go to Vietnam for two years, so they did and I brought my wife Traudel to Fort Louis, Washington, along with our son Wayne and she was pregnant with our daughter Delores.

We only stayed a short time close to Fort Louis and then I came down and there were orders sending me to Fort Carson, Colorado and later we bought our first home there at Colorado Springs until 1970 when I came again on orders sending me to Vietnam. We put our home up for sale and I moved my family to Fayetteville, North Carolina where we found a little two-room house, a block from where my mother Catherine lived, so she could help my wife and the children while I was in Vietnam. After being wounded two times while in Vietnam and staying there for one year, I was again sent to Germany with my family. After Germany, we came back to Fort Hood, Texas and stayed in Killeen, Texas first and then moved to Copperas Cove for a while then bought our home at 21 Hollywood Drive in Lampasas, Texas where we still are today.

I was sent back to Germany again and brought my wife and children over. Our last son, Corey Cyrus Hatchell was born in Bremerhaven, Germany and in 1981, we all came back to our home in Lampasas as I was again stationed at Fort Hood, Texas and many times, I went other places on temporary duty. One time back to Germany, but I left my family in Lampasas, Texas.

In 1985 on the first of September, I retired from the Army. First worked at a gas station along with Bobby Brown, my best friend. Then I did construction work, operating heavy equipment, in Austin, and then went to building homes for a builder in Lampasas,

from there back to the gas station. Then I was working at Lampasas Schools building and grounds. I left there and worked at Wal-Mart for five years becoming department manager. Then went back to school at the middle school cleaning it until my back went out and because of college, I had while in the Army, and after the Army, they made me a teacher's aid. That was by the high school and I worked there helping boys and girls form the 7th grade through the 12th grade until 1998 when because of health problems that I got when I was in Vietnam, I could no longer work, so veteran's administration would not let me go back to work.

Lampasas is a town of people who help others, a town of love, and many things to do. It is a town I miss so much, a town I would like to have a second chance in, as I do the will of God and be with my family and friends for the rest of my life. A town where I can again sing in the rain on bandstand and other churches also drive my old 1970 Ford Ranchero and the car and truck shows again; yes back to Lampasas, a town I love a tow that has become mine.

She Believed Castor Oil Cured Everything
By Mabel Edmondson of San Saba, Texas
Born 1924

School was in a two-room, white building, and four miles from my house. My sister, who was five years older than I, either walked or rode horseback. The first day I went to school I was either to shy or stubborn to go to the outhouse when the teacher, Mrs. Stroble, asked me if I needed to go. A little later, it was too late and I wet myself and she gave me a spanking and made me go out to the outhouse. The other kids never let me forget it.

Mama believed in castor oil for everything, from colds to constipation, but her dose consisted of putting the oil in coffee, black with no sugar. I have hated coffee all my life. We had no radio or telephone in the 1930s. The only water we had was in the river, which we carried in the buckets to the house. In winter, we bathed in a number three washtub by the kitchen wood cook stove. In summer, we went to the river to bathe and wash clothes. We had no washing machine, only an iron wash kettle that was filled with water and a fire built around it to keep it hot. This iron pot held about 20-gallons of water and was used to scald hogs for eating, making lye soap for laundry, and bathing and washing dishes, rendering the hog fat for lard and making cracklings out of the hog hide. For fun times like at picnics we made a pot full of Mulligan Stew, what was left over, everyone took some home. Everyone brought something to put in it, like potatoes, corn, beans, etc.

We lived 13 miles from San Saba and the road was a dirt trail, wide enough for a wagon or later a Model T truck. One day coming home from school I was riding the horse, the saddle turned and we fell off. My sister fell on top of me and when we tried to get up my right arm wouldn't work. It was broken an inch below the shoulder. We got it tucked into my overalls and Jo put the saddle back on. Somehow, we rode three more miles home and mama and daddy weren't there! I laid on the bed and way after dark they came and they took me to the doctor's office in San Saba. It was broken so bad that Dr. Pence couldn't set it. There was a new doctor in town, Dr. Failey and Dr. Pence sent for him and he finally got it put back together. I was taped up so tight I got sores under the tape. It took a long time to heal.

Pretty soon, after that, my sister died and we moved to town. My dad worked on the P.W.A., paving streets in San Saba for $1.00 a day. The depression was on and there was no money. We had had a few cows while living in the county and the government bought them for $5.00 a head and shot them and pushed them over a cliff. They let us keep one to dress to eat. We canned it in tin cans with a pressure

cooker and salted some of it in containers.

We didn't have an icebox till we moved to town. We bought ice when daddy had money, 50-pound blocks, wrapped it in all quilts and a wagon sheet, and we would chip off the block, sometimes we had ice cream in a hand cranked freezer. Sometimes when daddy had $0.05 to spare before we moved to town. We could go to the movie on Saturday while mama and daddy did the town errands, such as selling the eggs for $0.05 a dozen, selling some farm supplies and getting staples like flour, meal, and soda. The rest we raised and canned or preserved.

Sometimes during the bad 1945-1955 years, the feed companies started putting feed in material sacks. I made my children's clothes and mine from these sacks. I still have a few of the things I made in the 1940s. We stayed living on a farm in 1949 and there was no water much in the community. I had a Maytag Wringer Washer. It was a square tub made of heavy aluminum. Some were made with gasoline engines, but mine was electric. We had gotten electricity in 1945. We had a smoke house, which was originally for smoking meat to keep it usable all winter and early spring. I put in the washer, made a drain and all my neighbors came to wash for $0.75 an hour. That lasted till the smokehouse burned down from an electric short. Burned the grass to the wall of where we lived and stopped. We didn't know it burned till we woke up.

The Life of the Turns
Ruby Turn of Austin, Texas
As told to Jean Grady
Born 1913

From what we can gather, Henry Turn and Lillie Ann Hendryx met in the Pontotoc Community near Brady. A.J. remembers his mother telling that she and Henry communicated by exchanging notes put in a hole in a tree trunk Orville says his mother told him that Henry rode on horseback down the railroad track behind her house and when she saw him, she set her cap for him and finally caught him. Pauline says Lillie dated Henry's brother Andrew before she dated Henry.

Henry Turn and Lillie Hendryx and Timothy Landrum and Helga Mathilda Turn married in a double ceremony July 16, 1905. Each couple arrived at the East Sweden Church in their buggies and the preacher, J.A. Irvine, performed the ceremony as each couple remained in their buggy. First one couple was married, then the other. The couples witnessed for one another. We know that they had planned a formal wedding because of their dress, but we think that due to the fact that Henry and Helga's father died three weeks prior to their wedding date, they made their wedding as simple as possible. Henry and Lillie worked as tenant farmers on the Dutton, Shropshire, and Winnie farms in the Brady Community, but earning a living was not easy. To supplement their income, Henry corded wood for $1.00 a day and picked cotton, along with any other job he could get. Lillie raised turkeys and later canned food on halves, took in laundry, and worked out as a practical nurse.

Orville remembers that while living on the Dutton place, Lillie Turn raised turkeys. She had around 500 and it was the children's duty to keep up with the nests, which the turkeys were very adept at hiding. Orville says he would walk backwards toward the nests thinking the turkeys would think he was going away from the nests instead of coming to them; this must have been the origin of calling a person "turkey."

One year while Henry Turn was in Waco working, Lillie and the children stayed home on Winnie's place and got stranded by a snowstorm. Orville remembers Grandpa Ake bringing food on horseback and he can still see him coming across the pasture covered with prairie dog holes and snow up to the horses' belly. Pauline and Bea recall Aunt Claudie bringing food on horseback too. One year, as the family was following the cotton crops from Brady on south, they picked cotton for a doctor who owned a farm in Taft, Texas. Orville remembers this very well because they furnished all the milk, eggs, and butter they could eat. The doctor tried to get the family to stay on his farm and sharecrop, but they moved on.

During this move from Brady to Sinton in their wagon, the family had a little donkey that followed them all the way. When going through towns, boys would try to catch him, but he always outsmarted them and never was caught, much to the delight of the Turn children. To their dismay, Henry Turn finally sold the donkey for $15.00, which was a good price in those days. While on the Winnie place in Brady in 1919, they made over 200 bales of cotton, paid off all debts and moved into Brady where they bought a house and left their farm life. Farm life was too uncertain and by now the children were growing up and needed a permanent school, but Henry could not make a living there.

In 1920, Henry Turn went to work for a road crew that was building highways form Stephenville to Dublin, Cleburne, and Grandview. He had two teams of horses and two wagons and one saddle horse. The family lived in tents and they moved from job to job. Henry and family then moved to Mexia, Texas, where he worked in the oil fields, using his teams and wagons for hauling. Bonnie Ruth was born there.

This life was very hard and the children were still not getting proper schooling, so Lillie and Henry Turn made their final move. Del Barringer was moving to San Angelo, so he talked Lillie and Henry into moving there also. Of course, there were no moving vans or other means of transportation except by train, so they packed all their belongings, including horses and wagons, into a boxcar with Del Barringer's belongings and moved to San Angelo. Henry's driver, L.Q. Goodwin stowed away in the railroad boxcar and took care of the stock enroute.

The family made the trip in a Villi touring car. The roads were little more than trails, dusty and hot. They had one flat tire after another, but finally got to San Angelo. They had their last flat tire at the Pulliam Street underpass and while they were fixing the tire, a bus passed by and ran over and killed their little rat terrier dog that they had brought all the way with them.

After many moves from one rent house to another, they bought their permanent home at 15 East 8th. Ben, A.J., and LA Vaughn were all born there. Henry Turn still had four horses. He sold Dock and Dan, but kept on working Old Blue and Eagle until 1935. He hauled gravel, caliches, leaf mold, fill dirt, and whatever he could get to eke out a living for his family. By now, they had 11 children.

In 1935, Henry sold his horse and wagons and took up carpentry, a trade he followed until death. Although Henry and Lillie Turn lived the major part of their lives in San Angelo, Lillie's heart remained in East Sweden. She bought a cemetery lot in the East Sweden Cemetery and had a nice "Turn" stone erected thereon, but Henry Turn never wanted to be buried there. Out of respect for his wishes, since he died fist, the children talked Lillie into having Henry buried in San Angelo. Henry died December 31, 1951 in San Angelo. Lillie died November 24, 1964 in Austin, Texas where she had been in a nursing home after an extended illness. Both were buried in the Resthaven Cemetery in San Angelo.

Our Town Had Plenty of Filling Stations
By Faye Speight of Kerrville, Texas
Born 1933

I was born April 28, 1933 in Kerrville, Texas. The house where I was born was furnished by the Tivy School District as

Faye's parents, Adolph and Estella Ersch

my dad; Adolph Ersch was janitor at the elementary school. It was located on the school grounds near the corner of College and 3rd Street. I still have the address on the original mailbox. In that neighborhood, we had two grocery stores within two blocks of our house. The building is still there. It was called the Red and White Store owned by Roger Adkins. Later Mr. Bernard joined as partners and was called Adkins and Bernard Red and White. It served all that part of town. Mama charged groceries there during the depression. When groceries got rationed during the World War II time, Mr. Adkins always saved a bag of rationed items for Mama. Things like double bubble gum was scarce so Mr. Adkins always threw in several pieces in Mama's bag for me and my brother. There was a smaller grocery store owned and operated by Ms. Charolaise and her sister. There you could buy candy, tobacco, and a few other things. My grandpa bought his Prince Albert in a can and got free tobacco papers. He lived in a little house in our back yard when we moved in 1938.

The railroad tracks ran in front of our house. The train came every weekday around 11:00 a.m. Sometimes it had a cattle car or two and once in a while a passenger car for some special occasion. It went to the end of North Street and forked off on a sidetrack to be turned around and head back to San Antonio by 1:00 or 2:00 p.m. The turnaround was about where the McBride Oil Company is today. Volunteers from the neighborhood help to turn it around on the train table. A ditch ran alongside the tracks, but was paved over when the city widened and paved North Street. It is still a drainage.

Saturday night baths. Oh boy. Mom brought in the #3 washtub and heated water on the stove enough to warm the cold water. This was in the kitchen because our bathroom was too little. Daddy later remodeled it, made it bigger, and put in a bathtub with four legs. That was pure luxury. The area that now has the Garden Street was a huge field. We could cut across it for a shortcut to town. There were only about three houses on the north side of Jefferson Street. The one on the corner belonged to the L.T. Davis. They had a son killed in World War

Faye with her brother, Dayton Ersch

II and his body lay in state in the small room on the west side of the home. It still stands on the corner of Washington Street and Jefferson Street. Across from the Davis house was the big First Baptist Church. The Assembly of the God Church bought it and used it for several years before tearing it down and building the church that is there now.

The Council's house and the Smith's house were on the opposite corners. The Smith's owned the funeral home, a block down that is now Grimes Funeral Chapels.

The Presbyterian Church's newest addition is now on that corner where the Smith's house was. I believe the Smith's house was moved, in two sections, out by Highway 16 South. It was a huge frame house. The rest of Washington Street was filled with small houses all the way to Barnett Street.

We had a wringer washing machine with three tubs. The water was heated in a big black pot over a fire in our backyard. My grandpa, Olfen Feller (Opapa) would start the fire and fill the wash pot and have the water boiling by the time mama was ready to wash, every Monday. One tub was clear cold water, the second was too. The third tub had a few drops of bluing in it to make the white clothes even whiter. Each load was hung on clotheslines, strung across the backyard. If I wasn't in school or during summer, I helped hang clothes. After school though, when I got home I had to help fold clothes. Mama had made starch for our clothes we wore and she had them all sprinkled and wrapped in a bed sheet, ready to be ironed on Tuesday. How she did all that and had dinners on the table and supper too, I'll never know. The washing machine was outside under a tree on a wooden stand daddy had made. We didn't have a hot water heater in the '30s and most of the '40s. Mama drained all the water out with a garden house onto our grapevines. We had grapevine arbors across the backyard and a big long one on the east side of the house. It was long and high enough to park at least two cars under it. The grape were so good. We had

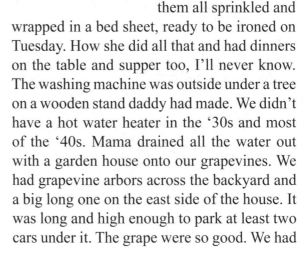

six to eight varieties on the big arbor. When they got ripe mama made jams, jellies, and at least one pitcher of fresh juice. She gave the peelings and pulp to the Trapp boys who lived next door and they made wine with it.

Our town had so many filling stations. When there was a loss of electricity in the 1940s, there was only one gas station where you could get gas. There were gas stations on every street and corner. On Saturdays, we got to go to the picture show. Cowboys and Indians were always showing at the Arcadia. We didn't get an allowance, but we would each get a quarter. It would get us in to the theater, plus one box of popcorn and a cold drink or candy bar. We would be there when it opened at 1:00 p.m. and stayed until mama told us to be home. Usually about 5:00 p.m. We would see the movie over and over during that time.

I was born during the depression years, but didn't know we were poor. We always had a hot meal on the table, morning, noon, and night. Daddy made $30.00 a month at the elementary school in the '30s. There were four of us kids, three girls, and one boy. We went to church every Sunday morning and Sunday night and on prayer meeting nights. Up until I was five or six years old, we went to the old tabernacle corner of Barnett and Clay Street. The original building is still there and belongs to the Zion Lutheran Church. It has been remodeled many times and is now a day care center. It was only four blocks from our house. After moving in 1938 we started going to a new church, being built by almost all the men members it was called the United Pentecostal Church. We have always called it the Rock Church. It still stands and is now owned by Crenwelge Motors. It had been used as the library and more than one other church. In the early '40s, we had a real bad storm with lots of hail. It broke out several windows in the living room. Daddy had us all get in the dining room and stay away from the window. No other damage was done

other than a lot of water and glass to clean up.

My brother, Dayton Charles Ersch and I made several homemade toys, such as wooden stilts to walk on; a scooter made with leftover lumber, and used old roller skates for the wheels. We would take the scooter to the high school, a block away, where there were lots of sidewalks and spend lots of time there. We also each had a pair of roller-skates and skated in front, on the sides, and around back of the school. There was also a long slide from the second floor at the typing room. It was a fire escape in case of fire. There were no outside steps to get to the top so we climbed up the pipes outside to the top of the slide and climbed over to the landing. Then we would slide down on waxed bread wrappers in order to go faster. Sometimes we would climb up the inside of the slide, but it was hard to hold on to since it was u-shaped. We had a huge swimming pool down town behind the businesses on Water Street. I went every day it was open during the summer. Mama finally bought me a season ticket for $7.00. I was a very blond kid, but I was in the pool so much the solution in the water turned my hair green. Took a while to get the green out.

Across the street from the cascade swimming pool was the Blue Bonnet Hotel. After leaving the pool my girlfriend, Loretta Carney and I always entered through the side door of the hotel to use the bathroom. It took a dime to open a stall door and we didn't have one so we put our towels down on the floor and side under the door. Then when we came out, we fixed the lock so it wouldn't relock. That was so someone else who didn't have a dime could get in. The elevator always had a girl running it. Her name was Gloria. She would let us ride to the top of the floors and then we liked to walk down the stairs. The roof of the hotel had a small room for the HAM operator. His name was Mr. Toler. More swimming holes on the river was across the bridge on Knapp Crossing. It was the road that goes down to the river beside Chili's. It was flooded over when the dam was built.

When "Homemade" is a Memory
By Gladys Krause of New Braunfels, Texas
Born 1932

The Hill Country is a marvelous part of the State of Texas. Marvelous because of the extraordinary display of its natural beauty. The evergreen forests, the waving of the many green grasses of the prairies and plains, and the fresh springs of crystal clear waters are in abundance. The terrain varies from rugged hills to ranges of small mountains. The hills and mountains are studded with the variety of the oak trees, elm, and mesquite and cedar trees. The open plains are of grazing grasses and a variety of wild flowers. The deep meadows and valleys are a haven located near the abundance of the crystal clear water springs and rivers. The many wild flowers to name just a few are the verbena, bluebonnets, black-footed daises, and evening primrose. The wild brushes are such as the wild sage, chaparral, the yucca, and cactuses grow here.

The small community of Sattler, Texas is located in Comal County. The German settlers established the community in 1847. The settlers took advantage in establishing their homesteads near the Guadalupe River and its many fresh water tributaries. There was an abundance of trees, mostly the oak, the ash, elm, hickory, walnut, and cypress to build with. The settlers were amazed to see the beauty of the long, graceful strands of the Spanish moss that grew on the low branches of the live oak trees.

My grandparents, Heinrich and Alwine Meckel, had their ranch and home at the base of a mountain range and near the Guadalupe River. Grandfather had a herd of cattle on his range of land. He obtained the required certification for his stock. This certification was his originated brand that was placed upon his livestock and was obtained at the Comal County District Court in New Braunfels, Texas on July 16, 1875. My dad, Frank A. Meckel, was born in 1902. He was the second youngest with two older stepbrothers, seven brothers, and two sisters. They all attended the Mountain Valley School near Sattler.

As a child, one of my greatest pleasures was to spend as much time as I could at my grandparent's ranch home. My three brothers, Lawrence, David, and Dennis and I met our cousins to spend many hours playing, fishing, swimming, and listening to our uncles spin many a tale or two.

The German families were frugal farmers and ranchers. They were very neighborly and shared their bounty of harvest and gain. 'They were gifted in building their homes, many barns, and also helped with building their neighbors' homes and barns as well. They made some of their own tools, home furnishings, and some of their children's toys. My dad, my uncles, my three brothers, and now my two sons, Paul and Glenn Krause have inherited the gifting of wood making. The custom was that if the parents were able, they would furnish each son with some farmland or tools of their trade upon marriage or leaving. The daughters were supplied with home furnishings, which included a new sewing machine.

Heinrich and Alwine Meckel celebrated their 50th Golden Wedding Anniversary at the Hancock dance hall on February 4, 1935. The celebration included a dinner and dance. Because of their German heritage for the love of music, they danced the night away to the many German waltzes, polkas, round dances, and the Paul Jones. The Paul Jones was popular in the unexpected exchange of your dance partner at the blow of a musician's whistle. The evening's celebration was concluded with a grand march with all that were there in attendance. A photographer was present to photograph the anniversary couple with their original attendants and the attending kinship numbering about 57 people. Also, a picture was made of the couple with their 12 children. A formal photo was made of the Golden Anniversary couple with the bride wearing her beautiful original wedding gown. At the anniversary celebration, the men all wore suits, dress shirts, and ties. The ladies wore their jewelry and pretty dresses. Slacks for the ladies were not introduced in this area until the ladies went to work at the many positions vacated by the men during World War II. Many of the ladies from this area commuted to work at the bases in San Antonio.

My grandmother, Alwine, was an excellent cook. Her chicken soup was the greatest. She cooked and baked on a wood stove, which was replaced by the glory of electricity! She made ever such delicious coffee cakes, homemade breads and an unending supply of molasses cookies. One of the staples in the cupboard was homemade molasses syrup, a sorghum made from sugar cane. I remember my dad and some of my uncles would go into the field with a team of gigantic, black mules and wagon to bring in the sugar cane. The team brought the wagon alongside a large crushing machine. The mules took turns to power the massive grinder. The cane juice ran into a metal funnel and emptied into a metal vat that looked like a small flat fishing boat. After the vat was filled, a fire was maintained under the vat all the daylong. The men stirred the cane juice with long handled wooden paddles. After the cane juice became a rich golden syrup it was poured into large crock-pots to cool.

Near the sugar cane grinder was the tobacco house. My grandfather used this small barn for the purpose of drying and storing of the large tobacco leaves he had harvested. The drying and the ageing of these leaves was a slow process. The tobacco leaves were attached upside down to the rafters of the barn. At the completion of this drying process the aroma of the leaves was poignant, their texture were as velvet and their color beautiful amber and orange.

I still can recall the times that our families would gather together to go camping along the Guadalupe River bank below the ranch house. The men would clear the riverbank, pitch a tent or two, cut wood for the fire pits, and set up the camping gear. As the sun slipped away and as we hung up our swimming suits to dry, we would be on the watch for the first darting of the fireflies (lighting bugs), and their glimmer. What a delight to capture them and to see their fluorescent glow. Mom would bring out the quilts and pillows, as we got comfortable around the campfire. There would be stargazing as we listened to the stories that the adults would recall. Later in the night the men would get into their fishing boats with lighted lanterns and would check the trout lines for fish or re-bait the ones that they had set out earlier in the evening. Usually a pot of coffee was put on the hot coals and the aroma of the coffee and the wood burning fire was so great.

Some of the stories the older uncles would tell were about the times that Indian braves would come at night. They would investigate why their watchdogs were barking and the horses were whinnying. They would find some Indians had come to barter their animal skins for food. They would give than a supply of staples because they knew they had come in desperation for food. Most of our uncle's stories were about their challenges in defending themselves against ferocious and wild beast on the forest trails. Their stories included their skills and expertise in stalking with the greatest of patience and their positioning themselves for the final kill of these wild beasts. Prevalent were the panther, cougar, wildcat, bear, black wolf, coyotes, and the red and silver fox. Their fish stories were as equally elaborated and concluded with great enthusiasm. These stories were to us children; a great delight and we would let our imagination hold with theirs.

Often my dad would tell of the very cold

and harsh winters that they did experience in his growing up years. He related that often the Guadalupe River and the creeks would be so frozen that they could ride their horses on to the river without any difficulty. Often times the winters were so cold with snow and ice that the Pastor would come to encourage these housebound families. He would pray for the ones that were sickly and in danger of the influenza or other infectious diseases.

Their social life was mostly fellowshipping among themselves. In the home or front yard was a game of the broom dance. A circle was made and with the clapping of hands or the accompaniment of perhaps a harmonica, fiddle, or accordion and the dance began. As a broom was handed off in the circle of participants, there was much laughter if you were in the possession of the broom at the end of the beat of the music. In my grandparent's front yard was a large date tree. Its leaves were similar to the mountain laurel. As children, we had to be patient until the dates turned dark brown and ever so sweet to tasting.

Some of the Burger Ball dances were held at the Echo Hall. The music and dancing would last far into the night. At the intermission time of the musicians, we would gather into the gleaming white basement with white painted tables and benches. Our moms would bring out shoeboxes filled with sandwiches to go along with the freshly perked coffee. Our moms came prepared with quilts to put us younger children to bed by the big, warm wood stove in the kinder (children's) room. There was a kindly, but stern lady as our sitter for the rest of the night. My sleep was always so sweet as I listened to the joy and laughter of our parents as they danced and visited with their many family members and friends.

My dad's family attended the First Protestant church in New Braunfels. At the time, all of the services were held in the German language. The Christmas Eve candlelight services were so memorable. I remember the sweet unison of the singing of the Christmas music and carols. The evening's service was concluded with Holy Communion at midnight. It was the custom for the Pastor to make his circuit visitations to the many members in the Hill Country. On the appointed day, the Pastor would arrive in his horse and buggy, which was later replaced with the Model T coupe. My dad's family held it an honor for the Pastor to come to their home to give them Holy Communion and pray for their welfare. Another memorial occasion for us children was attending one another's birthdays. Aunts, uncles, and cousins would come to bring special meaning to the celebration of life.

Our family spoke the German language fluently. I did not speak or learn the English language until I was five years old. Our conversations and our prayers were all in German. At the age of five, I was hospitalized for a few weeks with pneumonia. It was during my stay at the hospital that the nurses and doctors spoke only English with me. I was very capable to speak in English when I started to school at the age of six.

Life of a Central
By Carol Johnson of Brady, Texas
Born 1936

If you haven't lived where there was "central one central" you haven't lived in a small town in by gone days. Her husband was the telephone man. My mother ironed for central's husband, five-cents a shirt, 10-cents for pants. I had been in central's office, which was a little switchboard in a corner of her front room. She could keep track of everyone's location that way. I had even been privileged to sit in central's chair while my mother and she were talking. Central was up on everyone's location. You called her to tell her where you would be in case you got a

224

call; it didn't matter what your ring was-one long and two shorts. Most people would listen "quietly" to hear any gossip or news. In a small town it's important you don't say the wrong thing or let them know that you were listening and it would keep you from asking the wrong question or saying the wrong thing. Little did I know that in a few years I would be sitting on a position at a switchboard where I would work for 15 years during which time I became engaged, married, and had three children.

Mother walked to a little store to get soup for me and thought I could be left alone. I had a bad cold and didn't need to be out. It seemed that she was gone a long time, it wasn't, but it does take a little time to walk nearly a mile and back. "Well" I thought, "I wonder what central is doing." I buzzed her, made up a number, she rang several times, and I waited. Finally, panting, I heard a lady answer. "Hello!"(Pant, pant). Little girl's voice said, "What cha doing?" The lady said, "I am outside in the wash house washing." Oh. Lady said, "Carol, is that you?" I said, "Yes ma'am." Lady said, "Well you hang up that phone and don't you be playing on it again." Click. I'll bet central was laughing. I never did that again. I don't know if she ever

Carol Johnson as telephone operator

told mother about that incident, but later the couple moved to town after we did and I was scared of that sweet lady the rest of my life.

After graduation in 1954 Southwestern States Telephone Company hired me. There was not much turnover there as it was the best paying job for a lady in Brady. I took a lady's place that was very ill with Leukemia. There were still a few centrals but great transition was occurring. General Telephone Company bought Southwest States, which was later bought by Verizon. There were threats of strikes avoided only by just hours.

Some small offices closed and transferred their traffic to Brady and became dial phones. Couldn't call long distance but local calls. Central or the operator had to dial long distance. There were still a few private systems between neighbors but had to call central to be connected; they sounded like a tin can call but it was free to them. After a few years, other towns closed their local offices and Brady became their central, Junction, London, Mason, Menard, and possibly others. Pontotoc was the last "hold-out." When these offices came to Brady many of their operators transferred with them. That meant realignment of seniority. Hours were chosen by seniority. The girls who had been there the longest got the early hours of course.

We had been trying to train our customers to use numbers instead of asking for a person in Dallas or Austin or wherever. Although we were pretty good at tracking down people for our customers, people were more open and willing to help central than they are now. Once while trying to locate a number through information in NYC I got the number and in a sweet Texas drawl I said, "Thank you ma'am." That was a no, no and a great offense to the northern operator and she said I am not your ma'am. We finally got a person who called Pontotoc often to call by number because they were phasing out central Well I asked for that number and she replied, "Oh she is over at Aunt

Mae's," and when she rang she asked for the person I wanted at Aunt Mae's. It was funny I learned those 15 years that some people would say things to the operator that they wouldn't dare say to you in person hiding behind invisibility. There were mean customers and wonderful customers. I got to the place I knew your name, your voice, and your number, but didn't know your face. Once in Rudder Drug I heard a voice I recognized. I looked around the corner to see what that number looked like.

There were learning times and dull everyday times and scary times. On our staff there were engagements, marriages, broken hearts, disappointments, break ups, and divorces and deaths, some natural and others not so natural. We became sisters in spirit, loving each other sometimes having resentment or being mad at each other just like sisters. Some of us stay in touch; some have moved to other towns, some have died.

This was an end of time when people were still calling the operator to ask, "Where is the fire? Where is the ambulance going?" We knew we weren't supposed to tell. I was sitting on positron. Early one morning when a bomb exploded under a local lawyers car, it was loud. That switchboard lit up immediately. We didn't know what it was and we wanted to know. Every other positron had the same lights so it showed the length of that switchboard. You couldn't answer them quickly enough. That traffic department and plant department was inundated with local police state officers, newspaper people, and FBI.

During that time we were to never go back on a line if the customer flashed you back to unplug and let them call back because it might be thought of us listening. Many businessmen who needed to place several calls just flashed us back after the called party hung up, that way he got an operator without having to wait. We were scared to start our cars after that event for fear whoever set that bomb might think we knew something. We became paranoid.

The local police patrolled the office well, especially for the girls getting off late. Later when that lawyer was in the hospital, legend has it when he was asked, "Aren't you scared up here in the hospital without a guard?" His answer was no, as he showed a pistol from under the sheets. He probably smiled a little.

You had to know and say the right phrase for all situations. A supervisor was behind every three operators and would plug in with you if you didn't sound correct. Your tone of voice should be congenial but not personal and speak as if you were smiling and end your sentences with an upward tone, almost like a question. Speak clearly and distinctly. This was an end of time when people were still calling the operator to ask, "Where is the fire?

There were a lot of sorrows and joys among we sister Centrals. One girl had twins. She was expecting one baby and it was early. She had worked the day before. One girl lost a contact. The supervisor called the girls on break to come help hunt a contact; it was hard to find on a white floor at night. One girl, who turned 100 last August, was our blind cleaning lady and did a great job on her knees and with a great smile. She had two daughters that came to help when they weren't in school. One of the girls coming down the White Land Hill, sitting on the fender, slid off and was killed. We all grieved with her. One local girl was working in the summer to earn money for the fall college semester living with mom. She failed to wake up in time for work. Her mom checked on her and she had died in her sleep.

One friend and I both wanted a baby and the doctor said I was going to have one; I was so happy and I wanted to share it with her. At the office they told me the sad news that her husband had put poison into the sugar bowl and into her coffee. She was in the hospital under oxygen and didn't respond and died. Several of us girls went to see her in the hospital and her husband happily invited us all to go to his house for ice cream; everyone declined.

At the board as the evening progressed the rates became a little lower just at shift change. Where there had been regular traffic it got very heavy and fast. Circuits would be busy and there were lights shining everywhere. You were not to let a light shine more than 10 seconds. Well that was impossible. We would take the call, try, and many times had to call the customer back. They usually hung up and placed another call possibly with the same operator. It was like a fire ant bed that had been disturbed. After 10:00 p.m. traffic usually slowed down, usually having two or three girls until 11:00 p.m. One girl came on at 10:00 p.m. and worked until 6:00 a.m. We were only beginning to handle mobile calls in your car or boat. What a hassle it was, so new and wasn't always successful. It is so easy now. You can call anywhere without assistance, take pictures with your phone, and send them to a friend. We laughed then at the concept of possibly seeing the person you were calling. Wouldn't Central be surprised now?

As I said there were happy times, funny times, and sad times. We would bring things to the break room to share, exchange recipes,

Carol Johnson (142PR876)

family problems, and joys with that special friend. My little girl was going to be in Little Miss Farm Bureau. That night I had been making her dress and hadn't completely finished hemming it. It was that night. Everyone on their break helped hem that dress, being happy to be a part. My daughter didn't win, but she was the prettiest and sweetest little girl there, of course a momma would think so. She told the MC that Elvis was her boyfriend. Maybe that was the reason she didn't win.

It was sad when the traffic department was closed. Those who wanted to transfer did. Some got local jobs, some took severance pay; I didn't want to transfer as we had a dairy and it is hard to move and relocate 100 cows. We had three little girls' ages: 10, 7, and 6. I had loved being a central. Of course there were times when you just wanted to stay at home or get away from your job. But I was glad to be able to spend more time with my family and help with the dairy. I had an important job taking coffee to the workers in the field when they were combining, baling, or plowing. I had started working during Christmas rush at a florist and worked there during rush times for several years. That was fun, hard work and tales to be told if you paid me enough. There I didn't have to work Sundays. My sweet mother had been taking my girls to Sunday school and church. I had promised the Lord that if I didn't have to work on Sunday I would be in church with my girls and I kept my promise and God has blessed me and my family as well.

The Rivalry
By Patricia Haas of Spring Branch, Texas
Born 1952

I was born on August 22, 1952 and the day I was born, it started raining and did not stop for 7 days. The doctor who delivered me called me the Flood Baby. It had not rained for three years in Blanco County. I grew up

227

Patricia's father, Roy H. Byars

in a small Texas hill country town with a population of maybe 250 people. Our little town had a state park, which was built by the CC Camps, on the beautiful Blanco River.

My family came to this community back in 1917 when my father was only six months old. Grandmother Sybil Massey Byars became a widow in Rosebud Texas; she sold her farm there, loaded a wagon with eight children and a horse to pull the wagon, to transport her and her eight children to Blanco Texas, where she would have family to help her raise her family. She bought a small farm about seven miles west of Blanco. When the town of Blanco put in a telephone office the phone company needed someone to operate the office 24 hours a day, 7 days a week. Mrs. Byars sold her farm and moved to town and she and her three daughters were the first phone operators. Her sons did odd jobs until World War II broke out and all of her sons went to serve their country, proudly.

After the war, one son came home and ran the Wool & Mohair business, another moved to Johnson City and ran the telephone office there, one helped build Blanco State Park, one moved to the Austin, Texas area and

opened a restaurant, and my father ran the Blanco Lumber & Hardware store. When the family could be together, they had a family re-unions in the Blanco State Park. Mrs. Byars died in June of 1952, but still lived on the town square. When the telephone company modernized and built new phone offices the Byars' boys helped collect all of the old heavy phones from most of the houses. The phone company gave Mrs. Byars the house and property for all her years of service. That same house is now known as the Byars' House and is owned by the City of Blanco.

When my father was small (1920s), he shined shoes on the sidewalks of Blanco and when Blanco got a movie theater he would hand crank the movie reels and got paid 10-cents. That was the old silent black and white movies. The building on the square in Blanco was a school, bank, the County Seat Courthouse, and hospital; in later years, 1968, it was a Wax Museum. Most of us were born in the hospital there on the square. My father helped to get a historical marker put on that building so it could never be destroyed.

Blanco and Johnson City were rivals to each other and Johnson City, Texas managed to get the County Seat moved to their town because politics. Many people in Blanco are still mad about that! It's like the Hatfield's and the McCoy's. But in school football and other sports, the rivalry continued. At Halloween each year the school kids would drive to each town and throw eggs and put toilet paper on trees and buildings, just to be silly. Back in the day each town had a bonfire right before the big homecoming football games and each town would drive over and try to destroy each other's bonfire. Johnson City had a drive in movie theater and a downtown theater. Blanco only had one inside theater, but Blanco had a state park and back in the older days each town had a rodeo arena. Johnson City started having the Blanco County Fair and Rodeo every year. Blanco had some events but they were held in the State Park.

My mother was from Johnson City and with my father being raised in Blanco, when they married in 1944; we had family in both towns. The war took my father away and upon his return they settled in Blanco. I loved looking at all the wonderful old pictures of when my parents were young. The beautiful dresses, hats, and gloves the women wore back then. The men dressed pretty sharp also. Paton leather shoes, tailored pants, and all the men wore hats. You hardly ever saw a woman in pants back then. My parents went to boat races at Ink's Lake or Austin, Texas. They went out on picnics with family and friends.

Our grandparents went to house dances up until communities started building dance halls. This starts another part of history. Around Blanco County there were dance halls you could go to on weekends. I heard my parents talk about Bugscuffle, Albert, Flugarth's store, Kendalia Hall, Smithson Valley, Twin Sisters Hall, Pat's Hall, Fischer's

Patricia's mother, Marie Crider Byars

Hall, and many others. There are many of those old dance halls still going today. In fact my husband's family still helps operate Twin Sisters Dance Hall. I am proud to say there have been four generations of the Haas family still involved with the Twin Sisters Dance Hall. The hall was built in 1868, there was also a bowling alley on the same property, but the bowling alley burned down in 1968.

Growing up in the '50s, '60s, and '70s life was simple. The boys had the quarter-mile marked off on back roads and there were always races to go watch. We had our proms in the gymnasium as well as our Halloween carnivals at our schools. All the kids had to help decorate for the proms. In 1964 my oldest sister's prom theme was Hawaiian. I got to dress up as a Hawaiian dancer and we stood on an island made of sand with a palm tree and danced in our grass skirts. Plus Ricki Ware, a radio disc jockey from San Antonio, was the guest speaker at the prom. The music was so different back then also. We had sock hops in our gyms also, as well as Sadie Hawkins Dances.

As children we made our own kites to fly on a windy day; we made small sail boats to put in the flowing water in the street gutters. We played lots of baseball, volleyball, and touch football (if you were a girl). We use to go outside in the mornings during the summer, went home for lunch and in the evenings we had to be back home before the street lights came on at dark. Most of us were in the Blanco State Park most summer days. We all learned to swim at a young age and lots of fishing on that river. Someone had paddleboats and canoes to rent in the park. There was a concession stand in the main clubhouse in the park also. We had birthday parties and girls had slumber parties. We would go out at night when we had slumber parties and throw toilet paper rolls up in trees of friend's houses or a boyfriend's house.

Blanco had a water tower up by the

schools that every senior or junior would climb up on and you painted your name on the tower. My dad never knew how much paint he sold with brushes that were used for that purpose only. Every year a new name got put there. We would go and ring the big bell at the elementary school after winning a big important football game. One year the bell got stolen and stayed missing until the Blanco River went dry and some fishermen found that bell. In a small town everyone got talked about and it was a big scandal that hit the hometown newspaper about who actually stole the bell because when it was recovered that man was a County Commissioner and probably 50 plus years old. It scared his family name. The drag races we all went to watch ended with a sad story when some of the young men were killed in the races. One young man was so obsessed with having the fastest car that he died in a wreck and his speed odometer was stuck on 120 but he also crashed into a tree and was killed instantly. That really made the whole town very sad and taught the boys to stop trying to be fastest.

Blanco had a volunteer fire department and my dad had a fire station phone in our house and we got woke up many a night with the fire department phone. Downtown, at city hall, there was a siren that went off every morning, at 12 noon and 6 p.m. Everyone was so use to hearing it that even when they moved the fire station that the siren had to be hooked up to a timer to keep the tradition going.

As children growing up in a small town, if you were caught misbehaving, which ever adult saw you do whatever at that moment, they corrected you immediately and when you got home your parents knew about it also, so you got in trouble and punished again. We city kids learned to respect our elders as well as all kids from my area. Life was different back then. We went to church on Sundays; we had school events and grade school classes, and got to perform at

PTA meetings at school. I was in the square dancing classes at school. One evening at a PTA meeting and my assigned partner did not show up and I had to do the square dance with the elementary principal (a grown man) and I cried through the whole performance. I got teased terribly for days at school.

Another experience I had that my parents never knew about was one of the first times I got to drive our family car to a basketball game. A bunch of us kids were standing around the cars in the parking lot and someone jumped up on the fender of our car and broke off the radio antenna. Blanco had a gas station that stayed open late at night. I immediately drove to the station to see if they had a replacement antenna, and thank goodness they did. I paid for it and the station attendant even put it on for me and my parents never learned what happened. But I was nervous for weeks and weeks because of my guilty conscience.

We use to pull pranks at Halloween also. We would borrow an old outhouse and put it on the steps at the high school. We would pick on this kid who drove a Volkswagen car. If we were all at the local drive inn someone would distract him from the parking lot and four people would each pick up a corner of the car and move it. If we were downtown and the bowling alley we would carry it over to the courthouse square lawn or put it on the sidewalk somewhere. It was a funny prank and no one ever got hurt. Even back in the 1940s kids would move outhouses.

Medicines were different in the '40s and '50s. Most women awaiting the birth of a baby were generally given Castor Oil. My mom had to drink three bottles before my oldest sister finally slid out. We also had a snowstorm December of 1946. We had droughts where each family was given one barrel to fill with water from a spring in the state park and depending on the size of your family determined how often you could fill your barrel; that year was 1949. I remember stories of the depression from my grandparents and parents. Everyone shared food and did chores to earn a meal or to get a place to sleep. Everyone worked together and even though there might not be anything but water, day old bread, cornbread, beans, and vegetables if you had a garden, no one went hungry.

The Children Were Always Involved
By Karen Barrington of Austin, Texas
Born 1948

My grandparents had an outhouse and as a young child, I remember I could not quite understand why they did not have bathrooms in the house. I remember castor oil, camphoric, monkey blood, calamine lotion, and Vaseline that were the cure-alls for any and everything. I remember dad had a special Polio life insurance in case he contracted Polio so mom and me would have funds to live on if needed. Radio was the entertainment source for my grandparents. I remember listening to the original county music, Hank Williams Sr., Charlie Walker, Gene Autry, and many more. There was Pat's Hall for dancing in Fredericksburg that mom (Lena Alberthal)

Karen's father's side of the family
The Alberthals

and dad (Leroy Alberthal) and many other young couples of my parent's age would go to on a Saturday night. You could even bring your kids and just lay a blanket down behind their table and we would sleep. My grandma and grandpa had a party line phone in their home and you could hear the clicks on the line of the reserves picking up and down as you talked. Their ring was three shorts and one long. Windup record players and the record that was about a ¼ inch thick and my grandma was just amazed by it just as she was the first time she got her foot pedal sewing machine. I got a few spankings at home as did my brothers, but just seeing dad's belt hanging on the kitchen doorknob was enough to give us second thoughts before getting into trouble. The phrase of a "Time Out" was not around in those days.

My mother's two brothers were in the Philippines in World War II and she would read me some of the letters she got from them quoting: "You don't know what it is like until you are laying in one of those holes and the bombs going off a few yards from you and not knowing if the next one would land in your ditch." They were both in the medical core and they would tell her in their letters that sometimes after the flamethrowers were used it was hard to tell an American soldier from an Enemy soldier. I remember how upset she would get after reading the letters and how she had no right to complain about staying at home on the farm and doing the work that she had to do. My dad was in the Texas Division of the National Guard. He was two weeks from deploying to go to Korea when the conflict was ended and even though I was a small child I remember how mom & dad would talk and I did not quite understand everything that was meant by what they were saying about a war.

We had a Maytag Wringer Washer and every Monday was washday and bread baking day. She would set up a pot of brown beans, butter beans, or a pot of soup and bake a large pan of corn bread. Dad would start the bread dough when he got up at 4:30 and when mom got up at 5:00 she started the next step and got us up, fed, and off to school. She set up the beans or whichever that Monday called for and started the wash, got it hung on the lines, and that is how Mondays went and when I was old enough I was part of the Monday routine. In the summer months if Monday fell on a school holiday we still did the routine. I was eight years old and my brothers (Kevin, Sheldon, and Nelson) were small and it was like triplets around the house, since they were born in 1956, 1957, and 1958 and I remember three long wash lines filled with diapers, no disposables in those days. Thursday was ironing day and I was the one to do it. We ironed everything from dad's starched work pants, bed sheets, pillowcases, shirts, Dan's handkerchiefs, and so on.

Karen's mother's side of the family
The Müllers

We got a TV and I got to set up the ironing board in the front hall and could watch TV as I ironed. I could watch the daytime melodramas, like "As the World Turns," "The Guiding Light," "Search for Tomorrow," and so on. Also on Saturday was cartoon day, even if it was hard to get up on school days, on Saturday me and my brothers were up at 6:00 AM to watch Bugs Bunny, The Road Runner, Pepe Le Pew, Pop Eye, Donald Duck, Elmer Fudd or whatever cartoon was on in the 1950s, but we never missed them. Of course there was "American Bandstand" and "The Art Linkletter Show" too.

On some Fridays we would go over to my Opa and Oma's and watch wrestling (real wrestling), not like it is now. Mom also canned peach and plum jelly, pickles, okra, and beets. We always had a big garden

where I was the "potato digger upper" and the "green bean picker" since I was closer to the ground. We also had a number of Pecan Trees and when the time came to pick them after dad thrashed the trees it was all our jobs to do the picking up. Boy did our fingers get all stained and it took weeks for the stain to come off. My parents were born in 1918 and 1923 and being farm people they learned how to work the land and never wasted anything.

There was a drive-in movie theater in Fredericksburg called the "87 Driven In" and on one or two Saturdays a month dad, mom, and I would go. I don't remember the cost for adults. I got in free. The speaker was hung on the driver side window and we saw some great movies. I was an Audie Murphy fan and I loved Westerns. I remember the movie "Night Passage" where he starred with James Stewart and at the end Audie Murphy's character was killed and I was just crying crocodile tears and mom had to explain he was only playing that he got shot and killed, he was still alive. The next movie I remember was "Frankenstein" and I had dreams about the monster under my bed for weeks. We saw many movies, because that was the main entertainment in the 1950s for families and I think this is why I love the old movie classics so.

Mom, dad, and I would also take drives around town on Friday or Sunday nights, just to see what was going on and wave at other family and friends doing the same. But what I liked is that we always ended up at the Dairy Queen and we each got a vanilla ice cream cone topped with chocolate syrup.

Mom sewed all her dresses, as well as

mine, dad's and my brother's shirts and even shorts for my little brothers to wear in the summer. And we all got a new pair of shoes at the first of school. Mine were Saddle Oxfords; they were either black or brown. We could not wait until summer so we could go barefooted. Many of my dresses were made from the cotton 25-pound flour sacks. The flower designs were very pretty. When I was one or two years old mom made me some real pretty dresses from her wedding slip with embroidery on top.

School days they were good, but the 1st grade was the best. My teacher was Mrs. Urbanec and she was kind to all of us kids and I never remember her fussing at us. I got the chicken pox in the 1st grade and missed being in the class picture. Mr. Halamicek was my 3rd grade teacher and he was neat, as the kids would say now. I remember that he was left-handed and when he wrote he would hold his hand in an upside down style in lieu of how you normally see a left-handed person hold his hand when writing. He had beautiful handwriting. I remember once when at recess we were playing Red Rover Red Rover Come Over. Well I was called from the other side and one of the guys (Tim Hannemann) was called from my side to run over, well neither one was looking just where we were going and bang, we ran straight into each other. We also played Ring Around the Rosie.

There were and still are times that pull at the heartstrings. I remember when the oldest of my little brothers started 1st grade, we walked to school and I left him at his school room and I can still hear him hollering to me, "Karen don't leave, Karen don't leave me." His teacher said for me to go on, he would be okay, but I still can hear him and see him standing at his classroom door calling to me and me crying all the way to my class.

I remember hurricane Carla and how the wind and rain came all the way to Fredericksburg and mom and my brothers sat on the living room couch and mom told us to be quiet and sit still. That was very scary. We also had a space heater with a gas jet hose connected from the wall to the heater and we had to light it by turning on the gas and putting a match to the front of the grill.

When I was eight, the little girl that lived next door to us came over to me and gave me a calico kitty and since I was drinking a Pepsi at the time I named her Pepsi Mimzie Alberthal (my last name). I also had three parakeets, three gold fish, and a dog, but Pepsi-Mimzie was my favorite.

When my cousins and I were at my grandpa and grandma's farm we ran all over the place in the rocks and on the small hills around the farm and never even thought about encountering any snakes or anything like that and did not worry about it. There were not really homemade toys, but my cousins and I when up at the farm we would set up a playhouse. We would get one of grandma's old brooms and clear off the dirt and use some branches and line off rooms and mark off where the table and chairs were and play for hours or until one of the families went home. The family reunions were fun also. My dad, grandpa, and uncles would make BBQ and mom and my aunts would make all the other food. We would play baseball, hopscotch, marbles, and hide and seek. And for dessert we had all kinds of cakes and pies and watermelon from grandma's garden. We were covered with juice and not allowed to touch anyone or anything and all had to bathe before we went home, because between the dirt and the watermelon juice it was hard to tell just who was who.

Another thing we did when it was hunting season, all the men folks would go hunting, and then we made good old deer sausage and deer jerky and hung it in the smoke house for later; oh boy it was good eatin'. When it was time to make the sausage grandpa was at the head of the table and he would be grinding the sausage and as the meat went into the casing, one of the adults would remove a link, tie it off, and hand it down to the first kid, and so it went down the row until at the end it was handed to another adult to put on a wooden rod to be taken to the smoke house. They also went squirrel hunting and grandma would fix some gravy, cook some potatoes and some kind of greens and supper was on. Both my grandparents always wanted us kids involved, because that is how they learned when they were kids and they wanted it to be passed down the family since it was part of their heritage.

Random Recollections
By Marjorie Morgan of Kerrville, Texas
Born 1938

Random Recollections is what the title states, a random gathering of memories from my wonderful childhood spent surrounded with love in the Hill Country of Texas. I was born at home in Boerne on February 22, 1938 of German heritage. A doctor was in attendance and my father, Eddie Wille, administered an ether drip to my mother per the doctor's instructions. My "Oma" Emma Weidner Sueltenfuss, (my mother's mother) was also helping me enter the world. This was the story according to my mother, Agnes Wille. All the family spoke German, so naturally it was my first language. When we stayed with Oma Sueltenfuss in Blanco, (Opa Sueltenfuss was deceased and her youngest son, Arno lived with her) I recall bathing in a washtub behind the wood stove because it was the warmest spot in the house. She had an inside bathroom, but we never used it, maybe because she had no way to heat the room or the water.

I was always happy when Oma let me watch the milk separator. This milk separator consisted of a round metal container on legs that had a small glass window on the lower front portion that you could visually monitor. You poured the fresh milk into the top of the separator and then my job was to let her

know when the line between the milk and the cream became distinct. Then I thought I was doing a real job! Then you would let the milk out first and then the cream through a spout on the front. It was a real treat when she got a clothes wringer, no more wringing by hand. I remember when Oma wanted to have chicken for a meal, she would wring its neck by hand, and the poor chicken would then actually run around without a head for a while. Then it would be de-feathered and soon we would have the best chicken stew ever! All cooked on a wood stove.

My dad's parents, Herman and Emma (Marquardt) Wille, Oma and Opa to me, lived in Waring. I remember their new electric milk separator thinking that was really quite fancy. I was in awe of the milk coming out of one spout and cream coming out of the other! I remember mixing that wonderful fresh cream with homemade molasses into an incredible spread. I loved eating it on homemade bread.

Marjorie with her mother, Agnes Wille

234

I called it angareat, which in German means mixed together. Sometimes I would just eat it plain. I'm afraid I may never get to enjoy this wonderful flavor ever again. I remember helping out by gathering eggs and once in a while bringing in a not so fresh egg with the fresh ones. Oh, my I was told so quickly to take the bad egg back. Being the oldest grandchild, I was allowed to crawl high up into the barn and do all sorts of things the younger ones never got to do, Yea! I never learned to milk real well, I thought if I did, it would become a regular chore! When I visited Oma and Opa Wille when they were living in Kerrville for a short while, I remember feeding a tame fawn when I was about five years old. There's a photograph of me feeding the fawn and it really shows the beauty of the Texas hill country quite clearly. The deer are still plentiful in Kerrville where I live now; they come into our yard all the time.

I can still remember walking with both my parents on either side of me, holding my hands and lifting me up over curbs and as we walked we would hear people talking in their homes through their open windows, hearing the radios and the occasional click of a cigarette lighter being opened. That was such a very distinctive sound and one that really brings me back to my childhood. While living in Corpus Christi for a short time we experienced an air raid while eating supper. Mother opened the refrigerator door and the air raid caption knocked on the door and told us to close it. I don't know if it was a drill or what. It was rather scary because all the lights in the town were off. Since I really did not exactly know what was going on, but knew it something to do with the war, I was afraid.

I still hang clothes like my mother did. I hang all like things together. Sheets, towels and underwear all had their places. Underwear always hidden on the inside lines. There is also a certain place I place clothespins: on the seam area, so it doesn't pull the clothing out of shape. Starching is a chore of which I don't have fond memories; too much work and too hard to iron. Pants stretchers were something I really liked, make ironing my dad's pants so much easier. During wartime rationing, we completely opened the sugar bag, and got out every grain from the bag. This made for frugal people. When butter was rationed we got bags of white oleomargarine with a very small little round yellow dye pouch in the bag that you pressed until it popped and the dye made the whole bag turn yellow like butter. I guess they couldn't sell it yellow or people would think they were trying to sell fake butter. I still have some of my ration stamps from that difficult but character building era. During wartime, women could not get nylon hose to wear. Back then, the style was to have seams down the backside of each leg, so to mimic the hose; they used a special pen for drawing the seam lines. Rubber and elastic were also difficult to get, so us little girls had underwear with ties at the sides rather than elastic. Velcro was unheard of then. Of course, babies still used cloth diapers; so many moms had to hand-wash them because not all had washers. These diapers were dried naturally by sunshine and I'll bet babies had less diaper rash.

Another thing we did during the war was to collect all our newspapers and bring them to school for recycling. They also recycled cans. In Waring Oma Wille always gave her chickens eggshells to peck because she felt it would make their own developing eggshells stronger. Hand-me-down clothes were the norm. Since I was tall, the clothes were often too short but fit otherwise. My mom solved this by adding a ruffle to add some length. I had a lot of clothes with ruffles! I remember that we used almost all of a watermelon. We would make watermelon jelly from what people today throw away. Recycling is not new!

I recall my mom telling me a story about a neighbor lady that had just replaced her kerosene stove with a new gas stove. With

Marjorie Wille in 1941

a kerosene stove, she was accustomed to having soak the cloth like burners before lighting them. While visiting her one-day, mom asked about the gas smell. The lady said, "Oh I am soaking the burners before I light them." My mom probably saved her life by stopping her and reminding her about the new stove. She would have likely have been killed by the explosion. Oh, the new technology.

When my mom was growing up in Welfare, she had a most unusual job. Every day as the train passed slowly, she would throw the US mailbag to a worker on the train, and then he would throw the mailbag for the Welfare area to her. One day the mail had a special surprise in it from the gentleman who threw the mail: a rose for my mom. My dad meanwhile worked in New Mexico for the Civilian Conservation Corps (CCC camp). He sure worked hard at this job of conserving and developing our natural resources. He earned $30.00 per month and was required to send home $25.00 to his family. (This was before he was married) Money was so scarce back then. Those were the days of the big phones on the wall when we had to listen for our special ring. It may have been two long rings and one short or any number of variations. Everyone on the same line would hear the rings and many times

would pick up their phones to hear the "news" when you were talking. So your conversation was not private. They called these party lines.

Staying in Waring was always a treat, especially when the train came by. I would always wave at the trainman in the caboose; of course, he would always wave back and give me a thrill. I didn't have to know the schedule; I was outside ninety percent of the time, either exploring under the house or making my "kitchen stove," which was made out of boxes and lids or making a playhouse outline with rocks. Imagination was allowed to the fullest and no readymade toys were necessary, nor were many available. I also helped Oma with her garden work and laundry. When I was older, my memories of the railroad tracks changed quite a bit. The Wille boys had a very unusual pastime of first deflating their car tires and driving up onto the railroad tracks where the tracks intersected a dirt road. They continued, "riding the rails" until they came to another dirt road where they could easily exit. It helped that they had memorized the train schedule. When I was first married, they took my husband for a rail-ride and he didn't know quite what to think. This was over 53 years ago; I don't think anyone does that anymore.

Does anyone remember sitting close to the radio and listening to Bobby Benson and the B Bar B Riders? We were lucky to have someone read the Sunday funny papers to us on weekends. Back then, we did not call them the comics. It was so much fun and I would always look forward to the next episode the next week. Listening to the radio was the big pastime in my teen years too; all the hit songs and idols were not on TV because there was not TV until later. Even when TV became more common, not everyone had one, when the first programs came on there was a lot of wrestling, some children's shows and I am sure people my age all remember the test pattern that was aired when the networks closed down. They played the national anthem when the network went off the air. Yes, they actually went off the air. No TV. They did not have programming 24 hours around the clock.

Games were always fun, such as Jacks, where you threw a small rubber ball in the air and tried to scoop up as many small metal pointy "jacks" as you could before catching the ball with the same hand as held the jacks. Hop Scotch consisted of drawing a pattern of squares on cement and then hopping on one foot into each square in order. We all had fun playing Red Rover by throwing a ball over a house and yelling Red Rover and guessing where it would come from. When the Slinky craze hit we really thought that was something, a big spring that would "walk" down stairs, but oh, don't let it get tangled! I think my favorite pastime was roller-skating. We could skate on sidewalks or any smooth concrete area. In those days our roller skates had to have "keys" to tighten the front. Yes, we wore our regular shoes and tightened our skates to fit. When I played inside I often played with paper dolls, the dolls themselves were heavy paper or cardboard and their "clothes" were paper. You had to cut them out and they came with a supply of various outfits. The tops of the clothes had tabs that you folded over to secure them on the doll.

I tell people that I feel as I lived in an era that reminded me of the "Happy Days" TV show. Once you have the Hill Country experience, it stays in you. The right family and the right patch of community are really all one needs to have a wonderful life.

Here Comes Our Oak Groven
By Edna Taylor of Marble Falls, Texas
Born 1925

I am 87 years old and my favorite memory is about when my two brothers and I were young. We lived in the country and attended a country church called Oak Grove. We attended church Sunday morning, Sunday night, and Wednesday night. All three of us accepted Jesus as our Savior in the Oak Grove Presbyterian Church. People in our community attended different denominations but when a church had a revival, everyone in the community attended.

One night my family attended one, and during the invitation, a lady came to my youngest brother and asked him if he was a Christian. He answered "yes, I am, I am an Oak Groven."

We never let him live that down. We all married and went to different churches but every time we had our get together, we called him, here comes our Oak Groven.

J.V., Edna, and Hubert

Love of Family
By Lodie Carter of Seguin, Texas
Born 1950

My mother had me at an early age so she left me to live with my grandmother and my uncle and being that I was her only child, my aunt and her husband also stepped in to help my grandmother to raise me up with their five children which were my cousins, and we were all treated the same, they didn't treat me any

237

different than their children.

We all pulled cotton on the weekend to make our own money to help with things we would need for school, and if we wanted to go to the movies. We also picked pecans to make money but we didn't mind it, it just made me a strong young woman and made me aware that if you want something in life you must work for it.

Also, I would like to say that I am very grateful to my grandmother and my aunt and her husband for taking the time to raise me and show me the love of a family. They took us fishing, taught us to swim. I remember my grandmother cooking a big pot of pinto beans and corn bread and sometimes she would make homemade light bread and tea biscuits and on the weekend sometimes my aunt and uncle would make us homemade ice cream for me and my cousins. On Sunday, we would go to church and after church we would come home to a good Sunday dinner and my aunt would have a big lemon meringue pie and we played Hula Hoop, jump rope, jacks, hide and seek, and we were very happy children even though we didn't have much.

What we didn't know was that we had something more than most children have in their life and that was the love of our family and that is more important than anything we could have wanted or needed to play with or wear and that also helped shape my life as an adult.

Thanks Aunt Lillian, and Uncle Richard and Big Mama Hattie White.

The Last Graduation
By Louise McWilliams of Hext, Texas
Born 1919

Seventh grade graduation was a big event in rural communities in 1949. School was out on May 3rd, this was to be the last class to graduate, as the school had been transferred to Rochelle.

The teacher wanted to make this graduation extra special. Miss Stewart wrote what each was to say.

There were six students, Imogene, Charlotte, Louise, Clark, Billy, and Shaddy. Helen was to play a hymn, and she did, she played "Shall We March at the River."

We were to march in and go to the platform at the front of the room and sit on a long bench. Imogene was the first to march in; she sat on the incorrect end of the bench, so we all followed her. Mr. Stewart called the house to order and gave a welcome address.

Imogene was the valedictorian so she was to speak first. She was a fat girl, her mother had curled her hair, and she had a new organdy dress. Oh how dressed up she felt. She went to the little table where the trumpet flowers were on it. They were so pretty and so many sugar ants. The ants got on her. She began to scratch and could not remember what to say. She said a few words and sat down.

When we went to the bench, Charlotte gave her a push saying, "We don't want what you have."

Then Charlotte got up to say what she was supposed to say instead she said, "This is my last graduation, and I'm not going to school again!" She sat down and picked the ants off herself and put them on Imogene.

Now it was time for me, Louise. I went to the little table but didn't touch it. But what was the first page? Then I looked up at the picture of George Washington and said the second page and sat down.

Now it was time for the boys. Clark said a few words and sat down. He had touched the table and the ants had gotten on him. Then it was Billy, he got up took two steps and said, "I don't know nuting, and I ain't gonna say nuting," and he sat down.

Then it was Shaddy. He had gotten a new cap and was wearing and playing with it. He got up and Billy grabbed his cap, after a brief struggle Shaddy went to the table. He didn't say a word but put his cap on his head upside down, and made a face at the audience. Miss Stewart was telling him word for word but he wasn't saying them, working with his cap and making faces at the audience. His dad said, "Sit down son, before you ruin your cap."

Then it was time for Miss Stewart to give our diplomas. She came to the table and saw the ants crawling on the flowers, she picked up the flowers and said, "So that's where those dad burned ants were," and she threw them out the window.

We got our diplomas and went outside to eat homemade ice cream. All agreed that was the funniest graduation that East Sweden School had ever had.

Bouncing Baby Boy
By John Hoover of Burnet, Texas
Born 1932

About seven miles northwest of Marble Falls, Texas was a community called Tobey, Texas. Tobey was a schoolhouse and a cemetery as a lot of communities across Burnet County was. Some of the communities would have a church also. These buildings served as a place to have community parties, and meetings of all kinds. At one point there were eighty-one school buildings having school in Burnet County, some combined and other changed names over time.

Down the country road, about one mile north of the Tobey schoolhouse was a small farmhouse that my mother and dad lived in along with my eight year old brother and six year old sister. I was born March 10, 1932, in that little house. It came a big snow storm on the day I was born. I weighed a whopping 10 pounds and 4 ounces, and looked like a picture of health, but that was about to change. A week went by and my mother noticed this beautiful bouncing baby boy was throwing up all the milk every time she fed me. They waited a few days thinking this would get better, not so, my mother took me in to see Dr. Nanny in Marble Falls. He gave mother some medication to give me but it didn't help at all. Mother waited a few days and took me back to the doctor. He told her he thought I needed surgery and would need to be taken into Austin. He had a friend working at the University of Texas who was willing to operate, it would be experimental. What do you do? It was evident something needed to be done.

The news of a community travelled about pretty fast by way of the old rural telephone. One neighbor calls someone and two or three other people take the receiver down and listen. You had party lines so when you called a certain person it was heard by everyone on that line. The news was spread that a baby in the community was very ill and needed to get to Austin.

Six weeks had gone by since I was born. I was no longer a bouncing baby boy!

Two or three days later after the visit to the doctor, a funeral was held at the Tobey Cemetery. After the funeral was over a man stood up and told how his neighbors had a baby who was very ill and his only chance to live was to go to Austin, Texas for surgery. The hat was passed, some money was collected, another man volunteered his pick up, another would buy the gas, and a plan was put into action. Mother packed her bag and off she went with me in her arms. The doctor took me and off to the operating room. I don't know how long it took. The doctor returned and explained he had made an incision the length of my stomach. They found a blockage, and removed it and time would tell. I know my mother must have been ever so anxious. The days passed and I continued to improve. Mother ate only once a day trying to save her money. The day came when we could go home. She had enough money to buy a train ticket home. The train had to make a special stop for her to get off at Tobey.

Hookey Was a Hoot!
By Ann Bailey Mayfield of San Antonio, Texas
Born 1935

Ann Bailey Mayfield age 16

I moved to the little Hill Country town of Medina, Texas in the summer of 1948. It was not under the happiest of circumstances. My parents had divorced and mom had remarried shortly after.

My step-dad had a brother there and I suppose he and mom wanted to move away from Nixon, Texas to make a new start and escape the gossip about them.

My step-dad's brother lived about three miles out of Medina and my three step-cousins received me warmly. We lived with them a short time until a house could be rented.

We climbed the beautiful hills and swam in a clear creek that was dammed. It was so pleasant there.

In the fall, I enrolled in eighth grade and quickly made friends so my hurt about my parents became less.

I was a little above average student and a "good girl" never getting into trouble. That is until I became a freshman in high school.

We had an hour for lunch and were allowed to leave campus and walk "up town." It was only one main street where all the businesses were and less than a block away from the school. One spring day two of my girlfriends and I decided to skip all our afternoon classes and go to the river.

The Medina River was crystal clear with towering cypress trees lining the banks. As we were strolling away from the school a lady working in her flowerbeds called out to us "you girls playing hookey?" "Oh, no ma'am,"

was our reply, but of course she knew it was a lie.

It wasn't long until we realized we had been followed by one girl's pesky boyfriend and two of his dorky buddies. We decided to hide so when we heard them coming along the riverbank we did, and then we would run back the opposite direction. The bank was a little high in places so we could look down and watch them. They were spitting, cursing, and throwing rocks in the water. They were quite frustrated because they couldn't find us, and we of course were laughing our heads off! They never found us!

It was great fun but there was a day of reckoning. My math teacher went to my mom's work place and ratted me out! When I went home my mom wasn't even angry, she said "alright young lady when you go to school tomorrow, just take your medicine."

My medicine was staying after school a week and outlining the Constitution of the United States. The boys got paddled and it was over, but our principal didn't think it was proper to do that to young ladies.

Years later, I ran into the friend who had married the pesky boyfriend and she asked me if I remembered that day. We had another good laugh and I'm not repentant to this day. It was so fun, and this is only one memory of those happy years in Medina High School.

How to Raise a Cowgirl
By Jean Landers Wright of Menard, Texas
Born 1933

This story is dedicated to my father, Grover Landers, who, at the ripe age of 41 became a father for the first and last time in his life. This long awaited baby was a GIRL, so began his desire to make a cowgirl. We lived on Bear Creek in Kimble County, 33 miles from the home town of Menard. In mid-August of 1933, he brought his wife and baby, who was six weeks old, home. Mother decided to walk to the barn, but felt too weak to return to the house carrying the baby, so began my introduction to the back of a horse.

My first own horse was from a remuda of Shetlands that Daddy pastured for our town doctor, Dr. Davis. His name was Zack after his owner. When he moved the herd, Dr. Davis left a red and white Shetland mare for me. Her name was Bessie and we spent many hours together. She had a mind of her own with those who did not know her and would go to a corner of a fence and refuse to move without Daddy leading her out. However, she did not do that trick with me and demanded that I move fast to mount her. She lost me one time as she suddenly decided to run to the barn to the other horses, and then one time as we were going down a steep hill, the saddle slipped up on her neck and I dumped. When I was about six my daddy felt I was capable of riding alone. Bessie had very short legs and had to trot to keep up with other horses, so began my many miles in a trot. We were in several parades in Junction where I went to school. Bessie died when I was at Texas Tech in the mid-fifties.

Daddy decided that I needed a normal sized horse, so we purchased Sugar, a palomino mare when I was 12. Thus began a long-time friendship. We rode barrels, performed in a mounted quadrille and "cut" many cows and sheep in our life together. I never had a spill off her, but she refused to allow anyone to ride her bareback. My rodeo career came to an end in the fifties, when Daddy pleaded that he could not control Mother's emotions and watch me too. In 1948, I represented Junction in the Fort Worth Stock Show, riding in the Grand Entry at a rodeo performance. Even though my professional riding ended, I continued to love the life. When in college, the only "sorority" I was in was the Rodeo Club. Sugar had two colts in her long life and died at the ranch at the age of 27.

I married at the ranch in 1954 and after a year on a vegetable farm in the Rio Grande Valley, my husband and I came back to Bear Creek and joined the ranching business. We continued until 2003, even though my husband died in 1998. My whole family joined in helping me continue the business.

In 1999, a friend and I went on a Trail Ride on Utah's Bryce Canyon where we slept in tents and rode 127 miles in 5 days. It was a great experience. I fell in love with an easy riding mule, and attempted to train one on my own when I got home, but he was harder-headed than I.

Daddy did succeed in raising a cowgirl and horse lover, but at age 70, I retired from riding, due to difficulty with mounting. Thank you, Daddy, for developing my love of the land and horses.

Paw-Paw's Old Lake Victor Mercantile Store
By Billie Buck of Burnet, Texas
Born 1934

Paw-Paw was almost round; he was short and big around. He didn't show his feelings well, but he was always kind to me. Once he gave me a free piece of candy from the large glass case where what-knots, lemon drops, licorice sticks, and bubble gum lay in enticing boxes and jars. There were Hershey bars,

Peter Paul's Almond caramels, Beechnut gum, jellybeans, and gumdrop, a child's dreams come true. If I was lucky enough to have a penny or the windfall of a whole nickel, it took much careful thinking and deciding just which wonderful morsels were to be mine. Chocolate kisses, two for a penny, huge chocolate bars for a nickel, charcoal chewing gum in a box of twelve for a nickel. It was a delicious dilemma.

Then the war came, the big one, World War II. Great piles of scrap iron grew in the calf pen out behind the store. Paw-Paw paid for it by the pound. I crawled under our house and filled a box with old rolled up aluminum toothpaste tubes that we had dropped through a pipe hole in the bathroom floor. We kids gathered up old nails, tin cans, and pieces of rusty wire and took it to Paw-Paw for a penny or two.

People couldn't buy sugar, shoes, gas, tires, and other basic products without ration stamps. Every car windshield carried a reminder decal that said, "Use it up. Wear it out. Make it do, or do without." People had victory gardens raising their own food and sharing with the neighbors. All efforts across the nation were targeted to the armed forces.

Cereal box cartoons showed some children finding a bomb in the back yard and instructions of what to do if you found one. Mother didn't like that kind of scare and didn't buy that brand. She just told us if we found anything unusual to leave it alone and come get her. Also, she assured us that there were no "Japs" in or even near Lake Victor in the same way she assured us there were no bears around us. We were always safe and would always be safe. Mama and Daddy were there.

Tire test cars came streaming along the highways in long caravans testing tires for the military. Army convoys were regularly passing by. Once, one of my dad's cousins was in the back of a passing army truck and

someone saw him going through. All troop movement was secret and we had not known where he was. I was only about four years old and remember this only from hearsay.

I do remember being in the store when everyone was so upset about a young soldier who was missing or dead. I didn't understand, but I remember it because of the emotions in the store that day.

We were very poor, but I didn't have the slightest idea that we were. We were happy. We had enough food. We had wood for our fires. We had each other. We were snug and invincible to the world beyond Lake Victor. Everyone was poor together, so in essence, no one was poor.

These people from my childhood have remained for all of my 78 years. These, I love more than any others. They have been my friends the whole rest of my life. We were one together in a small country community, welded and twined by mutual history and love.

The store was still the center of social contact after the war. There were gas pumps out front; bread, cheese, crackers and soda waters inside. There were outdated old boxes of high button ladies shoes on the shelves. Piles of colorful feed sacks were near the back and Mother would let me choose the patterns and colors that I wanted for the dresses she would make for me. One of my favorites was of bright blue, red, yellow, and green stripes. She made a skirt with red buttons down the front, a pair of red shorts for a play-day we were having in fourth grade, and on the white blouse she cut a circle of red around a little hoot owl face and sewed it on the pocket. That was some get-up!

Daddy spent most of his leisure hours in the store playing dominoes, smoking and visiting. When Mother needed him, she always called the store first to see if he was there. If he wasn't, they usually knew where he was. The phone was in a wooden box hanging on the wall and the cast iron heater was a big winter draw to all the farmers and others who had little to do in the long winter days.

In summer it was a place to drink a cooling soda water, Cokes, Orange Crushes, Delaware Punches, New Grapes, Dr. Peppers, and Pepsi Colas. There was a chocolate one, but I can't think what it was called. These cold drinks were kept in the Coke box with a block of ice, which melted slowly, and often the bottles were deep in icy water. Good to dip ones hands in and dig around while cooling off from the dusty heat. They cost a nickel.

School Days in the Early 1940s
By Virginia Mohr of Fredericksburg, Texas
Born 1934

The Doss School was organized in 1884 by the early pioneer settlers in Gillespie County, a community nestled in the beautiful Hill Country in the heart of Texas. Location of the school was moved several times and finally in 1894 found its home at the county crossroads in the center of the growing Doss community.

In 1896, St. Peter's Lutheran Church was organized and a wooden structure was built north of the Doss school. Two country stores were built nearby the school in the early 1900s. As farmers and ranchers were moving into the Doss Valley, the population grew to about three hundred.

My story begins as an only child, living on a cattle ranch located eleven miles from Doss with no other children in the near vicinity. Therefore, my parents made arrangements for me to stay with my grandparents during the school week. Their homestead was located only two miles from the school. My older cousins lived nearby and we chose to walk through the wooded pastures, only a mile to school. We followed a cow trail that in earlier times had been a wagon trail, and at times, our walk became quite an adventure. We encountered snakes, skunks, and occasionally a jersey bull that chased us to a nearby fence for protection! We had harsh winters that left our fingers and toes numb form the cold. At school, we all gathered around a large, wood-burning stove for comfort. Whenever we got caught in rain showers, we huddled under trees or brush for protection, causing us to be tardy for school. Whenever the creek near my grandparents' home was flooded, my grandfather would be waiting for us after school and guide us safely through the muddy waters.

Most children walked to school, but those living several miles away rode horseback, leaving their horses on the churchyard to eat the grass. Very few of the older students were privileged to drive an old "Chevy" or "Ford" car to school, loaded with neighboring children.

Our school building was a sturdy concrete structure consisting of four large rooms with a wide hall in the center where we hung our coats and kept our lunch boxes. Of course, indoor restrooms were non-existent in those days; instead, outhouses were located about fifty yards away in both corners of the school property.

First grade at Doss School in 1940

243

Our classes were divided into three groups: primary grades in the "little room," early junior high in the "middle room," and senior high in the "big room." At first, we had only the first grade through eleventh grade a few years later the twelfth grade was added.

The fourth room had a stage and a piano. This is where we gathered for singing patriotic songs and recited the Pledge of Allegiance. Prayers were also allowed in schools.

There was only one water fountain outside the school entrance where we stood in line to enter the building after recess. Weather permitting we ate our lunch outside under the shade trees. Some of the games we played were, Andy Over, Fox across the River, Hide and Seek, Drop the Handkerchief, Baseball and marbles.

All of us brought our lunch to school, which usually included home baked bread, cured ham, or venison sausage, jelly or molasses and homemade butter, occasionally a few home baked cookies were included. Rarely did any of us have store bought fixings for lunch!

At the end of the school year, a picnic was held on the school grounds and under the open community center (tabernacle) adjacent to the school. A program of music, recitations and plays were performed. A delicious barbeque meal was enjoyed and best of all; soft drinks were provided by several of the local businesses in Fredericksburg.

Our teachers were courageous, dedicated people with a lot of patience! Each teacher was responsible to teach several grade levels in one room. In spite of the number of students in one room, the teacher was still able to give us the one-on-one attention we needed.

The old limestone school house constructed in 1905 being just a few feet from the new school building, was renovated to provide living quarters for the women teachers who chose not to travel the rough, dusty county roads to their homes each day.

I remember fondly, those early school days with great admiration for our teachers, usually young women, who were brave enough to teach in a country school.

Looking back to the early 1900s over forty country schools existed in Gillespie County, Texas. By the late 1990s, the Doss Common Consolidated School is the ONLY school still actively engaged in the education of our schoolchildren in Gillespie County and one of the very few still in existence in the state of Texas!

Foot Washings
By Gayle Hester of New Braunfels, Texas

Foot washings are very high on my list of memorable special events that have occurred in my childhood and adult life as well. As a barefoot girl in childhood, I treasured the times I got a good foot washing in lieu of a bath. In my early married life, foot washing was a sort of loving ritual. As a thirty-something daughter and with my family of origin, a foot washing took on an unexpected and very spiritual significance. In my present life, foot washings have evolved into foot massages with lotion though an occasional foot wash is still not out of the question.

My love of foot washing started when I was a young child, visiting my paternal grandparents in Pritchett, Texas. Grandsir and Granny Branch's old home place didn't have running water, so foot washings replaced baths at the end of a long day of play. I was a normal child, and as most normal children, I didn't want to take a bath every day that my feet got dirty! So, a foot washing was always an event that I anticipated with a certain amount of satisfaction.

My grandparents' house was miles away from available utilities in Gilmer, the town closest to their property. Their house was a converted army barracks that had been moved from a World War II dismantled army camp to their 40 acres in Upshur County. It was not plumbed for water, even if it had been available. A well was the only source of water for their drinking, washing, and bathing needs. Therefore, drawing and hauling water from the water well was part of the routine of daily living and somewhat of an unpleasant chore. Since water was not readily accessible and since much time was required to draw it from the water well, bathing was usually a weekly event with intermittent spot washing and or foot washing being the usual pre-bed routine.

The Number Two Washtub was reserved for baths while a small white enamel water basin edged in red was filled with water for washing feet. Since going barefooted was the trend of the day, my feet were usually crusted with dirt at bedtime, so I could rest assured that I would enjoy a daily foot washing when visiting my grandparents. The special thing about the foot washings at their house was that someone else would always wash my feet instead of me having to wash my own. As the millions of women who pay for pedicures today will attest, there is something very special about another person soaping, rubbing, squeezing, smoothing, and soothing your heels, toes, and soles.

I remember the foot washing process well. Someone would carefully carry the aforementioned shallow basin of water to a spot on the ground where spilling was okay. Then, I would sit on a bucket that had been turned upside down for a stool and put one dirty foot in the basin. After it was soaped and scrubbed clean by the two hands of a parent or grandparent, my foot was dried with a rag and then propped on the knee of my foot washer. It would remain there while the other foot was soaped and scrubbed. I can remember how good it felt to have clean feet and how the gentle rubbing and touching calmed me after a hard day of play, readying me for bed.

Of course, I was carried to bed so as not to put dirty feet under the covers. What a special childhood memory.

Carrying this foot-washing tradition into my early marriage, I would frequently treat my husband with a foot washing not only for the soothing effect, but because he tended to have very stinky feet! One of our funniest 48 millimeter home movies is of him sitting back in his oversized leather recliner in our apartment that wasn't much bigger than his recliner with his feet in a plastic tub while he waits for the foot washing. At that time, it was my pleasure. With laughter, I can truly say that by the time we were divorced, I wouldn't have touched his feet with a bar of soap if my life depended on it! As I understand it from Barack Obama's wife, Michelle, his feet stink too! Bill Maher was a little critical of her remark, but with Bill Maher, one has to consider the source!

As an adult, I suggested a foot washing as a family ritual while visiting at my parent's house one evening. Mom was near death but at home for a time between hospital stays. We all agreed that it would be a fun event and make us feel good. Once we were all circled around the living room and the water and soap were ready, we agreed to pass the basin and each person would wash the feet of the one sitting next to him. Right before we started, it occurred to me that it might be nice to read the biblical version of how Christ washed the feet of his disciples. Foot washing turned from fun to something with much deeper meaning.

Dad agreed to read John 13:5, which tells that Christ poured water into a basin, washed the disciples' feet, and wiped them with the towel he had with him. The verses that follow specify that "If I then, your Lord and Master, have washed your feet; ye also ought to wash one another's feet." Our family wept as we washed one another's feet. It was the most spiritually gratifying and unifying experience I ever remember feeling as a family. Shortly afterwards mom died, and I hold the memory dear in my heart.

Often I would wash my children's feet when they were tired from a day's play. As they grew older and when I became very interested in foot reflexology, the washings evolved into foot massages. Now we are all great foot masseuses who give treatments to our children and spouses. Even friends are sometimes treated to a foot massage. The foot washings are occasionally still in the picture, however.

Just this weekend, I washed my sixteen-year old granddaughter's feet and followed it up with a massage and toe-nail painting session. It was a great way to give her some special attention that I can no longer give her in the rocking chair.

I recommend everyone try foot washing on someone they love. Valentine's Day is the perfect time! And remember, it's a very special treat for any age. The event is the ultimate when you can get someone else to wash your feet! I haven't had a lot of personal luck with that since childhood, so I cherish the memories!

Stories from the Texas Hill Country
By Shirley Buck Smith of Kerrville, Texas
Born 1943

We lived ten miles from Bandera out on Winans Creek Road or about a mile off it. Our property, 216 acres, bumped up against my paternal grandparents' place on the north and against my maternal grandparents' fields on the east, which is one of the reasons my parents met. An uncle of mine had bought this land for investment when my paternal grandparents, Jeannie and Robert E. Buck moved into the area and later sold it to my dad, several years into my parents' marriage. Winans Creek wound through both of my grandparents' places, but the smaller creek, which ran through our place, ran into it. This was the scene of my early childhood. There was a two-room rock house with side porch, which was later screened-in when I was four. I may have been the reason for the bath being added because I told my first grade teacher, Mrs. Teel, that I didn't take baths. She mentioned this to my mom and that's when I let them know that an outhouse and frequent visits to a galvanized tub, which I had to help empty afterwards, was not my idea of a bath. To me a bath occurred when there was a porcelain tub, which the water drained out all by itself. Well, I was only six.

For a short time, we took a newspaper from San Antonio and it was dropped from an airplane onto our property. Sometimes on the day of delivery my brother, Robert, and I would wait on top of our butane tank. The butane tank was kind of the middle and made an excellent target for the pilot. It was amazing how accurate the drop was since the pilot didn't fly that low. The big attraction about the newspaper was the comics. We called them the "funny papers" and they were in color and they were a big section all by themselves. Not much like the comics of today. Then there was Red Ryder, and Little Beaver to read about. My brother even had a Red Ryder B-B Rifle, and today I have a Gene Autry cap pistol as a souvenir of those days.

About that outhouse, it had a small block of wood that turned on a nail that served as a latch to keep the door shut when no one was using it. My brother thought it a good trick to sneak up and turn that block locking me inside. If I hollered, he would let me out. It didn't take many times to teach me that I had to take a long nail or a saw blade with me so I could jiggle the block up enough to force the door open. Of course, he stopped doing it then. We had a very elaborate phone system rigged up from wire and tin can in an area behind the house under these two tall oak trees. We passed all kinds of secret messages from strategic can to strategic can. We were probably just shouting at one another, but there was a kind of humming echo that made it adventurous. One of these tall trees that we played in and under had this thick limb about a foot in diameter that stuck out from the tree about eight feet up. We had boards nailed to the tree trunk to climb that high and higher. One time when I was walking along this branch, I fell off, landed on my back, which knocked the wind out of me. My brother was in the house so no one knew what had happened. I remember lying there several minutes before I could breathe easily again. I was lucky I didn't break anything, but my walking on tree limbs became scooting along them. It didn't stop me from climbing around in trees though.

In the early '50s, Nabisco Shredded Wheat used to put two thin cardboards to separate the layers of biscuits. On these cardboards would be printed all kinds of North American Indian skills from building a campfire to putting up all kinds of Indian homes, tepee, wigwam, Hogan etc. to weaving, pottery, and making

Shirley's mother, Alice Bausch Buck

arrowheads and spears. One of these skills that we tried to develop was pottery. There was a caliche hillside exposed about a third of a mile from the house. We would dig out some clay and carry it back to our play area. We would mix a little water with it to get it where we could roll it out into long strips. Then we tried to imitate the pictures on the cards by winding these strips around and around- first the bottom and then the sides. These vessels were only air dried, so they didn't last long. We spent hours at this getting plenty dirty but it certainly kept us occupied.

We also spent our time in playing cowboys and Indians, cops and robbers in copying what we saw at the Saturday night movies. Bandera had an in-door theater and a drive-in back then. On Saturday mornings, we would drive into Bandera where my Dad was a butcher at Ryan's Red and White Grocery store. We would leave dad at work and mom would drive us home in our old international pickup to go about our usual chores. Then about an hour or so before closing time we all drove back to town, picked up dad, crossed the Medina River bridge just below where Highway 16 from San Antonio comes into Bandera, had us a picnic supper, then went to a movie. These suppers were an important weekly event there by the river. Today there is a park there, but then it was just the big old Cypress trees and the river going by. After supper, we chose either the in-town movie house or the drive-in depending on which movie was preferred. Besides the main feature, there was usually a serial, starring some hero, cartoons, and the new reel. Westerns won out most of the time. These were the days of Roy Rogers, Gene Autry, Hopalong Cassidy, and Lash LaRue- his weapon of defense was a bullwhip, and of course Tarzan. Today there are not any movie houses of any kind in Bandera. People have to drive to Kerrville, or Boerne, or even San Antonio. There is something about watching movies on a big screen, everything became

Shirley with her brother, Robert

larger than life.

Now rattlesnakes were a horse of a different color. They were real. Two encounters come to mind. One was on that mile walk from where the school bus dropped us off on Winans Creek Rd., nine miles from Bandera. We walked up the road along one field for about 150 yards. Here there was a gate to go through and the road turned to become a one-vehicle lane between two fields with high fences. One day Robert and I spied a rattlesnake right in the middle of the lane, sunning itself. Well, there was not a safe way to get past it and it was too far away from getting help from a grown-up. Besides, we needed to get home to listen to the Lone Ranger and Tonto on the radio. We figured the best thing was to chunk rocks at it, so we did, staying well out of striking distance. Finally, we annoyed it enough and it slithered into one of the fields. The other encounter happened one morning when we were playing down on the small creek at the end of the field where our dad was working. There was a sycamore tree with a branch that we could grab hold of and swing out over the creek. It was a miracle that all the noise we made didn't wake up this big rattlesnake that was curled up closer to the trunk of the tree. When we did become aware of the snake we quietly crept away and ran to get our dad. He came with his twenty-two rifle and shot the head off. That was exciting, but we both knew we had been very lucky. The snake was about five feet long and dad cut the rattles off for a souvenir.

And there was our dog Skippy. She was a black and white border collie. She helped our dad and mom herd the sheep when they had to be gathered in but she was our protector too. She would fight off snakes, even rattlesnakes by crowding them and barking up a storm, but with a chicken snake she would grab it in her mouth and shake it slinging the snake from side to side until it was dead. She knew the difference between a poisonous and a non-poisonous snake. One time when she had puppies it was during lambing season. One of the ewes died and left an orphan lamb. Skippy let the lamb nurse first and then fed her pups. We have this picture of her lying there giving nourishment to this lamb with its legs all spread out so it could reach her tits. The Bandera County Agricultural Agent, Mr. Slimmer, thought this action such a rarity that he kept a copy of this picture on his desk for a long time.

Probably the saddest thing I experienced as a child was the death of Skippy. It happened on a February day when dad brought mom home with my new baby sister Gayle in 1949. Before dad left to go to Bandera to get them, he had been checking the fence line between us and the ranch to the north of our place. Skippy was with him, but when he had to leave, she didn't answer his call. He figured she would return on her own. He dropped Robert and me at our paternal grandparents, which we called Daddy and Grandma Buck. Both Robert and I were born in their farmhouse and we used to tease Gayle that she had to be born in a hospital. The fascination of a newborn sister held our attention all evening, but by morning when Skippy still hadn't returned our joy became concern then worry. Upon checking with neighbors, dad discovered that one of them had placed a bounty on sheep killing dogs due to loss of livestock. One of his workers had shot Skippy, cut off her ears, and collected his bounty primarily for a Saturday night spree in town. He finally admitted that Skippy was not attacking their sheep but was really herding them. It was good that we could play with and watch our new baby sister in the following months after the cruelty of losing our best friend, Skippy.

We had another dog then, but it never captured a place in my heart and that was a good thing because it turned out to be an egg sucker. An egg-eating dog would generally turn into a chicken killing dog and when a good portion of your food supply comes from your chickens, the dog has to go. Anyway, one morning dad left for the back pasture with his twenty-two and the dog. The dog never came back. Not too long after this my grandparents Buck sold their place and moved to Bandera. They had purchased a yellow-gold and white male border collie that had been a littermate to Skippy. Daddy Buck didn't want to confine Ruff to a yard in town and we had always played with him when we visited. It was a solution made in heaven. Ruff became family, our protector, and constant companion to us and two more siblings born later. Ruff went where we went. He lived to be nearly 16 and never forget his "herding" skills. I can still remember him placing himself between my little sister Sandra and the street when she tried toddling down the driveway at our home in La Porte, Texas. He would let her get halfway and that was all.

Lifelong Friend
By Peggy Peese of Kerrville, Texas
Born 1936

My mother told me this story and I heard it many times. She went to a baby shower and they served ice cream. I am sure it was homemade, as you could not buy ice cream in those days. She liked it so much she wanted to share it with her children, so she wrapped it up in her handkerchief. Of course, we were all so disappointed as when she got home it was all melted in the hankie.

When I was about five years old, my sister took me to the one drugstore we had in town. It was called UpChurch Drugstore. My sister was going to treat me to my first ice cream cone. We got cones walked out of the store and my ice cream fell out of the cone. I cried and cried so my sister took me back in and got another one. In those days, people were so friendly and nice my sister did not have to pay for another one. When I got in high school each day, I had to walk by the drugstore to get home. As teenagers, we would meet after school and have cherry cokes.

Oh my, castor oil, my mother believed in it. One day she had her quilting friends over to quilt well I got sassy. Guess what she got the castor oil and orange juice took me on the back porch and gave me the castor oil. Well I spit it out on the porch floor. After that, she gave me another dose without orange juice. One other time I had to take it per doctor's orders to bring the new baby. He said to take it with root beer. I vowed I would never subject my children to castor oil and I have not.

The schoolhouse was red brick. It sat on a slight hill that you could see the town from there. I could also see it from my house. It had two stories. The first, second and third grades the restrooms, and the cafeteria were on the first floor. The fourth and fifth grades were on the second story along with the principal's office. We had a wonderful lady principal but we were all scared of her. The first grade was just the first grade, as I do not remember much about it being only six years old. I do remember about World War II starting, I was scared as I thought it was going to happen in our town. My parents spoke German so they discussed it and I knew something bad was happening. I had to walk home from school. I had to cross a railroad track. Many times a train was parked across the road taking on water at the water tower. I did not want to wait so I would crawl under the train so I could get home. I do not know if mom or dad knew I did that or not, usually there were several of us walking together.

The second grade was all right I guess. I remember a couple of incidents that still are with me today. My mom was not going to be home so I was to walk to my brother's house. While walking, two boys in my grade caught up with me, and walked with me one on one side and one on the other. One decided to kiss me on the left cheek and not to be outdone the other decided to kiss me on the right cheek. Also, one of the boys in my grade and myself caused the second grade to stay in. The boy sat behind me and for days, he would cut some of my hair out of the back until one day the teacher caught him and we all had to stay in. It was one of the boys that had kissed me. The third grade I do not remember much about.

The fourth grade came along and also came my lifelong friend. She was a little skinny girl coming out of a country school and she was so shy. I took her under my wing so to say. Took her to show her the restrooms, and went with her to the cafeteria. One day we were on the school ground and we looked toward town and saw this great big red dust ball coming. We ran as fast as our little feet would carry us to the schoolhouse. Little did we know that was a dust storm and it was bad. Oh, we were so scared. We had fire drills quite regularly. We had to go down from the second story this big metal outdoor fire escape. Boy was we ever scared. I did not like those fire drills at all.

We had a regular fifth grade nothing that I can remember outstanding. We were excited about going to another school but also afraid.

Life goes on when I went back home many years after being gone I was so saddened. My red brick schoolhouse had been torn down. In my mind, I can still see it today. Most of the kids that went there also finished high school

together. That's memories!

My friend and I entered sixth grade of what was called junior high. We had a wonderful teacher that was an old maid and she would let us stay the night with her. Oh, that was such fun. She had an upstairs apartment and an oval shaped dining area with a table and chairs. We would sit there and look out the windows. We played board games on that table.

We started band in the eighth grade. She played the clarinet and I played the flute. The school was small so we moved right into the big band so we could march for football games and parades. Those years were so fun. We went to many football games. Oh yes, we got to wear jeans on Friday and if it was a big game our band director would let us march in the halls and play to get the spirit going. During those years, one of the majorettes taught us how to twirl a baton. We stayed after school many days to practice. It paid off as we went to a state meet and won first class medals. We tried out for majorette in our freshman year and did not make it. We cried and cried. Also, that night my parents had planned a sweet sixteen party with guys and gals. She and I even cried at the party. The next time we could try out was in our senior year. We practiced and practiced. She was more popular although I could twirl better. The night before the big try out, she called and we talked for hours, should we or shouldn't we try out. We talked of our parents not being wealthy and we would need new batons, boots, etc. for just one year. The last thing she said before we hung up that night was I do not want it to tear up our friendship if one or the other would make it. We decided then not to bring shorts or batons to try out. The kids at school were shocked and wanted us to go back home and get our stuff. We stood our ground and to this day, I still have my dear friend for almost 60 years now.

Through those years, we have done many things together. We had to walk everywhere we went as my parents did not have a car and her dad used theirs to go to work. We finally got bicycles and rode all over town and downtown to the shows. One day I was at her house her mother had to go shopping and asked us to watch her little brother. We were into boys so we did not watch like we should have. He found an orange Crayola and scribbled all over the living room wall that just had new wallpaper put on it. We tried to wash it off but to no avail. For sure, I left before her mom got home. I rode my bicycle so fast to get home.

We double dated some and we thought we were so special as we dated some guys out of town and they had already graduated from high school and were working. We thought we were in high cotton as the saying goes. One year at our jamboree, they were our escorts on the football field. We at one time dated the same guy. I was the first and went with him through the ninth grade. Then she went with him. We still to this day laugh about that, as after he had married and he would see us like class reunions he would not hug either one of us.

I married first and moved to Georgia as my husband was in the service. She was a bridesmaid in my wedding and her husband to be was a groomsman. We sort of lost touch after she married. I could not be in her wedding as we were out of state. We had children and eventually we got back to Texas.

I got a divorce and for several years enjoyed her farm and cabin out in the country. My children loved the place. Later I remarried. Her husband and mine got a long so very well. They were so alike. Baldheaded, wore baseball caps, jeans, and boots. We spent many times at their farm cabin together. She and I planned many class reunions that were at the cabin. We lost her husband several years ago. We have been back to the cabin but it is just not the same. Life goes on and I still have my friend of 60 years. We are so blessed.

What is a wringer washing machine? My mom had a cast iron wash pot to wash clothes. Every Monday that it was not raining, dad would put a fire under the wash pot and mom would start with the white clothes, boil them in the pot, then take them out put them in a number two wash tub use lye soap on them, and then rinsed twice. The whites got what they called a bluing rinse. This was some kind of rinse that was blue that was supposed to whiten the clothes. After she washed the whites next came the rest of the clothes. All boiled in the wash pot first, transferred to the number two washtubs, and rinsed twice. The clothes were all hung out on a clothesline to dry. I loved to hang clothes on the line. Mom demanded everything be hung accordingly. Sheets on one line, towels, dishtowels, and underwear had to be hung together. My mom never had a wringer washing machine.

Guess I Shot the Wrong Buck
By Robert Buck of Hugo, Oklahoma
Born 1941

I was born on my Grandpa Buck's small dairy farm on Winan's Creek, Bandera County, Texas. Dr. Butler drove the ten miles to the farm that rainy morning on March 5, 1941, to deliver me into this world. He charged my folks $40.

My first memory was about two years later. My mother and grandmother Buck were washing clothes with an old wringer type washing machine. They went into the house and left the washer running. I picked up a washrag and stretched up to the wringer. It grabbed my fingers and pulled my arm in as far as my shoulder and ground on it.

I have a jagged four inch scar seventy years later that has moved down to the bend of my arm. What I remember was Dr. Butler coming out to change the dressing. I didn't

Robert's parents, Alice and Claude Buck

want him to touch me, and I still don't like doctors touching me.

My grandparents had eight or ten jersey cows, which they milked every morning and night by hand. Mom and dad helped with the milking and other farm work. The raw milk was run through a big cream separator turned by hand. The five gallon, metal milk cans were filled with cream and stored in a cool water vat. Butter was made in a big churn, also turned by hand. The agitating action of the churn on the cream separated the butter from the buttermilk. The skim milk and buttermilk was used either in cooking or fed to the chickens and pigs.

Twice a week grandpa would load his old red International pickup with all the fresh cream, butter, and eggs on hand and head for San Antonio. On the way, he picked up any additional butter, cream and eggs the neighbors might have. He had a route of happy home customers, which he delivered to.

Grandpa made a living and raised a family doing this. They raised most of their feed, a garden, and butchered hogs in the fall. We ate a lot of deer venison. When someone killed a deer, they shared it with family and neighbors.

The Winan's Creek schoolhouse was vacant, Dad rented it, and we moved in for a while. I remember the black board, the cistern outside and a litter of puppies that were born there. I was acting up one night and Mom told me if I didn't behave, I would have to sleep with the puppies, I hadn't thought about that, I got a blanket and headed outside and bedded down with the pups. After a while, Mom made me come back inside.

Later the old school building was moved into Bandera where it became the school cafeteria. Our next move was into the upstairs of my Grandpa Bausch's big house. I remember listening to the news on the radio. World War II was going on and it was the talk of the day. My folks and uncles discussed it at night and I sat there taking everything in, my imagination running away.

Folks were asked to make sacrifices. There was rationing on things like sugar, gas, rubber, and metal. Mother made a news-clipping scrapbook of all the boys from Bandera County that went to war. Many didn't return. Some got killed in car wrecks when they got home. I kept the scrapbook after Mom's death three years ago.

While we were living there, my little, infant sister, Shirley swallowed a Live Oak leaf and was choking. She turned blue. Dad grabbed her by the ankles and shook her with her head down. The leaf appeared and was retrieved. I don't know if the shaking had anything to do with it, but years later, she was valedictorian of her senior class.

I got to ride into Bandera with Grandpa Buck occasionally and he would take me into the Best Yet Café on Main Street. He would set me on a barstool and order us both hamburgers and cokes.

That little café was named right; to this day, I judge all hamburgers by those I ate as a kid sitting on that barstool, my feet dangling, with my Grandpa at my side. Those hamburgers and a coke for twenty-five cents

Claudin Mae, Shirley, Robert, and Gayle
on Old Bill

are worth a million dollars in memories today.

Along about this time my Dad acquired 216 acres from Arthur Edmonson, another uncle. It was a piece of Hill Country Heaven that joined both places belonging to my grandparents. Lee and Pugmore Creeks entered, came together, and exited on the property to become part of Winan's Creek on Grandpa Bausch's place.

There was a beautiful spring coming out of the ground near the top of a limestone canyon. It was called Tenor Spring, and had never gone dry that anyone living knew about. Spanish Oaks and wild grapes shaded the sparkling fern and mint lined pools of clear, cold water.

Dad and his brother, Uncle Raymond, framed up a two-room house with a porch running the length of it, later to become two more rooms. They roofed it with tin and walled it with outside sheetrock. The rock veneer would be added later. We moved in. Dad had a well drilled on a slope above the house and installed a windmill and a metal tank to catch water. We were blessed with the best water in the world in every direction. We had a wood cook stove and a wood heater. Dad bought a kerosene refrigerator and we used kerosene lamps.

Up to the age of four, I had a lot of stomach cramps. During one of those bouts of sickness, Dr. Butler sent me to a doctor in San Antonio and I ended up in Santa Rosa hospital. The doctor decided my appendix needed to come out. They put me under with ether and went to whacking. The doctor said my appendix was on the verge of bursting. Every time I get to wishing I'd lived in an earlier, more romantic time, I remind myself that I probably would not have lived past the age of four. That causes me to appreciate the here and now, the most exciting time in human history.

Besides helping my granddad with his cows and farming, dad rented some fields to farm and sheared sheep and goats about six months of the year. During the depression, he was paid one to one and a half cents per head. He could shear about one hundred head a day. When he quit, because of his back, in about 1950, he was getting thirty cents per head.

Grandpa Bausch had lots of sheep and when it was his turn, I got to stomp the wool into the sack. The sacks were about five feet tall and because of my size, I had to wait until the sack was half-full of wool before I could climb in and do my stomping.

Aunt Alma always fixed a good meal and there were sandwiches for an afternoon snack.

Shearing sheep kept my dad out of the service during the war. Mr. Thalmann, who

Robert Buck and his Bandera Co. champion lamb

253

was on the draft board had a lot of sheep and goats and realized that there were not many able bodied men left that could shear. That kept dad out.

My uncle Hugo Bausch had a thrashing machine. It was powered with a flat belt that ran from a pulley on an L Case Tractor. The grain was cut with a binder pulled by either horses or a tractor. After the binder cut and bundled the grain, the bundles were stacked into shocks to dry.

When time and moisture were right the neighbors came together to help each other. The threshing machine would be set up and several crews, using pitchforks, loaded the wagons with the bundles. The bundles were then pitched into the thrasher, which separated the grain from the shaft.

The grain came down a chute with a bagger on the end. One burlap tow sack was being filled while the other was taken off and replaced. The sacks of grain were hauled to bins and dumped and the empty sacks returned to use again. At five years old, I witnessed a time that was soon to end. Uncle Hugo bought one of the first six-foot pull behind combines in the county. Then my grandpa bought one.

Guns were a way of life when I was growing up. We kids knew not to touch them unless supervised. I started hunting with an old Remington Rolling Block single shot .22. Someone had shortened the barrel, smoke belched out of the chamber every time it was shot. It wouldn't shoot through a 2 by 6 board, but I was happy to be hunting at age six.

It was Christmas Eve and I was ten years old. Uncle Buster and I went deer hunting. I borrowed a bolt-action single shot from him. Grandpa Bausch caught a ride with Uncle Buster so he could visit with Mom while we hunted. We drove to a clearing where we left the 1936 Chevy that my uncle drove.

I loaded my .22 with a long rifle shell and dropped some in my coat pocket. Buster walked toward the west and I turned in the opposite direction. I eased down the canyon to a ridge called Saddlegap Ridge, which deer were known to travel. I found a place to sit and wait. Beings it was Christmas time, waiting got to be a chore, so I eased back up the canyon to Tenor Spring and checked it out.

I didn't see anything so I eased back to the car. It was starting to get late, but my uncle wasn't back yet. I crawled up and sat on the fender. I was holding the rifle with the barrel up. I stood up and the gun slipped from my grip. The hammer hit the bumper and went off. I found myself getting up from the ground, my left arm was numb, and blood was dripping from my coat sleeve.

I took stock of my situation and tried to honk the horn. It didn't work. Panic was starting to creep in, but I tried the horn again, this time it worked. It was starting to get dark and Uncle Buster hadn't showed. I made a decision, which could have been fatal, to go look for him.

The pasture road made a big circle; a trail cut through the rough cedar brush and intersected the road on the south side. I followed the trail and when I came to the road, luckily I ran into Uncle Buster walking back to the car. He figured out what had happened, told me to wait and ran back to get the car.

Back at the house, Uncle Buster yelled for my mother, and she jumped into the back seat with me. Grandpa stayed with my two sisters, Shirley, and the newest one, Gayle. Shirley made a phone call to my dad. He was at the Ryan's Red and White Grocery Store in Bandera, where he worked as a butcher. The doctor's office was just around the corner.

Dad was waiting in front of the doctor's office when we drove up. Dr. Meadows had just started practice in Bandera, right out of Korea, he knew about wounds. He patched me up.

The bullet had gone through my left wrist and I had a two inch long wound across my ribs. I had two small holes under my left arm. My grandpa Buck came into the doctor's office about the time the doctor got through bandaging me up. "What happened son," he asked. I grinned back, "guess I shot the wrong Buck!"

Two weeks later when I had about healed up, doctor Meadows took me to another doctor who had a fluoroscope, and he was able to locate the bullet, which was found dangerously close to a main artery. He took it out and I survived another adventure.

The McCoy Family in 1952

Recollections of Martin and Nettie McCoy
By Benita Lane of Pipe Creek, Texas
Born 1942

During the 1950s, I used to drive my grandparents, Martin and Nettie McCoy from Leakey, Texas to Temple, Texas in order for Martin to have doctor check- ups every four months. Martin had cancer. Traveling for several hours, we would pass the time by them telling me about the old days.

In the early 1900s, Martin and Nettie had a covered wagon when they first got married. They often traveled with Barney and Ethel Rowan who where their brother and sister-in-law along dirt roads all around Texas. The wagons were driven by mules and one day they all came upon this wooden bridge. When the mules looked between the cracks in the floor of the bridge, they would not step on it. Barney's wagon was in the lead, and he tried to no avail to get the mules to cross the bridge. He pulled and pulled on the reins, he blindfolded them and whipped them. The mules would not budge. Martin said he would give it a try. Martin built a small fire under the mules; they raced across the bridge.

They camped on a cleared place on a bluff, which overlooked a river. They slept out in the open beside their covered wagons. Martin was known to be a sleepwalker. That night, he was dreaming that Indians were chasing them and he was awakened in the nick of time. He had his baby girl, Ethel Emma, in his arms running from the Indians but toward the bluff! Naturally, he was trying to save his daughter from the Indians in his dreams.

Martin and Nettie settled for a while near a town that happened to have a carnival. So,

Martin McCoy, his wife, Nettie McCoy, and their baby, Ethel Emma McCoy

255

Martin, Nettie and two of Martin's brothers went to the carnival. There was a hawker loudly describing how durable the dollar pocket watch was, "buy your watch here, it won't break, cost only a dollar." So, Martin and his brothers each bought a watch. On the way home, (Martin was a prankster too), Martin told his brothers, "let's see how good these watches are." Unknown to the brothers, Martin put a silver dollar wrapped in a handkerchief on the ground and stomped on it real good. Then he quickly by sly of hand exchanged the silver dollar for the watch and showed it to the boys. They were so impressed they took their watches and stomped on them and of course, they broke into pieces. Martin did not intend for the brothers to smash their watches to pieces. He was just trying to entertain them.

Martin was born on December 13, 1891 and as a young lad, he lived with his grandparents, William Jefferson and Phoebe Jane Jewell Bybee on a ranch near Leakey. He went to the Cypress Creek one room schoolhouse. He had an aunt, Elizabeth Bybee who helped with his up bringing.

William Davis "Martin" McCoy married Nettie Arminda Rowan on 21 November 1911 and they eventually settled at Leakey, Texas. From 1940 to the mid-1960s, they owned several pieces of property around Leakey, one being the General Store and Gulf Service Station on Highway 83 south of town. He bought and sold furs, pecans, and cedar posts. They also owned a house with a few acres where they grew vegetables and had fruit trees. This was the work they enjoyed most. Martin and Nettie had a granddaughter, Benita McCoy Casey (Lane), who lived with them. She would watch the store while Martin and Nettie would gather the produce. During the summer months, another granddaughter, Zelma Preece (Walsh) would help in the store and around the living quarters.

Martin had a grandson, Sammy Preece

who lived near the Gulf station. Martin would teach Sammy how to measure cedar posts and how to judge furs. People would bring in ringtail hides and raccoon bodies to sell. Once a nephew, John Pendley, brought in a raccoon body however, later on it was discovered missing! It apparently recovered from its wounds enough to walk away. Martin would take Sammy to Junction, Texas with him to sell the furs.

Martin served as Constable of Real County. When Martin had prisoners in jail, he would often feed them breakfast at his own expense, which would consist of bacon and Nettie's famous buttermilk biscuits and gravy. Benita often went with Martin during the night when he was called to restore law and order. Martin was the only law in town at night since the sheriff lived in Camp Wood. Whenever problems arose, Martin was the man to go to. Martin died in May 17, 1963

Memories of Goldie

We were all crowded into a small room, trying to be respectful of each other's feelings, taking turns to be near Goldie. She was the center of attention that day. The doctor was giving a lesson on death and grieving. He was saying, "We all grieve differently, some may experience depression, and sadness right away whereas others may grieve months later. The things to focus on, he went on, were the good memories you have of your loved one. For instance, say, if Miss Goldie made good fried chicken, then you try to…" as sad as we were, we all burst out laughing. The idea was so funny thinking about Goldie frying chicken.

As Goldie lay dying, I thought about so many different things. One of her favorite stories was to tell about the end of her cooking days. This was when she caught an iron skillet of grease on fire, and Jay told her to just forget about cooking. After that she would say, "Boy, I do what I'm told! You know, those iron skillets are heavy. Jay told me to not cook

Benita with her mother, Goldie McCoy

anymore and I sure don't." Goldie would give us one of her beautiful smiles and laugh. Goldie, Jay, Josh, and Jesse ate breakfast every day at the town house in Uvalde. She would visit me and I loved to cook for her. She was always so appreciative of my meals. She especially enjoyed the desserts and cornbread.

Memories of our times together were so special. When I was about four years old, I lived with her parents, Martin and Nettie McCoy) Goldie and her husband, Tate Burleson came to visit us at the old Gulf Station in Leakey. I was in the kitchen pouring corn flakes into a glass. Goldie came into the room and went to the refrigerator, she was looking for something, and then she noticed me. She was wearing tailor made western clothes and handmade boots. The boots had her initials on each one above the heels. She looked as always, beautiful. I told her that I could read the letters on her boots and I

stooped behind her and read "G.B., G.B." She was so surprised! "I can read other letters too," I said. Feeling excited, I read all the letters off a Clorox container. She could make me feel so special. Then she put 4 teaspoons of sugar in my cereal for me.

One warm fall day, Tate and Goldie went hunting. But Goldie stayed in the car while Tate and a friend went on out into the woods. While they were in the woods, a buck deer comes up to the car where Goldie was dozing on and off. Goldie saw the deer just standing there looking at her, she eased down the window and using her rifle, killed the deer. When Goldie and Tate got back to town, the town people asked, "Well, Tate did you kill a deer?" He said, "no, but Goldie did," and he would just laugh his big laugh telling the story.

Goldie and Tate moved into one of Papa's rent houses, which were right next door to the station. My sisters, Brenda and Rosemary were babies at the time. We would visit daily. Tate liked to play poker and one night he came in from a poker game and he went to bed forgetting to turn out the light. Goldie said, Tate, you forgot to turn out the light. He said, "Oh Hell," and reached under his pillow, pulled out his gun and shot out the light. Rosemary told us the next day that "daddy killed the light."

Once when Tate was taking a nap, I very carefully rolled and pinned his hair with bobby pins. He left some time later unawares to go to a poker game. When he took off his hat, he got the ribbing of his life. Goldie enjoyed telling that story too.

Goldie and Tate had racehorses. We would go to the races in towns nearby. We loved to go to the horse races. One morning I got up to go to school and Papa said "look out back." There was the most beautiful horse that I had ever seen. This was Queen B, a new racehorse that Tate had bought. She was black with a white star on her forehead. When Tate's horse won, he would have his picture taken with the winning horse and the little girls, Brenda and Rosemary. Sometimes Goldie and Tate would travel with the horses to other states. When Goldie refused to drink her usual orange juice in the mornings; Tate said that he knew that it was time to go back home to Texas. That was her sign of being homesick.

I once asked Goldie how did she meet Tate Burleson. She said she and Mama were in Casey Jones café having lunch when Tate was there having an argument with the owner about the service. Goldie and Mama were taking in the scene when Tate told the man that he would throw him out of the café. Goldie told me admiringly that she thought, what nerve, to say he would throw the man out of his own café.

I loved to draw pictures and give them to Goldie and Tate. Once she showed me a picture of a horse that I had drawn when I was about six years old and we laughed till we cried. The horse that I had drawn had fat red lips. Goldie took my artwork so seriously. I did improve, she used to say "my daughter is an artist, but I can't draw a straight line on my lips."

I think the best gift Goldie ever bought for me was a pair of blue boots, which I wore almost every day until I outgrew them. I had them on when class pictures were taken. I did tell Goldie, about 40 years later that I really appreciated her buying me those boots.

In the summer of 1954, Papa was in the hospital at Scott and White in Temple, Texas and he was not expected to live through the night. The whole family was gathered around the bed and out in the hallway. Everybody was crying. Goldie looked at me and said "come with me." We pulled up to an outside payphone. Goldie called a friend of the family's Mutt Brooks. Goldie asked Mutt to call the elders of the Church of Christ and join together to pray for Papa. Papa made it through the night, recovered his health, and

became a Christian, and a faithful member of the Church of Christ at Leakey, Texas.

Goldie and Jay attended church in Uvalde, Texas. They had a great relationship in their marriage of 35 years. As their usual habit, they were eating breakfast at the Town House when suddenly she could not swallow or talk. She was rushed to the hospital where she later died at age 77. What an interesting life she led.

The famous baseball player Mickey Mantle came to Leakey to go hunting on a ranch nearby. He was staying at the Frio Canyon Lodge and our mother, Goldie worked there. Goldie told Arlie my brother where Mickey Mantle was staying. Arlie knocked on the door of his room and Mickey Mantle opened the door. Arlie said that he was very gracious, talked to him a few minutes, and gave him his autograph. That was so special for Arlie.

Texas Hill Country Events Recorded by My Mother, Alice Bausch Buck
By Sandra Buck of Kerrville, Texas
Born 1953

Many Germans immigrated to Texas in the late 1830s through the 1850s and beyond. One such family was that of Johann Heinrich Andreas Meier who with his wife Johanna Friedricke (nee Dettmar) and their three oldest children arrived from Bodenstein Hanover, Germany by ship at Indianola, Texas on September 5, 1852. The ocean voyage lasted thirteen weeks. They traveled over land by ox team to Luckenbach and settled there. Their home was a two-room rock and log house with an open hall. Their cellar was a dugout with a barn for saddles and harness built over it. They used oxen to work their land; faced the many hardships of early Texas pioneers, but were happy in their decision to immigrate. Their first child born in Luckenbach, a daughter

Claude Buck in 1940

named Wilhemina who with her three siblings born in Texas were baptized in the Lutheran faith at the Vereins Kirche in Fredericksburg, Texas. Wilhemina later grew up and married Andreas Bausch, whose family came to Texas from southern Germany in the late 1830s. This couple settled in the Sisterdale area.

Johann Heinrich Meier at the age of 51 after about 12 years in his new homeland on July 21, 1865, was driving a wagon to his married daughter's home to get cypress logs to make shingles. He was accompanied by his 16 year-old son, Heinrich, who was on horseback. They were attacked by a stray party of Indians. The Comanches had a treaty with the German settlers, so it was believed not to be them. His son rode to his sister's home for help, but when this group returned, it was too late to prevent his father from being killed and scalped.

Another German family was Ferdinand and Emma Hohenberger whose son Wilhelm married Rosa Alisa Anschitz. They had a daughter named Adela who married Henry Andrew Bausch, the son of Wilhemina and

Andreas Bausch. Adela and Henry Bausch were the parents of Alice Bausch Buck, my mother.

As a young man, Henry decided to buy land in Bandera County on Winans Creek in 1901. The first purchase was 160 acres. There he built a one-room log house, which had one door and two windows high up, one each in the north and south ends. It measured about 18 feet by 20 feet. He hired two Mexican families to help him grub and burn trees to clear land for fields. After several years, he returned to Sisterdale where he had been born and raised to help out his mother. He did this for a year and during this time, he met Adela Hohenberger. Adela worked at the Nimitz Hotel in Fredericksburg and she knew Chester A. Nimitz who later became the famous Admiral of the Pacific Fleet during World War II.

Henry and Adela were married on May 10, 1908. He was 34 and she was 20. A custom of those days was once a girl was wedded she was no longer able, as a "married lady," to work with single girls. I doubt Henry wanted Adela to continue working at the hotel anyway for he wanted to return to his land in Bandera County.

Their first home there was three rooms in a row built of lumber, with stairs on the south end of the porch leading to a bedroom

Robert E. "Daddy Buck"

259

above. The three rooms downstairs were two bedrooms and a living room. Across an open walkway were two more rooms, a kitchen with a dining area and another bedroom. In the next ten years six children were born. As land was sold and more purchased, the farm/ranch grew to over 1000 acres. In the over 150 acres that had been cleared for fields the main crops raised were cotton, oats, corn, and cane for molasses. He also raised cattle, sheep, goats, and hogs. Adela raised chickens and turkeys. She also kept a flock of geese to pluck their feathers for pillows. When the children became school age and there was not a school close by, the solution was to rent a house in Bandera. Dad moved Mother and the children to town for the school year but always brought them home for the summer.

In 1918, the year Alice was born, the family lost the oldest son, Arthur. He would have been nine that year. There was a rising inside an ear and it burst causing his death. Modern medicine could probably have prevented this from happening.

During World War I the country needed mules, so Dad sold most of his mules to the Army. He was called to serve after Alice was born in August, but the Armistice was signed November 17, 1918 so Dad didn't have to go to war after all.

Every Christmas Dad sold a large load of oats, and Mother sold all her turkeys. With this money they would buy our Christmas gifts and lots of fruit: big boxes of apples, oranges, two huge stalks of bananas, and raisins, dried apples, and prunes. The gifts could include tin dishes, dolls with hair, miniature furniture, small tractors, and trucks.

Then in 1922 our parents decided to build a large rock house, so they hired Otto Meyer from Comfort, Texas to build it on top of the hill. Mr. Meyer had a large tent that he put up under the large live oak trees next to our current home. We were to live in the tent so they could start tearing down the house so they could use the lumber in the new house. They left the kitchen area, but it was gutted out to later become a corn crib. They got the rock out of the Hanson ranch now known as the Kyle ranch. The rock was sawed out 18 inches square and two to five feet long. After the foundation was dug, Alice, age 4 and Ida Mae, age 6, had lots of fun chasing each other around in it. It took almost a year to build the house. The first floor raised at least four feet above ground consisted of the front porch, a bedroom, the dining room, the back screened porch with its entrance to the cellar, connected by the kitchen and hallway to another bedroom, bath, bedroom and living room. All these rooms were large with ceilings at least 12 feet high. The upstairs was open and in winter was excellent for roller skating. In later years it was the scene of dances when barbeques would be held.

Four more children were born between

Sandra Buck in 1962

260

1922 and 1930, but one of the twin girls died in 1927. Only the surviving twin girl, Irene, is living today at age 89.

One bad event happened while we were herding sheep in the field across the creek. Ida Mae, Hugo, and Alice were out close to a ditch where snakes had been seen before. A turtle was in a hole and Hugo was sitting on a tree limb poking a stick at it. Ida Mae and Alice were just standing there about three feet apart. A big rattlesnake crawled up between them and started to rattle and bit Ida Mae. Alice ran away and Ida Mae and Hugo followed. The snake kept on chasing us until our dog fought it off. Then we stopped. Hugo took off his belt and wrapped it real tight around her leg. We got to the gate and looked over to the house and yelled to our mother who was out in the yard talking to Elden Fries. We yelled, "Ida Mae got rattlesnake bit." Elden got on his horse and rode to the post oak field to get Dad while Mother called Dr. Butler. When Elden got back to the house he took his pocket knife and lanced one of the bites, and Dr. Butler lanced the other one. Her leg swelled big and turned dark. A tourniquet was kept on her leg, but it had to be loosened periodically to let blood flow to her leg. Her body had to fight off the poison. She was a very sick girl for ten days, and our Dad stayed the whole time at her bedside.

Another scary event happened when Harold was five years old. He was playing close to where Hugo was cleaning something with gasoline. A cup of gasoline was sitting there and Harold thought it was water and drank it down. He could barely breathe and was turning blue in the face. Ida Mae and Alice shouted to Mother. Our place was over nine miles from town, so Mother called Dr. Butler. He told her to get egg whites down him and make him vomit. She did and it worked. Thank goodness it worked. When Harold was older but still just a kid, he built an airplane up in the loft of the big barn. When he got

finished Buster told him it would not fly, but Harold just knew it would. Out he pushed his plane and down to the ground it went and broke all to pieces. Harold got up and said, "It didn't fly" and that was that.

We also had to do the washing. Our washing machine wasn't working anymore, so we had to rub everything on a rub board. One Saturday Alice and Ida Mae put water in the wash pot, started the fire under it, and collected the bed sheets, towels, and all the clothes together. We called Alma to help us, but she didn't come. We had all of the washing to rub out ourselves. Not fair, so we decided to make a dish pan of real stiff starch. We took all of Alma's clothes; underpants included, and starched them so stiff they hung on the lines like boards. From then on she always came out to help wash the clothes.

One cold night we had long icicles hanging off of the barn, almost three feet long. We decided to gather them and make ice cream. Norma mixed up the ice cream and we took turns rotating the handle on the freezer. The temperature was down in the teens, so Alma and Alice would go out and turn the handle for a while, and then Ida Mae and Norma would take our place. Finally, the mixture was frozen and we surprised our parents with a gallon of ice cream. We really enjoyed it.

One night Hugo and Buster went hunting and saw smoke drifting all down the Winans Creek but did not realize at first what was on fire. There was a large barn where we kept about 300 sheep, ewes, and lambs, during the lambing season. It was very cold so inside a 50 gallon barrel with a foot of sand in the bottom a fire was built to keep the newborn lambs warm. The barn had a wooden floor and there was sheep manure on it. The manure got hot enough and set the floor on fire. Luckily the barn door burned down and the ewes and lambs got out. When the fire was out, it was discovered that only one little lamb was lost. That was a miracle.

261

Dad liked sports so he put up a basketball goal and made a tennis court, and we played baseball. Dad always played ball with us on Sunday evenings. He got us roller skates and we skated upstairs in the winter, but we would also drive to Shotts Skating Rink in Pipe Creek. Our mother was always busy cooking and sewing. She made our dresses, shirts, and quilts. At night Dad would sit down and help her quilt. Mother passed away at the age of 52 from a brain hemorrhage in 1940. I, Alice was married to Claude Buck by this time. Alma took over the housework. Harold, only ten, helped with the sheep and goats. Buster fed the hogs, and Buster and Hugo did all the field work. Irene did what she could to help out and life went on at this Hill Country ranch.

Leroy F., Walter F., Esther, and Fred Fuhrmann

Walk Home Seven Miles from School?
By Walter Fuhrmann of Fredericksburg, Texas
Born 1924

It all started in the spring of 1930 when Honey Creek School, located in the western part of Gillespie County, closed its doors again after having a school term with 3 students in the school for the year. Those students were my brother, Fred Fuhrmann, Oswald Preiss, and me.

Oswald was 16 years old and in the sixth grade, but hadn't been to school for a few years. No other students had come forth during this year. Our teacher Miss Norma Hohenberger, we called her Miss Norma, had agreed to teach there one year, and try to establish a school, but that didn't develop.

So now, it was time to consider our options for the next semester of school. We could go to town school, but we couldn't drive yet and staying in town would mean dad would lose his help. So it was finally decided Live Oak School was the best option, even though it was seven miles away. Our options for getting

there were numerous, such as dad would take us in the model T, drive the buggy with Prince, our thirty-three year old utility horse, or we could walk, the least favorite way.

As the time of action arrived, we were duly enrolled in the fall of 1931 that is the three of us, Fred, Walter, and Leroy, our schedule unfolded. Dad would drive us to school after we had finished our milking chores, and then we would walk home, getting there in time to do more chores such as getting kindling, shucking corn, feeding the hogs, milking the cows, and separating the milk and cream, all before darkness arrived and we had supper. The schedule worked fine until fall crept in and we boys shouldn't be exposed to the cold and sometimes wet weather for so long. So dad gave us Prince, and hitched him to an older buggy with one seat and a storage bin behind for books, blankets, and coats. This worked fine for a period of time until the weather turned real cold. Our innovative dad then installed a "heater," without gas, kerosene, or wood, merely by cutting a rectangular rock just smaller than the oven of our wood stove.

This stone was placed in the oven after supper was over. A good fire during the night assured a "warm" stone in the morning, which was then wrapped in an old blanket and placed on the footboard of our buggy. So we had warm feet when arriving at school and when your feet are warm your body is also. Of course, there were many blankets and coats for warmth as well. This combination worked well for all concerned for several months until Prince came up lame, and needed a rest period.

So we were down to our next alternative, walking the seven miles in the evenings after school. Dad would take us to school in the mornings and we would do what we had to in order to get home after school.

Walking a distance of seven miles can be quite an adventure for three youngsters. For example, we knew of a short cut lane, but it passed by the residence of a "colored" man or family, it seemed too "spooky" for us. This family had a large black dog and no yard fence. So we never used this shortcut.

We had schoolmates to walk with us on the main road for the first mile or so and then they turned east and we turned west. Walking along a new U.S. Highway, four years old, in God's creation can be quite an experience, especially for the young. There was always something new over the next hill, be it man or nature, such as a prairie snake that needed to be killed, or chased off, the highway. There were many other distractions as well. But, Thursday was a special day. After leaving our friends and turning west, we would start looking for a nearly new car, one that had windows that rolled up and down! The older gentleman driving this car would shop for his groceries, etc. every Thursday morning and return home about the time we would be walking. He would stop and pick us up, even if it was three of us, and on occasion, he would offer each of us a peppermint stick and then drop us at our gate. We loved that man!

I must remind the readers that this highway, US 290, was the shortest route from Florida to California. So on the average only 5 or 6 cars would pass us in the approximately 2 hours we were on the highway.

But, we'd arrive home just in time to help milk a few cows, with stronger legs and bodies. The next afternoon we'd face another seven-mile walk.

Index A Hometown

Clinton B. Solbrig	Amarillo	Texas	191
Barbara Browning Young	Amarillo	Texas	83
Rodger Cunningham	Atascosa	Texas	27
Karen Barrington	Austin	Texas	231
Wanda Lancaster	Austin	Texas	63
Ruby Turn	Austin	Texas	217
Dorothy Callahan	Bandera	Texas	32
Charles Crawford	Bellville	Texas	152
Emma Jewel Goodwin	Bertram	Texas	128
Jerry L. Harkey	Bertram	Texas	122
Lucille H. Hough	Bertram	Texas	181
Diana L. Johnson	Bertram	Texas	158
Lowell Johnson	Bertram	Texas	88
Ken Odiorne	Bertram	Texas	209
Deanie Smith	Bertram	Texas	125
J. C. Smith	Bertram	Texas	125
Bob Wilson	Bertram	Texas	64
Dorothy Lee Howe Dillon	Blanco	Texas	71
Larry W. Seiler	Blanco	Texas	65
Mona Carol (Bates) Workman	Boerne	Texas	53
Alberta Elliott	Brady	Texas	61
Mary Sue Fields	Brady	Texas	153
Carol Johnson	Brady	Texas	224
Penny Pennington	Brady	Texas	189
Roy Kemp	Braunfels	Texas	44
Irma Lange	Braunfels	Texas	44
Judy Maersch	Braunfels	Texas	23
Joan Johnson	Brownwood	Texas	27
Zada Jahnsen	Bulverde	Texas	99
Lillian Mayer	Bulverde	Texas	197
Glen B. Bates	Burnet	Texas	141
Billie Buck	Burnet	Texas	241
Virginia Hammond	Burnet	Texas	49
John Hoover	Burnet	Texas	239
Vivian Hoover	Burnet	Texas	133
Leona McDaniel	Burnet	Texas	176
Dorthy Steadman	Burnet	Texas	128
Loys Tippie	Burnet	Texas	132
Linda Wiley	Burnet	Texas	109
Adele Matthews	Caldwell	Texas	26

L. K. Walker	Canyon Lake	Texas	67
Martha Smith Carlson	Center Point	Texas	135
Robert D. Sevey	Center Point	Texas	111
Mae Durden-Nelson	Comfort	Texas	74
Joy S. Hawkins	Comfort	Texas	33
Theron C. Hawkins, MD	Comfort	Texas	37
Arturo Alvarez	Converse	Texas	93
Jim Godat	Del Rio	Texas	48
Thelma Gutierrez	Del Rio	Texas	96
Joe Morales	Del Rio	Texas	142
Guy Daugherty	Denison	Texas	105
Leo Cardenas	Denver	Colorado	202
Jim Runge	Eldorado	Texas	164
Vickie J. Williams	Eldorado	Texas	171
Ralph Hatchell	Fort Stockton	Texas	215
Donald Bauer	Fredericksburg	Texas	140
Hazel Castonguay	Fredericksburg	Texas	210
Elizabeth Sieckmann Ellebracht	Fredericksburg	Texas	157
Cynthia Engel	Fredericksburg	Texas	56
Verna M. Engel	Fredericksburg	Texas	31
Walter Fuhrmann	Fredericksburg	Texas	262
Lorene Harmon	Fredericksburg	Texas	103
Gertrude J. Klein	Fredericksburg	Texas	176
Bob Lee	Fredericksburg	Texas	23
Joe A. Moellendorf	Fredericksburg	Texas	103
Virginia Mohr	Fredericksburg	Texas	243
Elmer Wahrmund	Fredericksburg	Texas	209
Charlene Dickerson Heim	Haven	Kansas	127
Doris Craven	Helotes	Texas	79
Louise McWilliams	Hext	Texas	238
Robert Buck	Hugo	Oklahoma	251
Robert Bell	Hunt	Texas	55
Richard G.Smith	Hye	Texas	107
Victor Ammann	Ingram	Texas	188
Clarence Ray Lee	Ingram	Texas	58
Joel Ayala, Sr.	Kerrville	Texas	182
Weldon Baker	Kerrville	Texas	20
Charles H. Bierschwale	Kerrville	Texas	178
Larry Borchers	Kerrville	Texas	91
Sandra Buck	Kerrville	Texas	258
Regina Caulk	Kerrville	Texas	186
Paul Kane	Kerrville	Texas	168
Claudell Kercheville	Kerrville	Texas	53
Marjorie Morgan	Kerrville	Texas	234
Frank F. Ordener	Kerrville	Texas	55

Peggy Peese	Kerrville	Texas	249
Winnie Scott	Kerrville	Texas	62
Shirley Buck Smith	Kerrville	Texas	246
Clarabelle Snodgrass	Kerrville	Texas	81
Faye Speight	Kerrville	Texas	219
Loretta Carney Treadwell	Kerrville	Texas	118
Janet Beam Chase	Killeen	Texas	25
Audrey Perry	Kingsland	Texas	141
Leon H. Sims	Kingsland	Texas	69
Claire Johnston	Lago Vista	Texas	34
Chester Bagby	Lampasas	Texas	39
Elizabeth Bettle	Lampasas	Texas	159
Jerry D. Blalock	Leakey	Texas	195
Dean Kothmann	Leawood	Kansas	38
Linda Carta	Llano	Texas	136
Melvin Glenn, Jr.	Llano	Texas	114
Wanda Holloway	Llano	Texas	212
Shirlene Rogers	Llano	Texas	214
Joyce E. Scott	Llano	Texas	129
Janice and G. L. Mays	London	Texas	120
Hildegarde Gebert	Manor	Texas	145
Patricia Magerkurth	Marble Falls	Texas	90
Edna Taylor	Marble Falls	Texas	237
Leroy Trussell	Marble Falls	Texas	106
Shirley Wright	Marble Falls	Texas	116
Charles Cale	Marion	Texas	77
Thelma Traveland Cardwell-Cale	Marion	Texas	193
Helen T. Hahn	Mason	Texas	149
Lorine K. Metz	Mason	Texas	130
Robert H. Kensing	Menard	Texas	204
Jean Landers Wright	Menard	Texas	241
Lanny Leinweber	Mountain Home	Texas	57
Austin Barber	New Braunfels	Texas	24
Tommy Barganier	New Braunfels	Texas	50
Barbara C. Bird	New Braunfels	Texas	144
Joan R. Cielencki	New Braunfels	Texas	158
Cora Millett Coleman	New Braunfels	Texas	126
Michael Collins	New Braunfels	Texas	60
Betty Ann Geren	New Braunfels	Texas	140
Gayle Hester	New Braunfels	Texas	244
Gladys Krause	New Braunfels	Texas	222
Rebecca Mendoza	New Braunfels	Texas	48
Sonja Reeh Moore	New Braunfels	Texas	52
Carl D. Scott	New Braunfels	Texas	45
Melba Simmons Shaw	New Braunfels	Texas	40

Sandra Tarleton-Goll	New Braunfels	Texas	54
Barbara Touchstone	New Braunfels	Texas	177
Joyce Weatherby	New Braunfels	Texas	30
Beverly White	New Braunfels	Texas	18
Gerald R. White	New Braunfels	Texas	162
Daniel Woodson, Jr.	New Braunfels	Texas	167
Peter Writer	New Braunfels	Texas	15
Diana Ingram	Odessa	Texas	35
Dorothy Parker	Pearland	Texas	104
Benita Lane	Pipe Creek	Texas	255
Frances Schneider	Pleasanton	Texas	62
Ronnie Holloway	Pontotoc	Texas	53
Christine Anthony	Richland Spring	Texas	80
MiMi Hardwick	Rio Frio	Texas	59
Helen Deeds	Rochelle	Texas	58
Jane Ann Myers McBee	Rochelle	Texas	161
Bill E. Seale	Rock Springs	Texas	160
Jack W. Clark	Rockdale	Texas	102
Lavon Clark	Rockdale	Texas	211
Richard Clark	Rockdale	Texas	210
George Seeburger	Rockport	Texas	108
Carolyn L. (Weegie) Cottle	Rocksprings	Texas	183
Gloria Duarte	San Angelo	Texas	85
Edward Anderson	San Antonio	Texas	89
Fred C. Anderson	San Antonio	Texas	148
Shirley A. Barbe	San Antonio	Texas	199
Patricia Canellis	San Antonio	Texas	56
Olivia Valderaz Herrera	San Antonio	Texas	169
Steven B. Kensing	San Antonio	Texas	104
Ann Bailey Mayfield	San Antonio	Texas	240
Larry Edwin Mayfield	San Antonio	Texas	173
J. Driana Redwood	San Antonio	Texas	143
Irene A. Scholz	San Antonio	Texas	124
Thomas Lou Whisenant	San Antonio	Texas	146
Mabel Edmondson	San Saba	Texas	216
Jymmie Linzey	San Saba	Texas	43
Marjorie Turner Wagner	San Saba	Texas	110
Lodie Carter	Seguin	Texas	237
Lina M. Davis	Seguin	Texas	213
Patricia Haas	Spring Branch	Texas	227
Wendell Pool	Spring Branch	Texas	36
Lo-Rena Scott	Tarpley	Texas	54
Roberta Smith Wallace	Victoria	Texas	126
Kathy Whitney	Victoria	Texas	157
Gary A. Smith	Visalia	California	206

Index A Year of Birth

Frank F. Ordener	1930	55
Bill E. Seale	1930	160
Patricia Magerkurth	1931	90
J. C. Smith	1931	125
Mona Carol (Bates) Workman	1931	53
Arturo Alvarez	1932	93
Thelma Traveland Cardwell-Cale	1932	193
Mae Durden-Nelson	1932	74
Alberta Elliott	1932	61
MiMi Hardwick	1932	59
John Hoover	1932	239
Gladys Krause	1932	222
Clarence Ray Lee	1932	58
Leona McDaniel	1932	176
Dorthy Steadman	1932	128
Victor Ammann	1933	188
Vivian Hoover	1933	133
Joy Jenkins	1933	159
Faye Speight	1933	219
Loretta Carney Treadwell	1933	118
Bob Wilson	1933	64
Jean Landers Wright	1933	241
Weldon Baker	1934	20
Billie Buck	1934	241
Emma Jewel Goodwin	1934	128
Virginia Hammond	1934	49
Virginia Mohr	1934	243
Deanie Smith	1934	125
Gary A. Smith	1934	206
Barbara Browning Young	1934	83
Patricia Canellis	1935	56
Leo Cardenas	1935	202
Michael Collins	1935	60
Betty Ann Geren	1935	140
Helen T. Hahn	1935	149
Lorene Harmon	1935	103
Zada Jahnsen	1935	99
Gertrude J. Klein	1935	176
Ann Bailey Mayfield	1935	240
Dorothy Parker	1935	104
George Seeburger	1935	108
Robert Bell	1936	55
Cora Millett Coleman	1936	126
Verna M. Engel	1936	31
Jerry L. Harkey	1936	122

Carol Johnson	1936	224
Roy Kemp	1936	44
Claudell Kercheville	1936	53
Lanny Leinweber	1936	57
Ken Odiorne	1936	209
Peggy Peese	1936	249
Leon H. Sims	1936	69
Beverly White	1936	18
Tommy Barganier	1937	50
Barbara C. Bird	1937	144
Mary Sue Fields	1937	153
Lowell Johnson	1937	88
Bob Lee	1937	23
Roberta Smith Wallace	1937	126
Gerald R. White	1937	162
Shirley Wright	1937	116
Joe A. Moellendorf	1938	103
Marjorie Morgan	1938	234
Shirley A. Barbe	1939	199
Janice and G. L. Mays	1939	120
Jane Ann Myers McBee	1939	161
Frances Schneider	1939	62
Richard G. Smith	1939	107
Austin Barber	1940	24
Jerry D. Blalock	1940	195
Elizabeth Sieckmann Ellebracht	1940	157
Adele Matthews	1940	26
Christine Anthony	1941	80
Charles H. Bierschwale	1941	178
Robert Buck	1941	251
Martha Smith Carlson	1941	135
Linda Carta	1941	136
Diana L. Johnson	1941	158
Joan Johnson	1941	27
J. Driana Redwood	1941	143
Barbara Touchstone	1941	177
Elizabeth Bettle	1942	159
Joan R. Cielencki	1942	158
Benita Lane	1942	255
Judy Maersch	1942	23
Kathy Whitney	1942	157
Charlene Dickerson Heim	1943	127
Shirlene Rogers	1943	214
Jim Runge	1943	164
Shirley Buck Smith	1943	246

Hazel Castonguay	1944	210
Melvin Glenn, Jr.	1944	114
Thelma Gutierrez	1944	96
Olivia Valderaz Herrera	1944	169
Lo-Rena Scott	1944	54
Larry W. Seiler	1944	65
Peter Writer	1944	15
Sonja Reeh Moore	1945	52
Wendell Pool	1945	36
Marjorie Turner Wagner	1945	110
Claire Johnston	1946	34
Linda Wiley	1946	109
Ralph Hatchell	1947	215
Ronnie Holloway	1947	53
Karen Barrington	1948	231
Larry Borchers	1948	91
Cynthia Engel	1948	56
Daniel Woodson, Jr.	1948	167
Richard Clark	1949	210
Robert D. Sevey	1949	111
Lodie Carter	1950	237
Carolyn L. (Weegie) Cottle	1950	183
Rodger Cunningham	1950	27
Gloria Duarte	1950	85
Jim Godat	1950	48
Lina M. Davis	1951	213
Diana Ingram	1951	35
Paul Kane	1951	168
Dean Kothmann	1951	38
Joyce Weatherby	1951	30
Vickie J. Williams	1951	171
Patricia Haas	1952	227
Sandra Buck	1953	258
Janet Beam Chase	1953	25
Steven B. Kensing	1953	104
Regina Caulk	1954	186
Larry Edwin Mayfield	1954	173
Joy S. Hawkins	Unknown	33
Gayle Hester	Unknown	244
Irma Lange	Unknown	44
Joe Morales	Unknown	142
Carl D. Scott	Unknown	45
Joyce E. Scott	Unknown	129
Melba Simmons Shaw	Unknown	40
Leroy Trussell	Unknown	106